First Pages

Giancarlo Maiorino

First Pages
A Poetics of Titles

The Pennsylvania State University Press
University Park, Pennsylvania

Maiorino, Giancarlo, 1943– .
   First pages : a poetics of titles / Giancarlo Maiorino.
       p.   cm.
Includes bibliographical references and index.
ISBN 978-0-271-05874-0 (pbk. : alk. paper)
1. Titles of books.
I. Title.

PN171.T5M35 2008
801′.95—dc22
2007043228

Copyright © 2008 The Pennsylvania State University
All rights reserved
Printed in the United States of America
Published by The Pennsylvania State University Press,
University Park, PA 16802-1003

The Pennsylvania State University Press is a member of the
Association of American University Presses.

It is the policy of The Pennsylvania State University Press
to use acid-free paper. This book is printed on
stock that meets the minimum
requirements of American National
Standard for Information Sciences—Permanence of
Paper for Printed Library Material, ANSI Z39.48–1992.

FOR
Grace,
HER NAME AND HER TITLE

CONTENTS

List of Illustrations / ix
Acknowledgments / xiii

Introduction: The Frontispiece of Literature / 1

MODERN

1. At the Top of the Page and Below the Frame: *Arcadia, Concert Champêtre,* and Pastoral Titles / 9
2. The Title's Novelistic Birthmark: *La vida de Lazarillo de Tormes y sus fortunas y adversidades* / 30
3. From Title to Genre: Essaying at the Threshold of Form / 48

MODERNIST

4. Title Translated into Title: *Ulysses* / 65
5. *The Waste Land:* The Archaeology of Titles / 95
6. Off the Page and onto the Stage: *Sei personaggi in cerca d'autore* / 124
7. Between Expectation and Explanation: *Waiting for Godot* / 141
8. The Dustbin of Titles: From "The Literature of Exhaustion" to "The Literature of Replenishment" / 160

POSTMODERN

9. "La biblioteca de Babel": The Archititle in a Library of Titles / 189
10. Cervantine First Pages: The Inadequacies of Retitling / 220
11. The Picaresque and the Quixotic: An Adventure in Titology / 240
12. *Se una notte d'inverno un viaggiatore:* Et cetera, Et cetera / 262
13. *After the End of Art:* The Obituary of Titles / 284
14. The Literature of Titles / 299

Notes / 309
Index / 355

ILLUSTRATIONS

FIG. 1   Copy of Heliodorus, *Pan Teaching Daphnis to Play the Syrinx*, c. 100 B.C.E. Naples Museum of Archaeology. (Photo: Alinari / Art Resource, New York) / 16

FIG. 2   Titian, *Concert Champêtre* (also known as *Pastoral Scene* or *Fête Champêtre*), 1510–11. Louvre, Paris. (Photo: Réunion des Musées Nationaux / Art Resource, New York) / 17

FIG. 3   Pietro Perugino, *Apollo and Marsyas*, c. 1495. Louvre, Paris. (Photo: Réunion des Musées Nationaux / Art Resource, New York) / 19

FIG. 4   Raphael, *The Parnassus*, detail showing Apollo and the Muses. (Photo: Scala / Art Resource, New York) / 20

FIG. 5   Titian, *Sacred and Profane Love*, c. 1515. Galleria Borghese, Rome. (Photo: Scala / Art Resource, New York) / 21

FIG. 6   Leonardo da Vinci, *Annunciation*, detail, 1472–75. Uffizi Gallery, Florence. (Photo: Scala / Art Resource, New York) / 21

FIG. 7   Giorgione, *Sleeping Venus*, c. 1510. Gemäldegalerie, Staatliche Kunstsammlungen, Dresden. (Photo: Erich Lessing / Art Resource, New York) / 23

FIG. 8   Titian, *Concert Champêtre*, detail of Figure 2. / 24

FIG. 9   Titian, *Concert Champêtre*, detail of Figure 2. / 25

FIG. 10   Raphael, *The Parnassus*, 1510–11. Stanza della Segnatura, Stanze di Raffaello, Vatican Palace, Vatican State. (Photo: Scala / Art Resource, New York) / 27

FIG. 11   Henry Moore, *Tube Shelter Perspective*, 1941 (HMF 1801). Tate Gallery, London. (Photo: Tate London / Art Resource, New York) / 121

FIG. 12   Giacometti, *Annette*, "Portrait of Annette," 1950. © 2007 Artists Rights Society (ARS), New York / ADAGP, Paris. (Photo: Visual Arts Library / Art Resource, New York) / 167

Illustrations

FIG. 13   Giacometti, *The Forest, Seven Figures and a Head*, 1950. Kunsthaus, Zurich. © 2007 Artists Rights Society (ARS), New York / ADAGP, Paris. (Photo: Bridgeman-Giraudon / Art Resource, New York) / 168

FIG. 14   Giacometti, *Femme debout* (*Standing Woman*), detail, 1956. Yale University Art Gallery, New Haven. Gift of Susan Morse Hilles. © 2007 Artists Rights Society (ARS), New York / ADAGP, Paris. (Photo: Yale University Art Gallery / Art Resource, New York) / 169

FIG. 15   The Destruction of the Pruitt-Igoe Public Housing Project in Saint Louis, 1972. *The Saint Louis Dispatch.* / 181

FIG. 16   The Destruction of the World Trade Center, September 11, 2001. *The New York Daily News.* (Photo: Todd Maisel) / 181

FIG. 17   Michelangelo Pistoletto, *Venere degli stracci* (*Venus of the Rags*), 1967. Hirshhorn Museum and Sculpture Garden, Smithsonian Institution, Joseph H. Hirshorn Bequest Fund, 1999. Washington, D.C. (Photo: Lee Stalsworth) / 183

FIG. 18   Pieter Brueghel the Elder, *The Small Tower*, 1563. Kunsthistorisches Museum, Vienna. (Photo: Erich Lessing / Art Resource, New York) / 192

FIG. 19   Pieter Brueghel the Elder, *The Big Tower*, 1568. Museum Boymans van Beuningen, Rotterdam. (Photo: Kavaler / Art Resource, New York) / 192

FIG. 20   Lucas van Valckenborgh, *The Tower of Babel*, 1594. Louvre, Paris. (Photo: Réunion des Musées Nationaux / Art Resource, New York) / 193

FIG. 21   Frans Francken II, *The Construction of the Tower of Babel*, 1620. Museo de Santa Cruz, Toledo, Spain. (Photo: Erich Lessing / Art Resource, New York) / 193

FIG. 22   Saul Steinberg, *A View of the World from 9th Ave.* Cover drawing for *The New Yorker*, March 29, 1976. © 1976 The Saul Steinberg Foundation / Artists Rights Society (ARS), New York. Cover reprinted with permission of *The New Yorker* magazine. All rights reserved. / 199

FIG. 23   Giuseppe Arcimboldo, *The Librarian*, c. 1566. Skoklosters Slott, Balsta, Sweden. (Photo: Erich Lessing / Art Resource, New York) / 209

FIG. 24   Jasper Johns, Installation view of the exhibition "Jasper Johns: A Retrospective." The Museum of Modern Art, New York. October 15, 1996 through January 21, 1997. © Jasper Johns/Licensed by VAGA, New York. (Digital Image © The Museum of Modern Art/Licensed by Scala / Art Resource, New York) / 211

FIG. 25   George Herms, *The Librarian*, 1960. Norton Simon Museum, Pasadena, California. Gift of Molly Barnes. / 213

FIG. 26   Robert Smithson, *A Heap of Language*, 1966. John Weber Gallery, New York. © Estate of Robert Smithson / Licensed by VAGA, New York. / 214

FIG. 27   Constantin Brancusi, *Endless Column*, 1937–38. Târgu-Jiu, Romania. (Photo: Jacques Faujour. CNAC/MNAM/Dist. Réunion des Musées Nationaux / Art Resource, New York) / 265

FIG. 28   Arata Isozaki, *Art Tower Mito*, 1988–90. Mito, Ibaraki, Japan. / 266

FIG. 29   Andy Warhol, *210 Coca-Cola Bottles*, 1962. Synthetic polymer paint and silkscreen ink on canvas. © 2007 Andy Warhol Foundation for the Visual Arts / Artists Rights Society (ARS), New York. (Photo: The Andy Warhol Foundation, Inc. / Art Resource, New York) / 266

FIG. 30   Saul Steinberg, *Summer Table*, 1981. Mixed media collage on wood, 57 × 80 × 36 inches. Private collection. © The Saul Steinberg Foundation / Artists Rights Society (ARS), New York. (Photo: Kerry Ryan McFate, courtesy PaceWildenstein, New York) / 273

FIG. 31   Roland Barthes, "Doodling . . . or the signifier without the signified," 1972, from *Roland Barthes by Roland Barthes*, translated by Richard Howard. Translation copyright © 1977 by Farrar, Straus & Giroux, Inc. Reprinted by permission of Hill and Wang, a division of Farrar, Straus and Giroux, LLC. / 291

FIG. 32   Cy Twombly, *Fifty Days at Iliam: House of Priam*, 1978 (seventh of ten parts). The Philadelphia Museum of Art. Gift (by exchange) of Samuel S. White 3rd and Vera White, 1989. (Photo: The Philadelphia Museum of Art / Art Resource, New York) / 293

FIG. 33   Cy Twombly, Untitled. 1970. The Museum of Modern Art, New York. Acquired through the Lallie P. Bless Bequest and The Sidney and Harriet Janis Collection (both by exchange). (Digital Image © The Museum of Modern Art / Licensed by Scala / Art Resource, New York) / 294

FIG. 34   Jasper Johns, *Gray Alphabet*, 1956. The Menil Collection, Houston. © Jasper Johns / Licensed by VAGA, New York. / 295

FIG. 35   Robert Rauschenberg, *Erased de Kooning Drawing*, 1953. San Francisco Museum of Modern Art. ©Robert Rauschenberg / Licensed by VAGA, New York. / 296

ACKNOWLEDGMENTS

For their encouragement and expert help, I would like to acknowledge Peter Burgard, Lois A. Cuddy, Eugene Eoyang, David Hertz, Emanuele Licastro, Terence Martin, Richard Thompson, and Stephen Watt. They all read parts or versions of the manuscript. The improvements are theirs and the shortcomings, mine.

Edward Shaughnessy read the Pirandello and Beckett chapters, even though his health was failing. I am honored that my pages were among the last that he read. Generous to the end, he was a scholar and a gentleman of the old school.

Among the gentlemen of the old school who have inspired me as an academic and a human being, I was lucky to have known Newton P. Stallknecht and W. W. Beyer. Their friendship and humanity did a lot to keep me focused on academics as a vocation.

Gerald Gillespie urged me to publish a paper I read at Stanford University. His suggestion spurred me to work it into the chapter on picaresque and quixotic titology. This is but the latest contribution to an intellectual dialogue that has extended through the years.

The first Penn State University Press reader, Theodore Ziolkowski, whose books on literary thematics I have admired since I was a graduate student, has strengthened my commitment to the type of interdisciplinary scholarship that fosters synthesis and interpretation in the Olympian realm of the history of ideas. The second Penn State University Press reader, Marjorie Perloff, made valuable suggestions about titological "gradation," which forced me to reread the chapter on Cervantine titles by paying greater attention to those instances in which the fit between titles and texts is problematic.

I was lucky to benefit from the help of Anthony Lichi my last graduate student in comparative arts, who has confirmed my faith in interdisciplinarity and the selective survival of academic professionalism. Elizabeth Clark's help with revisions, illustrations, computer expertise, and library transactions has been invaluable.

Throughout my research, the reference librarians of the Wells Library at Indiana University have helped me beyond the call of duty. I have relied on their collaboration and expertise to an extent that cannot be quantified. Among such outstanding professionals, I single out David Frasier and Gabriel Swift, who never failed to make me feel better than royalty every time I stepped into the library. For those who are committed to research, it does not get any better.

As always, my severest critic was Grace Farrell: Rhode Islander, wife, soul mate, feminist, Americanist, scholar, teacher, master weaver, mother (to Elizabeth, Matthew, and Lisa), mother-in-law (to John), and nana to our grandchildren, Massimo and Samuel.

I do hope that my astute friend Joe Bernardo will find the title of this book acceptable, for he alerted me to the potential earnings that an eye-catching title could yield. I know that Marge, their children, grandchildren, and extended family are eager to congratulate him on his insight. We all are waiting for him to prove the point by putting his money where his mouth is and buy them each a copy.

Different versions of Chapters 2 and 3 appeared, respectively, in *The Eye of the Poet: Studies in the Reciprocity of the Visual and Literary Arts from the Renaissance to the Present,* edited by Amy Golahny (Lewisburg, Pa.: Bucknell University Press, 1996), and in my *At the Margins of the Renaissance: Lazarillo de Tormes and the Picaresque Art of Survival* (University Park: Pennsylvania State University Press, 2003).

For plates and permissions, I acknowledge Art Resource, *The Saint Louis Dispatch, The New York Daily News,* Hirshhorn Museum and Sculpture Garden, The Saul Steinberg Foundation, Artists Rights Society, Vaga, Norton Simon Museum, Pasadena, California, and Hill and Wang.

Introduction: The Frontispiece of Literature

The title is a key to the book and, thanks to the book, a key to language and to society.
—MICHEL BUTOR

In a lively exchange of ideas about literary craftsmanship, Octavio Paz told Carlos Fuentes that the development of the modern novel "can be told between two titles: Dickens' *Great Expectations* and Balzac's *Illusions Perdues* (*Lost Illusions*)."[1] Their minds set afire by republican idealism, middle-class ambitions, and the heroics of Napoleon Bonaparte, the novelistic youths Pip and Lucien dreamed of a brighter future in the midst of a mediocre present. The defeat at Waterloo, however, hastened either the consolidation or the restoration of power structures that were in place before 1789, the earth-shaking year of the French Revolution. From England to France, titles encapsulated a poetics in which hopes of individual distinction met with disillusionment. The heroic gave way to the bureaucratic once Bonaparte's nephew, Charles-Louis-Napoleon Bonaparte, known as Napoleon III, reigned under the diminutive nickname *le petit Napoléon*. Moved by conciliation rather than decisiveness, he tried to please everybody but ended up displeasing the whole nation. It could not be otherwise, if we only pause on a remark attributed to him: "How could you expect the Empire to function smoothly? The Empress is a Legitimist; my half-brother, Morny, is an Orléanist; my cousin, Jerome, is a Republican, and I am said to be a Socialist. Among us, only Persigny is a Bonapartist, and he is crazy."[2] Between myth and misunderstanding, materialism dug deep into the middle-class culture of the Industrial Revolution. In the aftermath of policies first progressive and then repressive, the extraordinary surrendered to the ordinary, which crushed most illusions and raised few expectations. In the post-epic age of disenchantment,[3] titles could be at once palimpsestic and prophetic.

By chance or by choice, we may not read an entire book, but we do read its title. While some maintain that it is unfair to judge a book by its cover because the first page cannot do justice to the ones that follow, this study argues that interpretation begins with the title, which is the seed that contains the tree. As a literary nutshell that offers an introductory overview of etymological roots, semantic complexity, and literary echoes, the title ought to loom as large in the reader's mind as it does on the book's spine. In my own mind, this study began to take shape when, having become familiar with the scholarship that has linked allusions and references in *Ulysses* to the Homeric epic, I asked myself a simple question: Why did James Joyce entitle his book *Ulysses* instead of *Odysseus?* The answer first generated the chapter "Title Translated into Title," and then the rest of the book.

Granted that the value of many titles is merely indexical, this study sets out to show that "good" titles are as significant as "good" texts. Between the indexical and the significant we can find an array of titles that are more or less successful in raising textual expectations. Likewise, there are texts that grow beyond what titles seem to have promised. From *Oliver Twist* to *Nicholas Nickelby,* the titles of Charles Dickens's novels often take up social issues that exceed the protagonist's concerns. A landmark narrative such as *Madame Bovary* heightens the inadequacy of onomastic titles. Although Gustave Flaubert charges *Madame* with irony and *Bovary* with a bovine-like ordinariness, the title of his novel does not quite do justice to the text. Nor does the title of Miguel de Cervantes's master story mention Sancho Panza. These examples can be multiplied, especially when titles are strictly conceptual or overtly allegorical, from Henry James's *The Wings of the Dove* to *Light in August* by William Faulkner. The relationship between title and text covers complexities and contradictions that cannot be overlooked. At their best, Michael Seidel would suggest, titles are apprehensive and comprehensive.[4] Because it aims at making a case for titles as texts, this study may verge on "overkill" inasmuch as my selection hopes to make the best case for this emergent field of literary studies.

Whenever we wonder how to discuss books, titles come to the rescue, because they are the signposts of plots, characters, themes, and motifs that are resilient in the world of art and relevant in the archive of cultural landmarks. Indeed, titles create zones of transaction between readers and writers as well as zones of transition between literary traditions.[5] The most comprehensive of common denominators in the arts, titles spur interpretation, stir criticism, and entitle literary history. While scholarly practice has enforced the belief that texts command most attention,[6] calls for a focused study of titles already were heard in the 1970s, first by the Yale poet and academic John Hollander[7] and then by Harvard's Helen Vendler, the reader of modern poetry who noted that the titles of Wallace Stevens are a "form of caption, seizing the whole in a glance."[8] In spite of such authoritative statements, critical practice has remained tentative.[9] The following chapters will make a case for "titology," a term coined in 1977 by the comparatist Harry Levin when he decided to give a title to the yet unexplored field of title studies.[10]

The first step in literary interpretation is the title, which sets up a critical perspective on the text. Insofar as my own methodology is concerned, I suspect that my approach betrays a weakness for aesthetics and a preference for the history of ideas. Nevertheless, I shall not speculate on whether I have tried to reconcile the irreconcilable, that is to say, New Criticism (smartly exhilarating, though a bit ethereal) with New Historicism (evidentially impressive, though a bit boring). At any rate, the time has come to do for titles what Leo Spitzer did for literary linguistics and Roland Barthes for semiology.[11]

In this age of structuralism, deconstruction, and fragmentation, the symbolism of architecture in the language of the arts has become pervasive. To put it in terms of a visual image, I would like to frame this study by suggesting that the title is no less important to the text than the façade is to the building.[12] First pages are the frontispiece of literature.

1

In our own day, development has given way to exhaustion, which has affected the production of art. We have been thriving on belatedness to such an extent that Jacques Derrida has championed the idea that the retrospective has no original source; instead, what we have is an endless sequence of beginnings. Once the dynamics of culture relapsed, the titological focus of literary interpretation shifted from the present-future to the present-past; the "Promised Land" of Thomas More's *Utopia* made room for *The Waste Land* of T. S. Eliot, who describes a place where drawn-out processes of decay generate heaps of refuse. The end yielded aftermaths, and the linear continuity of humanist progress coiled into the circularity of procrastination; modernism stretched out into postmodernism, which spurred interest in those thresholds where history taught significant lessons about foundations and conclusions.

This study pins the contextuality of titles to the beginning (modern) and the end (modernist-postmodern) of modernity, which has unfolded westward from Mediterranean to Atlantic waters since the Renaissance. Instead of offering a systematic synopsis that might acknowledge ancient titles and do justice to a more inclusive list, this study focuses on highlights and crossroads. It is quite possible that some will resent the highlights and object to the crossroads; but then again, agreement and resentment are the dynamic poles of any interpretation that is successful, at least to the extent that it is provocative.

The structural makeup of this study finds a precedent in a recent title, *From Dawn to Decadence,* which Jacques Barzun introduces by pointing out that, by 1914, "the impetus born of the Renaissance was exhausted."[13] Barzun's subtitle, *Five Hundred Years of Western Cultural Life,* foregrounds the intellectual changes of modernity *from* dawn *to* decadence. They are the Renaissance, the romantic period, and the contemporary age. Similarly, I shall consider a comparable triad: modern, modernist, and postmodern. I have anchored dawn to the humanist tradition of authoritative narratives, linear histories, artistic individualism, and sociocultural amelioration, which declined at the antihumanist threshold of discontinuous narratives, fragmented archaeologies, and authorless production in the art market of conspicuous consumerism. Focused as it is on Renaissance beginning (modern), modernist end, and postmodern ending-after-the-end, this study is about titles that shed light on dawn *and* decadence.

The Renaissance found in antiquity a source of inspiration for fostering a more earthbound worldview. Once that impetus waned and rebirths no longer were possible, modernism turned to the myths of antiquity to make decadence at least more bearable.[14] My opening reference to the debate about *Great Expectations* and *Lost Illusions* highlights two titles that upheld the enduring validity of renaissance as the carrier of forthcoming success and of decadence as the harbinger of impending doom. As the intellectual translation of the biological concept of naissance (*nascita*), re-naissance (*rinascita*) spurred experiments in recovery and renewal that drew together the Greco-Roman and the Judeo-Christian traditions at a time when the heliocentric universe of Copernicus had discredited the Ptolemaic worldview of an earth-centered cosmos. To experience Renaissance culture, Stephen Greenblatt writes, is to feel "what it was like to form our own identity, and we are at once more rooted and more estranged by the experience."[15] Ascent and decline take us to the student of philosophy, who defines modernity as "the epoch in which simply being modern became a decisive value in itself." Gianni Vattimo traces its inception back to the end of the fifteenth century, when "an increasingly intense cult of the new and original emerged that had not existed before."[16]

The most significant crossroad in the literary map of this study separates representation from simulation. The first fastens the section on the "modern" to *Mimesis: The Representation of Reality in Western Literature* (1946), Erich Auerbach's epoch-making overview of Western literature. The second has grown from significant to dominant in *Simulacra and Simulation* (1981), in which Jean Baudrillard has linked modernism to postmodernism under the aegis of fictional representations of representations. From text to context, we can say that this study edges on the boundary where the "neo" and the "post" merge in a spirit of either renewal or exclusion.[17]

2

As the most enduring of literary microstructures, titles are the etymologies of literature. I would like to believe that, when it comes to practical criticism, titles provide a degree of accuracy in matters of literary interpretation that is comparable to the certainty that DNA provides to our understanding of biological codes. From biology to physics, Italo Calvino takes up the matter of beginning on a cosmic scale: "Let's say that to tell everything that happened in the first second of the history of the universe, I should have to put together an account so long that the whole subsequent duration of the universe with its millions of centuries past and future would not be enough; whereas everything that came afterwards I could polish off in five minutes." The first second of the universe is pregnant with the rest of creation: "Thus the universe, from being an infinitesimal pimple in the smoothness of nothing expanded in a flash to the size of a proton, then an atom, then a pinpoint, then a pinhead, then a teaspoon, then a hat, then an umbrella."[18] In the universe of literature, the first second is foundationally etymological, while the rest of creation is transformationally semantic. The expansion that links protons to umbrellas—a *rapprochement* that juxtaposes Jackson Pollock to René Magritte—can give us a fair idea of the dynamics that relate the first page to the rest of the text, and this introduction to the chapters that follow.

MODERN

1

At the Top of the Page and Below the Frame: *Arcadia*, *Concert Champêtre*, and Pastoral Titles

> The pastoral ideal shifts on the quicksands of wishful thought.
> Wishful thinking is the weakest of all moral and religious resorts;
> but it is the stuff dreams, especially daydreams, are made of.
> —RENATO POGGIOLI

Short-lived "renaissances" are as recurrent as they are of little consequence, should we agree with George Steiner that Western culture has evolved in the mode of loss and diminution after the achievements of Greek art and literature. Thereafter, "all renascences were only partial, strained spurts of nostalgia for a lost mastery over intellectual and aesthetic expression."[1] The Renaissance, by contrast, was unique and lasted for more than two centuries. Its contribution to the development of Western culture was so significant that much of the very structure of modernity still rests on its foundations.

The first section of this study begins with titles published during the Renaissance,[2] when the Gutenberg revolution spearheaded the culture of printed books (between 1475 and 1480) on a scale that medieval scribes who spent lifetimes copying manuscripts by hand could never fathom.[3] Matters of technology aside, the humanist tradition of paradigmatic orations, treatises, and panegyrics set canonical standards that enforced a cohesive, human-measured, and progressive view of reality. Throughout the fifteenth century, as naturalistic a genre as pastoralism drew together the literary with the pictorial on grounds where the *natura naturata* of urban topographies was set against the *natura naturans* of bucolic milieus that never portrayed reality at face value, because shepherds were urbanites in disguise who never thought of trading the cultural for the agricultural.

At the turn of the sixteenth century, bucolic poetry and pastoral art were "reborn" to a vernacular aesthetics. Thematic correspondences between Jacopo

Sannazaro's *Arcadia* (1489–1500, published in Venice in 1502 and in 1504 after a 1502 pirated edition) and Titian's *Concert Champêtre* (1505), previously attributed to Giorgione, updated the classical penchant for inter-arts comparisons under the aegis of *ut pictura poesis*—as is painting, so is poetry. I take these titles as microstructures whose anachronism and anatopism offer an intriguing point of entry into the aesthetics of pastoralism. *Arcadia* transformed a geographical region of Greece into a landscape as idealized as the topography of Thomas More's *Utopia*. At once inclusive and placeless, these titles staked new spatial markers on the map of Western literature. It suffices to add that Renaissance pastorals inspired later approaches to the genre, which turned out to be imitative (Montemayor), emulative (Sidney), nostalgic (Watteau), and parodic (Manet).

In Polybius's classical description, rugged Arcadia is a "poor, bare, rocky, and chilly country devoid of life's amenities" (*Historiae* IV, 20). Idylls and eclogues were Greek, even though Theocritus wrote his *Idylls*—"little pictures"—elsewhere. A Mantuan by birth, Virgil also published bucolic verses about herdsmen prone to trade agrarian work for singing contests that were all too familiar to Pan,[4] the woodland deity who invented the syrinx.[5] According to Bruno Snell,[6] Virgil created a mindscape when he gave literary presence to the remoteness of Arcadian forests away from Arcadia,[7] which he populated with Roman friends—Gallus, Lycoris, and Pollio—who reconciled cultivation with culture throughout the north Italian countryside.[8]

Between 1484 and 1486 the Neapolitan humanist Jacopo de Jennaro wrote *Pastorale*,[9] a collection of eclogues that gave a vernacular title to ancient bucolics. Still during the fifteenth century, Matteo Maria Boiardo published two collections of vernacular eclogues that bore the kin titles of *Pastorale* and *Pastoralia*.[10] As an adjective, *pastorale* describes a state of mind that has created an enclave of choice. While it points to poets-shepherds who have found a way out of the city, *pastorale* also plays down the prosaic tasks that burden anyone who attends to agricultural tasks.[11] Pastoral verses deal with an elite disguised under the tattered clothes of shepherds who, rather than shear sheep, prefer to engage in poetic contests and musical performances. Sannazaro's title gave generic status to a kind of poetry that translated ancient precedents into a form as distinctively modern as Boiardo's own *Orlando inamorato*, the vernacular *poema cavalleresco* that gave a modern twist to the chivalric narratives of the Carolingian and the Arthurian cycles. Whether the protagonists be knights or shepherds, the experiential was overshadowed by the wishful, which had deep roots in the literary heritage.

Antiquity already had divided the introduction—or *accessus*—to commentaries on classical texts into categories, and one of them dealt with *titulus operis*.[12] Later, one of Giovanni Boccaccio's Florentine lessons sought "to establish the title" of Dante's *Commedia*. Amid a variety of commentators, the task at hand was either to explain or to interpret why "the author felt he should so entitle his book."[13] While naming the completed act of artistic birth, titles engender art's rebirth into the flow of cultural changes that heighten gaps between texts and subtexts, artists and readers. Instead of harking back to harsh mountainous terrains that test goats and shepherds alike, *Pastorale* and *Arcadia* translate utilitarian deeds into recreational activities that satisfy the wishful rather than the necessary—*otium* over *negotium*. Sannazaro's underlining of the title stands out as a hermeneutic trace that favors "mythological transfers" from the literal to the conceptual. The title points to the authority of origins, which pastoralism linked to autochthonous Arcadians who had inhabited that region of Greece before the creation of the moon. Pelasgus had been their first ruler, and he had sprung from the earth like the food they ate and the animals they hunted. Ancient idylls, eclogues, and georgics refer to landscapes with herdsmen, animals, and pre-Olympian woodland deities, with Pan at their forefront. From Theocritus to Moscus and Bion, the bucolic verses of ancient poets included in their literary geography the Greek Magna Grecia, which extended from Sicily to the Neapolitan foothills of Mount Vesuvius.

Because they never strayed from urban centers, pastoral memories paid tribute to the lure of antiquity no less than to the demands of modernity.[14] By the end of the Quattrocento, Sannazaro had underlined *Arcadia*, transforming the place-name into an evocative title by far more ubiquitous than its geographical counterpart. The titological underlining extended the spatial outreach to the shores of Albion, where Philip Sidney entitled his own bucolic *Arcadia*. Etymologically speaking, topography means "the writing of a place," an inscriptive deed that presents Arcadia as an imaginative region inhabited by shepherds with the hearts of poets who herd flocks of verses rather than sheep.[15]

Titles as naturalistic as *Pastorale* or *Arcadia* countered titles that advertised urban splendor in the humanist culture of civic learning, which thrived within the sheltered architecture of *studioli* and *accademie*. Leonardo Bruni's *Laudatio Florentinae Urbis* (*Panegyric to the City of Florence*, 1402–3) stood at the forefront of texts that called Florence the New Athens, Rome the New Jerusalem, and Venice the New Byzantium. In a way, *Arcadia* was a New

Arcadia that alluded to Greek origins even though the action was set near Naples. Like the transferential mechanism of the Greek *metaphora,* the underlining of the title takes writer and reader "somewhere else." As the place-name of a region, literary toponymy allowed poets to map their own topographies of bucolic leisure.[16]

1

In the tradition of narratives about timeless Golden Ages and Gardens of Eden,[17] Sannazaro recovered tales of wishful exile to places of chosen, not given, origin. As a title, *Arcadia* is at once retrospective and deceptive. Instead of being faithful to the rugged landscape of the mountainous Greek region, it presents sunny enclaves at the edge of modern towns. As usual, Erwin Panofsky is right when he writes that the underlining of a pastoral title transforms Arcadia into a variation of "Golden-age primitivism. But of Arcady as it existed in actuality, and as Greek writers described it to us, the opposite is true at least insofar as the underlining of the title enacted metaphorical transfers to a place where devotees of art have always outnumbered real shepherds."[18] Indeed, the title takes us to another place, where the geographical has been translated into the scriptural. This is not Arcadia "represented," but Arcadia "reconstructed." Accordingly, Arcadians chart poetic geographies that disregard physical distances because what they write is literature about literature read and written in places where the terms urban and pastoral inspire reciprocity rather than exclusion. Sannazaro's title is a compound word-sign that sets the artist's present at the crossroads between Utopia and Golden Age; between prosaic descriptions and poetic effusions, the generic hybrid created a vernacular form that echoed Dante's *Vita Nuova,* another title that marked a threshold between different modes of human existence.

Pastoralism could be as ubiquitous as the books written about it, and *Arcadia* found its own sense of tradition among contiguous tomes that Sannazaro read before he wrote his own. *Arcadia* coexists with other books in which journeys are undertaken back and forth on the same bookshelf without going anywhere.[19] The etymon no less than the semantics of the pastoral title spells out a literary mode as well as the generic protocol of pastoralism, which fulfills titological expectations by weaving together verbal and visual signs that set Arcadia at the summit of Mount Parthenius, where the narrator utters:

> A pleasant plateau, not very spacious in extent, since the situation of the place does not permit it, but so filled with tiny and deep-green herbage that, if the wanton herds with their greedy nibbling did not pasture there, one could always find green grasses in that place. There, if I am not mistaken, there are perhaps a dozen or fifteen trees of such unusual and exceeding beauty that any who saw them would judge that Mistress Nature had taken special delight in shaping them. These trees, standing somewhat apart and arranged in non-artificial order, with their rarity ennoble beyond measure the natural beauty of the place.[20]

Trees planted at orderly intervals outline a measurable landscape in which "a straight cypress" soars like a "lofty obelisk" (30–31). By way of paradox, geometry describes growth, and the living tree gives way to a petrified sun's ray. In the humanist world of rational proportions and "golden sections," the literary is more geometric than natural. Among Neapolitan humanists, Giovanni Pontano's Latin dialogue *Aegidius* (1501) traces the Latin term *dispositio* back to Virgil, whose eclogues describe agricultural techniques for planting trees in straight lines and at measured intervals.

Between Mount Vesuvius and Naples, palatial gardens and adjacent woods mix nature with architecture, for the humanist tendency has always been to build *giardini* where vines are pruned and bushes are trimmed into geometric shapes. In the humanist mindset, nature exists as background to human deeds that give meaning to a manmade environment where Sannazaro subordinated the biology of *natura naturans* to the constructions of *natura naturata*. As the leading theoretician of humanist aesthetics, Leon Battista Alberti took up the pastoral dichotomy of primitivism and sophistication when he wrote that Arcadians "invented games, as a means of refining the minds of their citizens; when they abandoned games, they became so uncouth, according to Polybius, that they were despised by the whole of Greece."[21] The ludic drew a line between the agricultural and the cultural. An expert in "antiquities," the eighteenth-century Neapolitan philosopher Giambattista Vico reminds us that "bucolic poetry appeared only in the most civilized times, among the Greeks with Theocritus, the Latins with Virgil, and the Italians with Sannazaro" (*The New Science*, par. 1059). As a tile, *Arcadia* accommodates the cultural journey of an urban elite into fictional woods whose roots are willfully literary. Learning and playfulness stood out as indicators of cultural sophistication long before Johan Huizinga reached a similar conclusion in his exemplary study of the ludic component of civilization.

If pastoral enclaves are predominant at the beginning of *Arcadia,* urban longings come back midway through the narrative:

> I call to mind the pleasures of my delicious
> homeland, among these Arcadian solitudes in
> which—by your leave I will say it—I can
> hardly believe that the beasts of the woodlands
> can dwell with any pleasure, to say nothing of
> young men nurtured in noble cities.

Even the shepherds' songs carry Neapolitan echoes:

> Though I came with my ears replete with the songs
> of Arcady, yet in order to hear those of my own
> native land and to see how nearly they approached
> the others, it seemed to me not unsuitable to pause,
> and to add (to so much other time so badly squandered)
> this brief space also, this little delay.
>
> (Eclogue 10)

By the end of his journey, Sincero, a *coltissimo giovane*—very learned young man—bids farewell to Naples, not to the wilds of nature. We read about the *nostos*—exile followed by return—of an educated urbanite who, having joined friends such as Gian Francesco Caracciolo, Cariteo di Barcellona, and Pietro Summonte,[22] gives an educational slant to the literary myth of the courtier as lover and poet:[23]

> My friend, I was between Baiae and great Vesuvius,
> in the pleasant plain where drawn into a little flood
> the lovely Sebeto joins himself with the sea.
> . . .
> But among them all in the manner of a splendid sun
> shines Caracciol, who in sounding sampogna or cither
> would not find his equal in all of Arcady.

Whenever they journey to Arcadia, noblemen wear humble clothes that seem to shed aristocratic superiority. Yet we do not witness a transformation into prosaic modes of popular existence that might suggest an early alternative to the grand narrative of affluent privilege. Appearance is deceptive. Let us not forget that literary shepherds are literary; they are created through a scriptural act that is rooted in learning and is meant to expand beyond the urban perimeter without losing much of its learned core. The title entails humanist expansion rather than naturalistic escape. Arcadians are not born to colonize faraway countries. Their country of choice lies within reach of their pen and paper, and the underlined title makes them appear suddenly in the place and moment of literary creation. In the humanist mode, Arcadians stage and perform; their rugged clothes do not warrant any kind of empirical growth in the novelistic mode that is familiar to modern readers.

Accordingly, the topos of bucolic friendship takes the form of devotion to the calling of poetry and music, which find a suitable milieu at the base of Mount Vesuvius. "When it comes to the resuscitation of texts," Geoffrey Hartman writes, "Neapolitan sorcerers" lead the pack.[24] It suffices to add that the resuscitation of pastoralism thrived on "mythological transfers" that reconciled the bucolic place, Arcadia, with the human activities in which Arcadians engage themselves. Outstanding among them is music, and Virgil's pipe hangs from a pine limb at the end of *Arcadia*.[25] In the Epilogue, Sannazaro hangs his own pipe,[26] repeating a gesture that goes back to Pan, the woodland deity. In spite of what melancholy can voice at times, Pan's pipes do not remain silent for long. Pastoral conventions represent him as a teacher, which is the way he appears in the sculpture by Heliodorus, *Pan Teaching Daphnis to Play the Syrinx* (100 B.C.)—a Hellenistic marble group that yielded several Roman copies (Fig. 1). The classical sculpture illustrates endeavors that are as timeless as mythology itself. By hanging their pipes, Virgil and Sannazaro bring the literary experience to a close. Although a timeless escape, the bucolic world comes to life and fades away together with the literary representation of one poetic creation at a time.

Virgilian traces evoke a palimpsestic country where texts presume the existence of subtexts. *Arcadia* and *Pastorale* stand side by side on bookshelves where tomes quote, comment, and engage in dialogue with one another. Pastoralism had to be remembered in order to establish heritage and continuity alike. Since antiquity, literary images and pictorial scenes have stirred complementary forms of expression. Accordingly, Ergasto sings a song that Fronimo writes "down on a green beech bark" (63). The tree is a page that records human deeds at a time when the bucolic activity of carving names on trees enlisted Ludovico Ariosto and a host of poets who assumed that

FIG. 1 Copy of Heliodorus, *Pan Teaching Daphnis to Play the Syrinx*, c. 100 B.C.E. Naples Museum of Archaeology.

agricultural cultivation and artistic practice were equally necessary to make natural milieus pleasant. Through a process of spatio-temporal sedimentation, Sannazaro's title highlights a *titre citation* that lodges a place, a tradition, and a myth in the blueprint of rereadings and misreadings.

Amid bucolic environs of poetic resurrections, death witnesses but does not terminate the better life of art. Whenever pastoral resurrections affect the arts, the modern poet upgrades *ekphrasis*, a term that describes attempts at translating visual into verbal objects.[27] The eleventh chapter of *Arcadia* presents a wrestling game that rewards the winner with a cup painted "by the hand of the Paduan Mantegna (an artist cunning beyond all other and most ingenious)" (124). Sannazaro's bucolic world is inhabited by contemporary writers and artists. Not for a moment does he stop to consider the anachronism of a classical milieu depicted in a fifteenth-century artifact. Because it was more imaginative than archaeological, remembrance served *rinascita*, which was an experiment in cultural advancement toward a reality of superior models. By presenting a modern object instead of an ancient one, he gave priority to the vernacular vessel over ancient urns, as John Keats did in the wake of the romantic revival of Greek art. Both artists drew from the Horatian tradition of "inter-arts" correspondences. Under the aegis of *ut pictura poesis* (as is painting, so is poetry), art capitalized on art itself by becoming its own source. Rather than progress, pastoralism sought expansion in a topography of choice where past and present could blend flawlessly, at least for a while. Pastoralism charts an artificial reality tailored to the artist's personal longing.

At the northern and southern periphery of Florentine humanism, juxtapositions between bucolic husbandry and leisurely education unfolded in the ekphrastic mode,[28] and *Arcadia* found a visual counterpart in Titian's *Concert Champêtre* (1505), which popular acclaim has indexed as the landscape that best reconciles the mythological with the secular under the aegis of what the Venetians called *poesia* (Fig. 2). While *Arcadia* outlines the imaginative boundaries of the genre, *Concert Champêtre* focuses on a single event that is likely to take place within those boundaries. Together they provide an overview of the range, texture, and content of pastoralism.

FIG. 2   Titian, *Concert Champêtre* (also known as *Pastoral Scene* or *Fête Champêtre*), 1510–11. Louvre, Paris.

On such interdisciplinary grounds, Richard Brilliant has focused on the relevance of titles under the rubric of "titulature,"[29] which, etymologically and semantically, seems quite close to titology. Criticism has paid due attention to the title of Titian's painting, and Francis Haskell has reached a thoughtful conclusion on the matter: "By calling it *Concert Champêtre* I have accepted a name which has been conventional for about 170 years, but which has meant nothing to the lucky man who commissioned the picture, and which may well give us a misleading impression about what it actually represents."[30] The first citation by the court painter Charles Lebrun, in 1638, identified *Concert Champêtre* as *Pastoral*, a title that held up until the picture was moved to the Louvre in 1804. Closer to our own days, Kenneth Clark set the painting in the tradition of *fêtes galantes* by calling it *Fête Champêtre*.[31] Recently, David J. Wilkins has remained divided on the issues of attribution (Giorgione or Titian) as well as of title: "*Pastoral Scene* now known as the *Fête Champêtre*."[32]

Without implying either physical or intellectual work, *Fête* disregards the agricultural labor that is typical of Virgilian georgics and points to places where festive events resonate with musical sounds that are familiar to the work-free world of pastoralism.[33] In fact, bucolic fellowships ignore the ills that plague the "real" world of economic activity and material exchange. Conversely, the adjectival qualifier *champêtre* points to a somewhat rustic landscape where *champ* is agricultural. The clash between noun and adjective exposes the innate ambiguity of the genre, which makes the ascendancy of leisure over work essential to the very nature of pastoralism. Since shepherds make artistic rather than utilitarian efforts, the titological *fête* well captures bucolic teleology. Likewise, *concert* reinforces an event that offers an alternative to the discharge of ordinary tasks. *Champêtre* makes Titian's title locative, whereas *concert* makes it performative; their combination outlines a landscape that sets the human subject in front of nature. Because it is human-made, *fête* complements *concert*, and both "redeem" the prosaic *champêtre*. What is highlighted is a lifestyle that draws people and deities into an event symbolic of Renaissance aestheticism.

In an age when the *rinascita* of antiquity thrived on the recovery of the classical past, Sannazaro discovered his own pastoral clearings by recovering Virgil's bucolic exile. Titian, however, had no "pictorial" Virgil to draw from. Given the limited survival of ancient paintings, the Venetian master became a precursor in his own bucolic enclave. For Titian no less than for Sannazaro, it was enough to let the spirit of their classical forefathers be reborn in the midst of a more congenial culture that found expression in the mythic lyricism of the Umbrian painter Perugino. The open space and lyrical mood of *Apollo and Marsyas* (Fig. 3) bridged the gap between the Florentine geometries of Piero della Francesca and the Venetian naturalism of Giovanni Bellini.[34] None of them felt any anxiety about the authority of older models. Nor did they feel any Freudian compulsion to kill ancestral parents in order to shake literary filiations. Beyond the constraints of natural parenthood, Renaissance artists adopted foster parents of their own choice. Memory drew from a fellowship with the dead, which turned oblivion into the more constructive experience of nostalgia.

In terms of the social makeup of the Venetian *Concert*, we look at a group of four figures engaged in a musical performance. While the elegantly dressed man plays the lute, his rustic-looking cohort listens and learns. Standing by, the nude women could be goddesses who oversee the musical event. While holding a pitcher,[35] one muse turns away from the group to pour water into a cistern-like sarcophagus, thus adding sounds to musical notations.[36] She performs an act whose very uselessness transcends need, foregrounding a scene in which humans are seated next to deities in a place that is overtly

FIG. 3 Pietro Perugino, *Apollo and Marsyas*, c. 1495. Louvre, Paris.

fictional. Physical nudity and mental aloofness project the classic standard of impersonal style, much as the water that the deity pours seems to refresh Winckelmann's metaphor: "Perfect beauty is like pure water, which has no particular taste."[37]

Because of the muses' presence, *Concert* blends natural and manmade sounds. Water echoes the opening line of Theocritus's first idyll: "The whisper of that pine that sings by the springs is sweet, shepherd, and sweet, too, is the sonorities of your piping." Forests and rocks amplify human-made sounds in ancient pastorals. Likewise, a spring gushes forth near Apollo in Raphael's *Parnassus* (Fig. 4). In all of them, water makes nature sing, and by so doing it moves humankind to answer in kind. In the words of the poet-critic John Hollander, the muse pours:

> with a glowing faith,
> In one portmanteau, fame and death
> . . .
> The dead, whom we are shouting at,
> Though silent to us now, have spoken
> Through us, their stony stillness broken.[38]

FIG. 4 Raphael, *The Parnassus*, detail showing Apollo and the Muses.

Acoustics suggests that the sarcophagus, as water falls into it, is there to echo older voices, which disinter ancient memories that make pastoralism willfully posthumous. On pastoral ground, elegy can easily turn into eulogy.

The unadorned geometry of Titian's sarcophagus lacks the ornamental relief work of Titian's own *Sacred and Profane Love* (Fig. 5) or Leonardo da Vinci's *Annunciation* (Fig. 6). Because they were often carved with figures of the muses, ancient sarcophagi, to follow Paul Claudel, stands for one's cultural stature.[39] In *Concert Champêtre* the sarcophagus serves a function as elusive as the fiction it represents. From a thematic point of view the emptiness of ancient vessels accommodates modern contents, suggesting that life could be lived on the poetic plane of a more imaginative humanism. By pouring fresh water, the standing muse makes the sarcophagus life giving. Her gesture is one of rejuvenation, for it points toward grounds where the death of any bucolic poet—like that of any one nightingale—gives way to

FIG. 5 Titian, *Sacred and Profane Love*, c. 1515. Galleria Borghese, Rome.

FIG. 6 Leonardo da Vinci, *Annunciation*, detail, 1472–75. Uffizi Gallery, Florence.

the renewal of pastoral poetry in that no-man's-land where art has resurrected life on the stage of a more imaginative topography. Titian thus found it easy to set his pastoral somewhere between fact and idea. In one's mental Arcady, urns and sarcophagi could be a womb for the mind amid a landscape of symbolic markers. From Sannazaro to Keats, bucolic verses have been couched in the fertile urn of the poet's own imagination, which has never failed to craft vessels of its own.

The underlining of *Arcadia* plays up the symbolism of pastoral anachronism, which affects people as well as the objects they use. Accordingly, the juxtaposition between the pipe and the sarcophagus echoes the future-oriented resilience of the genre by preserving "traces" of inscriptions that stir mute contemplations. Death witnesses but does not terminate the better life of art, which belongs to the poet's present. He alone can give life back to the vase reliefs of bygone *fêtes,* which otherwise would be no more than cold decorations on clay pieces of Greek archaeology. In a way, Arcadian enclaves are graveyards where the human imagination performs acts of spiritual resurrection. In the bucolic images of Titian, Guercino, and Poussin,[40] skulls and inscriptions warn shepherds that all things human are bound to end. But art is there to replenish memories, and Titian has removed lids to let the embodiments of human creativity replenish life.

Titian's muse reminds the poet of tombstone epitaphs that inspire recreation beyond the undying ghosts of yesteryear.[41] Her elegant pose foregrounds "doing" as a dreamlike form of poetic renewal. The art historian Sidney Freedberg values memory over presence when he discusses Giorgione's *Sleeping Venus* (c.1505) (Fig. 7), whose "sensuous existence" is "no longer present to the touch. . . . Venus denotes not the act of life but the recollection of it." We could as well say that sensuality "has been distilled off."[42] In the Venetian hinterlands, only a wisp of cloth hides the nudity of muses and goddesses alike, because the folds of myth suffice to shield them from wearing clothes that would otherwise measure rank, wealth, and mortality.[43] Because she knows how to foster deeds that might rejuvenate poets, painters, and educators, Titian's muse guides us toward a better world where facts have become feelings. Yet that world is not better because ancient figures are guarding it; it is better because it has been visited by the modern paragon of cultural excellence.

Arcadia introduces a country where urns, tombs, and sarcophagi inspire unwearied melodists to sing songs that resonate with the heartbeat of what is most elusive in human life. With reason, Walter Pater's influential essay "The

School of Giorgione" reminds us that the arts aspire to disembody themselves by reaching out toward a more abstract plateau. Writing was the gift of Mnemosyne; her function was to commemorate, and Arcadian sarcophagi mark the last words, the very burial of voices. On Venetian grounds, the muse would remember a past that, unlike its Florentine counterpart, was less informed by historical memorials but more suffused with an impalpable sense of aesthetic self-renewal. Both acts were authoritative; to bring the vision back, in fact, could be greater than to attain it. Once it is underlined, *Arcadia* outlines an intellectual milieu that a titologist would describe in terms of the Proustian remembrance of things past.

Human acts of creation die in Arcadia as they do everywhere else. But the pastoral muse is there to announce the rebirth of the pastoral tradition from its own ashes. We can rest assured that the pastoral world dies only when the poet turns his back on Mnemosyne. She never forgets, and her act of remembrance gives life to the artist, who celebrates a vision of reality laid out at the foothills of a more familiar Parnassus.[44] The Venetians knew this better than most; and they would suggest that to read an epitaph is to be reminded of life. Thus they erased funeral epitaphs and made of musical language a recreational performance for the living, which Titian painted in the belief that bucolic images imitated art for life's "better" sake.

FIG. 7   Giorgione, *Sleeping Venus*, c. 1510. Gemäldegalerie, Staatliche Kunstsammlungen, Dresden.

As a deity who oversees a bucolic event, the seated muse holds a reed and joins the artist-courtier in the communal sharing of the musical event. She could be Euterpe, discoverer of the pipes. While owning the memorial language of the past, she plays music in the present. Since her seated pose is similar to that of the courtier-musician, *Concert* defines a "covenant" of deities and people. At once aural and aerial, language is as muffled as the density of dreams that let godly voices play in concert with human melodies. Likewise, silence holds on to the residues of songs that hover between the experience of what has been played and intimations of what might, or could not, be uttered. *Concert* unfolds the "harmonic time" of a musical performance that is set against the "customary time" of the transient shepherd in the background of the picture.[45]

The moment of suspension in *Concert Champêtre* blended pastoral "mode" and "mood" at a time when myths about the Pythagorean music of the spheres made room for more hedonistic forms of communication in the culture of northern Italy.[46] Of all the purported attributes of music, that of bringing relaxation was the one most familiar to the humanists. Otherwise, they trusted the power of words to be their forte.[47] *Concert* is enacted by wind instruments that detract from any "educational value" because they exclude the use of voice. According to Aristotle, "Athena invented the flute and then

FIG. 8   Titian, *Concert Champêtre*, detail of Figure 2.

threw it away. . . . the acquirement of flute-playing contributes nothing to the mind, since to Athena we ascribe both knowledge and art."[48] Much as the poet's literary persona went to Arcadia "not as a rustic shepherd but as a most cultured youth," so did Titian focus on a player-teacher who favors exchanges in the form of what Sannazaro calls "unsophisticated elegance" and "unassuming grace" (*Arcadia* 104–5).

Since Hesiod's *Theogony*, the muses have inspired pastoral poets, framing a cluster of relationships that affects rich and poor in *Concert Champêtre*. Social hierarchies echo stylistic classifications, and Virgil's shift from the epic grandeur of the *Aeneid* to quotidian praxis in the *Georgics* is updated in Titian's figures. One is what the Mantuan Battista Spagnoli, Virgil's Renaissance heir apparent, would call *pastor bonus;* he is as committed to his flock as he is oblivious to mundane calls. The other is a *pastor felix* who appreciates the "soft" life of intellectual leisure under the muse's tutelage. Titian echoed the common belief that rustics remain ignorant only until talent steers some of them away from the group. By taking over a pedagogical legacy, the nobleman educates the young shepherd seated next to him. He holds the "high" string instrument, which is superior because it allows the use of voice.[49] The uncouth appearance of the rustic youth comes through by way of unkempt hair, humble clothes, and bare feet, which play up those attributes of *champêtre* that touch on unsophisticated social mores. Unlike the other shepherd

FIG. 9 Titian, *Concert Champêtre*, detail of Figure 2.

who attends to the flock, he responds to art, and the artist-teacher is there to stir a latent potential for the appreciation of beauty.

Elegance and rusticity point to a culture in which clothes, language, and music identify "differentiated" social types. They enact the dualism of high and popular culture, which the title suggests through the noble *concert* and the rustic *champêtre*. If rusticity has unperfected the vision, reality has been ennobled in the pictorial pastoral. By giving the rustic "naive" and the urban "sentimental" a chance to meet, Venetian art bestowed earthly gravity on the more abstract ideals of Tuscan humanism. While the Neapolitan Sannazaro came back to a world where bees produced "unperfected honey" (Epilogue), the Venetians held on to a dream world in which people would have to part ways at the end of common experiences. Pastoralism could be sympathetic and even critical, but it rarely set out to be revolutionary.

Within the more popular perimeter of Venetian culture, the pictorial also drew from the theatrical. Angelo Beolco, known as Ruzante, wrote *La pastoral* (*The Pastoral*), which was staged for the first time in Padua in 1517. The play upgraded the depiction of rustics, who usually appeared as crude human beings in a tradition that went back to the Sienese *Congrega dei Rozzi*. Ruzante raised the reputation—if not the prestige—of *letteratura subalterna*, a kind of lower-grade literature that mixed dialect with vernacular. The comedy, in fact, opens with a double prologue. One introduces classical deities, nymphs, and the dignified language of Tuscany (*in lingua tosca*); the other is in the rustic style (*a la villana*) of shepherds, farmers, *pastori*, *agricoltori*, and *Ruzante villano*.[50]

Pastoral journeys therefore explored popular enclaves and stopped at the threshold of old myths. Discovery and recovery often stood next to each other. As a geographical and literary title, *Arcadia* retained the classical emphasis on places loaded with meaning, and, like Delphi, Olympia, or Cuma, it grew into a shrine of Western literature. Titling exiled pastoralism to the pages of written journeys that had become familiar to bucolic shepherds. They knew much of what they were going to find, confident as they were that progress was being made toward a place created not at the other side of the world but in the better corner of this world. In a sense, titles came of age inasmuch as modern artists had learned to draw their myths from their own vernacular past.

Popular acclaim resorted to the qualifier *divino* in the case of Raphael, who in turn sanctioned Sannazaro's reputation by including him in *Parnassus*, one of the three frescoes in the Vatican's *Stanza della Segnatura*. At the end of *Arcadia,* we read that the muses are dead. As ancient forms, they are indeed. After all, classical progenitors were recovered so that emulation would yield emancipation. The result was an array of conceptual and stylistic gaps. While creating confusion, artistic endeavors shifted back and forth between past and present.

Still, in the Epilogue we read that the *sampogna* is dead; yet could it ever die within an artwork that had just established itself as the modern paradigm for a genre caught between the rustic presence of a plausible *veduta* and the dreamlike wakefulness of an evanescent *visione?* At the edge of such a nostalgic imagery we may find an answer to Renato Poggioli's thoughtful remark: "Sannazaro did not lie when he named Sincero the hero of his *Arcadia.*"[51] Sincerity is not a sign of instinctual naiveté but of intellectual accomplishment. Onomastics spells out a transcendental sincerity divorced from, and elevated above, the drudgery of everyday existence. In fact, the Neapolitan shepherd, the Venetian courtier, and the Mediterranean muses body forth one of those rare eras "of more favorable conditions" when, to borrow from Walter Pater, "the thoughts of men draw nearer together than is their wont, and the many interests of the intellectual world combine in one complete type of general culture."[52]

FIG. 10   Raphael, *The Parnassus,* 1510–11. Stanza della Segnatura, Stanze di Raffaello, Vatican Palace, Vatican State.

Vernacular humanism thus named its own Arcadian enclaves in places and times that were uniquely modern. Pietro Bembo, the leading Venetian humanist at the turn of the sixteenth century, presents two beautiful girls at the outset of *Gli Asolani;* one sings after the other has started to play the lute.[53] The title has a double edge. It refers to the dialogues that took place in Asolo, but it could also refer to the "symbolic" citizenship of the speakers who are involved in the text. Painting and literature join forces in shaping a transient vision in which a happy few "disport in the open air" at Queen Caterina Cornaro's court in the little town north of Venice. At once inspirational and recreational, bucolic enclaves could be located in some of those Palladian villas that were built on the *terraferma* with mounting frequency after the Cambrai war.[54] Especially for the Venetians, pastoralism in the arts did not emerge until the *Serenissima* began to foster a culture of rural farmhands between the *laguna* and the Alps.

With regard to toponomastics, the etymology of Bembo's title, *Asolani,* created *asolare,* a neologism that describes a leisurely demeanor quite akin to the kind of cultural aestheticism that inspired the semantics of Castiglione's courtly *sprezzatura*. Upon revisiting the Renaissance enclave, Robert Browning translated the infinitive *asolare* into the gerund *asolando*.[55] It is the title of one of his poetic collections (*Asolando*), and it best encompasses the semantics of a lifestyle that spurred readers to do things in the manner of the sophisticated elite. "Titling" named places of the mind in which human presence left topographic accuracy behind. *Locus* was important because it was *amoenus,* and it was *amoenus* because of man's intervention in nature. An aristocracy of learning emerged in the heart of older towns, in gardens adjacent to palaces, or just outside the city gates. As the "other" place, *Arcadia* could not be written in Arcadia itself. Underlining turned places into titles, and landscapes were ploughed with the markings of anachronistic journeys from Arcadia to *Arcadia,* where nouns and verbs uttered an aesthetic logology that we still find resonant. If we agree that to imagine a language is to imagine a form of life, the humanists coined charismatic words—*lauro, virtù, grazia*—that defined an artistic culture.

Titian's image of detached nobility lets us enter a world of barefoot shepherds, elegant courtiers, and nude deities who translate casual encounters into a poetic vision. Titologically speaking, they have underlined *Arcadia,* which might as well be their Olympian initiation into the aesthetic of education.

Knowledge and beauty went hand in hand in Venetian whereabouts as well as in nearby courts where everybody read *Il libro del cortegiano,* in which Baldassar Castiglione portrayed the humanist elite at its very best in the material presence of the book itself. Whether scriptural or visual, such educational models paved the way for Schiller's *Über die Ästhetische Erziehung des Menschen in einer Reihe von Briefen* (*Letters on the Aesthetic Education of Man*), the emblematic title of cultural maturity for humanists young and old. Pregnant with wishful aestheticism, these titles outline a literary context in which *Arcadia* and *Concert Champêtre* magnify what pastoralism could inspire us to do. Both house a spiritual homeland where shepherds know much of what they are going to find. Confidently they colonize a place at the edge of an imaginative geography where they can resurrect the past in order to remember a "better" present of their own making. At once escapist and transcendental, part of that inclusive present is the humanist synthesis of education and aesthetics in the performative mode of *asolando.*

As an authoritative voice that paused on matters of titles, Patricia Egan opened her study of the Louvre pastoral by recognizing two titles: *Fête Champêtre* and *Concert Champêtre.* Having found them inadequate, she remained hopeful that someone would come up with a title that could express "the harmonious entirety of the scene and the thematic union among its parts."[56] Perhaps that title could be the one that Dante Gabriel Rossetti gave to his ekphrastic poem *A Venetian Pastoral,* which blended the Virgilian echoes of Sannazaro's *Arcadia* with the Venetian uniqueness of Bembo's *Asolani.* Hopefully they all rejoiced with Titian in dissolving space and time into the self-fulfilled plenitude of a daylight dream.

2

The Title's Novelistic Birthmark: *La vida de Lazarillo de Tormes y sus fortunas y adversidades*

To give a name, is that still to give?
Is that to give some thing?
—JACQUES DERRIDA

By definition, pastoral journeys ignored empirical concerns with money, income, and employment. Fictions of poetic rusticity expressed fulfillment at the other side of the materialist practice of everyday existence. Whether in the low or the high style, much Renaissance literature traded empirical paths for the wishful geographies of Latin and vernacular texts, from Petrarch's *Africa* and Leonardo Bruni's *Laudatio florentinae urbis* (*Panegyric to the City of Florence*) to *La città del sole* (*The City of the Sun*) by Tommaso Campanella. Such place-name titles anchored exemplary narratives to the rhetoric of praise, which took political dominance and economic affluence for granted.

To a significant extent, the Renaissance wavered between the fiction of static topographies and the reality of geographical explorations. The navigational journeys of the age of discovery claimed legitimacy for colonial expansion on the authority of the Roman heritage. Under the rubric of Christian imperialism, aggression crossed the Atlantic Ocean and landed *conquistadores* on American shores. Heathen souls were saved after Spain's hegemony in their homelands had been secured. At home, however, picaresque narratives in the "low style" charted paths littered with the footprints of indigent folks who would never believe that theirs was "the Golden Age."

In 1492 the Catholic kings began to conquer vast territories in the Americas. In that same year the Spanish Crown forced entire populations of non-Christians to leave their ancestral homeland in Spain itself. They were Jews and Arabs, many of whom converted to Christianity out of convenience while keeping their faith in secret. Like the great navigators of the time, some *conversos* turned out to be writers who ventured on desperate rather than unbeaten paths through the crowded geography of poverty. Outsiders in their own country, they gave literary form to a destitute humanity that nobody wanted to discover because everybody already knew it. Indigenous people in the Old World were as marginalized as the native populations of the New.

Outside Italian enclaves, where canonical standards were upheld with a vengeance, more unconventional minds favored the creation of literary fictions that depicted poverty in all its crudeness. Covering the range between the anonymous and the notorious, the excellent and the roguish, the affluent and the impoverished, the new genre of the novel brought into the light of day the utter destitution of poor people who struggled for survival in the streets and towns of Castille. Novels exposed readers to the chores of life in the making in places hitherto bare of historical markers. At the opposite pole from elitist escapes, the Renaissance produced titles that shed light on the material condition of ordinary folks all too familiar with the trials and tribulations of life in the raw. In its title, the anonymous *La vida de Lazarillo de Tormes y de sus fortunas y adversidades* (*The Life of Lazarillo de Tormes and His Fortunes and Adversities*) centers on the significance of name and place. Written in the 1530s and published in 1554,[1] this autobiographical fiction emerged as the prototype of both novelistic prose and picaresque tales rooted in popular culture. The humanist was lodged in courts and academies, whereas the merely human survived in dusty streets, forgotten hovels, and destitute neighborhoods. Insignificant places such as Tejares and Alfarache led rogues by the name of Lazarillo and Guzmán to Toledo and Seville long before nineteenth-century novels mapped out the working-class topographies of Paris and London.

The geography of these places called for a new kind of explorer, not one who would discover Florentine utopias or Venetian dreamlands but one who would wander through the landscape of common laborers who never benefited from Medician gestures. The picaresque text of *Lazarillo de Tormes* exemplified Toledo's poverty as much as the humanist treatise did the affluent merchants of Florence, where Leon Battista Alberti created a character—the family leader—whose conduct he described hypothetically in *I libri della famiglia* (*The Books of the Family* or *On the Family*). In Toledo, existence itself gave form and content to the toils of indigent folks who lived beneath the privileged culture of a vastly unproductive minority that kept popular voices silent. To the very end of the Spanish Golden Age, which drew strength from the gold and silver that financed it, the aristocracy upheld epoch-making myths that ignored the mediocre, overlooked the normal, and favored the elite. The fellowship of the happy few stood against crowds of impoverished folks.

Novels proved that the longest journeys often take place within the shortest distances. Whether historical or archetypal, picaresque adventures always pointed away from promised lands. On Spanish soil, the material condition of underprivileged people inspired writers and artists, from Alemán and Quevedo to Ribera, Murillo, and Velázquez. They brought to the fore anonymous folks who lived at the margins of productive society. It took a long time to map the outer reaches of the picaresque, where rogues by the name of Lazarillo and Guzmán made omelets with eggs as rotten as the corrupt society in which they lived. With a passion, prose narratives gave voice to water carriers, town criers, and outsiders of all kinds.[2] Titles such as *La Celestina* (by Fernando de Rojas) or *Rinconete y Cortadillo* (by Cervantes) identified a popular culture of servants, prostitutes, and criminals that stood side by side with the aristocratic tradition of epic and chivalric onomastics—from El Cid and Amadís de Gaula to Don Quixote.

By focusing on an individual whose fortunes and misfortunes led him to journey from a little village to the big city, this chapter will show how the title's onomastic (*Lazarillo*) and toponomastic (*Tormes*) markers touch on problems of genre formation (*vida*), socioeconomics (*fortunas y adversidades*), and the art of survival.[3]

The plot line tells us that Lázaro left his hometown of Tejares once his father was sent to prison for stealing grain. As a result, his mother decided to move to the university city of Salamanca in the hope of mixing "with respectable people" (*arrimarse a los buenos*). When things did not work out, she gave her son away to a blind beggar (*ciego*) who initiated him into the "career of living" (*carrera de vivir*). In the minor—or marginal—key of the picaresque, the narrative introduced an early version of lost illusions and great expectations, which spurred Lázaro to test instinct and ambition alike. After painful trials that sharpened his street smarts, Lázaro outwitted his master and moved to Toledo, a center of commercial power and religious authority. There he served a succession of priests, a dispossessed squire, and a seller of false indulgences before landing the job of water carrier. *Adversidades* gave way to *fortunas* once Lázaro established a routine that, for the first time in his life, yielded a steady income. Success, however, spurred him to give up steady employment in order to pursue a better, though uncertain, future. After a while he landed the job of town crier (*pregonero*) with the help of the local archpriest, who offered him a "package deal" that included a marriage with a young woman who, curiously enough, turned out to be the archpriest's mistress. Such a profit-sharing agreement was suspect, and the prologue tells us that, years later, Vuestra Merced, the highest ecclesiastical authority in the narrative, called on the town crier to explain his situation.

Lázaro was accountable for his marital arrangement; he had enjoyed its advantages, but the time had come to face up to its liabilities. However vague about the pseudolegal character of the written request (*caso*), the prologue turned out to be an indictment. To defend himself, Lázaro wrote the first European novel.

1

For Victor Brombert, the onomastic title *Père Goriot* is "distinctly plebeian and even vulgar." Because *goret* means young pig, the title points to a mimesis of ordinary life that underscores Honoré de Balzac's "realistic intentions."[4] Almost three hundred years earlier, realistic intentions inspired the first European novel, which also bore an onomastic title. An underdog by birth, Lázaro became a model for worthy heirs such as *El Buscón* (by Francisco de Quevedo) and *Guzmán de Alfarache* (by Mateo Alemán), a title that popular acclaim shortened to *El Pícaro*. Character and title established the picaresque as a genre that had undergone both evolution and settlement across a population of ordinary folks and forgotten villains.

Most *pícaros* never transcended mere survival, but a few did. They made a difference, and Lazarillo de Tormes was one of them. He was not a hero, and his onomastic diminutive left no doubt that the first picaresque text was neither epic nor chivalric, because neither genre ever presented diminutives of "epic" El Cid or "chivalric" Amadís de Gaula. In sixteenth-century Spain, onomastics was relevant to secular and religious writers who paid attention to the symbolic value of names. Luis de Léon wrote, "There are two different forms and manners of names; those which are in the soul and those which are on our lips."[5] Among contemporary readers of *novelle*, *novelas*, and novels, Lázaro de Tormes was the name on everybody's lips. Once the picaresque peaked at the turn of the seventeenth century, Guzmán de Alfarache asked, "Quieres conocer quien es? Mirale el nombre" (Wouldst thou know who this is? Behold his name).[6] Whether the narratives be popular or aristocratic, novelistic characters often bear names that stand out as points of entry into the reading of literary texts.

Lázaro's story makes a case for people whose daily routines fall below either the memorable or the extraordinary. Let us remember that *historia* (*storia* in Italian and *histoire* in French) is a portmanteau word that describes not only exceptional stories but undistinguished tales as well. Neither great expectations nor lost illusions ever fell within range of Lázaro's struggle to survive one day at a time. The protonovelistic form of the Spanish picaresque brought to the fore the poorest of society. Impoverishment was economic as well as onomastic. From Lazarillo and Pablillos to Guzmanillo, the title introduces a diminutive suffix that points to the low status of picaresque characters: ordinary at times and downright inferior most of the time. The title confronts readers with a preliminary contradiction. *Vida* refers to the entire life, and Lazarillo's blind master instructs his *mozo* in a *carrera de vivir* that unfolds through a series of *fortunas* and *adversidades*. But why does the title use the diminutive *Lazarillo*? Why not the adult Lázaro, who is, after all, the subject of the book? Only the *ciego* uses the diminutive—twice in the first *tratado*, where he tricks the boy out of a piece of sausage: "Que es esto, Lazarillo?" (39). Lazarillo, however, grows to adulthood and is never called by his juvenile diminutive again. So why *Lazarillo* in the title? The diminutive points not to his boyhood but to some kind of ominous demotion.

From picaresque to quixotic narratives[7] the diminutive implies demotion. Don Quixote pits two conditions of life against each other when he meets a famous man who has been condemned to ten years in prison: "This fellow is the famous Ginés de Pasamonte, alias Ginesillo de Parapilla." Ginés has become Ginesillo. Having rejected this surname, the galley slave looks at his future as a wishful recovery of onomastic integrity: "One day somebody may learn whether my name is Ginesillo de Parapilla or not.... I'll stop them calling me that or I'll pluck them" (*Don Quixote*, I, 22). The autobiographical book he is writing will bear the title *La vida de Ginés de Pasamonte,* which will remove onomastic no less than physical shackles. In fact, onomastics can be as complex as the novelistic form itself. After his initial sally, Don Quixote unabashedly proclaims: "I know who I am." Yet he says this immediately after assuming a new identity. Throughout, the knight's name shifts amid onomastic signposts—Quexada, Quesada, Quijote—that Quijano rejects once he recovers his mental health. Likewise, he calls his Ariostesque model "Roland, or Orlando, or Rotolando" (I, 25). Names seem to slip by under Cervantes's pen, the implication being that the instability of names is typical of human identity. "Borges and I" were always two for the Argentinean writer, and when people in the street asked him whether they ever were one, the answer was: "At times!" Indeed, one can grow into and out of a name.

Lázaro de Tormes, however, has no choice, because Toledans know what his name has always been. At the height of his prosperity as town crier, one of his duties is to march criminals out of town. Literally and metaphorically, he walks just a few steps ahead of them, discharging a duty that must remind him of his father's shameful past. The title tells us that Lázaro cannot separate his socioeconomic growth from past adversities, however much he sets out to sever the inherited family line from his own timeline.[8] Ironically, his lifelong task is to break the traditional continuity that ties parents to their offspring and birthplaces to workplaces. The title suggests that he has been reborn to some form of childhood, which entails either immaturity or inferiority. At any rate, Lazarillo's life is incarnated in the proper name, whose range and depth are dwarfed by the diminutive suffix *-illo*. In a way, to write a name is to chart a destiny; to acknowledge that Lázaro yields to Lazarillo is to accept belittlement as a verbal sign of self-punishment.

As a spokesman for religious authority in the sixteenth century, Antonio Nebrija wrote in *Gramatica Castellana* that quality—*calidad*—sorts out common from proper names. Actually, the picaresque narrative tests the qualitative fit between individual selfhood (Lázaro) and social identity (town crier). Indeed, names tell stories; Roland Barthes believes that to read is "to fold the text according to one name and then to unfold it along the new folds of this name."[9] Onomastics in the Spanish narrative brings to the surface the textual ripples of both inheritance and emancipation.[10] If the anonymous narrator (Yo) in the prologue can convince Vuestra Merced that he is just *a* destitute Lázaro, which describes a social type whose assets and liabilities are typical of the society in which he lives, his case will be strengthened. To do that, he lets the milieu absorb him.

Yet terms such as *fortuna* and *adversidad* are problematic in the picaresque title because they point to an outcome at once uncertain and propitious. Since it begins with an adolescent and ends with an adult, the trajectory of Lázaro's growth is pinned to the first word of the title, *vida*. However discreet the text's motive and the title's representation, even as popular a narrative as Lazarillo's *fortunas y adversidades* refers to historical events (the battle of Las Gelves, the emperor's entrance into Toledo) and raises the issues of famine, nobility of blood, ecclesiastical corruption, labor exploitation, bureaucratic inefficiency, and outright criminality. The title reins in the conflictive nature of Lázaro's socioeconomic growth, which covers lifelong deeds in tune with the ebb and flow of existence before the last chapter depicts his ability to secure a profitable job.

The title begs the question why and how Lázaro has become Lazarillo. Is the shift from one to the other a sign of fulfillment or failure vis-à-vis the fortunes and misfortunes of an entire life? Lázaro's whole life is intertwined with popular culture, which lets picaresque "continuations" proliferate side by side with Cervantine *hidalgos*. The word *vida* in the title prompts us to speculate about the novel, which constructs the world around a character that moves between the ordinary and the exemplary.[11] In the experimental mode of realistic parody, the new genre bridged the gap between story and history. Since the emergence of "realism" is linked to literature about common people, we might reflect on Antonio Gramsci's comment that the "heroes of popular culture, when they have entered the sphere of the intellectual life of ordinary folks, detach themselves from any literary origin and claim the validity of historical characters. Their whole life is interesting, which also explains the popularity of 'continuations.'"[12]

In a circular way, themes that appear at the beginning of the narrative come to fruition by the end of the story. One is the belief that marriage ought to be a profitable investment. As it turns out, marriage is a *fortuna* as well as an *adversidad*. Lázaro considers it an investment that entails profits and obligations alike. Having secured the job of town crier, he marries the archpriest's mistress. His social climb begins, but neighbors spread rumors about the "unholy" triangle in which he is involved. The town crier has no choice but to defend his wife's reputation by swearing on the Holy Ghost. After all, she is as good a source of economic fortune as anyone could find in Toledo, where everyone seems to trade principle for convenience; sign and coin seem to coincide.

Monetary and sexual exchanges merge in the culture of the picaresque. Since he cannot afford honor, Lázaro invests in the economic potential of dishonor. The fact is that luck is predetermined in Toledo, where work depends on favors either received or rendered. Because the corrupting powers of the authorities affect the whole body politic, the job of *pregonero* is a form of lawful work as well as of institutionalized parasitism. From nine to five o'clock, the *pregonero*'s words beget money; before and after hours, everybody points to Lázaro's shame. While testing ingenuity no less than honesty, profit comes with strings attached. *Provecho* holds the key to the balance of Lázaro's life, which the title sets between *fortunas* and *adversidades*. He can neither discuss nor debate; he can only acquiesce, because the archpriest alone controls the production of discourse. Only by adjusting to hypocrisy has the town crier secured the material benefits of a profitable conduct (*manera provechosa*) that entails choices at once lucrative and blameworthy. Although it is a utilitarian concept at heart, *provecho* implies progress, prosperity, and utility;[13] from a titological point of view, it is material *fortuna* and moral *adversidad*. To the very end of the picaresque narrative, *provecho* remains a source of integration and exclusion; it is bread and host, that is to say, a *pharmakon* at once poisonous and curative.

Together with its attendant verbs *ganar, ahorrar, recaudar, comprar, trocar,* and *negociar*,[14] *provecho* spells out the vocabulary of Lázaro's standard of living, which blurs the distinction between the good man and the business man, the *hombre de bien* and the *hombre de negocios*. The equation of moral good with material goods proves to be teleological. In the first chapter, Lazarillo manipulates the "liquidity" of fast-moving coins when he tricks his blind master by switching half *blancas* for whole ones. Just as quickly, the writer invests in a novelistic coinage that may turn out to be as valuable—as *bueno*—in discrediting Vuestra Merced's indictment as the ownership of "goods" is in empowering people not because they are good but because they own "the goods." Standing as it does at the heart of the corrupted socioeconomic mores of Toledo, *provecho* is bait and trap; the moral has been overshadowed by the material.[15] Instead of creating productive conditions that would transform society for the better, *provecho* consolidates the abusive status quo; and Lázaro falls hostage to it. We are reminded of Balzac's question in *Modeste Mignon:* "Combien de fois un mot n'a-t-il pas decidé de la vie d'un homme?" (How many times has a word decided a man's life?)

If words can be bait, places can be traps. As a picaresque locus, Lázaro's birthplace, Tejares, does not stir Medician pride, nor is the river Tormes conducive to Proustian longings. Lázaro remembers his place of birth only because people keep reminding him of it. The river Tormes and the village of Tejares blend into an enclave that is neither a comfortable shelter nor a safe harbor. From Tejares and Alfarache to Salamanca and Toledo, the picaresque sense of place bears heavily on the cultural symbolism of the novel. Whether he likes it or not, Lázaro is and remains the one "from" Tormes. The inference is that the verbal structure of names parallels that of human experience. At the turn of the seventeenth century, Guzmán, the most popular of *pícaros,* confessed, "In order not to be recognized, I did not want to use my father's last name; they called me Guzmán after my mother, and Alfarache after my birthplace."[16] By way of parody, the journey along the river Tormes recalls the biblical Moses and the Roman twins Romulus and Remus, who performed memorable deeds after they were rescued from the river. On dry land, picaresque narratives turned chivalric correlations between names and places upside down; the noble origin of the chivalrous Amadís de Gaula stood against the ordinary heritage of Lazarillo de Tormes.

Let us remember that Tormes refers to the river in which Lázaro is born—*dentro del río*. Birth *in* rather than *by* the river is symbolic inasmuch as "fluvial" mobility carries downstream a youth who is destined to swim against the current for the rest of his life. Although the text is about a journey from Tejares to Toledo via Salamanca, the title, which is pinned to Tormes, makes it clear that questions of toponomastics touch on matters of structure and ideology. It is no accident that the prologue, written years after the events of the last chapter, closes the narrative by praising those few who can reach a safe harbor—*con fuerza y maña remando salieron a buen puerto*.

Once in Toledo, the archpriest's insistence on attaching the locative "de Tormes" to Lázaro's name tells us that his status as town crier is that of an outsider in the heart of a city where he is welcomed only insofar as he serves someone else's *picadillo*. For Lázaro, Tejares and Tormes are places to forget, but the title suggests that this will never happen. If one thinks of the proper name as a composite "milieu,"[17] Lázaro de Tormes is the initial place-name against which the *pícaro* contends for the rest of his life. Having lodged its dynamics between the land-based economy of Tejares in the first chapter and the urban mercantilism of Toledo in the last, the plot reflects widespread migrations from the country to the city, where resourceful individuals stand a better chance of finding a birthplace of merit. In the city, people exchange knowledge and trade commodities. However unwittingly, they enact the humanist myth of man as a socially integrated citizen. In terms of topographical accuracy, the title should read *La vida de Lazarillo de Tejares*. Insofar as the town crier is concerned, the title that would most aptly describe his success is *La vida de Lázaro de Toledo*.

Amid picaresque milieus, the counterfeited currency of rumors and whispers puts Lázaro de Tormes on trial in Toledo. As a cuckold, he is socially reprehensible; as the object of an indictment, his freedom is in jeopardy. As an author, he is about to create a narrative in which a dishonorable *ménage à trois* turns into a source of material prosperity and intellectual distinction. It may be less than accidental that the novel settled down in Toledo, which was enthroned as the *catedra de la picaresca real y literaria*—the headquarters of the real as well as of the literary picaresque.

While periods of crisis in the Christian tradition linked onomastics to saints,[18] secular achievements in the age of mercantile affluence favored such auspicious names as Bonvicinus, Bonaventura, Moneta, or Divitia—"good neighbor," "good luck," "money," or "wealth."[19] Value-laden names reflected a culture of treatises and panegyrics that relished the praise of individual excellence and financial success.[20] The Florentine humanist Leon Battista Alberti recommended that parents not underrate names: "It seems to me that a graceless name may well have the power to detract from the dignity and grandeur of a man, even if he is an excellent person." While some names are unlucky, others are "propitious. They somehow add luster to our virtues and our dignity."[21] Conversely, names could also point to inferiority or alienation; in the case of Lázaro the town crier, his name implied both. At the margins of society, Lázaro's "belittled" name is mirrored in his own "belittled" position as a half-outsider who keeps masters and employers anonymous. Birth bestows the gift of life, but picaresque naming warns us not to expect too much from it.[22] The title spells out an abbreviated description of a plot in which *fortunas y adversidades* highlight material deeds that played a role in the economics of Renaissance Spain,[23] an era in which the novel gave literary form to the resilient culture of poverty as well as to the corrupting influence of privilege.[24]

Before their abject condition became typical of the picaresque, poor wretches who answered to the name of Lázaro already existed in popular culture. *Lázaro existia antes que Lázaro* (Lázaro existed before Lázaro), which is another way of saying that poverty has been around since time immemorial. Poor neighbors give the boy the name of Lázaro because it speaks to their own culture of impoverishment. In fact, Lazarillo echoes the acoustics of poverty—*laceria*.[25] While it suggests that the boy's name is a matter of public charity, the homophonic association also resonates in the priest of Maqueda's appellative, *el lacerado*. His lack of money echoes his lack of compassion,[26] and the phonetic reference Lázaro-*laceria*-*lacerado* confirms that a character is the noise of his name.[27] For Arnold Weinstein, the very word *laceria* reminds us that "the self as hunger is a terrifying lens to place on society,"[28] and its sound is just as strident.

Toward the middle of the seventeenth century, the terms *lazzaroni* and *lazzari* were quite current in the Hispanic culture of Naples, where *lazzaretti* sheltered the sick and the poor. Two aspects of social pathology merge into a single word. Sickness upsets physical health in much the same way that begging undermines financial solvency.[29] The meek shall inherit the heavenly kingdom; here on earth, however, popular wisdom has it that "llamarse Lázaro ya era una predestinacion" (to be called Lázaro already was a matter of predestination). Lázaro's fate is his name, and its "popular" iconography points to Lazarus, the sickly beggar who enjoyed neither health nor wealth (John 11:1–45; Luke 16:19–31).[30] This extreme case of socioeconomic indigence stands behind the onomastic association. At the most impoverished boundary of society, Lazarus stands as a symbol of those regressive forces that are at work wherever mobility is impossible and productivity is deficient. The gift of a second life on earth "resurrects" Lazarus to neither wealth nor learning; his return to the world entails no change of fortune. Lazarus is and remains disinherited.[31] Unlike his Christian homonym, Lázaro gives up begging at a rich man's door, but his pursuit of a better future is fraught with more trials than he anticipates.

The Lázaro-Lazarus connection hints at a harsh future for the youth.[32] If there is truth in the assumption that every "nomen" conceals an omen, the Lázaro-Lazarus symbolism upholds themes of pain and privation that grow to prominence in picaresque onomastics. From a literary point of view, Lazarus is a paragon without a story; he has no *vida* to tell. Was he always a beggar? Was he always sick? The *pícaro* is not born "like" Lazarus, but the onomastic diminutive is there to remind us that the gap between the two is narrow indeed. Lazarus-like figures point to a popular model of economic destitution. Absurd as it may seem, the suggestion is that the poor would have something to be thankful for if they compared themselves to Lazarus.

Later in the seventeenth century, Quevedo compared Pablos Buscón to Lazarus only because they both smell. Once he is smeared in human waste, Pablos draws a lesson: "'When in Rome, do as the Romans do,' says the proverb, and how right it is. After thinking about it I decided to be as much a tearaway as the others and worse than them if I could" (92). The resurrection of one wretched soul does not erase the misery of the poor, and the last thing one should ask of them is that they wait for a miracle.

The genealogy of human archetypes has given us Lazarus, the Christian beggar who receives the miracle of a new life, and Sisyphus, the mythical pagan whose endless labors go unrewarded; both echo picaresque narratives. The improvement of the lot of humankind takes more than the multiplication of loaves and fishes. In practical terms, wages are needed more than alms, contracts of exchange more than gifts, and purchases more than gratuities.

The juxtaposition of Lázaro and Lazarus casts a shadow on a culture that is responsible for many varieties of social and economic illness and *laceria*.

The resurrection of one wretched soul does not offset the marginality of poor people at large. In a fundamental way, the onomastics of titles thrives on the disheartening connotations of the Lazarus etymology, which makes a case for literary creation in the mode of "negative idealism."[33] In a way, the *pregonero* is a kind of futile laborer in Toledo, where his modest achievements are liable to fail. At the same time, moral resentment is not good enough, and resignation often strengthens the status quo of class discrimination. One might say that underprivileged folks are especially prone to wait for miracles to dispense unhoped-for "gifts." Actually, gifts and miracles are escape valves that trade one form of dependence for another. The real miracle of ordinary people who want to improve their lives will not take place unless the Lazarus myth is transformed. Instead of waiting for the rewards of heaven, it would be more practical, and certainly more profitable, for the destitute of society to empower themselves, so as to partake of the bounty—*fortunas*—they help to create.

Renaissance and post-Renaissance experience teaches us that society should do away with the lure of heavenly rewards. The real miracle would be to acknowledge that the Lazarus analogy has become obsolete. In the Toledan culture of selfish cunning, a miracle occurs only when the uneducated town crier produces a written document that answers Vuestra Merced's indictment. What emerges is a narrator who exposes the corruption and hypocrisy of the society that is trying to put him on trial. *Fortunas* and *adversidades* mint a literary coinage that crosses the threshold between naiveté and resourcefulness. Although ostensibly comic at times, *Lazarillo de Tormes* is a trenchant critique of socioeconomic discrimination. But what is funny to some can be deadly serious for others. When the book first appeared, the general readership read it as comical. But this reception did not last long, and one may wonder whether the book's success—it went through three editions very quickly—can be attributed to its comic episodes, or whether its irony struck a deeper chord in readers all too aware of the kind of life led by people at the margins.[34] Mikhail Bakhtin warns us that laughter itself "means abuse, and abuse could lead to blows."[35] By 1559, when it was added to the Index of forbidden books,[36] those in charge of the master narratives no longer found the picaresque story at all funny.

Roguish tales in the largely "comic" world of popular culture surfaced in short stories (*novelle*) before novelists began to string out episodic plots into full-length novels. From text to context, a direct link exists with the secular world of Boccaccio's *Decameron*.[37] The issue of diminutive onomastics takes us to Andreuccio, a youth from Perugia who goes to Naples to buy horses. In the market square, a prostitute carries out an elaborate deception in order to steal his money. Later the same night, Andreuccio steals a ring of equivalent value from the finger of a dead bishop. His Neapolitan "education" reduces his naiveté, but whether "little" Andrew (Andre-uccio) will mature to be called Andrea is anybody's guess. Boccaccio could have included stories about Andreuccio's life back in Perugia so as to trace his development; but the short story could not accommodate such development. The picaresque, by contrast, is able to cover an entire life. By the end of the last chapter of *Lazarillo de Tormes*, we know that Lazarillo has outgrown his onomastic diminutive.[38] Its reappearance in the title points to a diminution of Lázaro the author, who refers to himself as Lazarillo to let readers know that Toledans would never permit him to rise beyond a "diminutive" position in society. It is not by accident that the picaresque *Yo* reminds us of the maxim that one man's meat is another man's poison. Meaning is literary as well as socioeconomic. The caste's meat, in fact, can be the class's poison, and vice versa. Applied to the protagonist himself, the moral poison that Lázaro has to swallow in order to survive economically turns into precious meat when the writer translates his travails into a literary narrative. To the best of his abilities, he is both meat and poison, victim and victimizer.

A number of years intervene between the events of the last chapter and the writing of the prologue. We must infer that much literary education has taken place in the interval in the house next door to the archpriest's. The *adversidad* of an unfaithful wife is offset by the *fortuna* of a clandestine education. Since the text is not explicit about Lázaro's schooling, we must surmise that the linear progression of the plot stands above a subplot that unfolds in the unwritten gaps between episodes. It is in those gaps that the *pregonero* steers away from the chivalric deeds of Amadís de Gaula as well as from the Boccaccesque ordeals of Andreuccio da Perugia. Slowly, the Salmantino *mozo* has transformed himself into a writer in Toledo.

Having left the most prestigious seat of Spanish learning behind in Salamanca, Lázaro goes on to prove that education can be acquired in Toledo, the city of business, to an extent that neither Vuestra Merced nor anyone else ever imagined. From nine to five the town crier suffers commercial transactions, moral indignities, and social marginality. During the lonely evening hours, however, he reads and studies, and his "hidden" investment pays off when Vuestra Merced asks him to explain his marital situation. The written request is vague, and Lázaro chooses to answer it by detailing the causes of his transgression. Like his father, who did not deny he was a thief, Lázaro the *pregonero* does not deny the charge against him. Unlike his father, however, he unleashes a counterindictment that puts everybody at risk. Having struggled in the world of production, the town crier becomes the anonymous narrator who can exercise judgment in the world of reproduction. Is the insightful narrator content with a secondhand wife and worn-out stockings? Is he content to remain a cog in the exploitive society that he understands so well? Such questions presume a freedom of action that Lázaro does not have, trapped as he is in Toledo. His only escape is to use the indictment to his advantage by showing that everybody is trapped. The picaresque text is not another *libro galeotto* that falls back on chivalric escapism. Instead, it is a book that those as underprivileged and as ambitious as Lázaro de Tormes would be wise to read.

Because he lives in a place with few opportunities for academic instruction, Lázaro's achievement defies expectations.[39] Unlike the biblical Lazarus, he is reborn to the life of the mind; and he does it all by himself. Yet the city of commercial transactions proves to be a milieu in which the *pregonero* is an outsider.[40] He lives and works in Toledo, but he is not a Toledan. It is this estrangement that allows him to become a writer, and writing secures his rebirth into the better life of artistic creation. Lázaro de Tormes is reborn to the homeland of artistic fellowship, where the picaresque *Yo* can claim literary parents who bear the names of Pliny and Cicero. At last the anonymous author trades the heritage of those *buenos* who finance his daytime activities for the better humanity of letters. At night he befriends an elite of *buenos* who are good because of their intellectual excellence. As a writer he finds ways of rising above the world of circumstance. Amid priests and blind men, the pen achieves what *provecho* cannot afford. Beyond pagan and Christian epics, the author of the prototypical picaresque knew that the time was ripe for bringing a constituency of vagrants, cheats, weavers, prostitutes, and impostors into the literary fold. With their array of socioeconomic outsiders, picaresque writers introduced the novel, the most radical outsider in the world of literary genres.

By the end of the final chapter, Lázaro's *buena fortuna* has made desire manageable by trading values for things. The upshot is a profitable arrangement that secures his "good luck." Because the picaresque novel foregrounds clashes between expectations and results, onomastics points to the facts of poverty as well as to the pretensions of wealth. Social and artistic priorities merge: "I beg Your Honour to receive this little gift from the author who would have written it better if his desire and skill had coincided" (24). *Suplico* describes a verbal act of begging that takes author and reader all the way back to the adolescent *mozo*. He toys with the assets and liabilities of religion to the point that neighbors call him *pecadorcico*—a term for sinners and rascals alike. The benevolent appellative *niño inocente* is bound to become obsolete, because the adolescent Lazarillo of the opening chapter has lost his innocence by the time he becomes town crier. The *pregonero* wants to become a *hombre de bien* more or less like the city folks he admires. But then again, how admirable are they? Popular wisdom and literary texts warn against false heroism. "As the sea washes away all the sins of mankind," Erasmus writes, "so war covers over the dregs of every crime."[41] For his part, Lázaro refuses to see himself as either the miller or the soldier that his father was; instead, he is determined not to let inheritance plot his future. While Lázaro the town crier endures manifold indignities, Lázaro the writer takes an assertive stand and makes a case on his own behalf. Vuestra Merced writes to a *pregonero*, but the answer reveals a person whose intellectual sophistication has been vastly underrated. In the end, the mature author chooses anonymity so as to conceal the blemishes of his previous life. Nevertheless, the title reminds us that, at the end of the story, people still call him Lazarillo de Tormes. They put Lázaro on trial in the world of Toledo, but he puts himself on trial in the world of art. The authorial pronoun of the prologue rejects onomastic impositions, and the anonymous *Yo* makes himself known with reference to a birthplace of limited merits. Because the self-portrait is pegged to a *nonada* (little trifle), proper names are wiped out, authorial signatures become impossible, and narration disappears into the gap that separates the chapters from the prologue.

Since his honor is questionable, Lázaro cannot legitimize himself any more than he can legitimize the literary form he has brought to life. The narrative raises self-defeating expectations: "I think it's a good thing that important events which quite accidentally have never seen the light of day should be made public and not buried in the grave of oblivion. It's possible that somebody may read them and find something he likes and others may find pleasure in just a casual glance; and as a matter of fact, Pliny says there is no book, however bad it may be, that doesn't have something good about it" (23). The anonymous *Yo* heightens and debases himself. In a way, the prologue upholds the Spanish mode of *harcerse* and *deshacerse* (to make and to unmake) by keeping the pronoun at once assertive and reticent. In the words of the modern poet, the pro-nominal *Yo* can rejoice:

Que alegra más alta:
vivir en los prenombres!

What higher joy
To live in pronouns!

(Pedro Salinas, *La voz a ti debida*, 1933)

If we take artistic creation to be an act of rebirth, could the picaresque narrator sign his name without falling prey to the burden of onomastics all over again? The pronoun *Yo* enacts a rhetorical strategy of concealment and exposure. Since too many people harp on Lázaro's bankrupt morality until the *caso* threatens to discredit him, Lázaro as narrator finds it more convenient to exchange name for namelessness. Only through anonymity can the prologue assert familiarity with Pliny and enforce the Ciceronian dictum that honor encourages the arts. Lázaro's rebirth into the nameless *Yo* does not proclaim the glory of a new name, but it does make a case against the retention of old ones. The *pregonero* endures moral indignities and social ostracism by day but has his revenge, as it were, by night, in the company of his books and papers. Once he is called upon to defend his *buena fortuna*, the town crier-turned-writer falls back on the cultural capital he has accumulated over the years. Thus he produces a literary text of value and beauty; and he does it better than many a student in Salamanca.[42]

While the name Lazarillo retains both ancient and modern echoes, the rest of the title reminds us that misfortune and adversity have not come to an end. Anonymity as a form of onomastic suicide leads to an act of rebirth once the prologue fashions an authorial persona that reconciles survival with culture.[43] In the hiatus between Lázaro and *Yo*, Tormes and the book,[44] we confront the paradox of a notorious namelessness that foreshadows a split between name and person in the culture of sixteenth-century Spain. The inference is that onomastic instability is but another measure of the complexities of human identity. We verge on the emergent breakdown of the medieval unity between inner and outer man. While Niccolò Machiavelli exposed the duplicity that governs life, Erasmus and Montaigne took notice of disparities between being and seeming, names and things.[45]

Gustave Flaubert later devalued fixed currencies in the matter of names when he wrote, "One dies almost always in the uncertainty of one's proper name, unless one is an imbecile."[46] On matters of naming and writing, we know how bovine Charles Bovary must be long before we meet him, and what kind of schoolteacher Dickens's McChoakumchild is even before he steps into a classroom. Names describe personal features as well as social milieus;[47] and anonymity at the end of the picaresque text denies the possibility of taking up a new name as vulnerable as the old one.[48] Against all odds, anonymity flouts the dismemberment of names, things, and values, making an ironic case for "onomastics by default."[49] By denying his own name, the narrator leaves Lazarus-like resurrections behind. What finally emerges is a man who has weathered the trials of existence and who has been ennobled by his own literary achievement.[50]

Picaresque selfhood can bear names only by undermining identity. Such a self-destructive bent plays up denial, and Roland Barthes would add that the denial of names brings forth a distinctive feature of modern narratives. "What is obsolescent in today's novel is not the novelistic, it is the character; what can no longer be written is the Proper Name."[51] Ironically, the first novel about the sustained development of a character opens with the rejection of as basic an asset as the name itself. By denying names, the narrative *Yo* denies much of life—as much of it as people deny him whenever they call him Lázaro de Tormes. Any "achieved" identity, therefore, harbors the seed of its own subversion. If proper names default and authorial signatures become impossible, the picaresque *Yo* is rewarded with the knowledge that his work can be bought, read, and praised. We do not know the outcome of the novel, but we do know the effects that *fortunas* and *adversidades* have had on names and titles.

Postmodern readers familiar with popular culture could raise pointed questions. Did it take a pseudolegal indictment to give artistic form to everyday life? Is it possible that the value of a picaresque life can become meaningful only under the threat of punishment? Should we not reflect on the dominant role that the economics of affluence has played with regard to matters of artistic representation? In other words, on whose backs was the New World "discovered"? Whose skin paid for the gold and silver that enriched commercial dynasties and Catholic kings?

2

The Renaissance scholarship of Jacob Burckhardt and Walter Pater focuses on humanist aestheticism, which gave order, clarity, and form to a vision of the state as "a work of art." The picaresque genre showed that, for the majority of people, the state was anything but a work of art. In Hapsburg Castile, the state let a few prosper while many toiled. Rich and poor lived drastically different lives within the same city walls, and the wealthy had plenty to be embarrassed by whenever light was shone on the strategies that secured their prosperity.

Picaresque titles about specific names and places clashed with humanist titles about ideas—*The Prince, The Courtier, Utopia, In Praise of Folly*. This opposition, which some may see as exclusive and others as dialogic, raises questions. How do we account for the shift from the conceptual to the practical and from the heroic to the ordinary? What is ordinary in Renaissance culture, with its awe-inspiring praise of human dignity, models of perfection, hyperbolic comparisons, and Godlike similes? How long could society ignore mundane deeds and basic existence? Insofar as artistic mimesis is concerned, it may be that the very idea of common people with ordinary values leading inconspicuous lives is itself a fiction. Under the aegis of "mobility studies," Stephen Greenblatt has written on the need to develop a literary history of "the groups marginalized by the hegemonic cultures of the ruling elites." Such a history should pay greater attention to accidental judgments, carnal and bloody acts, and "the fierce compulsions of greed, longing, and restlessness." In fact, these "disruptive forces, not a rooted sense of cultural legitimacy," shape history.[52]

The renaissance of civic humanism rediscovered the ancient world by excavating the artifacts of Roman antiquity. Now we face a similar task with regard to the renaissance of popular culture, which, though it left few historical documents and even less artistic evidence, shaped history well beyond what we have cared to investigate. Picaresque narratives about the practice of "life in the making" have shown us that the "common man" never tired of taking one more step into the future, and the title of Lazarillo's story has given title to our own lives, warts and all.

For Claudio Guillén, the picaresque gave literary form to the lifelong growth of a single individual by taking up a challenge at once aesthetic and ontological: "How does one shape a life?"[53] Such an achievement was unprecedented. The very title of the novel brings to the fore deeds we all experience under the heading of *fortunas y adversidades* that are as earthbound as the river Tormes and as driven as the imperative of survival itself. While this chapter titles an "entire" life, the next takes up the complementary task of entitling a "whole" mindset. A quarter-century after the publication of the first picaresque novel, Michel de Montaigne invented the essay once he set out to answer what I consider the kindred question "How does one shape a thought?" Taken together, these two literary genres, which grew to prominence in the culture of the late Renaissance, gave birth to much post-Renaissance experimentation.

3

From Title to Genre:
Essaying at the Threshold of Form

> The text is its own criticism, its own explication, its own application.
> —MICHEL SERRES

The picaresque art of survival favored individuals who trusted common sense and relied on proverbial wisdom to cope with the hardships of existence. Lazarillo's character development consists of his learning to get along in society as it is. Having grown into adulthood by using his street smarts, the picaresque author becomes a humanist who can quote Cicero and Pliny. During the quiet evening hours, his lonely dining room turns into a *studiolo* where he cultivates the life of the mind. Whether pauper's hovel or nobleman's palace, places of learning take us from Petrarch and Federigo da Montefeltro to Michel de Montaigne. In the seclusion of his "tower," the French aristocrat wrote his intellectual autobiography by creating a literary genre whose title, *Essais,* charted the map of the thinking mind, enacted its own methodology, and produced its own criticism.[1]

The age of discovery began by clearing grounds that were erudite in Petrarch's *Africa,* which celebrated Scipio's victory over Hannibal in the second Punic War. Written in classical Latin, the Renaissance epic was the prototypical text that played up the *rinascita* (rebirth) of classical learning. It is as longwinded as it is poetically mediocre; it was never finished and was quickly forgotten. But it displayed the kind of learning that would be required of any respectable humanist, who was expected to be well acquainted with Roman history and ancient mythology.

Throughout the Renaissance, the high style of Latin literature was countered by vernacular prose fiction that took up medieval and contemporary matters of high and low, religious and mercantile, traditional and transgressive human exchanges in both palaces and the marketplace. Let us not forget that Boccaccio's *Decameron* opens with the words *Umana cosa è* (It is human). And human means humane. The "Human Comedy" of the *Decameron* was one of the earliest narratives to represent not only the privileged classes but also ordinary folks who performed prosaic deeds.

The epic and the short story, therefore, developed in tandem during the Renaissance. Toward the end of the sixteenth century, the learned and the popular, the humanist and the humane, converged in the *Essais* (first published in Paris in 1588) of Michel de Montaigne, who tested theory against practice at a time when idealism had to come to terms with empirical reality. The humanist was progressively humanized, and Montaigne resorted to writing essays when he proposed to focus on the complexities and contradictions of the *humaine condition*. Normally the adjective follows the noun, as in Malraux's *La condition humaine*. At any rate, Donald Frame translates it as "each man bears the entire form of man's estate."[2]

1

The dictionary defines *essay* as an experiment, attempt, or trial. The OED defines it as "the action or process of trying or testing," and Larousse equates *essai* with *vérification, experimentation, épreuve*. As a title, *Essais* introduces an experimental mindset that puts on trial the flawless clarity of the humanist lexicon by debating such qualities as "glory," "vanity," and "experience" itself. The title sets up an experiential point of view that throws into question the very concepts of clarity and certainty, the cornerstones of the humanist mindset.

The plural noun *Essais* suggests accumulation, introducing a literary form that enforces the axiom "I add, I do not correct" (736). In this way Montaigne avoids erasures and fosters expansion: "The titles of my chapters do not always embrace their matter; often they only denote it by some sign. . . . I seek out change indiscriminately and tumultuously. My style and my mind alike go roaming" (761). These are not synoptic titles but mere introductions to texts whose openness is so deliberate that the writer can foresee cases in which the text will discredit the title. Both point toward a search rather than spell out a goal.

The experimental nature of the essay is bound to the present, and its "operative mode" produced three layers (which Montaigne labeled A, B, and C): "My book is always one. Except that at each new edition, so that the buyer may not come off completely empty-handed, I allow myself to add, since it is only an ill-fitted patchwork, some extra ornaments. These are overweights, which do not condemn the original form, but give some special value to each of the subsequent ones, by a bit of ambitious subtlety" (736). Each textual addition tests the range and depth of the title, which does not pretend to be less tentative than each sentence or paragraph. The plural noun in the title foregrounds the open-ended nature of the emergent genre. Montaigne maintains that anyone can speak: "Truly; but to speak with order, wisely, and competently, of that only a few men are capable—*tout homme peut dire veritablement; mais dire ordonnéement, prudemment et suffisament, peu d'hommes le peuvent*" (708). In fact, adverbs describe a context wherein plan and opportunity adjust themselves to a mode of writing that calls for a balance of opposites.[3] The essayistic modus operandi relies on adverbs that privilege function over definition; one can speak of ignorance and knowledge "meagerly and piteously, the latter secondarily and accidentally, the former expressly and principally—*megrement et piteusement, accessoirement cette-cy et accidentalement, celle là expressément et principalement*" (809). Language treats categories of knowledge as adverbial matters that are incessantly operative. The continuous practice of essay writing so empowered the writer that Montaigne finally entitled his book *Essais*. While finding permanence in change, the title tells us to expect neither an anatomy nor a synthesis, but plenty of analysis, contradiction, and discussion. In favoring process over goal, Montaigne relied on adverbial forms of expression. Throughout the sixteenth century, a shift occurred from retrospective commentaries that thrived on intellectual analogues to experimental forms. Montaigne took his title and his text from life in the making.

During the last quarter of the sixteenth century, the essayistic method became an instrument of verification. Neither paradigm nor panegyric, the essay made it clear that the order of reality was different from the order of ideas.[4] What emerged was a new awareness of the disjunction between names and things. As Montaigne put it, "There is the name and there is the thing . . . the name is not a part of the thing" (468). Humanism was figuratively aesthetic and verbally "logological." To borrow from Kenneth Burke's study of epiphanic God-words, humanist rhetoric employed charismatic terms such as *virtù, grazia,* and *sprezzatura*. The title-as-essay spurred a critique of canonical systems of order that relied on treatises and orations to legislate perfection. Humanist poetics tended to postulate flawless forms, whereas the essay brought into being forms at once tentative and developmental.

We all know that perfection is not of this world, and Machiavelli distinguished between the learned *verità ideale* and the empirical *verità effettuale*. As an ideal model, *Il Principe* (*The Prince*, completed 1513–16, published 1532) flaunts the definite article *Il*, which suggests an absolute model of acquired knowledge. Montaigne, by contrast, wrote *Essais,* not *Les Essais*. By dropping the definite article in the title, he made his essays as heterogeneous and expandable as the array of practical realities that make up human experience.

Relativism settled in once the singular yielded to the plural. In the spirit of writers who elaborated a vocabulary that gave precedence to earthbound *prudenza* (Guicciardini) and *mediocrità* (Della Casa), the time had come for literary forms to accommodate ordinary life. Between treatises that offered theories meant to solve problems and novels that magnified the persistence of problems, compromises fell short of any panacea. From the fourteenth to the late sixteenth century, there was a general evolution from the theoretical to the empirical in literature. The *Essais* undermined the utopianism of humanist literature by presenting the ideal not of the theoretical man but of the ordinary man, whose stature is neither monumental nor insignificant, but proudly life-size.

It is significant that two Italian translators of Montaigne render *essais* as *discorsi*—Naselli's *Discorsi morali, politici, e militari* (1590) and Canini's *Saggi: Overo Discorsi naturali politici e morali* (1633). These translations give us an insight into the inability of Italian writing to break away from the authority of ancient canons. As a literary form, there was no Italian equivalent for *essai*, and the best that the translators could do was to consider similar forms. Canini did use the term *saggi*, but in a tentative way that in fact paraphrased *discorsi*. Appropriately, they turned to Machiavelli's *Discorsi sulla prima deca di Tito Livio* (*Discourses on the First Decade of Titus Livius*, 1513–19), a title that was original in terms of vernacular forms and displayed continuity with Roman historiography. Its preface opens with a literary challenge: "It has always been no less dangerous to find ways and methods that are new than it has been to hunt for seas and lands unknown, since men are more prone to blame than to praise the doings of others. Nevertheless, driven by the natural eagerness I have always felt for doing without any hesitation the things that I believe will bring benefit common to everybody, I have determined to enter upon a path not yet trodden by anyone." The novelty of literary forms went hand in hand with the exploratory ethos of the age of discovery. Montaigne, however, detected shortcomings in the *discorsi*, which are "solid enough for the subject, yet it was very easy to combat them. . . . The diversity of human events offers us infinite examples in all sorts of forms" (497). However valuable, ancient models are restrictive.

Against the humanist tradition of grids, plans, and topographies of fixed order, the literary methodology of the *Essais* moved beyond the reach of Italian orthodoxy. Montaigne began to write literary prose that echoed commentaries on classical texts. By emphasizing a flexible, if not downright opportunistic, approach to relationships, the very title of the first essay, "By Diverse Means We Arrive at the Same End," traces the evolution of vernacular prose back to Machiavelli. Hesitation inspires the opening essay, which takes an empirical approach to human motivation: "The commonest way of softening the hearts of those we have offended, when, vengeance in hand, they hold us at their mercy, is by submission to move them to commiseration and pity. However, audacity and steadfastness—entirely contrary means—have sometimes served to produce the same effect" (3). Whereas the Machiavellian method stresses confrontational dualisms (righteousness versus convenience, principle versus expediency), Montaigne believes that people "can easily maintain an opinion, but not choose one." As a result, he writes, "I keep within me doubt and freedom of choice until the occasion is urgent. And then, to confess the truth, I most often toss the feather to the wind, as they say, and abandon myself to the mercy of fortune" (496). Machiavelli's style is anchored to the certainty of the indicative mode, which orders thoughts sequentially. However concerned with details, he remains focused on general principles. In that sense, individual *discorsi* are tassels of the overall discourse on antiquity, which stands out as a guide for the conduct of modern affairs. Machiavelli's method is centripetal and reductive, whereas Montaigne's approach is formative, corrective, and centrifugal; it modifies itself according to individual volition and external events.

Whether their titles be pastoral or urban, humanist texts raise an immediate question: what would the future of art be after the incomparable achievements of Rome and Florence? History, however, teaches us that the gap between rebirth and adulthood often turns into a graveyard of broken promises, a lesson that inspired Francesco Guicciardini, Machiavelli's skeptical heir. Common sense told him that favorable moments come without guarantees; more often than not, they yield disappointment.

As the sixteenth century unfolded, Guicciardini, a favorite historian of Montaigne, wrote *Ricordi politici e civili*, not *I Ricordi politici e civili*. Again, the absence of the definite article in the title points to a growing preference for a less authoritative form of writing that reflected changes "not only in men's speech, vocabulary, dress, style of building, culture, and such things, but, what is more, even in their sense of taste."[5] Begun in 1512, the *Ricordi* were edited in 1528 and 1530.[6] They express views on a large number of issues and belong to a sustained form of intellectual autobiography that includes the *Ricordi* of Giovanni di Pagolo Morelli and the writings of Poggio Bracciolini.[7] In the Florentine tradition of familiar diaries that favored practical concerns and cautious judgments,[8] Guicciardini warns relatives and friends to profit from his example in a context familiar to the audience of the *Essais*.[9] The real remains subservient to the ideal in Machiavelli, whereas Guicciardini dismisses universals, believing that the effects of historical deeds do not shed light on human motivations. History proves that we learn very little from the past, because the gap between causes and effects cannot be bridged, at least not in any significant way. Guicciardini looks into things, not beyond them; above all, he does not focus on what human beings ought to do but on what they have always done.

By underlining the nature of things, Guicciardini focuses on the details—*particolari*—of people's actions, and his analytical method transforms history into a laboratory for the study of human nature. As a result, theoretical statements yield to opinions that stem from personal experience: "To judge by example is very misleading. Unless they are similar in every respect, examples are useless, since every tiny difference in the causes may be a cause of great variations in the effects. And to discern these puny differences takes a good and perspicacious eye."[10] Machiavelli's *discorso* speculates on what rulers and prudent men should have done. Guicciardini's *ricordo* outlines what he actually is and could not become. The *essai* portrays Montaigne as he is and wants to be. Through the lens of the essay, he analyzes himself in order to shape a *capable man* (*homme suffisant*) out of a "recomposed" self.[11] In the course of the sixteenth century laudatory genres declined, and a critical view of humanist utopianism inspired titles as overtly satirical as Desiderius Erasmus's *Moira encomium* (*The Praise of Folly*) and Giordano Bruno's *Lo spaccio della bestia trionfante* (*The Expulsion of the Triumphant Beast*). Their transgressive character played a role in Montaigne's own critique of titles that upheld the rhetoric of praise.

Montaigne ventures into unexplored territory once his *Essais* draw a sketch of the mind at work within its own mental space. The visual surface of the novel runs parallel to the introspective depths of the *Essais*. By confronting life through a vernacular form as changeable and resilient as human thought, their nonfiction prose lies between the narrower boundaries of literature and the larger ones of "writing." Because he understood that the "invisibility" of intellectual speculation could find its own written presence, Montaigne set out to give literary form to a mental autobiography with precedents in confessional titles such as Augustine's *Confessions* and Petrarch's *Secretum* (*The Secret Life*).

Since the essay's preliminary task is to give shape to shapelessness, Montaigne anticipated Blaise Pascal, who believed that "all our dignity consists, then, in thought."[12] Appropriately, the title of his book is *Pensées,* which makes explorations of the world *within* primary. From philosophy to history and science, Paolo Sarpi wrote *Pensieri* and Francis Bacon published his own *Essays.* Speaking for all of them, John Donne confirmed in *Problems and Paradoxes* that "our creatures are our thoughts, creatures that are born giants . . . my thoughts reach all, and comprehend all."[13] Since thought is an ineffable form that exceeds physical boundaries, the process of literary creation never tires of unearthing forms of the inner self.

Montaigne knew that the essay had to steer away from the dialogue form, which dominated the literature of humanism—whether the subject was aesthetic (Alberti), philosophical (Ficino), or scientific (Galileo). His choice also bore on the twofold tradition of classical rhetoric.[14] The ponderous structures of Ciceronian—or Asiatic—prose remained influential even into the late sixteenth century. Yet Justus Lipsius, Marc-Antoine Muret, and Francis Bacon leaned toward the familiar style of Seneca, whose Attic prose Montaigne found "undulating and diverse" (330). Anti-Ciceronian writers developed ideas naturally, flexibly, and freely.[15] In Joan Webber's words, thought unraveled in ways that suggested "work-in-progress," and the whole form of the book was "left open."[16] Prose style became suggestive, incomplete, exaggerated, and contradictory.

The rational pace of humanist *elocutio* no longer disciplined restless investigations. "In order to get more in," Montaigne piled "up only the headings of subjects" (185). The written word is the fragmentary survivor of intuitions that test the possibilities of literary discourse, to the point that he seems to lose control of his own thought processes. "Were I to add on their consequences, I would multiply this volume many times over" (185). Antirhetorical forms of expression are given new prominence: "The speech I love is a simple, natural speech, the same on paper as in the mouth; a speech succulent and sinewy, brief and compressed, not so much dainty and well combed as vehement and brusque . . . rather difficult than boring, remote from affection, irregular, disconnected and bold; each bit making a body in itself" (127). The space of the essay is the written page, but the space of the essayist's mind expands beyond it. In that sense, the title is as tentative as everything else: "I have always an idea in mind, and some blurred picture, which offers me as if in a dream a better form than the one I have employed, but I cannot grasp it and exploit it" (482–83). Unwritten words and unspoken thoughts represent yet another dimension of the fragmentary style and content of essays,[17] *pensieri,* aphorisms, and maxims.[18]

The *Cinquecento* began by attempting to shape the future, but it settled into acceptance of its own dynamics once Montaigne made of ignorance an incentive for improvement: "Ignorance that knows itself, that judges itself and condemns itself, is not complete ignorance. So that the profession of the Phyrrhonians is to doubt and inquire, to be sure of nothing" (372). Thus Montaigne crafted a form bound to materialize beyond the essays themselves.[19] Art shapes mental forms in order to make them communicable. Since an active mind "has impulses beyond its powers of achievement," and since its pursuits are "boundless and without form" (818), that elusive form might belong to art as much as to life itself. Because it fosters metaphorical transfers from the page to the street, the title turns out to describe what Stanley Fish has called a "self-consuming artifact." Semantically speaking, the title introduces a text that tests its own assumptions, and Montaigne qualifies its formlessness by means of adjectives such as *shapeless, disjoined,* and *grotesque.* These qualifiers call for flexibility amid controversies about ancient genres, their modern counterparts, and combinations thereof.

Individual titles are points of reference in the fluid structure of a book that thrives on incompletion: "In order to get more in, I pile up only the headings of subjects. . . . And how many stories have I spread around which say nothing of themselves, but from which anyone who troubles to pluck them with a little ingenuity will produce numberless essays?" Title headings call on readers to take a confrontational stand toward the text, because the concept of "essaying" is one of shared empowerment: "An able reader often discovers in other men's writings perfections beyond those that the author put in or perceived, and lends them richer meanings and aspects" (93). Educated minds are encouraged to undertake their own essays.[20] Headings, therefore, are titological tests that call for alternative rereadings and rewritings. The inference is that the universe of literary experimentation echoes the expansive world of geographical exploration and scientific discovery.

Montaigne deliberately challenges readers to compete with him along an uncharted path. The inference is that writer and reader are equally engaged in the experience of "essaying."²¹ *Essai* is the linguistic form of an operative mode of thinking that is as efficient as a surgical instrument for probing thought processes: "I expose myself entire: my portrait is a cadaver on which the veins, the muscles, and the tendons appear at a glance, each part in its place. It is not my deeds that I write down; it is myself, it is my essence" (274). Anatomy offers an analogy for psychology, and both contribute to sharpening literary tools apt to transform an inert body of quotations into an inventive undertaking. Matter itself should "make its own divisions. It shows well enough when it changes, where it concludes, where it begins, where it resumes" (119–20). At the same time, revisions express the mind's own meandering: "It is a thorny undertaking, and more so than it seems, to follow a movement so wandering as that of our mind" (273). In a roundabout way, the essay has always "essayed" on its own versatility by mixing creation, commentary, and criticism.

To visualize the shaping power of human thought, a metaphorical leap is in order. Repeated references to Lucretius introduce an aquatic vocabulary that is typical of Montaigne's way of giving literary expression to mental activities. "We float between different states of mind," he writes, "we wish nothing freely, nothing absolutely, nothing constantly" (240). The fluid imagery calls to mind the ever-changing shape of the octopus, whose form is designed to allow spontaneous motion. On dry land the octopus is a chaos of flesh, but free motion in its natural element allows its body to resume its natural shape. The mellifluous arms outline patterns that are unsettling and unsettled by definition. Form is changeable, adaptable, far-reaching, retractable, tentative in each posture, and always about to shift into another position.²² Mental signals change the form of the essay just as quickly as they do the octopus. Henri Focillon confirms that unrest is functional as well as aesthetic: "The mind is a design that is in a state of ceaseless flux, of ceaseless weaving and unweaving, and its activity, in this sense, is an artistic activity."²³

Antirhetorical patterns and the rise of new genres called for spontaneous connections between inspiration and expression. Since he knew that his was "the only book in the world of its kind, a book with a wild and eccentric plan" (278), Montaigne anticipated developments typical of baroque poetics. In *De vinculis in genere* (1591–92), Giordano Bruno integrated form and content into a new aesthetic relativism: "Just as the irregularity of a stone does not fit, coincide and join with the irregularity of any other stone . . . in the same way any appearance will not strike just any mind."²⁴ Likewise, Montaigne wrote about eggs: "Both the Greeks and the Latins, as we ourselves, use eggs for the most express example of similarity. However, there have been men . . . who recognized marks of difference between eggs. They could tell which hen the egg came from" (815). One of the etymologies of "baroque" refers to a pearl of irregular shape—the Spanish or Portuguese (?) *barrueco-berrueco*—and of low economic currency, which validated the more popular matrix of art and literature. From atoms to eggs and pearls, irregularity became a concept of interest. In Bruno's words, "there are as many genres and species of true rules as there are of true poets."[25] Poetry depends on individual minds that emancipate themselves from rules, and Montaigne admits that "popular and purely natural poetry has spontaneous effects and charms by which it may be compared with the principal beauty of poetry as perfected according to art" (227). Against the grain of classical and humanist conventions, art found form and content within the unrestrained act of creation that produced it.

At a time when Montaigne believed that progress was being measured "by disagreement more than by agreement, by difference more than by similarity" (703), there were artists who conceded that the true rule consists in knowing how to break rules according to contemporary taste—"la vera regola è saper rompere le regole a tempo e luogo."[26] Anyone could define beauty and become its critic. The plural title of the *Essais* also suggests that the form of each essay is uncanonical.

The essayistic text enacts the title by giving full exposure to the "physical" dimension of a new literary genre created by an unconventional mind: "I have no more made my book than my book has made me—a book consubstantial with its author" (504). The preface, addressed "to the Reader," makes an unprecedented equation: "I am myself the matter of my book." Hence, "I want to be seen here in my simple, natural, ordinary fashion, without straining or artifice: for it is myself that I portray." Montaigne knows that written language is effective as long as it is translated into action, which remains the foremost goal of human expression. In the *Essais,* imitations of ancient and medieval models gave way to the "incarnational" mode of baroque literature. Since words fall short of deeds, "What I chiefly portray is my cogitations, a shapeless subject that does not lend itself to expression in actions. It is all I can do to couch my thoughts in this airy medium of words" (274). In this sense, the title points to the "other side," silent and invisible, where "essaying" consists of deeds that leave words behind. The title does not refer to a "figural" representation of ideas but to the mimesis of "how" ideas find expression in language.

In the broader context of European culture, the incarnational mindset produced the ingenious biography of a mad *hidalgo* whose excessive reading of books spurred him to chase chivalric glories of old across the planes of Castille. Whereas the Spanish novelist took up an anachronistic subject, the French essayist grounded remembrance and hope in the present. Don Quixote, who believed that the crown makes the king, tried to flesh out an obsolete ideal; Montaigne, who never confused the crown with the king, shaped his literary identity from lived experience. His book ends with an image that privileges empiricism over idealism: "On the loftiest throne in the world we are still sitting only on our own rump" (857). The common denominator of our human condition is the rump; it is the "lower body" of Rabelaisian imagery, what Mikhail Bakhtin has designated the symbol of popular culture. In this sense, Montaigne's title takes a pragmatic approach that equates the mental and the physical, to the extent that intellectual birth and biological evacuation coincide: "Here you have, a little more decently, some excrements of an aged mind, now hard, now loose, and always undigested" (721). At arm's length from the extremes of institutionalized artifice (Tesauro, Marino) and ridicule (Cervantes, Tassoni), Montaigne valued the spontaneity of natural forms of expression: "I would naturalize art as much as they artify nature" (666). Art "de-artifies" the classical, chivalric, and humanist heritage in the anti-utopian realm of essays and novels, where knowledge relies on the testing of knowledge itself. The artwork contains a critique of creation within the created work. The *Essais* are an experiment in the mutability of human nature, which affects language as well: "If it had been durable matter, it would have had to be committed to a more stable language" (751). The heterogeneous semantics of the genre calls for variation and verification.

In fact, the word *essai* stems from the natural condition of Montaigne's conflictive mindset at the boundary between art and life, where experiment borders on self-effacement:

> If my mind could gain a firm footing, I would not make essays, I would make decisions; but it is always in apprenticeship and on trial. (611)

> My trade and my art is living. . . . Perhaps they mean that I should testify about myself by works and deeds, not by bare words. (274)

Wishfully, literary expression should take the living form of human beings. The very concept of representation at times nears collapse, and form bears the scars of that conflict. In the realm of "boundary genres" and "boundary works," artists often court parody. In fact, they create entire texts of uncertain status. Gary Saul Morson would suggest that such a threshold literature accepts "the possibility of continual progress of hypotheses and new hypotheses, with no final determination—no 'last number.'" In short, utopia claims to know, whereas the openness of anti-utopia "asks why we think we know."[27] Montaigne put himself on trial at both ends of the creative process, from what he found or refused to complete to what he did not write. The challenge was to revise the canon without becoming canonical.

As a test, the essay borders on error, vacillates between genre and anti-genre, and often appears illegitimate to its own creator. Because conventions are on trial, any written text is suspiciously paradigmatic. Without ignoring epistles, commentaries, treatises, and confessions, Montaigne settled on an antiliterary sketch that sought out "change indiscriminately and tumultuously" (761). Life could easily be absorbed into art, but the reverse was equally possible. The coexistence of invention and debate, illusion and disillusion, drew strength from the contemporary world when it became apparent that the discovery of a new continent was due to a geographical misconception. Science (Ptolemaic-Copernican) and religion (Reformation–Counter-Reformation) were pulling in opposite directions, even within themselves. While Bruno and Galileo had to pay for their convictions, Descartes was grateful to faith for his scientific method. The human mind could no longer build identity on the foundation of human dignity and praise of folly.

It was inevitable that doubt and Montaigne's testing question—"Que scay-je?"—would shape mental habits that took on controversial aspects of experience: "When I declare 'I do not know' or 'I doubt' they say that this proposition carries itself with the rest. This is more firmly grasped in the form of interrogation: 'What do I know?'—the words I bear as a motto inscribed over a pair of scales" (392–93). Between the extremes of seeing humankind as the masterpiece of creation and the quintessence of dust, Montaigne's question—"What do I know?"—leads from one to the other by suggesting an open-ended approach to the classical imperative "know thyself." Socrates moves from the certainty of knowing to that of not knowing, whereas Hamlet does not survive the clash between the two. Montaigne explores the range of human knowledge that takes us from one pole to the other. The interrogative mode best exemplifies a mind caught in the essayistic process of judgment and interpretation. The best way to overcome Hamlet's doubt is to acknowledge that life is not just silence, and humankind can be more than dust. Once the old circle of perfection began to break down, art contested itself; in the process, it was never more consciously artistic.

Stylistic as well as conceptual, Montaigne's question transfers content and authorship along a chain that is as continuous as life itself; and the title is there to become anyone's practice and everyone's text. Whatever the aim, it was generally agreed that to doubt "well" (Pascal) and "wisely" (Donne) was not to stray. Diversity and eclecticism were as necessary to method as they were to ideology. Montaigne's tightrope walk between moral philosophy and literary eccentricity made him suspect to philosophers, obscure to literary critics, but popular with sane people who needed guidance for coping with life in the raw.[28] Uncertainty and persuasion became significant in a culture where many a writer admired what Samuel Taylor Coleridge was to call "voluntary doubt, a self-determined indetermination."[29]

In terms of critical theory, Northrop Frye might agree that the essay fits the pattern of winter experiences, which foster "attempts to give form to the shifting complexities of existence."[30] Montaigne could have opted for satire, along with Brant (*Ship of Fools*) and Rabelais (*Gargantua and Pantagruel*), whose work he read "for amusement" (298). While it takes for granted a world that is full of anomalies,[31] satire still looks backward and rarely charts new paths. Montaigne had to go beyond satire, because his goal was to find a literary vehicle that would bridge generic categories. His essays contain satire and more. Unlike literary genres that bear the fingerprints of sociopolitical conditions, such as drama and epic, the essay can adapt to any context. If one only glances at essay writing after Montaigne, the genre has surmounted the restrictions of any other mythos. It was by reading Montaigne that Pascal found in himself what he read in the *Essais*, which made it possible for André Gide to gain a better perspective on his own self centuries later: "One never comes to an end with Montaigne."[32]

As his skepticism bottoms out in the *Apology for Raymond Sebond*, Montaigne can look only upward. Without reaching for the stars, he presents humankind as the fool of the farce, the victim of the universe, and the splendid sparkle that makes it all worthwhile. Transcending the constraints of other genres, his essays humanize theories and spur investigations of human nature. Looking for new paths that could overcome the limits of satire, the *Essais* provide endless resolutions to the continuity of life by defining a genre for all seasons as well as the best title for uncanonical forms of writing.

2

As a title, *Essais* has defined an experimental genre for scientists, philosophers, literary critics, and intellectual historians—from Bacon and Pascal to Ralph Waldo Emerson, Ernst Cassirer, and Michel Butor.[33] Whether written by Georg Lukács or Theodor Adorno, essay titles have often paraphrased the concept of "Essay on the Essay."[34] Perhaps as in no other title, meaning and method are one. When asked about the role of his essays in the culture of postmodernism, Roland Barthes answered that "the very form of these essays denies any 'doctrinal' intention; in my eyes they constitute a gathering of materials, a 'repertory' of critical themes intended for those interested in literature and modernity; to me, the reader is a virtual creator, to whom I offer an instrument for study."[35] Thus "doctrinal intentions" take us to widespread concerns with the paradigmatic "models" and "panegyrical" pages of humanist literature. Under the titological agenda of "Writing Itself," Susan Sontag believes that Barthes put forward "a poetics of thinking, which identifies the meaning of subjects with the very mobility of meaning."[36] This critical assessment describes Montaigne's essays as well.

The fact remains that panegyrical forms have always intrigued the human mind. However unwittingly, they present us with the lure of perfection. In 1931, however, Jorge Luis Borges resisted false assumptions about the nature of perfection when he wrote, "The perfect page, the page in which no word can be altered without harm, is the most precarious of all."[37] Since ancient times, culture has given us exemplary phrases and flawless pages under the guise of prophecies and proclamations. It is not by accident that Castiglione set out to describe the perfect courtier, "without defect of any kind." These literary forms are easily associated with the concept of the "definitive text," which Borges limits "to religion or exhaustion."[38] Of course, perfect pages often presume to enforce righteous dictates. Still mindful of perfect pages about exclusion and intolerance, Borges opens his brief comments on the *Aeneid* by pointing to a parable about two libraries: "One of a hundred different books of different worth, the other of a hundred books that are all equally perfect. It is significant that the latter consists of a hundred *Aeneids*."[39] Virgil made it the fate of the Trojan hero to fulfill a script mandated by the gods. For Borges, instead, "the page that becomes immortal can traverse the fire of typographical errors, approximate translations, and inattentive or erroneous readings without losing its soul in the process."[40] Imperfect pages are incomplete, nonlinear, or outright essayistic. They raise doubts and prompt alternative readings.

Having noted that neither Socrates nor Jesus ever published a word because their culture trusted only oral forms of expression, George Steiner writes that the result of this development toward the scriptural favored the "dictatorial" over the "didactic."[41] The same applies to dead or "perfect" languages, above all Latin. With linguists who maintain that dead languages do not condone mistakes, E. M. Cioran concludes that, during the Enlightenment, French had reached such maturity that it bordered on rigidity and fulfillment. After the revolution, it lost this "perfection" and made room for naturalness. In order to survive, "French needed to become corrupt, enriched by many a new impropriety, to move from the salon to the street."[42] Montaigne had already solved that problem when he chose to write in the impure French vernacular over Latin. Montaigne's essays leave no doubt about the validity of productive reading, much as they warn us about the danger of theoretical assumptions about correctness in all its guises and disguises.

Whether Renaissance or post-Renaissance, the essay gives priority to the tentative over the demonstrative, for the goal is to let the absolute become relative and for authority to give rise to understanding. The essay is not simply *a* test or *an* experiment. It is an experimental way of testing established ideologies. By writing himself down, Montaigne sets essayistic endeavors at the ground level of his own existence, not as he should be, but as he actually is, warts and all.

Between 1954 and 1958, Theodor Adorno wrote his own essay on the Essay as form.[43] His thesis is that the essay resists method and favors interpretation. Essay writing consists of *how* we deal with specific issues, whatever they may happen to be.[44] Accordingly, this most protean of genres stands out as the critical "other" of any paradigmatic model. But is it just an instrument for exposing the ironclad? Does it also show the way? Does it set goals? One can test, analyze, and dissect in the essay, but can one live, or plan, by it? Is the essay's relentless critique of ideology its weakness as well as its strength? Amid the culture of the new science, these questions resonated with a special urgency, which persisted amid modernist and postmodern uncertainties.

MODERNIST

4

Title Translated into Title: *Ulysses*

> The key to "Ulysses" is in the title—and this key is indispensable if
> we are to appreciate the book's real depth and scope.
> —EDMUND WILSON

By giving form to subjects as fluid as thinking and as unpredictable as human existence, essays and novels unraveled the tightly woven system of genre theory that dominated the Renaissance well into the sixteenth century. By the turn of the nineteenth century, the rebirth of neoclassical humanism paralleled radical experiments that changed society in the name of modern ideals of liberty and equality—from the American struggle for independence from the British in 1776 to the storming of the Bastille on July 14, 1789. At least in the short run, the French Revolution let violence get the best of brotherhood. Terror gained the upper hand and eventually put democratic ideals in the hands of Napoleon Bonaparte, whose ambitious agenda was less than brotherly and not quite republican. This intellectual heritage reached a point of exhaustion early in the twentieth century, when cultural disenchantment and political conflicts yielded dire consequences. At once escapist and indulgent, novelty became overwhelmingly referential once the aftermath of World War I spurred disappointment among the winners and despair among the vanquished.

Having written *Mr. Bennett and Mrs. Brown* at the end of 1923, Virginia Woolf dated the beginning of the modernist decline "on or about December, 1910," when the time had come for reconciling "ourselves with a season of failures and fragments." What was lost was the ability to "express character"; truth itself had reached "an exhausted and chaotic condition." By 1919 Paul Valéry had written that European culture would end up as "an infinitely rich nothing," *rien infiniment riche*.[1] From Malevich and Duchamp to Tzara,

Western culture tested invention and strained tolerance, because modernism steered individual talent toward forms of expression that were antithetical to the classical notions of clarity, restraint, and inclusion. New continents had been discovered, promised lands had been colonized, and ameliorative ideologies had run out of future. At the tail end of what many perceived as a historical downturn, Oswald Spengler wrote *The Decline of the West* (1926), a title that conveyed the eclipse of the belief that time marked a linear development toward a better future, at least insofar as the Western tradition was concerned.

What followed, instead, was the twilight of the artistic avant-gardes.[2] Speaking for a generation, T. S. Eliot made of difficulty a fashionable measure of excellence: "Poets in our civilization, as it exists at present, must be difficult."[3] Yet difficulty did not come in the way of genuine fellowships of the mind. However outrageous in his own ideas, Ezra Pound was unswervingly keen in promoting literary talent, whether T. S. Eliot or James Joyce,[4] who ended the "modern experiment" when he wrote the final words of *Ulysses* on October 30, 1921. Like *Ulysses*, *The Waste Land* was published in 1922, the year that marked the end of the Christian era for Pound, the breakdown of Western culture for Willa Cather, and the emergence of modernist experimentalism for F. Scott Fitzgerald.[5]

By the turn of the twentieth century, industrialization and the unfolding of Realism and Naturalism took steps toward narrowing the gap between highbrow and lowbrow, socially as well as culturally. It is within this trajectory that the epic Odysseus made room for the novelistic normality of life-size individuals. At the western edge of the British Islands, the title of *Ulysses* alludes to the epic story through the middle-class viewpoint of an advertising agent by the name of Leopold Bloom, who performs common tasks in the streets of the Irish capital. Years of momentous adventures dwindle to a prosaic routine, and the reduction of Odysseus's long journey to a single day leaves no doubt that the cosmological landscape of the epic had yielded to the urban milieu of the bourgeois novel. On June 16, 1904, there was no reason to believe that anyone would perform either clever deeds or extraordinary feats on what a 1922 reviewer described as "the dailiest day possible." The trajectory that links the Greek epic to the Irish novel parallels the translation of the classical Odysseus and Ulixes into the vernacular Ulysses and Ulisse. On matters of literary onomastics, Roland Barthes writes that "the proper name is in a sense the linguistic form of reminiscence." This remark highlights remembrance and recovery in the Proustian universe, but it applies just as well to "exploration" and "decipherment" in the Joycean one.[6] In fact, Joyce misread the old mythology, and the title of this chapter, "Title Translated into Title," highlights an experiment in etymological resilience and semantic transformation.[7]

By echoing the Homeric name, the title of the Irish masterwork weaves allusive threads into the fabric of modernist narrativity. Joyce himself asks a question that links personal to literary onomastics: "What's in a name? That is what we ask ourselves in childhood when we write the name that we are told is ours."[8] Some believe that a good name contains "everything." I trust that a good title contains, if not everything, at least everything that counts. Just as knowledge of a city is based on one's familiarity with its landmarks, the allusive range of the Joycean title brings to the fore cultural signposts that mark a daylong journey through the streets of Dublin at the turn of the twentieth century. While etymology brings together less than random juxtapositions between the ancient epic and the modern novel, the semantics of *Ulysses* foreground a "density of meaning" that thickens the layered contents of the book.[9] Gérard Genette has weighed in with a challenge: "How would we read Joyce's *Ulysses* if it were not entitled *Ulysses?*" This preliminary question emphasizes "the hermeneutic power of intimidation contained in just the title of *Ulysses.*"[10] I take intimidation to task by trading the virtual for the pragmatic: how should we read *Ulysses* exactly because it is entitled *Ulysses?*[11]

Since its model is the Greek hero, why did Joyce not title his book *Odysseus?*[12] Had he done so, modern readers would consider an array of references.[13] In spite of the romantic recovery of Greek culture by writers as diverse as Hölderlin, Foscolo, and Keats, the title's Latin etymology points to the resilience of neoclassical influences.[14] Before the turn of the nineteenth century, archaeological excavations at Pompeii added fresh evidence to our knowledge of Roman civilization, much as the authoritative studies of Johan Winckelmann and Edward Gibbon on Greco-Roman art and history stirred new interest in the classical heritage. A title such as *Ulysses* makes it clear that tradition and transgression affected Joyce at a time when Roman terminology was the standard practice among Victorian and Edwardian writers.[15] In the wake of fascist celebrations of Virgil and Augustus, the soul and mind of imperial Romanism, W. H. Auden set his description of postepic times: "Among the ruins of the Post-Vergilian City" (*Memorial for the City*).

Although the text alludes to the Greek *Odyssey,* Joyce's title spells out the Anglicized form of the Latin Ulixes.[16] Translation adds layers of meaning to the etymological source, whose onomastic geography points to a migration from Greece to Ireland via Italy. A student of topographical narratives, J. Hillis Miller, takes up the significance of names and places: "There must be lots of deer, one thinks, on Deer Island."[17] This assumption points to "mimetic" correlations between language and reality. In *Ulysses,* however, the correlations are strictly literary. Since it takes up associations between names and texts, the title presumes a readership capable of relating Ulysses to both Ulixes and Odysseus.

My approach to the title as text sets out to explain why the Greek Odysseus became the Irish Ulysses. The onomastic shift takes us to the retrospective core of Western ontology, which the poet Michael Longley, of Northern Ireland, has condensed into a memorable verse:

"I am walking backwards into the future like a Greek."[18]

Mindful of the ancient heritage as much as of modern challenges, Joyce made his title both retrospective and groundbreaking. Ulysses added a "modernist" stage to the epic development that linked the pagan mythologies of Greek Odysseus and Roman Ulixes to the spiritual worldview of medieval Christianity.

Although we find Ulisse near the bottom of hell in the *Divine Comedy,*[19] Dante reinterpreted the Greek wanderer at the very end of the Middle Ages, when Florentine culture began to thrive amid a mercantile economy that would finance the artistic flowering of the Renaissance. However critical of it, Dante was too smart not to know that what Vittore Branca has called the *epopea dei mercanti* (the epic of merchants) was bound to carry the future. Almost unwittingly, Dante crossed the Renaissance threshold when he approached the adventurous hero not as the old-fashioned Greek trickster but as an explorer whose pursuit of new horizons delayed his return to Ithaca. At the sunset of the Middle Ages, Ulisse undertook a hell-bound voyage in Dante's medieval epic. The opening image of the twenty-sixth canto of the *Inferno* shows Florence as an eagle spreading its wings over Tuscany and the rest of the world in the wake of Ulisse's journey, which dared to break through the pillars of Hercules (Gibraltar), beyond the "known" world around the Mediterranean Sea and out into the "unknown" waters of the Atlantic Ocean. Dante condemned such a challenge as much as he denounced the overland trips of merchants and scoundrels like Ciappelletto, who opens the "human comedy" of Giovanni Boccaccio's *Decameron* on the eve of the age of discovery, which pushed the westward exploration of the Atlantic Ocean toward American shores.

Having transgressed the self-contained mold of the epic as Dante adapted it to medieval geography, Ulisse set up a precedent for adventurers whose precapitalist ingenuity opened commercial venues across the European continent. At the height of the Middle Ages, he sailed beyond Gibraltar to defy the finite boundaries of the old Ptolemaic universe. His daring journey stood not for return but for direction:

> Consider what you came from: you are Greeks!
> You were not born to live like mindless brutes
> but to follow paths of excellence and knowledge.
> (*Inferno* 26, translation by Mark Musa)

Perhaps Ulisse is in hell not because he sailed beyond Hercules' pillars once, but because he would dare again to venture through the forbidden waters of the Atlantic just before the great navigators of the Renaissance became equally adventurous. For John Freccero, Ulisse's journey ended in death because it fostered a "novelistic" progression that strayed from the epic circularity of a "providential" homecoming—*nostos*.[20] The title of John Freccero's essay, "Dante's Ulysses: from Epic to Novel," tells us that "the transformation of Ulysses's circular journey into linear disaster is a Christian critique of epic categories."[21] However unaware of the novelistic as a literary genre, Dante foresaw such a transformation and gave the hero the vernacular name of Ulisse.

Thereafter, the Renaissance grew to convince itself that the time had come for displacing the epic sense of place in order to make room for the more ubiquitous character of novelistic journeys, picaresque and quixotic alike.[22] By the turn of the sixteenth century, memories of the "disaster" could stop neither novelists nor navigators from steering linearity toward secular endpoints. Like seafaring explorers, bankers and merchants vied with kings and emperors in financing the conquest of new territories. Once Christopher Columbus opened the way toward the Americas, the "Mediterranean" *repubbliche marinare* of Genoa, Venice, Pisa, and Amalfi resigned their economic supremacy to the emergent "Atlantic" powers of England and Spain. Charles V consolidated the ascendancy of the Spanish monarchy when he spearheaded the colonization of the American Indies under the leadership of ruthless *conquistadores*. After the disastrous defeat of the Armada in 1588, however, England took control of the seas and oversaw the creation of a modern brew of aristocracy and middle class that took full advantage of the socioeconomic potential of mercantile opportunities and industrial technologies.

If the world was falling down and humankind feared its demise, artists could take refuge in the relative stability of literary artifacts that favored imaginative leaps. Legend, in fact, refers to something that belongs to myth as well as to the Latin etymology of *legenda*, which describes that which is to be read.[23] In the wasteland of obsolete ideologies, a title such as *Ulysses* confirms that myth is the first and last foundation of literary mimesis. The Greek etymology of Odysseus belongs to the oral epic, whereas Ulysses belongs to the written tradition of novelistic literature. Since the past is rewritten and reread, modernist writers took liberties with history because they were interested in the past in the specific way in which they wanted to revisit it. Accordingly, translation updated linguistic transitions as well as cultural transformations. In a letter to his brother, Stanislaus (18 October 1906), Joyce, having discussed the plot of a story in progress, finds its title, "Chamber Music," unsatisfactory because "it is too complacent—I should prefer a title which to a certain extent repudiated the book, without altogether destroying it."[24] In a way, this titological comment is an apt introduction to the historical, etymological, and semantic tensions—attraction and repulsion—that "energize" the relationship between Odysseus and Ulysses.

In Greek culture Odysseus is known as the "man of many turns." His central attribute is *polytropos*, which describes a multitalented individual whose intellectual curiosity informs ancillary qualifiers: *polymetis* (of great intuition), *polyphron* (of many thoughts), *polyplanes* (of many adventures), *polymechanos* (of great cunning), and *odyssamenos* (thief and liar). Among the Greeks, "name" and "character" had the same meaning (Giambattista Vico, *The New Science*, 433). Whenever they pondered names, the Greeks upheld the conviction that the proper understanding of a name would reveal its hidden nature. *Onoma eponumon* describes a name that corresponds to the person or object designated. In the case of Odysseus, the old nurse Eurycleia suggests the name Polyaretus, which means "much prayed for," whereas Autolycus, the boy's grandfather, chooses a name with the opposite meaning. Odysseus, in fact, is derived from the verb *odysasthai*, which means "to have hostile feelings or enmity toward someone." In a way, the name is both active and passive, so that *odyssamenos* should be understood as "angry at many" or "incurring the anger of many." The name thus refers to the cunning Autolycus, the troublemaker known as the foremost liar and thief of his day, as well as to the passive victim of divine wrath.[25] Dualism also inspired

Sophocles, who presents Odysseus as a somber and compassionate statesman in *Ajax* and as a scheming politician in *Philoctetes*.

The first words that Odysseus utters are *allo ti* (something else). In his own voice, the hero can be "other" than what he appears to be. Odysseus is one and many, no one in the cave of Polyphemus, and anyone as he wanders from place to place. Having disguised his own identity upon returning to Ithaca, Odysseus is torn between the comforts of domestic life and the adventures of the quest. We can wonder whether the king measured up to the journeyman, for he probably found the open seas more challenging than familiar shorelines.[26] George Seferis rephrased the Odyssean dilemma in a verse written in modern Greek:

> The secrets of the sea are forgotten on the shores (Erotikos Logos)[27]

As a name of "many turns," Odysseus bodies forth the resourceful individual who can beat the odds as he makes his way out of the war, even if home is not his immediate destination. Long after the fall of the Roman Empire, Joyce chose the Anglicized Ulysses to introduce a long day's journey through the streets of Dublin. As he stopped by local pubs, Leopold Bloom exchanged trivialities that alluded to epic deeds.[28]

Along with Montaigne's *Essais,* Joyce's one-word title is the most restrictive in this study. This chapter takes up the onomastic latitude of the Odyssean title by exploring its mythical resonance, allusive outreach, linguistic changes, and geographical symbolism. The implication is that the ease or difficulty with which we read titles reflects the ease or difficulty with which we read history and map out literature.

1

Although he gives the epic hero titological stature, Joyce does not let him enter the novelistic text. Whether the etymology is Greek or Latin, the epic hero remains pagan. Just as Dante cannot let Virgil enter Paradise, Joyce excludes Ulysses from a text that begins by trading the invocation to the pagan muse for a prosaic deed that fuses and confuses secularism with religiosity: "Stately, plump Buck Mulligan came from the stairhead, bearing a bowl of lather on which a mirror and a razor lay crossed. A yellow dressing-gown, ungirdled, was sustained gently behind him by the mild morning air.

He held the bowl aloft and intoned: *Introibo ad altare Dei*" (*Ulysses*, 1:1–5). Scholars tell us that the rhythm of the opening sentence evokes the dactylic hexameters of Virgilian verse (*Arma virumque cano*) as well as the ritual gestures of Christian liturgy.[29] The journey has been "reread" as a procession, and parody becomes physical once Mulligan utters the opening lines of the Latin Mass while he raises the shaving bowl as if it were the sacramental Eucharist.[30] To the extent that title and text join forces in rejecting the inherited habit of translating the heathen into the Christian, the first two pages of Joyce's novel reverse direction and warn readers to expect a rather secular assessment of the religious heritage.

While we are reminded of the sustained analogy between the role of the artist and the priestly office,[31] the dualism of ritual is extended to human identity. By way of introduction, the writer warns us that novelistic deeds and characters are willfully allusive. Like translation, allusion is transformational. If Odysseus is the man of many turns, Bloom is "a cultured allround-man" (*Ulysses*, 1-10:581). His ambition, however, is to "lead a homely life in the evening of his days, permeated by the affectionate surroundings of the heaving bosom of the family" (*Ulysses*, 1-15:908–9). The Irish Bloom, whom Mulligan describes as "Greeker than the Greeks" (*Ulysses*, 1-9:614),[32] alludes to the Greek Odysseus; both resemble, but do not identify themselves with, the Latinate Ulysses. This triadic relationship sets up much of the symbolic meaning of the novelistic narrative, which tells us that Ulysses is somewhere else than Odysseus, and Dublin is somewhere else than Ithaca. Displacements are magnified in the "Proteus" chapter, where everything is changed into something else.

Joyce's inclusive approach is made clear in his choice of Dublin as a general model: "If I can get to the heart of Dublin, I can get to the heart of all the cities of the world."[33] The coincidence of micro and macro entails metaphorical transfers that make history and geography panoptic; they exist simultaneously as Ulysses and Odysseus, Stephen and Bloom, Joyce and Shakespeare. Synchronicity favors present-oriented allusion over past-oriented allegory, to which Walter Benjamin paid extensive attention in his discussion of the origin of German tragic drama. Published in 1928, this influential study played up the role of allegory in baroque literature before its modernist decline. Benjamin concluded his historical overview with the statement that "allegories are, in the realm of thoughts, what ruins are in the realm of things."[34] It could not be otherwise, because allegorical works uphold the validity of paradigmatic premises.[35] Since they are preexistent, premises are retrospective. Given Joyce's skeptical overview of historical events and traditional wisdom, the title could not be allegorical, because the author had lost faith in the exemplary authority of the past. For Joyce, history is a nightmare; for Eliot, it is a wasteland. Allusion, however, allows both writers to make discrete references without any ideological commitment. We can rest assured that there is no "better" land after the Waste Land, nor is there a "better" Ulysses after Leopold Bloom!

Allegorically speaking, Odysseus overshadows Ulysses; allusively speaking, Ulysses can coexist with Odysseus. The pairing of characters reminds us of the Joycean dictum: "Where there is a reconciliation . . . there must have been first a sundering" (*Ulysses*, 1-9:334–35). Plurality is common to language, structure, and characters. And plurality begins with the Janus-like co-presence of Ulysses and Odysseus in the title. In fact, allusions foster parallels without trying to recover the past. The Oxford English Dictionary defines allusion as "a play upon words, a pun" or "a covert, implied, or indirect reference." The mythical and the allusive merge when Eliot writes that they are "a way of controlling, of ordering, of giving a shape and a significance to the immense panorama of futility and anarchy which is contemporary history."[36] While calling for a reader who can appreciate literary echoes, allusion highlights change and continuity through a "dual-voiced discourse"[37] that Joyce himself describes as "stolentelling."[38] Whereas Eliot is always ready to favor the past,[39] Joyce gears allusiveness to the present, which pivots between Daedalus and Stephen, Ithaca and Dublin, Homer and Joyce.

We know what Odysseus did, and we read about what Leopold Bloom does. But what would Ulysses do in their place? We might say that translation unsettles language and *what* language translates. In other words, translation calls everything into question. Helpful here is Umberto Eco's recent question: "Should a translator lead the reader to understand the linguistic and cultural universe of the source text, or transform the original by adapting it to the reader's cultural and linguistic universe?"[40] Scholarship has tied the inclusive structure of *Ulysses* to ancient Homer no less than to medieval Thomas Aquinas, just as etymology links Ulysses to Greek and Latin sources. While reflecting Joyce's flair for assemblage, title and text favor pastiche-like techniques that are especially evident in the "Aeolus" and the "Lestrygonians" episodes.[41] The onomastic title could have moved Joyce to find a Homeric counterpart to the lengthy Shakespearean pastiche, "Rutlandbaconsouthemptonshakespeare" (*Ulysses*, 1-9:866). Throughout, mixture and referentiality affect the pagan-Jewish-Christian core. Odysseus belongs to the oral tradition of Hellenic culture, whereas Ulysses belongs to the written heritage of Judaism.[42] Joyce mixed them when he wrote "Jewgreek is greekjew. Extremes meet."

In a world that has had more than two thousand years to change some of its ways, comparisons and contrasts translate the mythical heroics of Ionic Greece into the bourgeois routine of Edwardian Dubliners in twentieth-century Ireland.[43] Much as the noble character of Odysseus is congruous with the age of heroic royalty, Bloom is as middle class as the writer himself. Studies of mythical intentions in modern literature suggest that Ulysses had to change into Bloom if mythology stood a chance of surviving in a postepic age that forced the Homeric to make room for the Joycean.[44] Allusiveness in the title *Ulysses* also relates here to there, the earlier to the later; in fact, there is a distinctly topographical dimension to Joycean names. Odysseus points to a Mediterranean journey, which Ulysses links up to the Irish Bloom, who is citified into "Bloomusalem." Here the linguistic compound goes back to the onomastics of meritorious places. In Rome, Coriolanus took his name from his heroic deeds at Corioli. In Bloom's case, the Judeo-Christian heritage takes Bloom back to Jerusalem, even though he never performed extraordinary feats. When it comes to the names of Ulysses and Bloom, Joyce suggests that it is inappropriate to concentrate solely on the literal sense or even the psychological content of any document to the neglect of the "enveloping facts themselves." The upshot was a semantic "soultransfiguring" (*Ulysses*, 1-7:771)[45] that translated the extraordinary into the ordinary. If we were to toy with titles that mix grand narratives with daily incidents, we could suggest the Shandean *Ulysses: Twenty-Four Hours in the Life of Leopold Bloom, Irish Sales Representative, Told Using Various More or Less Original Narrative Strategies*.[46] At their constructive best, double-coded titles foster duplicitous rules of reading.

In Dublin, Bloom and Dedalus live in the ordinary time that characterizes everyday life in contemporary Ireland.[47] One might say that the Joycean title echoes the lower frequency of an epic name; not to echo anything at all, however, would have been unwarranted. Since writing could not be mere chronicle, Joyce exploited the resources of what Eliot calls the "mythical method," which entails a treatment of mythology at once allusive and elusive. To hang on to the mythical by way of symbolism, parody, allusion, or parable is a way of coping with the mediocrity of everyday life for Flaubert and Pater or of surviving the shortcomings of history for Pound and Joyce. By reminding everyone of bygone legends, myth makes life intellectually bearable.

At the end of the second millennium, the discontinuity of the modern approach to myth has made room for its leftover, the *mythical*. Such a downturn entailed a recovery of everyday life over the elitism of past-oriented narratives. Likewise, the novelistic is a mode of expression that is present-bound, nonlinear, not necessarily progressive, and therefore contrary to the novel. In fact, the novelistic is a mode of discourse unstructured by a story, a mode of notation, investment, interest in daily reality, in people, in everything that happens in life.[48] This gives us a fair idea of why we have *Ulysses,* and why Joyce felt the need to write that "nobody in any of my books is worth more than a hundred pounds." Daily realities mixed the commercial with the aesthetic, and Joyce's ballad verses foreground his attempt to bring

> to tavern and to brothel
> The mind of witty Aristotle
> (*The Holy Office*)

Notwithstanding the objections of the Holy Office, Joyce details a mediocre routine.[49]

Although it is the title, Ulysses is mentioned only twice in the text. One quotation refers to the subplot of *King Lear,* in which Edmund is "lifted out of Sidney's *Arcadia.*" At issue is the juxtaposition of literary texts: "We should not now combine a Norse saga with an excerpt from a novel by George Meredith. *Que voulez-vous?* Moore would say. He puts Bohemia on the seacoast and makes Ulysses quote Aristotle" (*Ulysses,* 1-9: 993–96). By literary chronology, the older Ulysses, who here stands for Odysseus, should not quote the younger Aristotle. It suffices to add that Joyce's defense of historical consistency runs against the postmodern view of literature as a spatial grid open to arrangements that need be neither chronological nor linear. On the map of memory, things can be mixed at will.

The second reference occurs in the "Scylla and Charybdis" episode, which deals with literature, the library, the mind, rhetoric, and London. The speaker is Stephen Dedalus, and the subject matter is the spirit of reconciliation: "If you want to know what are the events that cast their shadow over the hell of time of *King Lear, Othello, Hamlet, Troilus and Cressida,* look to see when and how the shadow lifts. What softens the heart of a man, Shipwrecked in storms dire, Tired, like another Ulysses, Pericles, prince of Tyre?" (*Ulysses,* 1-9:400–404). As a humane character at the mercy of circumstances, Ulysses points to individuals who have overcome adversities. If history is a nightmare for human beings, time can be hell for literary characters once art and life show analogous features. The muscular deeds of Odysseus are part of the nightmare, whereas the bourgeois routine of Ulyssean chaps rests on a more inclusive understanding of the "human condition." They have read, as Odysseus could not, Michel de Montaigne and John Donne, whose acknowledged and unacknowledged statements about "the human condition" have become part of our cultural mindset.

History has always stirred echoes across the centuries, and a title such as *Ulysses* suggests that we have moved beyond the geography of the Greek *nostos* (exile and return). The text spurs us to roam around modern Dublin, where Leopold Bloom,[50] a Dubliner who is "anythingarian" (*Ulysses*, 2-15:1711), goes out on a stroll on June 16, 1904. The royal palace of epic Odysseus finds a bourgeois counterpart in Number Seven, Eccles Street. By means of allusions that affect title and text alike, readers embark on a westward journey from Mediterranean to Atlantic shores.

In a world where the classical tradition of humanist narratives at once linear and ameliorative was disintegrating, mythical allusions brought to the fore Joyce's attempt to shore up fragmentary avatars: "The most beautiful, all-embracing theme is that of the Odyssey . . . only the Odyssey stuck in my memory. I want to be frank; at twelve I liked the supernaturalism of Ulysses."[51] Somehow the stories of the oldest literature found modernist spin-offs. After all, names such as Oedipus, Medea, or Antigone are microtales that have generated plenty of sequels,[52] and Joyce grew to believe that the worlds of Ithaca and Dublin could buttress one another because literary constructs are transcultural.

Confident about his work but arrogant about its accessibility, Joyce willfully put in "enigmas and puzzles" that would keep the professors busy for centuries.[53] He was right.[54] Although mindful of Eliot's warnings about the deceptiveness of neat symmetries,[55] literary criticism has highlighted the role that mythic themes have played in the poetics of the twentieth century.[56] By presenting an introductory puzzle that makes sustained references to the ancient narrative, *Ulysses* updates the Homeric theme in the title, authorizes it in the notes, and validates it in the text, which confirms that much literature is reconstructed mythology.[57]

As a linguistic virtuoso, Joyce could have molded his title into a "proteiform graph"[58] of unprecedented originality, but he did not. Since it translates a title, a literary tradition, and a cultural mindset, *Ulysses* suggests that the Homeric *Odyssey* has been adapted to a postclassical narrative as tortuous as the hero's epic voyage.[59] *Ulysses* is the translated title and the translated name of an oral saga translated into a modern vernacular.[60] Because allusion makes it possible to compare and contrast without imposing tight correspondences, readers can weigh how significant is the "allusive latitude" of a name that spans seas and centuries by bringing to the fore tensions between etymology, which is source-bound, and semantics, which is history-prone.[61]

The Joycean title assumes that readers are familiar with the novel and know something about the epic. To gauge the impact *Ulysses* had on generations of educated people, it suffices to mention Joseph Campbell, the student of mythology who read *Ulysses* in 1927. He did not know how to approach it at first. Once Sylvia Beach came to the rescue, his search for a world of referential signatures turned out to be a lifelong project. He found the book "a kind of terminal moraine in which lie buried all the myths, programs, slogans, hopes, prayers, tools, educational theories, and theological bric-a-brac of the past millennium."[62] Yet the success of one protean mythologist has not offset the failure of multitudes of common readers unprepared to confront the elitist referentiality of the "mythical method."

2

Joyce's interest in mythology was inclusive, to the extent that he paired the titological onomastics of Odysseus with the earlier mythology of Daedalus, the prototype of the "universal man." On January 7, 1904, Joyce wrote a story in a single day and called it "A Portrait of the Artist." On February 2, Stanislaus noted that his brother had decided to turn it into a novel by the title of *Stephen Hero*.[63] Ten years later, *Stephen Hero* became *A Portrait of the Artist as a Young Man*, and the protagonist's name was Stephen Dedalus. The onomastic cluster Odysseus-Ulixes-Ulysses set up a parallel with Daidalos-Daedalus-Dedalus. Myth validates the artist-as-hero by reference to Daedalus rather than Prometheus, for Joyce serves art rather than humanity.[64] Odysseus and Daedalus still belong to the immutable world of what Mikhail Bakhtin calls the "absolute past" of deities and heroes. Conversely, Bloom and Dedalus belong to a world where names are as precarious as letters. Bloom has no preprinting precedents, and his onomastic vicissitudes—Leopold, Siopold, Stoom, Bloohoom, greasebloom—are markers of a novelistic complexity that subjects the name to duplications, aliases, mutilations (*Boom*), variations (*Jollypoldy*), and declensions (*Bloowho, Bloowhose*).[65] Relations between names and titles could not but extend the "mythical method" to the archetypal artist.[66]

The ensuing narrative confirms that Stephen has become, if not a hero, as the earlier title suggests, at least an artist who belongs to a culture in which his name carries Christian connotations as well. In the Christian tradition of onomastic naming, the last name is part of the Christian name. As a result, the pagan inventor merges with the first Christian martyr, Saint Stephen. Dedalus-*daidalos* means "cunningly wrought," and Stephen-*stephanos* means crown; the compound name reads "cunningly wrought crown." As a result, names—Stephen, Dedalus, Ulysses—link Joyce's titles to the novelistic progression that begins with *A Portrait of the Artist as a Young Man,* in which Stephen sets out to "[e]ncounter for the millionth time the reality of experience and to forge in the smithy of my soul the uncreated conscience of my race."[67] Once the word "forge" equates art with fiction as fakery, Stephen brushes shoulders with Daedalus and Odysseus. One created the deceptions of the wooden cow at Knossos, and the other came up with the deception of the wooden horse at Troy.[68] Between Daedalus and Dedalus, however, much has happened; one vowel does a difference make! The oral story has given way to a written text in which Joyce could not let the literal overwhelm the literary.[69]

On matters of language and nationality, Stephen Dedalus tells his Jesuit dean of studies that "his language, so familiar and so foreign, will always be for me an acquired speech" (189). About Gaelic as the ancestral language, Stephen writes that his "ancestors threw off their language and took another," allowing "a handful of foreigners to subject them." Resentfully, Stephen pauses: "Do you fancy I am going to pay in my own life and person debts they made?" (203). The inference is that the same language voices different cultures. A case in point is the distinction between the "English" *funnel* and the "Irish" *tundish* (188). Such an awareness spurs Professor MacHugh to concede that he speaks "the tongue of a race the acme of whose mentality is the maxim: time is money" (*Ulysses,* 1-7:556).[70] Hugh Kenner points out that *home* is a castle for the Englishman; for the Irishman, it is a tenement from which he is likely to be evicted.[71] In Trieste the Joyce family was evicted from apartment after apartment. Lucia Joyce had lived at five different addresses by the age of seven, and by age thirteen she had lived in three different countries.

Seamus Heney tells us that Joyce voices the Irish spirit of the English vernacular in the first sentence of "The Sisters," the first story in *Dubliners:* "There was no hope for him this time." This desperate utterance takes us to Joyce's trenchant statement "The Irish were doomed to express themselves in a language that is not their own." In fact, their level of excellence "is called

English literature."[72] Joyce shared with Oscar Wilde the experience of a literary language at once "so familiar and so foreign." If Irish, that is to say, Gaelic, was the national language, W. B. Yeats conceded in 1901 that English was his mother tongue: "I might have found more of Ireland if I had written in Irish,"[73] but he found more of himself by writing in English. Language forced the leading writers of the age to wrestle with individualism, nationalism, colonialism, and mixtures thereof. By 1930, scholars tell us, English had become the language of international modernism, which included the literary language of Ireland, America, and England itself.[74]

Less than unwittingly, Stephen and Professor MacHugh give history lessons that center on the theme of usurpation and on leaders who guided nations out of bondage—from Moses to would-be Irish liberators such as Charles Stewart Parnell. For his part, Joyce could not trust the future to any Moses-like character because he did not believe that the culture of his time gave him reasons for fictionalizing what was not there. In his Italian essays on Ireland, Joyce acknowledged that British rule had contributed to the reduction of the population from eight to four million people, the quadrupling of taxes, and the aggravation of agricultural problems. He questioned the advantage that Ireland gained from its loyalty to the papacy and disloyalty to the British crown. His bitter conclusion was that the time had come either to be reborn or to descend into the tomb forever.[75] The hope in *Finnegans Wake* was that language and literature would be the weapons of choice in the liberation of Irish minds from the corruption of Saxon modes of thinking. What persisted was the aftermath of colonialism: historical paralysis and cultural amnesia.

However briefly put, this was the intellectual background to both the 1916 uprising and the cultural phenomenon known as the Irish Literary Revival.[76] Joyce had grown resentful of British imperialism, but he remained ambivalent toward the English language and the English as well as toward Gaelic and the Irish. Slowly he invented an English of his own in *Finnegans Wake,* which introduced a kind of Hiberno-English that helped an Irish writer who either would not or could not write in "Irish."[77] Perhaps Joyce was too commercially minded to think of Gaelic as an alternative at once viable and profitable. He thought of English as the language of literature, and Borges reminds us that "he, an Irishman, recalled that Dublin had been founded by Danish Vikings. He studied Norwegian—he wrote a letter to Ibsen in Norwegian—and then he studied Greek, Latin.... He knew all the languages, and he wrote in a language invented by himself."[78]

Visually, the Anglicized etymology and linguistic intricacies of *Ulysses* take Joyce back to the indigenous grounds of illuminated manuscripts. Outstanding among them is the medieval Book of Kells, which dates from the end of the eighth century. Joyce considered it a "scriptural model" of his own Irish tradition: "It is the most purely Irish thing we have, and some of the big initial letters which swing right across a page have the essential quality of a chapter of 'Ulysses.' Indeed you can compare much of my work to the intricate illuminations."[79] Comments are made on the book's "weird and commanding beauty; its subdued and goldless colouring; the baffling intricacy of its fearless designs; the clean, unwavering sweep . . . through the mazes of its decorations."[80] The first of Joyce's lectures in Trieste was on the Book of Kells, which he must have seen at Trinity College. By Christmas of 1922, he had given a copy of it to Miss Weaver. Together with *The Book of the Dun Cow* and *The Book of Durrow*, it shaped what has come to be known as the "Hisperic aesthetics," a style that affected the whole area between Spain and the British islands. It emphasized the Asianic style, convoluted and ornamental. It found its roots in Quintilian's *Institutio Oratoria* (xii, 79), and let Jerome unleash his irate criticism: "Everything is caught up in such inextricable verbal knots that one could quote Plautus here: 'Here nobody except the Sibyl could understand anything.' What are these verbal monstrosities?" Indeed, it was a Hisperic aesthetic that was labyrinthine, and Umberto Eco sets up oppositions that clarify its context: "If the ideal of classical aesthetic was clarity, the Hisperic ideal would be obscurity." Preference was given to "the gigantic, the monstrous, the unrestrained, the immeasurable, the prodigious."[81] Here we have a source for *Ulysses* as well as for *Finnegans Wake*. What counts is the artistry of intricate patterns, which, in Joyce's case, begin with language.

Molly renders Aristotle as Aristocrat, which is a pun on a name as well as on a level of readership. It suffices to add that *Finnegans Wake* is replete with onomastic changes: from Faustian to fustian and from Nomad to Namar, Numah, and Nomon, not to mention the erroneous equation of metamorphosis with metempsychosis in *Ulysses*.[82] Radical experiments aside, the name Ulysses implies a literary topography that edges on what Hugh Kenner considers the province of the lexicographer: "A scholiast writing marginalia to the *Odyssey* may pause over a single word to consider how Homer is using it; but a lexicographer abstracts it from all particular usage."[83] In the epic mode, knowledge is linked to itinerant experiences; in the lexicographic mode, knowledge is drawn from, and written in, books. The geography of the lexicographer wavers between the stability of the dictionary and the dynamics of alphabetical combinations. We have reached a point where the transformational power of "rewording" on matters of Homeric translation assumes that languages leave traces, comprising the literal and the symbolic status of voyages, uncertain homecomings, marital fidelity, survival through cunning, disguise, the reversal of fortune.[84]

As a title, *Ulysses* is a word thick with etymological erasures, semantic grooves, and textual palimpsests; they all point to a strategy of transfers that takes us from Troy and Ithaca to Dublin. Just as Odysseus hides royal authority under a pauper's clothes upon his return to his island kingdom, so is *Ulysses* a title that hides meaning beneath earlier meanings that shelter construction and foster deconstruction.[85] Ulysses is the Other of Odysseus. He is the one who would dare neither Sirens nor one-eyed giants; by so doing, he would make the epic improbable and the novel possible.

Language also tells us that Homer's epic is entitled *Odyssey*, which links the individual story of Odysseus to the cultural geography of heroic Hellas. *Odyssey* and *Aeneid* are collective nouns that draw individuals and groups together. In Aristotelian terms, plot (*peripeteia*) claims priority over character (*êthos*) because epic themes celebrate nationhood.[86] Joyce did not entitle his work *Ulyssesead*, nor did he name his character Ulysses Bloom. By the same token, he followed the tradition of individual names for novelistic narratives, whether picaresque, realistic, or romantic—Lazarillo de Tormes, Tom Jones, Oliver Twist, Emma Bovary. In spite of his penchant for linguistic experimentation, Joyce did not go out of his way to create a neologism of comparable latitude. Yet his literary map of Dublin is so accurate that, as we all know, it could serve for an accurate reconstruction of the city, should disaster strike. In this sense, one might do justice to the relationship between character and place by combining two titles in one: *Ulysses the Dubliner*.

Inevitably, textuality and onomastics warrant an array of possible changes. A translated name entails loss of identity; Ulixes no longer is Odysseus, and Ulysses is even less than either the Greek or the Latin precursors. We know what Leopold Bloom does on June 16, 1904, but would Ulysses do the same? Could such a name, and such a title, be so downgraded as to collapse into the representation of one day in the life of an advertising agent? What we do know is that Ulysses functions as a translational bridge for names, genres, epochs, and geographies. Believing as he does that historical memory is all we have to set the literal against the literary, Joyce draws on the past to make contemporary experiences more palatable. The best that Leopold Bloom can do is to perform familiar tasks. Title and text, that is to say, Ulysses and

Bloom, support each other to keep literary form alive on the written page, where narrative text and mythical subtext elevate otherwise ordinary events. At least on June 16, 1904, there was no new ideology to uphold in Dublin.

3

W. B. Stanford entitled his diachronic study of the Homeric hero *The Ulysses Theme*. Along its thematic groove, this chapter unravels a journey that starts in the wine dark sea of Greek Odysseus and navigates toward Latin coasts, where the dialectical form of *Olusseus* yielded to the Latin *Ulixes* (which also drew from the Etruscan *uluxe* and the Seculian *oulixes*).[87] The *Ulixes* etymology is Etruscan, but scholarship has yet to ascertain whether the meaning was similar to or different from the Greek. At any rate, we can assume that by the time of Virgil, Odysseus and *Ulixes* were semantically equivalent. The title's etymological shift from Odysseus to Ulysses points to a divide where direct "translation" yields indirect echoes. Fritz Senn calls them "dislocutions" that thrive on "switches, transfers, and displacements." "The hybrid Latin form," Senn writes, "became Joyce's suggestive title, which intimates that the work so named is also a transmutation of Homer's epic—which in turn we surmise to be the outcome of previous reshapings."[88] In this sense the onomastic dislocution points to the vicissitudes of the epic hero in a postepic world where allusion sets the title against a modern—and modernist—landscape.[89] It is no wonder that Senn has learned not to ask who Ulysses "is," but what *Ulysses* "does."[90] For a "man of many turns," each turn re-qualifies identity, which is yet another sign of Odysseus's ability to meet diverse circumstances. Eclecticism sets him apart from monolithic characters like Achilles or Ajax. In light of the diachronic trajectory of this study, Odysseus's cunning spirit of adaptation is clearly protonovelistic.

Odysseus takes us to Troy and back to Ithaca, whereas the Latinate Ulysses steers us toward Virgil and Aeneas. The Trojan hero took the theme of the journey to Italy, for he was duty bound to settle in Alba Longa before his heirs would found Rome. From the ashes of Troy an even greater city rose on the banks of the River Tiber, well in the spirit of the phoenix-like mythology of death and rebirth. Joyce himself brings up "pious Eneas."[91] The name's spelling stands halfway between Virgil's *pius Aeneas* and Dante's *pio Enea*, who bodies forth the model of compliance with providential plans. In our own age of heightened anticolonialism, it is ironic that Joyce began to think about writing *Ulysses* while he was in Rome, where Aeneas's heirs built the most powerful empire of antiquity. Against the grain of stories in the tradition of naturalistic slices of life, the young Joyce gave the title of "Ulysses" to a tale about a certain Mr. Hunter, which he conceived in Rome but did not develop beyond the title itself.[92] Then he mentioned *Ulysses in Dublin*,[93] which he dismissed because he was still uncertain about its allusiveness. From the very beginning, therefore, Ulysses left footprints on first pages, but he never became a textual character. The inference is that Joyce developed an allusive approach to the relationship between title and text early in his literary career.

In fact, some would subtitle *Ulysses* "Tradition and the Individual Talent."[94] In terms of tradition, Joyce so contextualized his novel in a letter to Mrs. William Murray (10 November 1922): "I told you to read the *Odyssey* first.... Then buy at once *The Adventures of Ulysses* by Charles Lamb. You can read it in a night and can buy it at Gill's or Browne and Nolan's for a couple of shillings—Then have a try at *Ulysses* again."[95] In terms of individual talent, Joyce wrote to Carlo Linati (21 September 1920):

> It is an epic of two races (Israelite-Irish) and at the same time the cycle of the human body as well as a little story of a day (life). The character of Ulysses always fascinated me—even when a boy. Imagine, fifteen years ago I started writing it as a short story for *Dubliners!* For seven years I have been working at this book—blast it! It is also a sort of encyclopaedia. My intention is to transpose the myth *sub specie temporis nostri*. Each adventure (that is, every hour, every organ, every art being interconnected and interrelated in the structural scheme of the whole) should not only condition but even create its own technique. Each adventure is so to say one person although it is composed of persons—as Aquinas relates of the angelic hosts.[96]

The Latinate title—Ulixes-Ulisse-Ulysses—takes us to Rome, where Joyce confronted the visual presence of history in all its layered complexity. In 1906 he spent seven "unhappy" months in the city of the seven hills and seven kings. The city of paralysis, Dublin, found a counterpart in Rome, where paralysis as archaeology had reached universal proportions. In Rome Joyce pitched the "impoverished country" of Ireland against the bygone grandeur of classical culture. Rome reminded Joyce of "a man who lives by exhibiting to travellers his grandmother's corpse."⁹⁷ Rome sheltered what Joyce considered the main contributors to the nightmare of history: the Roman Empire and the Catholic Church.⁹⁸

At the heart of Latin culture, Joyce, who considered Latin his "first second language,"⁹⁹ created his own variations of Latin names; *Octavian Augustus, Lepidus,* and *Mark Antony* became "Oxtheivious, Lapidous and Malthouse Anthemy."¹⁰⁰ The importance of Latin culture in the heritage of the West is such that the onomastics of *Ulysses* could not help but remind Joyce that, much as Dublin stood for Ireland, so Rome stood for the classical tradition of imperialist narratives. The stratified depths of Roman palimpsests provided Joyce with the logistics as well as the linguistics for thinking about colonialism,¹⁰¹ which he readily identified with Great Britain.¹⁰²

If the political capital of monarchical Italy did not impress Joyce, the Roman Forum probably did. There he would have found counterparts to the epoch-making excavations that Schliemann and Evans carried out at Troy and Knossos. In the tense dialogue between science and mythology during the nineteenth century, archaeological digs gave a semiscientific credibility to the lore of legend, which drew history and literature into the realm of the provable. In light of evolutionary theories, the Homeric tradition shouldered some kind of primeval unity at the source of Western thought, and many a romantic looked at Greece as the "primitive" place of cultural origins. At the turn of the twentieth century, excavations undertaken under the direction of Giacomo Boni revealed more than twelve strata in and around the Roman Forum. This kind of evidence calls for "thick readings" that anchor memory to a place where myth is embedded in the texture of arches, bricks, walls, and ruins.

According to his biographer Richard Ellmann, it was in Rome that Joyce conceived "The Dead," the most complex story of *Dubliners*.¹⁰³ The title makes inaction permanent in a city where realistic trivialities open up to deeper levels of existence. For Joyce, realism consists of the "facts on which the world is based: that sudden reality which smashes romanticism into a pulp. What makes most people's lives unhappy is some disappointed romanticism, some unrealizable or misconceived ideal. In fact you may say that idealism is the ruin of man. . . . Nature is quite unromantic. It is we who put romance into her, which is a false attitude, an egotism, absurd like all egotisms. In *Ulysses* I tried to keep close to fact."¹⁰⁴ Although romanticism could be too much, and romance spawned self-deception, the pulp of mere reality was not enough. "The Dead" echoes *The Waste Land* as well as Gabriele

D'Annunzio's *La città morta* (The Dead City), an appropriate title for a play that mixes history with archaeology.[105] Some believe that Joyce found early inspiration for his own reliance on mythology in the Italian writer, who wrote about classical myths and was a mythmaker himself.[106]

At any rate, the journey from *Dubliners* to *Ulysses* seeks a middle ground where allusion, epiphany, and myth can make the ordinary less mundane. To look into the flotsam of a city was common enough after Zola, but to find Ulysses there was reckless and imprudent.[107] To quote from *Finnegans Wake*, the ordinary partakes of a diverse landscape of "gentes and laitymen, fullstoppers and somicolonials, hybrids and lubberds."[108] More than elsewhere, it was in Rome that the epic outreach of *nostos* and *fatum* stood in stark contrast with the daily activities of men without too many qualities. It is ironic that Joyce chose not to see Rome as the place where the past has shown the greatest resilience, displaying as it does architectural and sculptural landmarks that link antiquity to modernity. Since he saw the past as an unredeemable catastrophe,[109] Joyce could neither vindicate myth nor redeem history,[110] in Rome or elsewhere.

While in Rome, Joyce must have thought of Odysseus in the translated Ulixes-Ulisse-Ulysses etymology, which is closer to the neoclassical style to which Rome contributed with the eighteenth-century architecture of Valadier and the sculptures of Canova. It is perhaps the fate of exiles, whose point of view is intrinsically bifocal, to be aware of the spatial, temporal, and psychological complexity of distance as difference. From the Capitoline Hill to Piazza del Popolo, the Irishman could appreciate the Renaissance and neoclassical faces of Rome. Nevertheless, the monumental evidence of the past reinforced his conviction that Roman power contributed decisively to shaping history as a nightmare. While Stephen Dedalus tries to awaken from it, Professor MacHugh vilifies Roman antiquity:

> 'We think of Rome, imperial, imperious, imperative'. . . . He extended elocutionary arms from frayed stained shirt-cuffs, pausing: 'What was their civilisation? Vast, I allow: but vile. Cloacae: sewers. The Jews in the wilderness and on the mountaintop said: *It is meet to be here. Let us build an altar to Jehovah.* The Roman, like the Englishman who follows in his footsteps, brought to every new shore on which he set his foot (on our shore he never set it) only his cloacal obsession. He gazed about him in his toga and he said: *It is meet to be here. Let us construct a watercloset.*' (*Ulysses*, 1-7:484–95)

A blunt equation binds imperialisms old and new. Even the inane victims of colonialism are not spared: "Ireland, however, is still the brain of the United Kingdom. The foresighted and ponderous English provide humanity's swollen belly with the perfect instrument of comfort: the Water Closet. The Irish, doomed to express themselves in a language that is not their own, have stamped it with their genius and compete for glory with other civilized countries. This is called 'English Literature.'"[111] Memorial signposts of failure describe Dublin, and the water closet finds a counterpart in the urinal that stands by a statue of the protonationalist poet Thomas Moore.[112]

The last generation of Irishmen who lived under the empire lingered on the fringes of education, trade, culture, and social services, a posture that led Joyce to denounce blind obedience in "The Dead." Joyce lets trams, mail cars, and printing presses dominate the mechanized "HEART OF THE HIBERNIAN METROPOLIS" (*Ulysses*, 1-7:1–2), where many stand by, waiting for someone else to take the lead. Speaking for his own social enclave, Professor MacHugh recognizes that "success for us is the death of the intellect and of the imagination" (*Ulysses*, 1-7:553–54). For Joyce, politics in Ireland wavered between arrogance and daydreaming.[113] Just as wishfully, Bernard Shaw still hoped that *Ulysses* would be effective, on the Irish principle that one can train a cat by rubbing its nose in its filth.[114] In "The Home Rule Comet" (1910), Joyce unleashed an invective against Ireland.

> For seven centuries she has never been a faithful subject of England. Neither, on the other hand, has she been a faithful subject to herself. She has entered the British domain without forming an integral part of it. She has abandoned her own language almost entirely and accepted the language of the conqueror without being able to assimilate the culture or adapt herself to the mentality of which this language is the vehicle. She has betrayed her heroes, always in the hour of need and always without gaining recompense.[115]

By contesting structures of authority, this statement alludes to the British Empire and echoes Haines's condescending utterance: "An Irishman must think like that, I daresay. We feel in England that we have treated you rather unfairly. It seems history is to blame." (*Ulysses*, 1-1:648) Dubliners knew whom to blame when, in 1916, British gunboats came up the river to bomb Henry Street and adjacent neighborhoods.

As an Irishman who did not ignore the troublesome issue of national independence, Joyce knew who was responsible for history's wretched downturns. Thus he pitched the obsolescence of Greco-Roman mythology against the materialism of modern Dublin, a city that had always been divided between the dead past of powerless legends and a modern technology at the service of an establishment that did not necessarily serve Irish interests. The aftermath of the Easter Rising of 1919 curbed Joyce's hopes no less than Yeats's, who wrote a poem whose title, *Nineteen Hundred and Nineteen,* leaves no doubt about the historical reference:

> We too had many pretty toys when young:
> A law indifferent to blame or praise,
> To bribe or threat; habits that made old wrong
> Melt down, as it were wax in the sun's rays;
> Public opinion ripening for so long
> We thought it would outlive all future days.
> O what fine thought we had because we thought
> That the worst rogues and rascals had died out. (lines 9–16)

By 1928 Yeats had expanded his own poetic voice about political responsibility under the heading *Meditations in Time of Civil War.* If history is a nightmare from which Stephen Dedalus is trying to awaken, Yeats so describes his own dejected view of history in *The Second Coming.*

> That twenty centuries of stony sleep
> Were vexed to nightmare by a rocking cradle,
> And what rough beast, its hour come round at last,
> Slouches towards Bethlehem to be born? (lines 19–22)

In terms of the cultural journey that transformed the Homeric Odysseus into the Joycean Ulysses, things were permanent in Homer's days, and change was always for the worse. Michael Seidel closes his study of the epic geography of *Ulysses* with a comment on the recognition scene between Penelope and Odysseus, whose bed "is rooted in the ground, carved out of the trunk of an olive tree around which the bedroom was constructed. The olive tree, so important a symbol in the Homeric epic of domestication, is Athena's civilizing gift to the city of Athens. Penelope accepts Odysseus fully only when he identifies the structural rootedness of the bed—it cannot be otherwise in an epic of fidelity. But Joyce wants direction more than he wants rootedness."[116]

Penelope demands that Odysseus return to what he had been, because rootedness lets neither time nor space tamper with the identity of people and places.

After years of travel, Odysseus returns home, where dog, nurse, and wife recognize him through signs that vindicate his original identity. The problem with recognition is that it *re*activates continuity but cannot erase difference.[117] At the surface, recognition scenes reestablish order. Underneath, however, they stir disruption, because a lapse at once chronological and ontological has occurred.[118] By the end of the Homeric saga, the name of Odysseus proves inadequate to describe what the hero has become. His name is like his scar; it digs a furrow that plunges him into the past. Like the old rags he wears to enter the royal palace without being recognized, his name is another disguise. Physically, he looks aged; onomastically, he needs a new name. The thought slowly creeps in that he also needs a new place, if not a new wife who would appreciate what has happened to him between exile and return. One can fulfill one's name but one can grow out of it as well.

Because of Poseidon, his maritime foe, Odysseus is tossed around by the waves in such a way that he ends up seeing and learning what he could not have fathomed otherwise. From Athena, his ally, Odysseus inherits *metis*, and cunning is instrumental in conquering Troy and regaining Ithaca's throne. Yet there still is one more journey in store for Odysseus, and his destiny is to tell landlocked people about life at sea. Closer to our own days, Constantine Cavafy, in his poem *Ithaca*, has gone back to the epic voyager:

> Ithaca gave you the marvelous journey,
> Without her you wouldn't have set out.
> She has nothing left to give you.

Another city and another genre were needed for the journey to continue. In fact, Odysseus was on his way to becoming more Odyssean, that is to say, less epic and more novelistic.

Of course, some scholars would suggest that the shift from Odysseus to Ulysses begins to take place in the *Odyssey*, which itself is a book of many turns. It has been pointed out that the *Odyssey* should be divided into two parts. The first includes the five books of the Telemachia, whose mythical subjects focus on the marvelous and the monstrous: Cyclops, sirens, lotus-eaters who fog out memory as knowledge, witches, and animal transformations. These early books bring up the heroic ideals of the *Iliad* inasmuch as characters are moved by honor and loyalty, regardless of the consequences. It is a world of individual feats without any long-term teleology. Motivations are rather selfish, and Menelaus makes of a personal case of age-old cuckoldry the occasion for a war that drags along most of the other Greek tribes. Likewise, Paris makes a whole city pay for his adulterous lust. Some might suggest that the "incident" of Helen is just an excuse for the inevitable showdown between Greeks and Trojans, which is about political and economic dominance. In light of what happened after the fall of Troy, such an argument appears quite weak. The Greeks who made it home met rather tragic fates without any national cohesion to compensate for their drawn-out effort. Their deadly struggle at Troy could not be compared with the rivalry between Rome and Carthage, which had a socioeconomic base of lasting influence.

The switch begins when the gods decree that Odysseus should abandon Calypso and continue his homeward journey. Obediently, the hero leaves the sorceress (Book V, lines 215–24).[119] Once he comes ashore by the land of the Phaecians, a fundamental change occurs. He is less heroic and more human, less of a warrior and more of a home keeper. He moves from being the destroyer of cities to the restorer of Ithaca. Odysseus's restoration of the culture of Ithaca is the preliminary step that the epic takes before Aeneas sets out to fulfill his destiny by serving a universal mission destined to change the world. Beyond such settlements, a more "bourgeois routine" is bound to emerge at the edge of the novelistic.

Joyce himself downplayed the heroic as he internalized the theme of the journey and eliminated violent confrontations that were incompatible with the peaceful nature of Leopold Bloom. The only bloodletting at the end of Joyce's book is menstrual. For this very reason, Joyce leaves out of his allusions the opening episode of the Ciconians, in which Odysseus still acts out the epic qualities of ruthless killing, on which he would rely one last time to regain control in Ithaca. Between violent endpoints, the more peaceful episode of the lotus-eaters is expanded.

With an eye to the ongoing interest in the recurrence of myth, scholars have highlighted the linkage between Vico and Joyce. Accordingly, the *ricorso*-repetition of cultural cycles would strengthen the connection between Homer and Joyce. From a standpoint at once titological and onomastic, I would add that the pair Odysseus-Ulysses confirms the *ricorso*. It should be pointed out, however, that *ricorso* is more spiral than circular; it spins repetition into development. Dante and Shakespeare are as universal and outstanding as Homer, but they are "different" from the epic bard. Dante and Shakespeare express a postepic and postmedieval ethos. Repetition and development altered but did not sever the connection between Odysseus and Ulysses, which turned out to be at once significant and resilient. Odysseus and Ulysses might be called the double helix of the DNA of Western individualism. As Richard Ellmann put it, Joyce was aware that naming his book *Ulysses* "was like calling one's book the Bible."[120]

Vis-à-vis the mythical story, the humanist tradition of Athens and Rome exhausted its westbound thrust in Eliot's London and Joyce's Dublin, which became the last Babel and the second Troy of the islands facing the Atlantic Ocean. The flight of the eagle, first mythic in Greek lore and than historical at the dawn of the Renaissance, tired itself out by the time Eliot wrote *Ash Wednesday* in 1930:

> (Why should the agèd eagle stretch its wings?)
> . . .
> Because these wings are no longer wings to fly
> But merely vans to beat the air
> The air which is now thoroughly small and dry
> Smaller and dryer than the will
> Teach us to care and not to care
> Teach us to sit still.

Let us not forget that the epigraph of *The Waste Land* is about the Cumaean sibyl, who invokes death in the dead language of Latin. It is the death of the humanist tradition at its European border, where Joyce understood that there was no sea left for Ulysses. Like Eliot, Joyce would concede that there is no escape from the "prestige of beginnings," the prestige, that is, of myths that have claimed authority for centuries on end.

On matters of onomastic beginnings, it has been noted that the names of Leopold Bloom, Stephen Dedalus, and Molly Bloom are not Irish. As we turn to the Irish tradition of *The Book of Invasions,* we realize that indigenous mythologies draw nutrients from distant roots. Bloom is a counterpart to the Goidels invaders, and Dedalus represents invaders of Greek heritage, the Tuatha De Danann. Molly, by contrast, embodies the Spanish presence in Irish culture.[121] At the Western outpost of the European world, Joyce did not look toward the American continent, which attracted adventurous as well as destitute Irish immigrants.

Geography exhausted the resources of language inasmuch as *Ulysses* pointed to the outermost Western "dislocution" of Homeric onomastics. Somehow Joyce's allusive mode drew together epic and modern domesticity as well as Odysseus's sea voyage and Bloom's urban stroll. The civilization of the Mediterranean Sea was inscribed in the foundational tale of Odysseus-Ulysses, which set the epic against the novel. The civilization of the Atlantic Ocean, which started with Columbus's voyage rather than with a mythical text, was bound to find its novelistic bard in the counterepic of Herman Melville's *Moby-Dick*. Maurice Blanchot writes that Ahab crosses paths with Moby Dick only in Melville's text. Likewise, Ulysses introduces readers to Dublin only in Joyce's text. "The book," however, presents other encounters as well: "To unite in the same space Ahab and the whale, the Sirens and Ulysses—that is the secret wish that makes Ulysses Homer, makes Ahab Melville, and the world that results from this union the greatest, most terrible, and most beautiful of possible worlds, alas a book, nothing but a book."[122] Sequence makes room for simultaneity, which is reiterated by the temporal structure. Joyce's narrative begins at 8:00 A.M., with Stephen in the Martello Tower, and the first three episodes are centered on Stephen Dedalus. When Leopold Bloom enters the narrative (fourth episode), we go back to 8:00 A.M. in Eccles Street. In the tenth episode, "Wandering Rocks," Joyce again presents different people simultaneously. This simultaneity, I believe, is reflected in the title, whose allusive range does take in Odysseus, Ulixes, Aeneas, and Bloom. The titological underlining of *Ulysses*, therefore, is palimpsestic as well as panoptic. Its broad contextuality gives a titological slant to Fredric Jameson's rallying cry, "Always historicize."

Joyce understood that there was another way for an Odyssean narrative to unravel. It called on geography to abandon the surface and plunge into the depths of the human mind, where the "stream of consciousness" spurred the imagination to re-create more personal maps of the world. The very opening of the "Proteus" chapter heightens the modernity of the Joycean text. Late in the morning, Stephen arrives at Sandymount, where his meditations enact an "internal monologue." The Protean metamorphosis entails a shift toward the inner world: "Ineluctable modality of the visible: at least that, if no more, thought through my eyes" (*Ulysses*, 1-3:1–2). This concise statement takes up the traditional equation of sight with knowledge. To see is to know under the aegis of the "visible." The visual experience of exile and return adds to knowledge at the physical level of spaces and things theretofore unseen. From a retrospective point of view, however, the "ineluctable modality" of vision points to traditional limitations that stir the opposite urge to break free of inherited shackles. What emerges is the potential for a subjective view; the landscape faces up to a mindscape.

Still on visual grounds, the sight of two midwives on the beach prompts Stephen to guess the contents of the bag that one of them is carrying: "What has she in the bag? A misbirth with a trailing navelcord, hushed in ruddy wool. The cord of all link back, strandentwining cable of all flesh. That is why mystic monks. Will you be as gods? Gaze in your omphalos. Hello. Kinch here. Put me on to Edenville. Aleph, alpha: nought, nought, one" (*Ulysses*, 1-3:36–40). The birth of the individual links up to the birth of nationhood, from the Greek *omphalós* to the Martello Tower, which is the oracular navel of Joyce's mental universe.[123] It is by the Martello Tower that the archetypal journey moves from the visibility of the classical "without" to the interiority of the modernist "within." At last, visual sight shifted toward mental reconstruction. Joyce so mastered the center and the perimeter of his literary map that he could undertake the longest journeys without going anywhere. *Portrait of the Artist as a Young Man* came of age around the Martello Tower, where Ulysses stood by, the Godlike "persona" who drew together mythical adults, tired Dubliners, and youthful artists. Joyce as Ulysses hunkered down and reconstructed the map of modernity where the old and new *nostos* of the Western quest merged in the depths of the human mind. I would like to describe this shift by pointing to the title of a Stevens poem, *Phosphor Reading by His Own Light,* which transforms the Martello Tower into a light tower. After Joyce, Stevens also understood that "the stream of consciousness is individual" (*Adagia*, I). Indeed, light-givers read under the power of their own illuminations!

4

When all is said about June 16, 1904, what is left the next day is the belief that the mythical is there to save us from the realm of the untranslatable, which oversees the space of prosaic deeds and the time of intellectual idleness. Myth gives us the anachronistic freedom of nostalgia, offering metaphors that can *translate* us to somewhere else, where we shall find myth all over again.

At the end of his life, the last literary task that Joyce undertook was the translation into Italian of the washerwomen dialogue in *Finnegans Wake*. It is not a revision but a complete translation, and Jacqueline Risset entitles her introduction to the piece "Joyce *traduce* Joyce"—Joyce translates Joyce.[124] This title stands in symmetry with my "Title Translated into Title." Together they spell out Joyce's poetics by pivoting on the "idea" of translation as a transformational activity that is beginning and end, part and whole, past and future. Joyce, the Irish exile who did not speak a national language, began to translate himself into other languages, so that literary transfers and mythical allusions would continue to unfold.

However different the sources and the motivations, Eliot voiced a widespread interest—from Pound and Joyce to Mann, Yeats, and Valéry—in the resilience of mythology. They all trusted the "mythical method" to make reality more bearable by retaining a sense of history that offset the contemporary disintegration of cultural values after World War I, which turned out to be disastrous for the victors no less than for the vanquished. History was juxtaposed to mythopoetic history, which found pagan and Christian precedents: Herodotus and Augustine, Leonardo Bruni and Vico, Michelet and Burckhardt. At the beginning of the twentieth century, the ruins of history piled up in the Waste Land. To bypass its debris, artists, writers, and political ideologues rooted the future in the resilience of mythology. Its textual, subtextual, or contextual presence has tested a foundational aspect of human nature, which has always measured our experience of reality against a set of values that precede and survive the sheer facts of existence.

In a thoughtful study of "mythistory," Joseph Mali points out that Joyce's fascination with Vico's mythopoeic concept of history is apparent in *Finnegans Wake* as well as in *Ulysses*. The "Ithaca" chapter, in fact, outlines the relevance of myth as a "repository" of stories whereby humankind remakes its own history. It could be said that mythology "documents" the human mindset as much as actual deeds do. As he teaches a history lesson in the private school for boys in Dilkey, a village outside Dublin, Stephen remembers that there is a "Vico road" nearby (*Ulysses*, 2:25). The reflection reminds him of the mythology of Blake's *Vision of the Last Judgment*, arguing that vision and history coalesce because one can grasp the concept mystically rather than empirically. From Blake to the Pyrrhic victory at the battle of Asculum in 279 B.C., Joyce systematically undermines the uselessness of factual information that does not stir critical reflection. Hence he shifts toward poetic history, which retains dreams, hopes, and visions—what is called either "ghoststory" or "foundational narrative." It has been suggested that the entire ethnography of the Mediterranean originated from the big bang of the Trojan War and the consequent diffusion of the mythic *nostos* of exile and return.[125] For, as Borges reminds us, "In the beginning of literature is the myth, and in the end as well."[126]

From a titological standpoint, out of the big bang of the Trojan War came the foundational titles *Odyssey* and *Aeneid*, which have played a significant role in the literature of the West. Joyce understood that his novel, at once inclusive and conclusive, deserved a title that would enact the final *nostos* of a tradition he would transgress but could not reject.

And so it is in Joyce's masterwork, whose title is as onomastically itinerant as the journeyman it translates. The journey, however, had reached its westward limit, where the Odyssean epic settled down into the Ulyssean Dublin of middle-class everydayness. West of Dublin, the Promised Land remained a utopian dream that did not seduce Joyce. "Outcast from Ireland, scornful of Britain, and uneasy about the humanism of a Europe to which he could never fully surrender," Joyce became, to borrow from Declan Kiberd, "a nomad, a world author."[127] East of Dublin, T. S. Eliot landed in London, where he wrote memorable verses about an Unreal City at the center of *The Waste Land*.

5

The Waste Land: The Archaeology of Titles

Eliot's archaeological imagery presents the past as a collection of
dead and deadening memorials that anesthetize memory itself.
—MUTLU KONUK BLASING

Calvin Bedient opens his study of *The Waste Land* by asking, "What is the 'place' of a title, inside or outside the work?"[1] Inside the work, the title is textual; outside, it is contextual. At once noun and verb, *Waste* applies to both, for it describes *Land* as a site at once literary and geographical. Internally, it contains the modernist poem; externally, it reaches out toward the perimeter of Western literature. Likewise, *Land* is a synecdoche for earth as ground as well as for the whole planet. Just as important is the article, which tells us that the title is not about some generic waste scattered over just any land. Instead, it is *The Waste Land,* the prototypical model of a cultural landscape that exemplifies for modernism what *The Prince* exemplified for the Renaissance. But whereas Machiavelli was still capable of voicing idealism in the prophetic conclusion of his revolutionary treatise on human nature, Eliot pegged an epigraph to his title in which the Cumaean sibyl utters a death wish. By turning the humanist penchant for the panegyrical into a eulogy of eternal grief, the titological article, *the,* parodies the theme of the Promised Land. Title and epigraph introduce the space not of a dawn-renaissance but of a sunset-decadence that is further darkened by the title of the poem's first section, "The Burial of the Dead."

Equally relevant to this study is the title of Calvin Bedient's own book, *He Do the Police in Different Voices.* It quotes the provisional title that Eliot gave to his work when it consisted of a group of poems yet to be unified in a single frame. The source is Charles Dickens's *Our Mutual Friend.* In chapter 16 of that novel, Betty Higden claims that her son, Sloppy, "is a beautiful reader of a newspaper. He do the Police in different voices." The title promises literary experiments in different styles and disparate characters.[2] Because it alludes to a multifaceted assemblage, the title suggests that Eliot's London may turn out to be quite Dickensian.[3] It should be added that the original title had its own original epigraph, which quoted Joseph Conrad's *Heart of Darkness*: "Did he live his life again in every detail of desire, temptation, and surrender during that supreme moment of complete knowledge? He cried in a whisper at some image, at some vision—he cried out twice, a cry that was no more than a breath—'The horror! The horror!'"[4] Scholars have highlighted the clash between the unambiguous worldview of the "primitive" Africans and the complex worldview of Kurtz. The quotation reflects Eliot's attention to forms of nondualistic thinking that have become obsolete in modern society,[5] which has been trying to come to terms with relativism, indeterminacy, and chaos theories.

Back to the title, we confront the twofold semantics of *Waste*. As a noun, it defines the modernist grounds of advanced decline as Eliot experienced it in his own time. He is the insider who witnesses disintegration at the point where it begins to get out of hand. The word can also be turned into an adjective—wasted—which entails an external point of view focused on the acknowledgment of drawn-out processes of historical erosion. Once the spatial "waste" confronts the temporal "wasted," we understand why the *land* has become a desert guarded by

> the stuffed men
> Leaning together
> Headpiece filled with straw.
>
> (*The Hollow Men*, lines 2–4)

And what they stand guard over

> is the dead land
> This is cactus land
> Here the stone images
> Are raised, here they receive
> The supplication of a dead man's hand (lines 38–42)

These verses were written in 1925, three years after *The Waste Land* was published. In 1943, almost twenty years later, the *Four Quartets* so described Eliot's poetic grounds.

> There are flood and drouth
> Over the eyes and in the mouth,
> Dead water and dead sand
> Contending for the upper hand.
> The parched eviscerate soil
> Gapes at the vanity of toil,
> Laughs without mirth.
> This is the death of earth.
>
> (*Little Gidding*, lines 64–71)

Eliot himself conceded that the process of literary composition finds cohesion in the title: "One begins by choosing a title, in order to assure oneself that one has a subject: for a title is a kind of substitute or shadow of a subject."[6] *Land* is and remains scorched. Beyond it, there is no renewal, no renaissance, no resurrection.

1

At the western edge of the geography of European culture, Joyce translated the epic into the bourgeois and set his narrative in Dublin because his outlook was nationalistically Irish. Eliot, an American, acted out an eastward journey that started in his native St. Louis, took up residence in Cambridge during his education at Harvard, leaped across the Atlantic Ocean, bypassing Dublin, and reached its endpoint in London, the political center stage of modern Europe. Before becoming a British citizen in 1927, a convert to the Anglican Church, and a supporter of the monarchy, Eliot understood that epic and colonial quests had become obsolete. Heroism and imperialism had exhausted themselves by the end of World War I.

Published in the same year, *Ulysses* and *The Waste Land* form a pair that, Janus-like, point in opposite directions. Because of its emphasis on the narrative of human deeds, Joyce's title is Aristotelian, whereas Eliot's is an anti-Aristotelian description of stilled posthumousness. In Harry Levin's view, *The Waste Land* is "anti-epic in form as well as in purport, since it contains so little in the way of direct narration."[7] It has been suggested that the poem does have a chronology, perhaps because it does not have a story. Reverie structures the poem in Tiresias's mind, where time is "kaleidoscopic." A sequence of "symbolic incidents" does not a narrative make; what we have is a collage-like presence, a pastiche closer to Pound's *Cantos* than Joyce's *Ulysses*.[8]

It would seem that history has shifted from the narration of deeds to the description of their ruinous aftermath, which was eroding what Pound called a "botched civilization." In the spirit of an essay whose title, "Make It New," became programmatic for a whole generation, Pound left no doubt that "not all of us inhabit the same time." *The Waste Land,* however, made it clear that we all inhabit the same space. Joyce set the space of his novel in Dublin and dated the action June 16, 1904. On that day and in that place the Western experience was brought up to speed with the ordinariness of a middle-class humanity. The next day, Eliot turned his shoulders to Joyce and made of London the necrological epicenter of his cultural space. Set against the symbolic geography of the Western journey, *The Waste Land* turned *Ulysses* on its head.[9] Between the two, the "mythical method" offered some measure of aesthetic relief.

In London, the Anglo-American poet gazed neither eastward nor westward. Instead, he mapped out a geography at once memorable and memorial. It is there that the epigraph to the poem makes the cry of the Cumaean sibyl ever more trenchant. Her utterance in twentieth-century London is neither mythical nor historical, but literary. In the age of oral myths, she prophesied the future; in the modernist culture of the book, she stands guard over the debris of referentiality. Her Latin words are taken from Petronius's *Satyricon:* "For I once saw with my own eyes the Cumean Sibyl hanging in a jar, and when the boys asked her, 'Sibyl, what do you want?' she answered, 'I want to die.'" Apollo granted her eternal life, but she forgot to ask for eternal youth. The quotation demands attention. The Sibyl's Latin at the beginning of the poem is as foreign to most readers as is the Sanskrit at the end. In between, language contributes much waste to *Waste.* Unlike Joyce, who resorts to hybridism to expand the range of his literary tools, Eliot relishes erosion and outright phonic cacophonies.

The sibyl's attachment to life is pagan, her gods are abject, and she has no access to the metaphysics of asceticism. Her textual counterpart, which leads us out of the world of antiquity, is Madame Sosostris:

> Madame Sosostris, famous clairvoyante,
> Had a bad cold, nevertheless
> Is known to be the wisest woman in Europe,
> With a wicked pack of cards.
>
> (*The Burial of the Dead,* lines 43–46)

As the pedestrian version of the mythical figure, she makes poetry ironic, if not downright self-deprecating. She is more of a fortune-teller familiar with Tarot cards than an agent of Fate.[10] The juxtaposition between the sacred and the mundane leaves no doubts as to what eventually happened to the Latin prophetess who did not die with the rest of Latin civilization. However undignified, the sibyl moved into the practice of everyday life, where she had to make a living with a pack of cards. While some recognized the contemporary philosopher Bertrand Russell in her, I am reminded of the bourgeois "reduction" of the mythical Venus of Giorgione to a Parisian prostitute whom Manet named Olympia.

From beginning to end, the sibyl voices the haunting presence of modernist belatedness. She makes the mistake that the Renaissance was able to avoid. For the Renaissance, rebirth had to be for the better; modernist endurance and longevity, by contrast, thrived on the procrastination of what already had become old. The comparison makes it clear that the epigraph, instead of being initiatory, is as terminal as an epitaph. The irony is that *The Waste Land* has become as eternal as the sibyl's utterance. She endures old age by growing ever older, akin to Eliot's own typology of senescent titles. While J. Alfred Prufrock cries out, "I grow old . . . I grow old," Gerontion presents himself as "[a]n old man in a dry month." Let us not forget that, by the end of the century, Italo Svevo published *Senilità* (*As a Man Grows Old*) (1898). The age of innocence was long gone, and the sibyl knew that she would never enjoy a renaissance of her own. From myth to history, the Renaissance and neoclassicism had been overshadowed by the violence of the French Revolution and the Napoleonic wars. Thereafter, restorations and further revolutions led to World War I, which filled to capacity the *Land* with the *Waste* of armies and ideologies alike.

Standing as a pivot between title and text, the epigraph reinforces the referential structure of *The Waste Land*. By Eliot's own admission in the opening head note, his title echoed *From Ritual to Romance*. Published in 1920, Jessie Weston's critical book takes us back to the devastated land of the Arthurian Grail romance, whose origins are neither exclusively Christian nor uniquely folkloric.[11] Instead, they consist of a hybrid that strings out the shift from nature cults to Christian lore. Individual episodes include the Waste Land, the Fisher King, and the Hidden Castle. In spite of unique features and individual protagonists (Gawain, Perceval), the theme that holds the episodes together is the journey. If successful, it will heal the Fisher King and restore fertility to the wasteland.[12]

Vis-à-vis the literary source, Eliot focused on neither the journey nor the journeyman. Instead, he selected the wasteland, which is of such minor importance in the medieval saga that it often disappears in the background. Rather than favoring health regained, Eliot revealed his modernist markings by underwriting the pathological. The *Waste Land* does not recover its fruitfulness, because there is no hero to heal the sickly king. Tiresias knows, but he is too old to act. The title brings to the fore the shift from an ancient ritual, meant to unveil the secret of the physical and spiritual sources of life, to the lingering pathologies of the Arthurian romance. In emphasizing the ascendancy of Christianity over pagan and nature cults, Eliot foreshadowed his mature view of Christianity as the common denominator of Western culture. Yet such a philosophical context is ironic, because the poem does not portray Christian civilization at its best. In fact, it ends with the word *peace* written in a language that is neither European nor Christian.

Impatient critics might suggest that the *Waste Land* is where old scraps began to feed printed pages that recycled derivative materials. Mimesis so thrived on the imitation of used plots and abused story lines that Eliot wrote, "Immature poets imitate; mature poets steal." His elaborate assemblage, tedious footnoting, and collaborative editing paid due as well as undue homage to Ezra Pound in the dedication, which quotes the Dantean *il miglior fabbro*. At his caustic best, Robert Frost allusively noted that "one American poet living in England has made an Anthology of the Best Lines of Poetry."[13] Yet territorial claims are not easy to make in the *Waste Land*, where everything has been used, transacted, borrowed, stolen, and reused before being taken to the junkyard, where the likes of Man Ray and Jean Tinguely would stand by, ready to start their own recycling of bits and pieces. It is there, if anywhere, that the postmodern deconstruction of authorship took its start. Unhealthy by definition, the *Waste Land* is the place where the ameliorative worldview of humanism has spent itself. If plagues and wars disrupt the Promised Land, the *Waste Land* is the dumpster of the human experience, the place where devastation has played itself out. What is left is meaningless to Marcel Duchamp, perplexing to the Dadaists, but welcome to a postmodern artist by the name of Robert Rauschenberg.

The very concept of waste sets up a retrospective point of view focused on grounds where spent remains are inimical to human presence. By pointing to burned-out processes of physical, psychological, and cultural consumption,[14] waste is a threshold where the defunct can become significant once again. Eliot's title, therefore, describes a land where the fragmentary evidence of refuse constitutes the backbone of our knowledge of the past. Because *waste* refers to bygone artifacts, the *land* that accommodates it leaves no room for development. We do not discover; rather, we index, classify, and enumerate as if we were in an archive, a library, or a museum. The title introduces a cultural mindscape where poetry scatters the bones of tradition at the modernist edge of cultural residues.

> What are the roots that clutch, what branches grow
> Out of this stony rubbish? Son of man,
> You cannot say, or guess, for you know only
> A heap of broken images, where the sun beats,
> And the dead tree gives no shelter, the cricket no relief,
> And the dry stone no sound of water. (lines 19–24)

The *Waste Land* is unredeemable, and exhaustion creates its own ruinous future amid the last shreds of smoldering progress. Mythical journeys, chivalric adventures, and their parodic echoes relapsed in the wake of the destruction of World War I. The title tells us that, if the past has consumed itself (*waste*), the future has little else to offer, because modernist topographies privilege memory over discovery. *Waste* is a physical qualifier that makes the title topographical, and what it qualifies is scattered throughout the *land*.

Joyce's *Ulysses* is based on a name that itself has become the footprint of an epic map. Because of their layered symbolism, names such as Odysseus and Aeneas are at once onomastic and toponomastic. For his part, Eliot had neither an epic hero nor a bourgeois character to put forward. Instead, he mapped out the aftermath of the decline and fall of Western individualism. The very beginning of Eliot's poetry is anchored to an old man. Neither a prophet nor Prince Hamlet, Prufrock, having measured his life with coffee spoons, chooses to wear the bottoms of his "trousers rolled" (*The Love Song of J. Alfred Prufrock*). In the 1925 dedication to Jean Verdenal, Eliot added the words "*mort aux Dardanelles*," which refer to Troy and strengthen Homeric connections through the reference to the Ulysses canto in the *Divine Comedy*. In a way, Odysseus's journey is updated by Leopold Bloom and exhausted by Alfred Prufrock. In fact, the epigraph is but the first of Eliot's allusions to Odysseus.[15] Prufrock is an Odysseus-like character who has aged physically and mentally. By the time the twentieth century rolled around, Prufrock had failed to lead, to take on responsibilities, to act. No longer able to hear the sounds of the mermaids, he severed himself from the world of myth. In her comprehensive study of Eliot's poetics of evolution, Lois A. Cuddy makes it clear that Eliot, having traced the evolution of the Ulysses character, sets out to represent "the disintegration of the hero to an ordinary, insignificant, man."[16] Neither a leader nor an adventurer, Prufrock, like the Cumaean sibyl, echoes the memorial.

Aware of the ominous unrest brewing around him, Eliot drew antiheroic lessons from the past. Accordingly, Gerontion, who is as physically blind as Homer and Tiresias, is an antitriumphal embodiment of the spirit of antiquity:

> Unnatural vices
> Are fathered by our heroism. Virtues
> Are forced upon us by our impudent crimes.
> These tears are shaken from the wrath-bearing tree.
> (*Gerontion,* lines 45–48)

On matters of titology, Cuddy offers an overarching synopsis: "From Homer's Troy and the Dardanelles in the dedication, the reader moves to Plato's conception of Ulysses as a common man in the title of the poem, then on to the epigraph and the eighth circle of the *Inferno* where Dante's version of Ulysses resides."[17]

From the old to the older, *Gerontion* (1920) is "the old Greek man" who knows that it is too late to act. The title is explained in the opening lines:

> Here I am, an old man in a dry month,
> Being read to by a boy, waiting for rain. (lines 1–2)

In its wake, *The Waste Land* draws the knowledge of old age with the foreknowledge of prophecy into a mythical figure:

> Tiresias, though blind, throbbing between two lives,
> Old man with wrinkled female breasts
> . . .
> I Tiresias, old man with wrinkled dugs (lines 218–19, 228)

Against evolutionists and philosophers such as Hegel, Darwin, Spencer, Drummond, and Santayana, who still believed in some form of progress, Eliot put Ulysses to rest. His title is as axiomatically anti-evolutionist as "The Burial of the Dead," which paved the way for Hermann Broch's retrospective

Death of Virgil. From Proust to Spengler, *land* gave focal gravity to the vast spaces of remembrance and decline. Eliot saw that all journeys had been spent, and that there were no frontiers to dare. Thus he wrote his "epic of senescence" while recovering from nervous exhaustion in Switzerland. He was thirty-five years old.

2

Like a Janus figure, *Ulysses* and *The Waste Land* are the two faces of fraternal twins. One presents a backward-looking narrative and the other a deserted future of palimpsestic signs; one links up to humanist onomastics and the other to a nameless site. The *wasteland* is not just London or Dublin but a mythical enclave where *waste* enlarges space until it includes the waste of culture at large. Where *Ulysses* ends, a gap opens up; beyond it, *The Waste Land* expands to the edge of the horizon. The geographical mythology recalls neither the pastoral nor the edenic, but their negatives: from the plagued to the scorched. Eliot's title describes a place where the ashes of tradition are dispersed everywhere:[18]

> A heap of broken images, where the sun beats,
> And the dead tree gives no shelter, the cricket no relief,
> And the dry stone no sound of water.
> . . .
> These fragments I have shored against my ruins (lines 22–23, 430)

The debris of history saturated urban centers from London to Antwerp. Virginia Woolf witnessed a similar disruption in English villages where people were reduced to "scraps and fragments."[19] Gloomy cityscapes are an apt introduction to the "waning" of seasonal renewals at the edge of *The Waste Land,* which entitles an infernal vision of Europe at the end of World War I.

Ominous images of lifelessness open Eliot's poem.

> April is the cruelest month, breeding
> Lilacs out of the dead land, mixing
> Memory and desire, stirring
> Dull roots with spring rain.
>
> (*The Burial of the Dead,* lines 1–4)

As a human concept, waste modifies life-giving hopes that are usually associated with April as the month of natural rejuvenation. The predominant imagery is of despair, even though the feeble remnants of life-giving powers stir dull roots "with spring rain." Instead of baptizing new life, moisture brings forth the exhaustion of nature itself. Back in 1917 Eliot had written:

> Yet with these April sunsets, that somehow recall
> My buried life, and Paris in the Spring,
> I feel immeasurably at peace, and find the world
> To be wonderful and youthful, after all.
> *(Portrait of a Lady,* lines 52–55)

Five years later, seasonal renewal was just as ineffective in *The Waste Land.* By introducing "the cruelest month" of "the dead land," title and subtitle spell out the posthumous. *Ulysses* is about translation and the semantics of cultural change. *The Waste Land,* by contrast, sets the dried-up roots of words and the residues of things amid urban corruption, which has violated the ancient purity of the Thames.[20]

Wishfully, poetry cleanses the fluvial image by evoking pristine times.

> The river bears no empty bottles, sandwich papers,
> Silk handkerchiefs, cardboard boxes, cigarette ends
> Or other testimony of summer nights. The nymphs are departed.
> And their friends, the loitering heirs of city directors;
> . . . .
> London Bridge is falling down falling down falling down
>   (lines 177–80, 427)

Deities have departed so long ago that language can no longer do justice to bygone cleanliness. The fall of London Bridge anticipated

> Falling towers
> Jerusalem Athens Alexandria
> Vienna London (lines 374–76)

At the height of modernism, Eliot saw bridges and towers collapsing. As it happened, fiction turned into reality when Eliot experienced urban destruction during the German air raids over London in 1940–41:

> Between three districts whence the smoke arose
> I met one walking, loitering and hurried
> As if blown towards me like the metal leaves
> Before the urban dawn wind unresisting.
>
> (*The Four Quartets, Little Gidding,* lines 87–90)

Since devastation is historically literal and culturally literary, the title embodies memorial imagery that lodged its own demise between the devastations of the two world wars.

Urban debris links *The Waste Land* to the *Four Quartets:*

> Where is there an end to the drifting wreckage,
> The prayer of the bone on the beach.
>
> (*The Dry Salvages,* lines 54–55)

The *Waste Land* is Dante's *Inferno.* Contextually, the title tells us that what has become obsolete is the resilience of the Greco-Roman and Judeo-Christian traditions, with all their obsolete myths.

Vertical constructions that dared the gods proliferated well beyond the Tower of Babel. One of them was the Tower of Babylon, whose construction was undertaken under the reign of Nebuchadnezzar II (605–562 B.C.). The mythical tower became the bell tower of Christian cathedrals, some of which had four to symbolize the four Gospels. They projected power at the edge of *superbia* (arrogance), so much so that the Cistercians prohibited the construction of towers on their churches. With the advent of the Renaissance, towers became parts of secular buildings that offered military protection. Theodore Ziolkowski has coined the term *turriphilia* for the thematics of the tower, from Yeats to Rilke.[21] By 1927 towers that had not crumbled became insignificant in Virginia Woolf's *To the Lighthouse,* which emptied out the symbolism of power, authority, and metaphysical leaps.[22]

Because of disintegration, the urban imagery detracts from humanist landscapes, and the surface of the wasteland is either deserted or temporarily occupied by people who seem to emerge from the underground, as if in a Dantean landscape. Like hell, London has become an

> Unreal City,
> Under the brown fog of a winter dawn,

> A crowd flowed over London Bridge, so many,
> I had not thought death had undone so many.
> Sighs, short and infrequent, were exhaled,
> And each man fixed his eyes before his feet. (lines 60–64)

"Unreal" oscillates between myth and reality, where the flowing crowd echoes Baudelaire's "swarming city full of dreams." Eliot himself acknowledged that Baudelaire taught him to take up "the more sordid aspects of the modern metropolis," where the realistic blends into the "phantasmagoric."[23] In *The Waste Land*, the *polis* has become a necro-*polis* where people who have not died stare at their feet in a state of terminal isolation. The inference is that waste has a lot to do with the hellish underpinning of urban industrialization.

People have died in droves around London, and those still alive idle away in an underworld more familiar with death than with life. Such a state of abandonment lingered on, and it finally linked up to the *Four Quartets*, written between 1935 and 1943.

> Eructation of unhealthy souls
> Into the faded air, the torpid
> Driven on the wind that sweeps the gloomy hills of London,
> Hampstead and Clerkenwell, Campden and Putney,
> Highgate, Primrose and Ludgate. Not here
> Not here the darkness, in this twittering world.
>
> Descend lower, descend only
> Into the world of perpetual solitude,
> World not world, but that which is not world,
> Internal darkness, deprivation
> And destitution of all property,
> Desiccation of the world of sense,
> Evacuation of the world of fancy
>
> (*Burnt Norton*, 112–24)

The future is like the past, and both give form to the poet's vision of the city as the crumbling bastion of Western culture. Eliot set London at dead center of *The Waste Land*, making it more deadly than the historical metropolis. As it happened, London survived both world wars, and Eliot was there to witness it. But he never felt compelled to recant, because his mythic London stood for a cultural failure independent of, and juxtaposed to, reality itself. The gap between the historical and the unreal city measured the distance between fact and design.

Florence was hellish to Dante because it brought the culture of the Middle Ages to a close. For everybody else, Florence was the shining centerpiece of the emergent Renaissance. Similarly, London was unreal to Eliot because he saw it as the embodiment of the demise of European culture. Culturally speaking, Dante and Eliot were right, for they saw their respective cities at the close of major cultural epochs. But whereas Dante refused to accept the fact that a new age was dawning over the horizon, Eliot extended the dying Western tradition to the outermost horizon of *The Waste Land*, to an aftermath in which we still reside.

It has been said that the barren city, which Joyce described with a good dose of meanness in *Dubliners*, has much in common with Eliot's London.[24] Joyce strolled along the banks of the Liffey and gave us a sense of the allusive distance between Odysseus and Ulysses, whereas Eliot looked squarely at the distance that separated London Bridge from the uncontaminated sources of the Thames. Brown fog hinders visibility, and the "final stroke of nine" has been heard. Only corpses sprout. As in the case of Beckett's tree in *Waiting for Godot*, the biological impulse is there, but to what avail, if the surface is layered with deadness? Having ceased to interact, people no longer constitute a working community. Instead, they are mummified, each man's eyes fixed before his feet. The human, humane, and humanizing world of relations has been curtailed. Set in *The Waste Land*, any city must be "unreal" to the extent that, as a city of waste, it cannot be functional.

While a title such as Martin Buber's *I-Thou* proclaims that humanity consists of relationships, *The Waste Land* presents no *semblable*, no brother. Even Prufrock seems to have no interlocutor. Eliot wrote about London in *The Waste Land*, and Constantine Cavafy wrote *The City*, a title about an urban prison from which we will never escape because we carry it with us:

> How long will my mind remain in this wasteland.
> Wherever I turn my eyes, wherever I may look
> I see black ruins of my life here,
> Where I spent so many years destroying and wasting.
> . . .
> Always you will arrive in this city. Do not hope for any other—
> There is no ship for you, there is no road.

>   As you have destroyed your life here
>   in this little corner, you have ruined it in the entire world.
>   (lines 5–8, 13–16)

We carry within ourselves the city of ruins that we are desperately trying to leave behind.

In this sense, the unreal city also calls to mind a later title, Italo Calvino's *Invisible Cites*. They are just as unreal, and one of them presents the postmodern variant of Eliot's urban enclave. By giving visual presence to the debris of intellectual exchanges, Calvino takes us from causes to effects that paralyze the topography of Ersilia: "To establish the relationships that sustain the city's life, the inhabitants stretch strings from the corners of the houses, white or black or gray or black-and-white according to whether they mark a relationship of blood, of trade, authority, agency. When the strings become so numerous that you can no longer pass among them, the inhabitants leave: the houses are dismantled; only the strings and their supports remain."[25] Strings are visual signposts of bygone relationships. They have so cluttered communal living that the network of social interactions has turned on itself. The growth of human contacts has laid out ropes in the streets, one rope for each thought. Streets and squares have been encumbered with so many ropes that circulation has become impossible. As a result, people have been forced to leave the place, and their "shared" humanity is the cause of their own undoing. Houses have been dismantled, and multicolored strings stand out as visual traces of human stories that are forever bound to end in exile. The strings testify to a defunct community of thoughtful people who have been lost to the archaeological silence of a "mental city."[26] Ersilia resembles urban plans where no people are in sight, and none are expected.[27] The upshot is that citizens will repeat their foredoomed migration to places of temporary settlement. To preserve itself as a social body, humanity must run away from itself. The exercise of humanism as a collective good has yielded the signposts of terminal estrangement. Absurdity is presented, not explained. I suggest that this is as visual an image as we can find for illustrating the default of spaces where human relations ought to thrive. Calvino's city is a place where communication carries a death sentence.

However invisible, the urban grounds of modernity are hostile to human presence. Eliot's title is so lapidary in its inert deadness that the text can do no more than leave readers with an inventory of things abandoned. The title locates the debris of narrativity in the space of cultural leftovers. As time hardens into sediment, *waste* hardens into *land*. There is little doubt that the spatial dimension of Eliot's title presents London at its worst. River walks and downtown streets—lower Thames Street—are littered with the refuse of human existence. An agglomerate of hopeless people is crowded in a milieu that has disappointed human expectations. In the poem about a European city by an American-turned-Briton, London seems to have marked a later stage of Balzac's *Splendeurs et misères des courtisanes* (1847), in which nocturnal Paris is ominously destructive. It is another corner of Dante's Inferno, where, to borrow from Bernard Schilling, "we descend from the beau monde, the world of business and money, through the police and justice, to the circle of criminals and prostitutes below. Even a large part of the daytime action in *Splendeurs* is in courts and prisons, leading finally to death and the grave."[28]

Conversely, Carl Sandburg's *Chicago* stands out as a muscular adult with "Big Shoulders" that laughs like a young fighter who has never lost a fight. The city's gas lamps lure the farm boys who fall victim to painted women; yet life goes on and expands, because the midwestern metropolis is the city of the future, where construction by far outshines destruction. The Midwest is what Eliot left behind, only to find out that, at least on the European continent, the future did not promise anything appreciably new. Accordingly, *The Waste Land* closes with language of cultural dissonance.

> *Poi s'ascose nel foco che gli affina*
> *Quando fiam uti chelidon*—O swallow swallow
> *Le Prince d'Aquitaine à la tour abolie*
> These fragments I have shored against my ruins
> Why then Ile fit you. Hieronymo's mad againe.
> Datta. Dayadhvam. Damyata.
>   Shantih shantih shantih

Quotations remain unconnected, and broken images become even more breakable. Saturation, however, found a way of replenishing the arsenal of literary production, and artists found ways for recycling the fragmentary no less than the overfull. Referentiality and productivity won the day, because there was enough refuse around for everybody to draw on. So much so that waste is yet to run out of its own terminality.

3

For the modernists, Janus's door to the future is closed, whereas the threshold to the past harks back to Rome and Greece. Before Eliot, Gustave Flaubert probed into the remote past and set *Salammbô* in pre-Roman Carthage, where "the notion of 'the people' is as worn out as that of 'the king.'"[29] Before Joyce, Flaubert spoke against the era of bourgeois mediocrity and made the middle class the cornerstone of his poetics. The return to myth has played a prominent role in the literature of modernism through such titles as *Thésée* (Gide) and *La Jeune Parque* (Valéry). In a letter dated July 25, 1920, Joyce wrote to his brother from Paris, "Odyssey very much in the air here. Anatole France is writing *Le Cyclops*, G. Fauré, the musician an opera *Penélopé*. Giraudoux has written *Elpenor*. Guillaume Apollinaire *Les Mamelles de Tirésias*." George Seferis, a poet whose classical roots and modern voice have tried to reconcile myth with history,[30] entitled a collection of his poems *Mythistorema*. Title explains content. In a note by the poet himself, "Mythos, because I have used, clearly enough, a certain mythology; istoria (both 'history' and 'story"), because I have tried to express, with some coherence, circumstances that are as independent of myself as the characters in a novel."[31] It suffices to repeat that the mythical method, however tailored to individual needs, became a staple of twentieth-century literature.

The belief was abroad that mythology could make the present of *The Waste Land* at least more acceptable. Rather than a desert, the modernist wasteland is an immense necropolis filled with epigraphs and epitaphs that Joyce, Eliot, and Pound—to name only the outstanding trinity of what Samuel Beckett would have called the "Acacacademy of Anthropopopometry"—could not ignore. Literature was littered with stories about the death of God, the terminal agony of the author, and the residues of Babel-like structures that have upheld "higher" points of view since mythic times.

As title and subject matter, *The Waste Land* is our own exhausted space, which entitles us to indulge in the awareness that neither exile nor return will lead us anywhere. The wasteland is a continent surrounded by sea, which determined the fortunes and misfortunes of most of the people living there. When progress on the high seas finally waned, its wreckage floated ashore. Oceanic debris is typical of Eliot's imagery. While Prufrock presents himself as "a pair of ragged claws / Scuttling across the floors of silent seas" (*The Love Song of J. Alfred Prufrock*, lines 73–74), the late verses take notice of "[t]he starfish, the hermit crab, the whale's backbone" (*Four Quartets, The Dry Salvages*, line 19).

The imagery of marine debris takes us to the Ligurian seashores of the *Cinque Terre,* where the Italian poet Eugenio Montale added to the titological wreckage of *The Waste Land* when he published *Ossi di seppia* (*Cuttlefish Bones,* 1925).[32] As such, the title refers to a rather inconspicuous object, a downright godforsaken thing.[33] The first nucleus of three poems went under the title of *Rottami* (*Refuse*), which turned into *Cuttlefish Bones* when another three poems were added. The titological focus is on the sea rubble, which conveys the idea of neat, arid, and shining objects as well as things that have been washed ashore.[34] As one would expect on matters of Anglo-Italian relations, Mario Praz was among the first to relate the two poets by quoting Italian verses that echoed shared debris:

> all life and its torment
> consists in following along a wall
> with broken bottle shards imbedded in the top.[35]

Like Eliot, Montale pays attention to stones and dried objects:

> Oh, tumbled then
> Like the cuttlefish bone by the waves,
> To vanish bit by bit;
> To become
> A gnarled tree or a stone
> Smoothed by the sea; to blend
> With the sunset's colors.

Personal disintegration echoes Eliot's verses:

> I stand amid the rubble
> that scales down to you, down
> to the steep bank above you,
> prone to landslides, yellow, etched
> by rivers of rainwater.
> My life is this dry slope,
> a means not an end, a way
> open to runoff from gutters and slow erosion.[36]

In a significant way, Montale updated the poetic erosion of Eliot's senescent figures.

Smoldering by 1918, the waste of Western civilization points back to the ashes of Troy. Out of its destruction, Eliot retrieved a journey that, via Aeneas and the Roman Empire, eventually led to England, where Hadrian built a defensive wall whose ruins are still standing. If London's fate was tied up with the fall of colonialism, Dublin stood its ground amid the bourgeois everydayness of advertising agents who had much to resent whenever London was mentioned. The geography of aggressive imperialism was pitched against people who staked no territorial claims. It is there that Eliot and Joyce parted ways. The future did not look bright in either city, even though Dublin still longed for independence from British dominance. On balance, literary artifacts did not stir much hope.

Nor did human relationships break the future open. In fact, Leopold and Molly lost their young son, Rudy. In the "Circe" chapter of *Ulysses*, there occurs Bloom's vision of his son, Rudy, who, having lived for only eleven days, would now be eleven years old. The numerological symbolism is one of renewal, for it consists of a double "I." Thus Bloom sees "a fairy boy of eleven, a changeling, kidnapped, dressed in an Eton suit with glass shoes and a little bronze helmet, holding a book in his hand." (*Ulysses*, 15: 4957–59) His death precipitated estrangement, which Leopold tried to repair on June 16, 1904. The cumulative experiences of a long day's journey teach him to redefine his marital circumstances. Thus he sets out to reconcile with Molly, even after her latest adultery. From historical characters to mythic figures, Tiresias's bisexuality entails a more rounded human experience, even though his advanced age precludes fertility. It is here that Homeric allusions break down. Stephen is a Telemachus-like character, but he is not Leopold's son. In terms of human generations, *Ulysses* and *The Waste Land* are as ominously sterile at the height of modernism as the anonymous picaresque town crier, Lázaro de Tormes, was at height of the Renaissance.

As the outcome of drawn-out processes of aging, waste is the opposite of growth, which the Cumaean sibyl forgot to claim. She could have prophesied the healing of the Fisher King, but she did not. In a way, she is Eliot's "Other." When Eliot left Saint Louis, one of the gates to the west, it was for the East, where he studied under the tutelage of Irving Babbitt and George Santayana at Harvard. The early poetry mentions St. Louis, Cambridge, and Boston. London became as central to his poem as the Mississippi River was to *Huckleberry Finn*. Helen Vendler has caught geographical details that mark cultural divides. Accordingly, *The Waste Land* contains scenes set in Boston and Gloucester that were taken out when Eliot revised the poem. As a result, "the modernist European poem had been born."[37]

Even Eliot's American connection with Edgar Allan Poe was screened through the European symbolists, from Baudelaire and Mallarmé to Laforgue and Valéry. In a place exhausted by war but still resilient enough to prepare for worse politics and an even more disastrous conflict, the best that Eliot could do was to close his poem with the word "peace," though written in a foreign language. Like Cassandra, his warning went unheeded; like the Cumaean sibyl, he was bound to prophesy waste, waste, forever waste.[38]

To a significant extent, Eliot's title presents the modernist anatomy of Western civilization. As aging as the senescent J. Alfred Prufrock, the poem lays out corpses about to be sectioned out "[l]ike a patient etherized upon a table." In fact, the title foregrounds a heap of Babel-like residues. The waste of symbols, themes, and language tells us that the poet is powerless because waste cannot be metamorphosed in the transitive workings of authorized, if not authoritative, narratives. The title is intransitive because waste as noun is as self-contained as a rock or a grave—the "stony rubbish."

Imbued with tradition and individual talent, T. S. Eliot was a standard bearer of humanist Eurocentrism; so much so that he made London, to his father's deep regret, his land of residence and citizenship. Reversing the westward progress of Western culture, Eliot created a civilized enclave where he could pursue endeavors geared to a sophisticated, if not downright royal, elitism. The outcome, however, was *The Waste Land*. Did Saint Louis and Harvard catch up with him, or did he find out that the grass on the other side was no greener after all?

Westward journeys across the Atlantic Ocean were undertaken in the name of the new, of promises to be fulfilled—in California for Thomas Mann and in New York City for W. H. Auden. Although he did not know whether Auden was to be considered an English or an American poet, Eliot did know that, "whichever Auden is, I suppose I must be the other."[39] As in the case of Eliot, Christianity played a major role in Auden's life and poetry. But Auden objected to Eliot's belief, in *After Strange Gods* (1934), that society should be "homogeneous." Likewise, he objected to Eliot's *The Family Reunion* and *The Cocktail Party*, in which the Christian calling is typical of the upper class.[40]

Eliot's emancipation from his American heritage was never complete. Much as Ernest Hemingway found Gertrude Stein in Paris, Eliot had to wait for another American, and one as controversial as Ezra Pound, to show up in Europe and jumpstart his literary career. Between a laugh and a pun, Amy Lowell wrote *A Critical Fable*, which diagnosed the relationship between Eliot and Pound in the very year 1922. Each left his country of birth, and

> Both of them are book-men, but where Eliot has found
> A horizon in letters, Pound has found Pound.[41]

Eliot never doubted that he had found his sense of place, one that, instead of describing a room of one's own, sketched the vast expanse of cultural hubs. He did it through a poetic hybrid that depicted his culture of choice below royalty and at the edge of social breakdowns. Title and epigraph bear out all the contradictions of a neophyte who eulogized what he had just claimed to be his. In a 1959 interview Eliot stated, "I'd say that my poetry has obviously more in common with my distinguished contemporaries in America than with anything written in my generation in England. That I'm sure of. . . . In its sources, in its emotional springs, it comes from America."[42] Scholars have strung along influences from Poe and Whitman to Emerson and Williams in literature as well as Bradley in philosophy. If the sociopolitical Eliot had settled on Britishness, the poetic Eliot had not, and the split burdened him throughout his life.

In an essay on Henry James, Eliot concluded that the final perfection for an American is to become "not an Englishman, but a European—something which no born European, no person of any European nationality, can become."[43] Sometimes émigrés are carried away by their newfound sense of belonging, and it would seem that Eliot may have wanted to be more British than the Brits. He ended up vindicating the integrity of two literatures that found expression in a common language, but he made that statement while lecturing in Saint Louis. Otherwise, his construction of a super-European persona hovering over the *Waste Land* betrays a lingering dilemma, which his spiritual, political, and cultural rebirth as an Anglo-American (hopefully more Anglo and less American) could not wipe out. The Victorian era was over, and the decline of the British Empire was well under way. As an American abroad, Eliot could perceive it better than most, as *The Waste Land* proves.

The multifarious references pegged to the title of Eliot's poem magnified the retrospective character of his artistic project. In fact, he linked up to European culture when it was too late to hope for a change. But it was not too late for him to make it the subject of his poetry. It would seem to me that he was a literary archaeologist who took stock of the debris of World War I. *The Waste Land* turned out to be an archaeological still life, which, in those days, was the best that history could afford. Actually, posthumousness and archaeology are the signposts of a poetics that introduced the last signpost of a cultural tradition about to be obliterated from vision and memory alike.

> And other withered stumps of time
> Were told upon the walls; staring forms
> Leaned out, leaning, hushing the room enclosed.
> Footsteps shuffled on the stair.
> (*The Waste Land*, lines 104–7)

Of course, Eliot's essay "What Is a Classic?" presents Virgil as the only universal classic. The reason is that "a classic can only occur when a civilization is mature; when a language and a literature are mature; and it must be the work of a mature mind." That combination took place only when Virgil, Latin, and *Romanitas* converged in the *Aeneid*.[44] Consequently, "no modern language can hope to produce a classic, in the sense in which I have called Virgil a classic. Our classic, the classic of all Europe, is Virgil."[45] The classical standard was a source of emulation for Renaissance writers, who set out to outdo antiquity itself. For the modernist Eliot, instead, the classical standard was stifling. The past could not be used to construct a better future but to deny the very idea of improvement.

Since two world wars had demolished the idea of progress, W. H. Auden offered an apt description of post-Virgilian culture:

> Stretched ahead,
> Into our future till it is lost to sight,
> Our grief is not Greek: As we bury our dead
> We know without knowing there is reason for what we bear.
> (*Memorial for the City*, 1945, lines 29–32)

Virgil bodies forth the postepic age, which is historically Roman. The Greeks have given us mythology, philosophy, and aesthetics; for better and for worse, the Romans organized the juridical, technological, military, and political structures of society. More effectively than anyone else, they translated thought into action.

Even more interesting from a modern standpoint is the fact that Auden declares the failure of prophecy, because history teaches us that the future cannot be predicted. This, of course, was the lesson that Guicciardini learned when the facts of history showed him that Machiavelli's faith in mastering the principles of human conduct through the study of past deeds had failed. Accordingly, Auden wrote:

> No, Virgil, no:
> Not even the first of the Romans can learn
> His Roman history in the future tense,
> Not even to serve your political turn;
> Hindsight and foresight makes no sense.
>
> (*Secondary Epic*, 1959, lines 1–5)

These verses make a compelling case for the final demise of the ameliorative worldview fostered by the grand narrative of humanist history. The present was an age of decline, which took its own good time in consuming itself out in the wasteland. Virgil celebrated the Augustan age, even though he had begun to have doubts about the *pax Romana*.

Against the Victorian acceptance of Virgil as the perfect poet, the twentieth century emphasized his descent into the underworld and the discovery of history, two feats that brought the darker side of human nature into the light of day. Virgil's awareness of the shortcomings of political institutions did not cancel out his need for order, which, to borrow from Theodore Ziolkowski, binds us to the Latin poet "in a conspiracy of understanding."[46] Since he had no doubts that colonial narratives had done their work, Eliot probably was aware that their demise was as inevitable as it was righteous. Roman republicanism inspired American republicanism, which, unlike its European counterparts, was successful from the start. On the European continent, Roman imperialism inspired Fascism and Nazism, which cast much of European culture into oblivion.

Ironically, *The Waste Land* is covered with the footprints of memory, footprints that only the "greater European" could describe appropriately. In this sense, *The Waste Land* is the no-man's-land where loss allows the poet to re-create the past according to a modern view that is memorial rather than memorable. By the 1920s the debris of Western culture belonged neither to the Victorians nor to the Futurists; it belonged to Eliot and Pound, who did believe that the wasteland was the only place where civilization could be appropriated to the life of art. The Forum is a necropolis for the archaeologist, but the wasteland is where the likes of John Soane and De Chirico could translate archaeology into images bound to take in reality at large. In this way Eliot drew together the best that eighteenth-century history, archaeology, and antiquarianism expressed through Vico the philosopher, Gibbon the historian, and Piranesi the artist. Whereas eighteenth-century folks pitted the past against the present, Eliot found the ruinous past *in* the present.

Herein lies the aesthetic core of the "mythical method." As the old saying goes, it takes one to know one. Eliot's critical standard described the poetics of Joyce, but only because the mythical method described his own poetics to begin with. He himself said that, as a critic, his best writing was about writers who had influenced him, and the mythical method was a way of setting up "a continuous parallel between contemporaneity and antiquity." Both shared in "the immense panorama of futility and anarchy which is contemporary history."[47] Indeed, we edge on Joyce's assessment of history as a "nightmare" from which we have been trying to awaken. Alive, such a matter could not be controlled; as waste, it could be molded into artistic forms. Unlike Joyce, Eliot made sustained references to Homeric poetry and classical tragedy that bordered on the allegorical, for he favored the past over the present.

Of course, the classical tradition was there to heighten the deficiencies of the modern world.[48] And those deficiencies never went away. In the long dramatic poem, *Choruses from "The Rock,"* written after 1930, images of construction and deconstructions are pervasive. The poet revisits the Unreal City:

> I have journeyed to London, to the timekept City
>
> And the Church must be forever building, and always decaying,
> And always being restored.
> (*Choruses from "The Rock,"* lines 19, 172–73)

Outside the city, the wasteland becomes even more mythical:

> In the beginning GOD created the world. Waste and Void. Waste
> And void. And darkness was upon the face of the deep. (lines 371–72)

At the end of human time:

> Waste and void. Waste and void. And darkness on the face of
> The deep. (lines 399–400)

For Eliot, the past was identified with tradition, and America had very little of it. Scattered fragments aside, a handful of great novelists did not a tradition make! Eliot found the past in Europe, and the past was as contextual as the titological *Land*, which had to be European. But what could Eliot contribute to the future of tradition at a time when culture at large had been assaulting tradition itself? London's towers were falling down in wartime London as much as in his poem. He also knew that, on the European continent, the present was going to be the future as well. He wrote *The Waste Land* after World War I and finished the *Four Quartets* in the midst of World War II. Prophecies of doom were being fulfilled once again.

The prophetic utterance of the Cumaean sibyl takes up the dilemma of the speaking voice. By definition, she is the divinity's mouthpiece. And so is the epic poet, whose frenzy makes him sing the muse's song. But what was Eliot's voice? In 1942, the year in which he wrote *Little Gidding*, he also wrote an essay entitled "The Music of Poetry," in which he said, "I shall always remember the impression of W. B. Yeats reading poetry aloud. To hear him read his own works was to be made to recognize how much the Irish way of speech is needed to bring out the beauties of Irish poetry: to hear Yeats reading William Blake was an experience of a different kind, more astonishing than satisfying."[49] Well, what about Eliot's voice reading his own poetry aloud? In calling Eliot's poem the "quintessential poem of Anglo-American modernism," Calvin Bedient either splits or confuses the poetic voice. While she considers the poem European, Helen Vendler remains silent about the poetic voice. As late as 1945, Eliot called himself *métoikos*, the Greek word for an alien resident in Sophocles's *Antigones*.[50] He had been living in England as a British citizen for more than thirty years, and the modern experiment meant to make the past new never haunted Eliot. For him the new was rootless, and he needed rootedness. When he found it, rootedness spread out into an arid desert, where the last thing J. Alfred Prufrock did was "[t]o spit out all the butt-ends of my days and ways."

The variety of butt-ends brings us to an issue that sheds light on my approach to titology. The semantic range of the word *waste* in the title of Eliot's poem has spurred critics to consider a feature at once common and dominant in *Ulysses*, *The Waste Land*, and Pound's *Cantos*, namely the shared emphasis on what rhetoric calls parataxis, which, simply stated, consists of the absence of transitions.[51] I would like to suggest that parataxis is constituent of titles as well. *Ulysses* is a typical example inasmuch as its layered etymology reveals itself only when a titological analysis brings to the fore ontological transitions. Titology, I hope, provides all the hyphens that connect titles to texts.

4

On the Sistine ceiling, Michelangelo's Cumaean sibyl looks as old and as bisexual as Eliot's Tiresias, whose role in *The Waste Land* is so prominent that the poem itself could be his own dream. Almost twenty years later, the *Four Quartets* spurred Eliot to ask questions that criticism has slighted. The poetic timeline tells us that, by 1925, *The Hollow Men* stood guard over lifeless grounds. Almost a decade later, images raised more questions. Once again, the sibyl comes back, only that the pagan prophecy has yielded to the Christian annunciation. In the "future futureless," is it not true that what is left is:

> the unprayable
> Prayer at the calamitous annunciation?
> . . .
> In a drifting boat with a slow leakage,
> The silent listening to the undeniable
> Clamour of the bell of the last annunciation.
> *(Four Quartets, The Dry Salvages,* lines 57–58, 69–71)

What is the calamitous annunciation in 1942?

Of course, Eliot was too smart not to hint at his own answer. He was sibyl and historian:

> It seems, as one becomes older,
> That the past has another pattern, and ceases to be a mere sequence—
> Or even development: the latter a partial fallacy,
> Encouraged by superficial notions of evolution,
> Which becomes, in the popular mind, a means of disowning the past.
> The moments of happiness—not the sense of well-being,
> Fruition, fulfillment, security or affection,
> Or even a very good dinner, but the sudden illumination—
> We had the experience but missed the meaning,
> And approach to the meaning restores the experience
> In a different form, beyond any meaning
> We can assign to happiness. (lines 90–101)

Experience is internal, whereas meaning is external.

> A people without history
> Is not redeemed from time, for history is a pattern
> Of timeless moments
>
> (*Four Quartets, Little Gidding,* lines 236–38)

Meaning is redemption, which is as timeless as art. Conversely, temporality is life consumed, which fills *The Waste Land* to capacity. Not to waste time, we must stand outside the land, if we are to avoid the seductive nostalgia of the edenic as well as the false hope of the utopian. Only in the space of art can consciousness be critical.

Art takes us to the Cumaean sibyl, who led Aeneas to the underworld, where Anchises prophesied Rome's forthcoming greatness. Although London was the modern Rome, Eliot could not be Anchises. In the "unreal city," the final verses of *The Hollow Men* rephrase the Cumaean sibyl's death wish:

> This is the way the world ends
> This is the way the world ends
> This is the way the world ends
> Not with a bang but a whimper.

The whimper tells us that the apocalyptic theme has shifted toward the ordinary, and epic feats have given way to bureaucratic routines. Spatial extension in *The Waste Land* is as unlimited as it is inimical to individual presence and social exchange. By pointing to the posthumous instead of the progressive, Eliot's title tells us that the epic journey has become the figment of overactive imaginations.

In 1922 Eliot wrote of the many people who flowed by London Bridge, and who had died in World War I. In 1942, when Eliot wrote *Little Gidding* (the last of his *Four Quartets*), World War II was raging, and Britain was living its worst nightmare. Nazi Germany had invaded most of Europe, the defeated French and British armies had been evacuated from Dunkirk, the United States had not yet fully entered the war, and Britain was hanging on for dear life. The final section of the poem spells out the inevitable by rehearsing the darkest stanzas of *The Waste Land*:

> Every poem an epitaph. And any action
> Is a step to the block, to the fire, down the sea's throat
> Or to the illegible stone: and that is where we start.
> We die with the dying:
> See, they depart, and we go with them.
> We are born with the dead:
> See, they return, and bring us with them.
>
> (*Four Quartets, Little Gidding,* 228–34)

These lines are a meditation on the cumulative slaughter of two world wars.

Eliot's crowds flowed into the London underground during Nazi bombings, and it was amid such darkness that the sculptor Henry Moore recorded human suffering in his black-and-white drawings of Londoners taking shelter in the tube during German air raids (Fig. 11). For a while, the body count added dead to more dead, because there was no end, only addition. Eliot knew that he was in the eye of the storm. But he also understood that the wasteland was there to stay because what had been wasted was civilization itself.

Personally, Eliot tried to minimize the general disenchantment that many a reader of *The Waste Land* felt. For him, the poem voiced "the relief of a personal and wholly insignificant rouse against life; it is just a piece of rhythmical grumbling." Maybe he himself was awed by the enormity of what he faced. Better than most, the American-born writer could see just how unreal

FIG. 11 Henry Moore, *Tube Shelter Perspective,* 1941 (HMF 1801). Tate Gallery, London

the "unreal city" was. This does not mean that he either would or could change things. Like Tiresias, he saw disintegration clearly and expressed it poetically. As it turned out, his own literary production would be "wasted" on many of his contemporaries, who slighted his ominous message and quickly began to venture toward greater upheavals. Prophecies often warn about impending disasters that are exceptional in nature. By 1922, however, the disaster had overtaken everyday reality, and it could hardly be separated from ordinary living. *The Waste Land* had become the negative epic of European civilization.

Is the sibyl's voice, then, that of a restless poet who, having left the rusticity of the American prairie behind, found elective affinities that so enchanted him that his masterpiece ended up shaping a glorious death wish? The dedication to Ezra Pound was added in 1925. Again, was Eliot paying a personal homage, or was he recognizing a master from his native culture? If so, was that but a reminder of what he had turned away from? More confident about the validity of American culture, Wallace Stevens put it clearly when he wrote that "nothing could be more inappropriate to American literature than its English source since the Americans are not British in sensibility."[52] Statements of this sort would have been unnecessary for Whitman or Emerson, but not for Eliot. He had rejected American youthfulness; he could as well fade away in the lingering splendor of continental senility!

Modernism had come to an end, and Eliot knew it, but he could not foresee that the postmoderns would stretch the residual potential of meaninglessness to new lengths. The final rhetorical question is: "Shall I at least set my lands in order?" The title's topographical marker, *Land*, comes back to accommodate order. But it is the order of the *wasteland*, which cannot exceed the accumulation of debris and the arrangement of refuse. What follows is the breakdown of architecture, of urban spaces, and of language itself. To set his lands in order, Eliot would need a new ideology that could impregnate a fertile soil. To find it, he would trade the mythical method for a pathbreaking view of the future, an outlook that was not there for the modernists as well as for the postmoderns. What he could set in order was the *wasteland*; introductory in the title and conclusive in the final stanza, it contains the arid plains of the archaeological wreckage. East of Dublin, we can only retrace our path, which we have littered with the refuse of urban settlements. The land has been discovered, populated, and depleted.

In the spirit of Mediterranean images, Eliot's verses present "fishermen sailing / Into the wind's tail." The quest is purposeful and communal. But the closing lines of *The Waste Land* present a reversal: "I sat upon the shore / Fishing, with the arid plains behind me." The communal has gone, the sails are down, and the speaking voice, lonely and stationary, faces the sea but thinks about the arid plains behind him. Caught in the throes of hopefulness, many scholars have interpreted this last scene as one that shows the speaker turning his back on the wasteland in order to seek out some kind of purgatorial clearing.[53]

To suggest that the final image implies that the Fisher King has healed, that he has turned his back on dead people and is focusing on the restored health of the land, is implausible, for this would entail a rejection of the title's symbolism. What lies before the lonely fisherman is the ocean, which has muddled the wine-dark sea of the epic in the polluted waters of the novelistic. Poetic evidence suggests that the fisherman may have turned away from the *Waste Land*, only because

> We cannot think of a time that is oceanless
> Or of an ocean not littered with wastage.
> (*Four Quartets, The Dry Salvages,* lines 74–75)

Once waste has aged the ocean itself, the lure of exploration is bound to fade, and the lonely fisherman embodies an image of unfunctional futility. At the polluted edge of modernism, hopelessness coiled back on itself. At that point, it did not really matter in which direction the old man was gazing. Sitting upon the shore, he waited for luck to take pity on him.

6

Off the Page and onto the Stage:
Sei personaggi in cerca d'autore

> The great prefix of the day is *meta-*: metalanguage, metatext, metadiscourse.
> —ROBERT ALTER

Ulysses and *The Waste Land* were published during the *annus mirabilis* 1922, which also saw the rise of political ideologies that would yield tragic consequences for the next two decades. From literature to life, fascist squads organized, in October 1922, the Marcia su Roma, which brought Benito Mussolini to power. Under the aegis of a renewal of dictatorial arrogance and imperial ambitions, Italian politics dreamed of *pax Romana* as the fascist variant of the "mythical method," and it would not take long for Ezra Pound to try to reconcile Jefferson with Mussolini. Some rescued antiquity to support utter disintegration in the wasteland; others set out to construct a brave new world under the power of ideological fanaticism and technological ingenuity. At the peak of his creative talents as a playwright, Luigi Pirandello became a member of the Accademia d'Italia, the highest cultural institution created by il Duce. It was headed by Guglielmo Marconi and, upon his death, by Gabriele D'Annunzio. However moderate in his political views, Pirandello trusted experimentation, which made his theatrical innovations epoch-making.

Born within sight of the Greek temple dedicated to the goddess Concord at Akragas (now Agrigento), Pirandello pushed the Sicilian heritage of Greek myths aside when he became a writer. His prose bypassed the "mythical method" and turned to the contemporary world in the *verista* tradition of Giovanni Verga. As a dramatist, he put on stage contemporary characters who tested the playwright's authority. By and large, modernist experimentation was retrospective,[1] but there were exceptions that enlisted individuals as well as movements—from Picasso and Duchamp to Dada and Futurism. Pirandello turned the retrospective into the innovative when he staged *Sei personaggi in cerca d'autore* in Rome on May 10, 1921. Whereas *Ulysses* turned the epic into the novelistic, *Six Characters in Search of an Author*[2] gave a novelistic title to a theatrical drama.

The title of *Six Characters in Search of an Author* is a declarative phrase with a subject, an object, and a verbal action implied by the prepositional phrase *in search of*, which immediately calls for explanation. That the six *personaggi* are looking for an author suggests that they have lost one. How has this happened? The title introduces a drama that stages itself regardless of literary blueprints.[3] The "existential" question about the six characters is whether they can exist in the theater as theatrical characters *without* an author. Anonymity does not diminish their dramatic identity, and their search for an author is meant to legitimize them as they are, rather than by any reference to the kind of conventions that inspired the classical plays of Racine.

As a phrase, Pirandello's title offers a cluster of structural supports. To begin with, it challenges interpreters with the mathematical precision of six, a number that undergoes significant alterations during the play. While "characters" suggests conflictive relationships with actors and stagehands, the prepositional phrase "in search of" spells out a latter-day quest that turns artistic conventions on their heads once it makes of "an author" its hypothetical object. Authors create characters; why does Pirandello's title challenge such a given? Neither the preface nor the text itself reveals why the original author has been rejected. Although the search does not exceed the confines of the theater, meaning is disruptive because expectations are not met. Since they already exist on stage, the six characters cannot let actors play their parts without denying their very existence. If emancipation has severed their dependence on *autori* and *attori*, why are these characters looking for another playwright? Should their search be successful, would they not deny all that they have achieved? They have neither doubts nor regrets about the choice they made; why would they undo their accomplishment? Is the title parodic or paradoxical? The dilemma, of course, involves a drama in which searching unravels a process of self-discovery that denies both dependence and emancipation.

This chapter gauges the extent to which drama expanded its cultural space when Pirandello tested the legitimacy of literary authorship as well as the conventions of theatrical representation. Performance reached out toward the audience and probed behind the curtain. At once narrative, contradictory, and self-destructive, the title is a point of entry into the way the literary text is pitted against the live performance of the theater as theater. On opening night at the Teatro Valle in Rome, the audience was not ready to accept the idea of seeing theatricality burst at the seams. Nevertheless, the play survived the hostile reception and inaugurated a mode of representation that we have come to know as *Pirandellismo*.

Throughout the 1920s, Pirandello's innovative approach to drama yielded *Ciascuno a suo modo* (1924) and *Questa sera si recita a soggetto* (1930),[4] which completed the trilogy of "the theater within the theater." While *Each in His Own Way* is an incomplete comedy that sends "the presentation up in smoke," *Tonight We Improvise* is about an unrehearsed comedy. As a unified cluster, these titles comment on one another. It would indeed be reasonable to infer that each of the six characters would want to recite his or her own way—*a suo modo*. The inference is Beckettian inasmuch as we would expect performance to test any cohesive narrative. In fact, the Pirandellian titles highlight the impending demise of the "literary" component of theatrical works. Literally, the third title spells out an unswerving emphasis on improvisation. Taken together, these titles construct action and deconstruct structure in a modernist culture in which indeterminacy permeated literary texts, visual artworks, and scientific debates.[5] Pirandello's trilogy crossed the threshold where the theatrical made room for the metatheatrical.

1

The first word in the title of *Sei personaggi in cerca d'autore* sets the certainty of numbers against the uncertainty of a problematic search: why do we have a numerical count? Six doubles the perfection that is usually associated with the number three because it suggests the Holy Trinity. In a Greek sense, mathematics is spatial, and numbers are drawn in the sand. Number six is the sum of its component parts—1, 2, 3—and can be arranged into a kind of perfect triangle.[6] This way, one would expect the titological qualifier to foreshadow the recovery of family cohesion, to suggest comedy rather than tragedy. We have been told that "numerical identity is held to be inalterable."[7] This statement can be applied to the identity of the six characters, which stand against the mutability of physical identity. The father believes that he has changed, but the daughter does not want to hear about it. It is here that irony sets in. Numbers tend to "socialize" with other numbers, and this is what we would expect from a family of six that reunites after a rather long while. The numerical anonymity of six characters asserts a collective identity that has replaced individual names with group interactions. The stage directions, however, list a seventh character, Madame Pace. She runs the brothel where the stepdaughter meets her father. The "extra" number disrupts numerical no less than family unity; it is the "irrational" number that contributes to shifting comedy toward tragedy. In light of the age-old symbolism of the seven deadly sins, the introductory "numerology" suggests that the numbers do not add up. Yet they shape the architectonics of the drama, and the text enacts a tragic countdown that "diminishes" the family—physically no less than spiritually.

In the pluralistic universe of mathematics,[8] additions and subtractions make numbers interactive. This does not happen in the case of the six characters, and their long-awaited reunion does not lead to reconciliation. In this sense, the numerical count reveals a parodic displacement of family relationships. Once it loses wholeness upon the children's deaths, the family's breakdown parallels the demise of theatrical conventions. The *personaggi* exist as creatures of art; their identities are as fixed as numbers, and nobody can make them more artistic than they already are. The fixed ratios of mathematics echo the equally fixed nature of the six *personaggi*. The drama stages conflicts between the numerical and the psychological; and the father is troubled by circumstantial variations: "We believe this conscience to be a single thing, but it is many-sided. There is one for this person, and another for that. Diverse consciences. So we have this illusion of being one person for all, of having a personality that is unique in all our acts. But it isn't true" (231). In a way, numbers are authorless in mathematics, and so should be characters in the equally self-contained world of the theater, where they set out to stage their unscripted drama. Since they cannot accept authorship without giving up their freedom, it is not clear whether the elusive author would be asked to reconstitute the family by solving its conflicts or whether he would be asked to "legitimize" (or underwrite) exactly what is enacted on stage.

In a prefatory note to the novel *Uno, nessuno e centomila* (One, No One, and One Hundred-Thousand), Pirandello writes that his aim is to demonstrate, "by what might be termed a mathematical method, the impossibility of any human creature's being to others what he is to himself." Obviously the title uses numbers to heighten the "otherness" of one's identity, which can be reduced and expanded at will by means of either addition or fragmentation—two favorite techniques of moderns and postmoderns alike. Although "happiness is a question of proportion"⁹ in *Il gioco delle parti* (loosely translated as *The Rules of the Game*), much of the playwright's poetics thrives on disproportion, which serves a rhetorical strategy based on the *scomposizione della personalità*—the decomposition of personality.¹⁰ Numbers quantify the complexity of the human psyche by offering the comfort of precision and accuracy.¹¹ Their theatrical symbolism, however, points to the unreliability of precise assumptions. In the late 1920s, mathematicians such as Kurt Godel trusted uncertainty, and Max Planck warned that "certainty is not proof of truth."¹² On stage, Eugene Ionesco presented a professor who believed that "mathematics is the sworn enemy of memory" (*The Lesson*, 1951).¹³ To quote Marjorie Perloff on the modernist pursuit of numbers, the Pirandellian title resorts to the "generative device" of a false assumption that sets off the artistic process no less than the dramatic representation.¹⁴

In the 1925 preface to *Six Characters*, Pirandello noted that his restless maidservant, Fantasy, brought "[a] family into my house. I wouldn't know where she fished them up or how, but, according to her, I could find in them the subject for a magnificent novel." The task is to let the characters "[e]nter the world of art, constructing from their persons, their passions, and their adventures a novel, a drama, or at least a story." At first, the challenge is to find a point of entry into the art world. Such a threshold is the proper genre, which must allow the *personaggi* to express their personalities to the fullest.

Fantasia, which always scouts for new talent, brings to the author's attention a family that could provide the subject for a "magnificent novel" (208). The initial impulse is novelistic, but the outcome is dramatic. A conflict has erupted at the threshold of artistic form, and it is likely that author and characters have parted ways. Having been given lives that the writer could not take away from them, these *personaggi* are fully developed: "While I persisted in desiring to drive them out of my spirit, they, as if completely detached from every narrative support, characters from a novel miraculously emerging from the pages of the book that contained them, went on living on their own" (364–66). Narrativity, of course, begins with the title, which points to a variant of the quest theme. The shift from the novelist to the playwright allows the *personaggi* to "[m]ove and talk on their own initiative; already see themselves as such; have learned to defend themselves against me; will even know how to defend themselves against others. And so let them go where dramatic characters do go to have life: on a stage. And let us see what will happen" (366). Having imposed unacceptable conditions on the author to be, the *personaggi* undertake a search that yields more loss. If theatricality depends on live performance, there is a point at which the playwright might consider the possibility of doing away with the written text altogether. By creating characters in search of an author, the drama raises the possibility that characters can exist *without* an author. This critical stand borders on a death wish, but is the wish not worth the risk?

At the beginning of the play, the stepdaughter imagines that her encounter with her father will be enacted again, should they find an author: "I am dying to live the scene. . . . The room . . . I see it. . . . But you, gentlemen, you ought to turn your backs now: I am almost nude. . . . But I don't blush: I leave that to him" (223). Since the *capocomico* is confused about her frame of reference, the father tries to explain. But he is abruptly interrupted:

> THE STEPDAUGHTER: *Qui non si narra! Qui non si narra!* [Here you cannot narrate! Here you cannot narrate!]
> THE FATHER: *Ma io non narro. Voglio spiegarti.* [But I am not narrating. I want to explain to you.]¹⁵

Motives call for explanation:

> THE FATHER: But don't you see that the whole trouble lies here. In words, words. Each one of us has within him a whole world of things, each man of us his own special world. . . . We think we understand each other, but we never really do. (224)

The reenactment of past events assumes that characters know one another as they were rather than as they have become. In the father's words, a "character has really a life of his own, marked with his special characteristics; for which reason he is always 'somebody.' But a man—I'm not speaking of you now—may very well be 'nobody'" (265). Characters are fixed in their theatrical form, whereas individuals float in the shapeless stream of life, which is more likely to be novelistic. By pointing to a journey, the future-oriented title could paraphrase the title of a Calvinian novel, *When, on a winter's night, six characters in search of an author show up in a theater.*¹⁶ This is but a lighthearted approach to the proximity of the dramatic and the novelistic,¹⁷ a kinship all the more significant for a writer who often adapted short stories for the stage.

Even the stepdaughter falls into the novelistic "trap" when she recounts her childhood:

> THE MANAGER: A bit discursive this, you know!
> THE SON (*contemptuously*): Literature! Literature!
> THE FATHER: Literature indeed! This is life, this is passion! (228)

The word literature makes its appearance, and the father is there to defend it, because it is only through a narrative that he can hope to make a case in his own defense. He has become a "character" who is known for what he "did" in Madame Pace's brothel; and no reason is given why he would not do it again. "Acting" got him into trouble, and only "explaining" can get him out of it. Yet the drama is not likely to offer him a chance to make his case.

The title's *in cerca* suggests tensions between the novelistic desire to control the action and the dramatic impulse to let the characters dispense with the apparatus of script, actors, stagehands, and directors. In a way, the title is a decoy, and the action on stage proves that the search is futile. The performance that does take place is so dramatically real that the characters play themselves without any recourse to actors. The writer has taken it upon himself to present an authorless situation. The upshot is that Pirandello creates a revolutionary drama inasmuch as what takes place on stage is contrary to the stated goal of the title. Because it constructs and deconstructs, the title amounts to a critique of the theatrical mechanisms of production. Lionel Abel would call the prepositional phrase *in cerca* metatheatrical because it highlights shared concerns between author and characters that partake of "the playwright's consciousness."[18] On stage, six characters enact their own drama independently of scripts and actors. The threshold between life and fiction is blurred, and the public witnesses an impromptu performance. Technically speaking, the play "happens," and luck has it that an author-like "witness" is present to record it.

Pirandello's title moves along parallel lines that tease each other. I would suggest that one line is theatrical and runs in the written text outside the stage. The *personaggi* exist as characters precisely because an author has given them theatrical life by means of a scripted text. Yet the title also asserts an act of emancipation; having eliminated their own "creator," the characters still want an author to discharge a vicarious role, at least for billing purposes. The other line is metatheatrical and runs inside the theater, where six characters stage a drama in that no-man's-land where the "Demon of Experiment" produces a play even though the director is reluctant and the actors stand by. Pirandello appears as the problematic author who rejected the six characters as well as the improbable author who tests theatrical possibilities once he lets the unexpected commandeer much of the plot.

Toward the end of the first part of the play, the father tries to convince the manager to become the author the six characters are looking for:

> THE MANAGER: Yes, that's all right. But you want someone to write it.
> THE FATHER: No, no. Someone to take it down, possibly, while we play it, scene by scene! It will be enough to sketch it out at first, and then try it over.
> THE MANAGER: Well . . . I am almost tempted. It's a bit of an idea. One might have a shot at it.
> THE FATHER: Of course. You'll see what scenes will come out of it. (236)

A debate breaks out about the role of authorship.

> THE MANAGER: Well, well, that will do. But you see, without an author . . . I could give you the address of an author if you like . . .
> THE FATHER: No, no. Look here! You must be the author.
> THE MANAGER: I? What are you talking about?
> THE FATHER: Yes, you, you! Why not?
> THE MANAGER: Because I have never been an author: that's why.
> THE FATHER: Then why not turn author now? Everybody does it. You don't want any special qualities. Your task is made much easier by the fact that we are all here alive before you. (235)

The denial of authorial instructions lends itself to improvisation, which stands out in *Tonight We Improvise,* the last of the trilogy plays. Dr. Hinkfuss, who believes that the manager-director (Hinkfuss himself) should replace the author, explains that *his* actors make up their own parts along a basic story outline. However unwittingly, he leads them to convince themselves that they can act without following directions.[19] Since the *Avvertenza* announces an improvised event that remains authorless, the title's impersonal verb (*si recita*) asserts a self-sustaining will to theatrical action.

Six Characters in Search of an Author begins with a stagehand and a few actors who are about to rehearse a comedy. The director complains that, since no good theater pieces are coming from France, he is forced to stage the second act of *Il gioco delle parti,* a Pirandellian play whose title (*Mixing It Up*) is appropriate to the confusion that is about to erupt. It is one of those plays that are "purposely written so that neither actors, nor critics, nor the public" are ever satisfied.[20] In a mocking tone, the door is opened for the kind of theater that recalls a comedy by the baroque magician Gianlorenzo Bernini,

The Impresario (1643?). The main character is a playwright who first takes care of the "staging" and then sits down to write the plot at the beginning of the second act. Actors and stagehands gather for the arrival of the cloud machine, which fails to open upon arrival. While the theatrical apparatus malfunctions, the play remains unwritten and the text breaks off.[21]

Southern Italian minds relished the multifaceted life of the theater on and off stage. Before the Sicilian Pirandello, the Neapolitan Giordano Bruno wrote a comedy, *Il candelaio* (*The Candle Bearer*), with an "antiprologue" and a "proprologue" in which an authorial voice (perhaps the writer-director) cries out before the performance, "Didn't I prophesy that this comedy wouldn't be ready for this evening? That bitch who was to play Vittoria and Carubina has got some sort of woman's complaint. The man who is meant to play Bonifacio is so drunk that he hasn't known the difference between heaven and earth since noon." The author-director is so angry that he is "off to turn friar, and as for the prologue, whoever wants it can have it." The written text is held hostage by the whim of unreliable actors. As a result, the comedy will have no prologue, because "the theme, the subject, the method, the arrangement and the details will emerge in due order and in due order pass before your eyes."[22] While Bruno's actors are not quite up to the task of performing their roles, Pirandello's characters refuse to be played by actors. The fear that actors might fail to play their parts has always caused insecurity for playwrights the world over. But the reverse might be equally true. Who is to say that the struggle of a drunken actor who tries to play a role is not as valuable as the written part? Do we really know how much actors repress in their personalities in order to act? Can't they be *personaggi* in their own right?

Inasmuch as it exploits its own mechanisms, theatricality relies on its own resources. Dr. Hinkfuss's wishful remarks in *Tonight We Improvise* get to the core of the dilemma that motivates the six characters: "If only the work could stage itself, not with actors, but with its own characters, who, by some miracle, could acquire a body and a voice: then it could be judged directly in the theatre."[23] This statement highlights a defining moment in the poetics of artistic creation during the 1920s, when the Sicilian writer was well on his way to creating theater within theater—or meta-theater.

Like *Il Candelaio*, *Tonight We Improvise* opens with altercations offstage, while people shout in the audience. Conflicts between the director and the actors dominate two acts. In the end, they get rid of Dr. Hinkfuss, but their victory brings about confusion. Some guess that a quarrel is taking place, but a lady in the balcony screams that it might be a fire. The play is anti-author, anti-script, and focused on a director who finds it hard to re-create a performance out of a text that he dislikes. He is interested in theories and stage effects rather than actors who improvise from an unconventional work by Pirandello, the usual suspect: "Oh yes, it's him all right! He's incorrigible, isn't he!—always the same! You remember what he did to a couple of my colleagues? First he sent the six lost characters looking for an author: they turned the stage upside-down and drove everyone crazy."[24] At this point we learn that the *sei personaggi* have been searching for a while, and one can only guess that they have never left the theater. The inference, I believe, is that each play is but a single aspect of what "happens" on stage as well as behind it, which is a more elusive place than one might suspect at curtain time.

Offstage, the *personaggi* are and remain alive—*vivi*—because the life of the theater is a palimpsest of characters, actors, settings, and scenes that haunt and enrich the performance every time the lights are switched on. As the space on which the script is acted out, the stage accommodates the *personaggi* because they already are alive. Being alive, they need neither authors nor actors. In fact, the title should read *Six Characters Without an Author*. In other words, the title reveals a condition as ambiguous as the philosophical core of the play, which mixes work in progress, the staging of a drama about strange characters, threatened actors, lost authors, temporary writers, and sought-after playwrights who might be willing to compromise authorial prerogatives.

Actors may or may not succeed in "incarnating" the *personaggi,* and audiences should consider themselves lucky whenever characters act out their own drama. As early as 1899, when he published the essay on *azione parlata* (spoken action), Pirandello knew that he had reached a watershed where the literary narrative clashed with the dramatic action: "On the strength of an artistic miracle, the characters ought to stand out alive from the written pages of the drama." Words should be alive, and the characters' own deeds ought to energize a plot in which "page" means "stage."[25] The theater demands that the playwright should find "words that are spoken action, living words that move, immediate expressions inseparable from action, unique phrases that cannot be changed to any other." It follows that "the characters must not be made to appear ghostlike, but as live creatures, fantastic constructions which are immutable and thus more real and permanent than the volatile naturalness of the actors."[26]

In a 1921 production of *Six Characters in Search of an Author,* Georges Pitoëff had the actors use a lift to descend on stage in order to heighten the "idealistic" symbolism of the *personaggi*.[27] Three years later, Pitoëff set the *personaggi* apart by means of dark clothes.²⁸ In the preface to the 1925 edition of the play, Pirandello himself suggested that the actors should wear masks as a way of preserving the integrity of the *personaggi*. In 1936 he told the actor and director Ruggiero Ruggieri that the characters should either wear masks or heighten their facial immobility by means of heavy makeup and lighting effects.²⁹ Pirandello did not use masks in his own productions of the play, but the pervasive symbolism of *maschera* and *volto* was abroad in the contemporary culture of *teatro del grottesco* (theater of the grotesque). As a direct precedent, it suffices to mention a title as suggestive as Luigi Chiarelli's *La maschera e il volto*. Written in 1913, *The Mask and the Face* exemplifies a radical approach to social conventions.³⁰ For Pirandello, the very concept of "masking" ties together plays, critical essays, and prose fictions: "Nothing is true! Oh yes, the sea is true, the mountain is true; the stone, the blade of grass are true; but man? Unwillingly, unknowingly, he is always wearing the mask of whatever it is that he, in good faith, fancies himself to be: handsome, good, courteous, generous, unhappy, etc." People are "masks, they are all masks—a puff and they are gone, to make room for other masks."³¹ Henry IV (*Enrico IV*) believes that "we mask ourselves with what it seems to us that we are." The theater has always staged a constructed reality, and Pirandello seems to "load" the preface with requirements that restrict the actor's freedom.

At stake are not the traditional masks of the *commedia dell'arte*, which, in Pirandello's own words, let actors improvise whenever they play characters "with a completely defined stage life of their own." Instead, he calls for masks with holes for eyes, nose, and mouth cut in such a way as to project a defining sentiment. Since it is meant to interpret *il senso profondo della commedia* (the deeper meaning of the comedy), the play's most important device ought to be *l'uso di speciali maschere per i Personaggi* (the use of special masks) that would express the personalities of the characters: "They will help to give the impression of figures constructed by art, each one unchangeably fixed in the expression of its own fundamental sentiment, thus: REMORSE in the case of the Father; REVENGE in the case of the Stepdaughter; DISDAIN in the case of the Son; GRIEF in the case of the Mother, who should have wax tears fixed in the rings under her eyes and on her cheeks, as with the sculpted and painted images of the 'mater dolorosa' in church."³² It suffices to add that two key words in Pirandello's plays are "mirror" and "mask," which set up duplicity as a dominant theme. In "Avvertenza sugli scrupoli della fantasia" (1921), a short critical piece added to the novel *The Late Mattia Pascal*, Pirandello writes, "I think that I must congratulate my imagination, if, in spite of all its scruples, it has been able to pass for real defects those which it wished to be so. In fact, they are defects of that fictional construct which the characters themselves have laid upon themselves and their own lives, or that others have constructed in their stead. The defects, in other words, of the *mask* until it discovers itself *naked*."[33] The *maschera* (mask) has form without life, whereas *vita nuda* (naked life) has life without form. As the author of theatrical texts, Pirandello groups his plays under a title at once collective and contradictory, *Maschere Nude* (Naked Masks). Humankind's lot is to waver between the unstable shapelessness of life in the making and the achieved fixity of a character's form. The six *personaggi* challenge such a dualism because they are alive in the theater. Whether the focus is on the theater of Pirandello or that of Jarry, mounting concerns with masks touch on the friction between life and playacting. Even Eugene O'Neill concedes that masks project an incantatory power that might enhance the actor's performance: "One's outer life passes in a solitude haunted by the masks of others; one's inner life passes in a solitude hounded by the masks of oneself."[34] This is a comment on how actors and characters convey the complexity of human identity.

To complicate things, masks can be visible or invisible. Pirandello never tires of pointing to the invisible masks that society forces on people. *La maschera dimenticata* (*The Forgotten Mask*) is a story about Don Cirincio, whose unfortunate circumstances generate such rumors that he becomes known as a ridiculous person. He has no choice but to leave his hometown and start a career in politics elsewhere. Things work out quite well for him, until the appearance of an old acquaintance forces him back into his former self. The original title of the story is revealing: *Come Cirincio per un momento si dimenticò d'esser lui* (How Cirincio Forgot for a Moment Who He Was). The social "Other" could make unbearable demands on one's identity, which is what happens to the father in *Six Characters in Search of an Author*. To dramatize his point, Pirandello pits the *personaggi*'s search of an author against props, genre, and interpretation: "One thing is the drama, as a work of art already expressed and alive in its essential and unique ideality. Another thing is the scenic representation, translation, or interpretation of it in the guise of a copy more or less similar, and which lives in a material reality that is nonetheless fictional and illusory."[35] Adjustments between script and performance must be made if the characters are to enact their "being" rather than their "being played." In spite of the *capocomico*'s objections, the drama takes place; the *personaggi* bypass the requirements as well as the restrictions of theatrical conventions.

Normally, actors walk away at the end of each performance, forcing the characters to fold back into the written script. To reinforce his commitment to authenticity, Pirandello recommended that the six *personaggi* learn their parts by heart rather than rely on prompters. Audiences cherish actors who have played famous parts. Hamlet is a compound of Shakespeare's script as well as of all those "performed" Hamlets that each spectator has deemed memorable. Actors come and go, but characters inhabit the theater as ghostlike presences even after each performance is over.[36] Because the six *personaggi* ask to remain alive before and after curtain falls, I would describe their "problem" as a logistical one.[37] These ghostly figures have been roaming offstage all along, and stage instructions demand that, at the end of the drama, a green light should project *le ombre dei Personaggi, meno il Giovanetto e la Bambina* (the shadows of the characters, minus the boy and the girl). Shadows are weightless reflections. At once alive and ghostlike, these figures exist in the theater and for the theater.[38] As Rosalind E. Krauss said of twentieth-century aesthetics, we move in the space of the "drama without the Play, voices without the Author."[39]

We have reached a crossroads where drama transcends its formal restrictions and trades artifice for immediacy; we move in that no-man's-land where genre, author, and fiction melt away, so that characters and audiences can interact directly. This is the space where theatricality thrives on integration. Oedipus, Antigone, Hamlet, Cyrano have outlived their creators and have grown into different historical contexts, where audiences cannot help endowing them with new features. The inference is that theatricality takes in successive performances and diverse interpretations, which never cease to make theatrical progress. For better or worse, even Shakespeare has to accept the fact that there is Olivier's, Burton's, and Gibson's Hamlet.

Pirandello's preface concedes that the *personaggi* have taken on a life of their own: "First, the surprise of the poor actors in a theatrical company rehearsing a play by day on a bare stage (no scenery, no flats). Surprise and incredulity at the sight of the six characters announcing themselves as such in search of an author." This is a surreal encounter. As the *personaggi* translate text into performance, the actors who stand by look at what they would act, should somebody ask them to play the characters before them. However unwittingly, the actors survey an ultimate measure of their own artistry. Could they be as good as the characters themselves? Are these characters what actors would like to become, or what they fear they might become? The matter of actors who meditate on the assets and liabilities of their own craft is the subject of Pirandello's *Trovarsi* (*To Find Oneself,* 1932), a title that challenges the actor to carve out an identity apart from the roles that he or she plays. The focus is on Donata, a famous actress who lives the life of her characters with such intensity that she utters, "I am not myself." Emptiness lies between herself and the roles she plays: "That horror I am experiencing with my eyes wide open, every night in front of a mirror; as soon as the representation is over, when I go to my dressing room to take my make up off."[40] Her fear is every actor's fear. For some of them, it is easier to leave the makeup on.

We know that Konstantin Stanislavsky demanded that actors should *become* the parts they are about to play. By the same token, Pirandello opens his comments on the legendary actress Eleonora Duse by noting that, from the very beginning of her career, she "had one controlling thought—the ambition to disappear, to merge her self, as a real person, in the character she brought to life on the stage." Her tragedy was that "her age did not succeed in supplying her with her author"[41] who could have made it possible for her to express her talents to the fullest. She found the plays of D'Annunzio, Praga, and Gallarati-Scotti uninspiring, while Ibsen appeared too late in her career. There were times when Ibsen himself was surprised by what some of his characters did, much as Chekhov felt besieged by an array of characters waiting to enter his universe. Recently, José Saramago entitled his 1998 Nobel lecture "How Characters Became the Masters and the Author Their Apprentice." The Portuguese writer turned "ordinary people" into "literary characters" who define the multifaceted profile of the author's own autobiography: "Letter-by-letter, word-by-word, page-by-page, book after book, I have been successively implanting in the man I was the characters I created."[42] This is but another aspect of the Pirandellian challenge.

Early in his career, Pirandello sketched problematic characters who kept showing up in front of him under different guises.[43] In the short story "Colloqui coi personaggi" (Colloquies with Characters), Dr. Fileno proudly states that characters like him are "living beings—more alive than those who breathe and wear clothes. Less real but more alive. . . . The man who is born a character, the man who has the good fortune to be born a living character, may snap his fingers even at death. He will never die!"[44] In *La tragedia d'un personaggio* (*The Tragedy of a Character,* 1911), Dr. Fileno looks at reality from the point of view of a ghost who complains about a "first" author who forced him to marry the wrong woman. In fact, an array of *personaggi* surrounded Pirandello, who believed that an "original observation" could not generate a play. Nor could it be "built like a logical chain of reasoning. Art dies when it is based on an abstract idea or fact, when an author rationally and laboriously selects the images that will serve as symbols of some more or less philosophical conclusion." Here we reach a cornerstone of Pirandello's poetics: "A play does not create people, people create a play. So first of all one must have people—free, living, active people. With them and through them the idea of the play will be born, its shape and destiny enclosed in this first seed." Can rebellious actors become the characters they have played? Perhaps that is how the *sei personaggi* enact their "story," so that only the signature of a perfunctory author would suffice to legitimize a drama that has generated itself. Whenever these conditions are met, dialogue in the play is voiced by "the individual characters, not by their creator."[45] Less than two years later, Pirandello's concern with dramatic characters was echoed by Virginia Woolf, who believed that novels were meant "to express character" rather than preach doctrines. Characters come before writers "and say in the most seductive and charming way in the world, 'Come and catch me if you can.'"[46]

Theatrical practice is reversed when the *capocomico* tries to write down the parts that the *personaggi* act on stage. For a few moments, a technician takes over the playwright's role; performance precedes, does not follow, writing. Under these conditions, the title's *in cerca* points toward an author who will have to contend with real characters by relinquishing much of his own "generative" power. At that point, a drama is represented and a challenge is issued: "But can one present a character while rejecting him? Obviously, to present him one needs, on the contrary, to receive him into one's fantasy before one can express him. And I have actually accepted and realized them as rejected: in search of *another* author." The six characters already have a drama to act out, and the *capocomico* cannot be their author because they are complete: *Ogni fantasma, ogni creatura d'arte, per essere, deve avere il suo dramma* (every creature of fantasy and art, in order to exist, must have his drama). The action stems from *il dramma dell'essere in cerca d'autore* (the drama of being in search of an author).[47] To a significant extent, the title enacts Pirandello's penchant for *sconclusione* (inconclusion), his love for the kind of indeterminacy that he admires in *Hamlet* and in *The Life and Opinions of Tristram Shandy*. Indeterminacy is structural as well as grammatical. In fact, the title of *Six Characters* has no verb. The sentence fragment thrives on a contradiction that Pirandello turns to his advantage. That they are in search of an author does not mean that the characters cannot do something else on the way. In fact, the play itself warrants the title *Six Characters Who Stage Their Own Drama While They Search for an Author*.

At the end of *Each in His Own Way*, the *capocomico* announces that, "in view of unfortunate incidents which took place at the end of the second act, we shall be unable to continue the performance." Likewise, the *capocomico* at the end of *Six Characters in Search of an Author* has had it with the disruption that the *personaggi* have caused: "Fiction! Reality! To hell with all of you! Lights, lights, lights!" The stage direction to switch the lights back on reasserts the presence of the stage as the only stable reality. Actors and directors occupy it for a while, whereas the *personaggi* inhabit it.[48] Viewers may wonder whether they have been looking at a play that should not have taken place. In the end, the *commedia da fare* turns out to be a distraction, because what Pirandello wants to do is exactly what happens on stage, where a traditional play has been stopped for the sake of a revolutionary performance.

Such enigmatic titles as *Così è (se vi pare)* (*It Is So [If You Think It So]*) and *Il gioco delle parti* (*The Rules of the Game*) confirm that human pursuits demand unsettling choices that link representation to willful failure. Characters cannot find authors, authors cannot find characters, and titles are caught in between. In *Arte e coscienza d'oggi* (1908), Pirandello wrote: "The old norms have disintegrated, and the new ones have not yet been established. It is therefore natural that the concept of the relativity of everything has so expanded in us to cause us to lose judgment altogether. Nobody is able to set a steady and permanent point of view. . . . I believe that our life never was more disconnected, ethically and aesthetically."[49] The task is to prove that a play happens only when it is acted in front of the spectator who legitimizes what he or she sees.[50] The text fails to find an author but succeeds in staging the drama of the authorless *personaggi*. Whatever the outcome, *Six Characters in Search of an Author* is a title-action that voices a search beyond actors, pages, scripts, and directors.[51] The play itself, as Pirandello wrote upon completion of *The Late Mattia Pascal*, charts the action "at the very moment that the character plots and acts." Under those conditions, we ourselves "are a clumsy, uncertain metaphor of ourselves."[52] Consequently, *in cerca* becomes the linguistic marker of the wishful, which criticism has described through phrases such as "suspended animation" and "dynamic incompleteness."[53] Even the playwright is *in cerca* of a form better than the ones he has inherited. He has found it, of course, and we are looking at it.

2

At the beginning of *Six Characters in Search of an Author*, we are informed that the comedy that has been interrupted has a title. But what kind of title would Pirandello give to a drama that is not meant to have a script? Perhaps it was too early in the twentieth century for a playwright to put on stage characters with a life of their own.[54] Yet title and text fostered a search that pushed the theater beyond its traditional boundaries. The Pirandellian search is metatheatrical because it begins in the theater and exhausts itself in the theater.[55] Pirandello validated both the resilience of fiction and the novelty of metafiction, of theatrical staging and metatheatrical unstaging.[56] After Pirandello, Beckett took up the demise of theatricality, and Jean Baudrillard put its deconstruction on the agenda of things to come: "Who will the new playwrights and new actors be? Everyone seems to be saying 'I am setting up a new stage, but in this space, in this new light, no one will ever move, there will be no play.'"[57]

Whether their object is Ithaca, the Holy Grail, or the whale, traditional journeys justify both authorship and narrativity. The Pirandellian *in cerca,* by contrast, is self-defeating, because the title's quest for an author is a rhetorical device that allows the *personaggi* to exist without him. Within the autonomous perimeter of a drama that places a wedge between written scripts and live characters, *in cerca* is self-fulfilling. The action of the search goes nowhere, and the play takes place precisely because "searching" remains as unfulfilled as "waiting" in Samuel Beckett's play about two vagabonds.

7

Between Expectation and Explanation:
Waiting for Godot

What if one could create a work in which nothing happened?
—THEODOR ADORNO

Once Pirandello let six characters deny their author and look less than eagerly for another one, the death wish of modernist playwrights was out in the open. While the *personaggi* continued to search for an author in the hope of not finding one, the authors themselves brought to the stage the impoverishment of ideas. Better than most, Beckett gave theatrical presence to the process of denial. If one were to look at *Sei personaggi in cerca d'autore* from Beckett's point of view, the numerical reduction of characters would run itself out until no one was left on the stage.[1] Once Pirandellism had made its mark, Beckett updated the theme of the failed search by focusing on the aimless wait for an unfathomable God-ot. Experimentation tested the resilient as well as the residual when Beckett probed the limits of drama by means of a title as inconclusive as *En attendant Godot*. Begun on October 9, 1948, the play was completed on January 29, 1949, published in 1952, and "translated" by the author himself into *Waiting for Godot* two years later.

Pirandello's *in cerca* challenges the tradition of the Western quest, whereas Beckett's "waiting" stalls the quest in the quicksand of belatedness. The theatrical setting in which the two vagabonds wait for an unlikely deity to show up is an abandoned road that has become a dead end. The two tramps act out the exhaustion of the modernist experience in a "drama of disorientation"[2] that waits the title out, so to speak. Modernism left to postmodernism an inheritance of textual as well as theatrical fragmentation.[3] For Jean Anouilh, the opening of *En attendant Godot* at the Théâtre de Babylone on January 5, 1953, under the direction of Roger Blin, was as groundbreaking an event as the 1923 opening of Pirandello's *Six Characters in Search of an Author* under the direction of Pitoeff. Both plays came out of the *teatro del grottesco* and the theater of the absurd,[4] and both failed in their search for a superior authority, whether an anonymous playwright or a would-be deity. However pointless the quest, failure made it possible to stage theatricality.[5]

The absurdity of Pirandello's impromptu representation is effective, and the six characters perform their drama. Beckett, by contrast, stages irresolution. Didi and Gogo are waiting, and so is the rest of humankind. The title names an elusive character that does not end the wait; Godot does not appear. There is an action and its object, but while the subject is missing, the object of waiting is an onomastic distortion; God becomes God-ot. Both playwrights teach us that there are times when titles cannot be more explicit than the texts they introduce. It is a matter of historical irony, I believe, that Beckett uttered many of the answers that Pirandello kept to himself. What remained problematic for the Sicilian took a turn toward annihilation for the Irishman, who made of denial itself a foredoomed search.

This chapter relates the title's emphasis on delay (*Waiting*) to the thematics of procrastination as well as the elusiveness of an enigmatic character (*Godot*). The third component of the title is spatial: where does waiting take place? Stage instructions point to "a road," which turns out to be as problematic as the characters themselves.

1

For Beckett, "art has always been this—pure interrogation, rhetorical question less the rhetoric."[6] To take rhetoric away from art, however, is to undermine style and vilify expression. Should art probe the aesthetic or the philosophical? Does the elimination of rhetoric burn the bridge between them? Bert O. States rightly points out that the French title emphasizes "the interim" rather than the "expectation; not the act of waiting *for* something but the activity of waiting itself."[7] Because it lacks aesthetic context and historical background, the earliest title heightens a kind of anti-Aristotelian pursuit of nonaction; waiting is everything.[8]

The "translation" of *En attendant Godot* into *Waiting for Godot* maintains an unrelenting state of uncertainty, which makes it easy for Godot to bring in a world of allusions—comic, ironic, or downright absurd. At the same time, "waiting" could mean "wanting" in the sense of missing, lacking, and longing. Michel Butor suggests that, ambiguities not being the same from one language to another, "one never translates but a part of a word."[9] Because it often thrives on subtleties that resist explanation, semantics becomes as tentative as the best attempts at translation. In French, the preposition *en* activates the time of hopeless waiting.[10]

After all, "waiting" is the least one can do without taking responsibility for anything to happen:

ESTRAGON: Well, shall we go?
VLADIMIR: Yes, let's go.

Having decided to go, "they do not move." Knowledge and purpose have imploded, and the intransitive verb describes an intransitive title that introduces an intransitive text. To this extent, the title mocks the unities of dramatic representation (time, space, action) that have presided over theatrical composition since antiquity.

To Gogo's assertion that he "wasn't doing anything," Didi answers, "Perhaps you weren't. But it's the way of doing it that counts, the way of doing it, if you want to go on living" (38a).[11] It would seem that the title verb points to a domain that has become quite familiar. In fact, Beckett's verbs are intransitive and stand in isolation. They damn us to living, and the minimal living we can do is to wait in a world where language is rich in verbs and nouns have become secondary. At the philosophical core of Beckett's play, inanity is valuable because it cancels out promises of bliss and prophecies of doom.

The root etymology of Godot points to a transcendental principle that is belittled by the onomastic suffix that turns God into God-ot. Godot is a compound that tampers with etymology (God) and semantics (God-ot) alike. On stage, however, the linguistic failure turns into the artistic triumph of a theatrical action that thrives on its own purposelessness. Traditionally, "waiting for God" expresses a hopeful absence; "waiting for Godot," by contrast, transforms a spiritual quest into a rhetorical gesture that can elicit skepticism as much as lightheartedness. The God-Godot dualism confirms Roland Barthes's belief that "language is never innocent: words have a second-order memory which mysteriously persists in the midst of new meanings."[12] Such a parodic slant becomes overt when Lucky describes a white-bearded God as no more than a linguistic oddity: "quaquaquaqua" (29). In the biblical lexicon, God creates by the word. After the humanization of the divine, after secularism, materialism, and the deity's own death, the word has lost much of its transcendental connotations. From beginning to end, nothing changes, and the two vagabonds end up experiencing "Godotlessness."[13]

God-ot makes it clear that the biblical creation by the word has yielded to a vocabulary of de-formation, which has un-worded the Word itself. We can say of Beckett's theatrical prose what Gertrude Stein said about poetry, that it "is concerned with using with abusing, with losing with wanting, with denying with avoiding with adoring with replacing the noun."[14] Indeed, the stage representation seems to give visual presence to *Waiting*'s progressive attempts at "loosing" and "avoiding" the deity's unbecoming namesake. In fact, Godot is one of the most notorious signifieds of the "literature of the unword," which acts out de-creation: "Ever tried. Ever failed. No matter. Try again. Fail again. Fail better."[15] In fact, tradition would link God to a grand narrative, but parody links God-ot to the insignificant chronicle of two vagrants who have nowhere to go and nothing else to do.

Herbert Blau gave the title "Who Is Godot?" to the program notes for a production of the play at the Actor's Workshop in San Francisco—and commented that the less one says about *Waiting for Godot*, the better. Beckett himself confessed that, had he known who Godot was, he would have told us.[16] All of that remained unsettled in the 1950s. Half a century later, we have yet to tire of asking the same question. As a sentence fragment whose meaning is at once accessible and vague, Beckett's title presents a familiar condition on a simplified stage where uncertainty favors the breakdown of language and the obfuscation of meaning. These "shortcomings," however, spur readers to take an active part in the search for meanings that are both fun and serious.

It might be that Western culture has entered a new domain, where noun-based languages are no longer appropriate.[17] What Augustine considered the logological God-word became ever more postlapsarian during the Renaissance, when ontological breakdowns took on ludic disguises in the linguistic hybrids of Rabelais. One more step and the more sober Michel de Montaigne declared that "the name is not a part of the thing or of the substance, it is an extraneous piece attached to the thing, and outside of it."[18] In the wake of that heritage, it was inevitable that Ludwig Wittgenstein would court arbitrary associations in linguistics. Humankind can face reality for what it is in a culture in which, "when no questions remain . . . just that is the answer."[19]

Waiting for its own sake is the core of theatrical action, which still trusts the resilience of human existence even after all illusions have vanished. On stage, "waiting" is the most that can happen whenever subject, object, and meaning are about to cave in. In Beckett's words: "No 'I,' no 'have,' no 'being.' No nominative, no accusative, no verb. There's no way to go on."[20] While movement leads nowhere, reading and writing rein in but "lifeless words"[21] that invalidate illusory signifiers. Quite literally, language spells out the meaninglessness of the human condition. "Whenever an age loses its nerve," Robert W. Corrigan writes about the dilemma of modern theater, "more and more it reduces its language to the verb, that verbal expression which denotes action in its simplest and most concrete form."[22]

Waiting is the title, the form, and the content of the performance, which thrives on a paradoxical drama of inaction.[23] This, of course, is the Beckettian condition. Beckett's plays confirm that he who has waited long enough will wait forever. Waiting is a test about whether we are able to endure, even when we can expect nothing in return. As a Godlike hybrid, the noun Godot adds ambiguity to the wait. At first the focus is centered on "who" Godot might be. As the delay drags on, the title leads the audience to confront its own expectations by suggesting that Godot is only the modernist variant of some deity either as uncaring as Fate or as unreliable as Fortune. If *Godot* is the future, *Waiting* is the present, which gives permanence to uneventful experiences. While the title sets up a passive condition, the action on stage does not relent, and performance lowers expectations to the point of questioning the very idea of waiting for such an improbable figure to show up.

Twice a boy appears, calls the tramps "Mr. Albert," and brings the news that Godot will arrive the next day. There is a witness to Godot, but does anyone still believe that he will appear? We assume that the boy is too innocent to lie, but he could be too naive to know the truth! Gogo and Didi are "curious to hear what he has to offer," and both agree that Godot will promise something only after consulting with friends, agents, correspondents, books, and the "bank account" (12a, 13). Are the characters constructing through words what does not exist? The all-knowing God is in heaven, but the misinformed Godot is closer to earth. If the name points to the metaphysical, his alleged conduct is as physical as the list of menial tasks he would have to discharge. Perhaps the only thing we know about Godot is that he is a deity of procrastination, an attribute that he shares with Gogo and Didi. Assertiveness in the wasteland of cultural debris is hard to come by, and T. S. Eliot himself borders on it when he creates Alfred J. Prufrock, who still believes that there will be:

> Time for you and time for me,
> And time yet for a hundred indecisions,
> And for a hundred visions and revisions
>
> (*The Love Song of J. Alfred Prufrock*, lines 31–33)

Perhaps Godot is so familiar with Tiresias and Gerontion that he no longer finds it worthwhile to show up, because

> Unnatural vices
> Are fathered by our heroism. Virtues
> Are forced upon us by our impudent crimes.
> These tears are shaken from the wrath-bearing tree.
>
> (T. S. Eliot, *Gerontion*, 45–48)

These lines convey cultural exhaustion long before Eliot made popular the mythical method for Joyce and fellow modernists.

Since he will consult other people before making up his mind, Godot's own judgment can be erroneous. Details are parodic, and they account for the equally parodic name, which Pozzo downgrades into "Godin . . . Godet" (24). Godot names and unnames all at once. Everyone's task is to understand the semantics behind the onomastic hybrid. Much as Hamm is but a fragment of Ham-let in *Endgame*, the two nicknames of Vladimir and Estragon—Gogo and Didi—also go into the making of Godot under the onomastic synecdoches "Go" and "Di." Is this a way of providing a focus, if not a purpose, for idleness? Yet how could two tramps define Godot if not in terms of their own wacky marginality?

The suffix -ot shifts the onomastics as well as the ontology of the play toward grounds where one asks whether the title is parodic or prophetic. Is the "unknown" Godot sane, mad, or ridiculous? Since there is no subject in the title, the assumption is that everyone is waiting for Godot. To the extent that he fails to appear, title, text, and performance carry out what Beckett acknowledged as "the key word" for interpreting his plays: "perhaps."[24] While it is enough to sustain uncertainty, *perhaps* unsettles logic, shreds knowledge, and keeps the imagination in a holding pattern. The preposition curbs thought, while the drawn-out action of waiting becomes itself the subject of the play.[25] It would seem that *perhaps* motivates *waiting*; their interaction plays down commitment and heightens procrastination.

One way or another, everyone has been waiting for a Godot of one's choice, and each of us will have to complete the title by giving it an object. The gerund activates proximity and spells out a delaying strategy. Time as waiting proves to be futile, but futility intensifies what Robert Champigny calls "the basic way to live what-has-to-be-lived, the gerundive aspect of existence."[26] The indirect object of waiting is Godot; its direct object, however, is the aimlessness of a suspended state of being.[27] But the "visitation" does not take place. No vindictive ghost hovers around to deliver instructions, much as no deity descends to the stage to solve the impasse. Because Godot fails to show up, the title maintains a position of prominence vis-à-vis the text. Expectation does not lead to resolution, but this is exactly what waiting entails. Waiting creates a state of suspension that is purposeless by definition. Neither titological nor textual shortcomings are at stake, other than an artful staging of the way procrastination has the best of achievement. The inference is that the audience ought to appreciate what theatrical action *is* rather than what it ought to mean. In this sense, Beckett's experimentalism follows in the wake of similar attempts by Flaubert and Mallarmé with regard to prose and poetry a century earlier.

Unlike Oedipus or Medea, Godot has no theatrical story of his own to act out. Ambiguity is linguistic as well as ontological, and the protracted wait raises concerns. By the end of the day, the performance has not overshadowed the title's implicit question: how long should we wait? Why wait at all? In a way, waiting implies presence, which triggers Beckett's talent for dramatizing the paradoxical dynamics of inertia. Godot is an intransitive deity, "unwitnessed witness of witnesses," a testimonial representation of man's endurance in a world where action erases itself in the play no less than in short prose texts: "No, something better must be found, a better reason, for this to stop, another word, a better idea, to put in the negative, a new no, to cancel all the others, all the old noes."[28] The rhetoric of persistent negatives is self-destructive, and a "new no" that overrides old ones is no more than an exercise in futility; it calls for the annihilation of something whose existence is doubtful to begin with. In a desolate milieu where intransitivity fosters aimless speculations, the title sets up a passive condition, and the action on stage plays with the idea of waiting for such an improbable figure as Godot. Actually, the play enacts a sense of nonplace that is typically Beckettian: "No place but the one. None but the one where none. Whence never once in. Somehow in. Beyondless. Thenceless there. Thitherless there. Thenceless thitherless there."[29] Presence becomes its own raison d'être because it upholds a language of immediate visibility.

The action goes nowhere even though the play takes place by a country road, which implies motion as well as direction. On the road, people pass by; if they wait, they do so before heading somewhere. Much as Godot is not God, the country road is not like any other country road. Because a rock and a tree stand in the middle of it, Beckett's road has evidently fallen into disuse. For a long while, neither traffic nor travelers could disturb Vladimir and Estragon, the homeless vagrants who walk around, discuss food, fall asleep, and keep on waiting. Action yields a routine that is bearable only because "habit is a great deadener" (58a).[30] Since the site of movement has become a dead end, the theme of the road fosters a roundabout movement that draws the boundaries of its own circularity. The two tramps keep on circling each other; turns, counterturns, and detours give visual form to intellectual misdirections. As in the rest of Beckett's oeuvre, little or nothing happens, but visual presence does not let theatricality lapse.

The title of Beckett's *Act Without Words I* stands out as the emblematic title of visual language, which tests the coexistence of word and gesture. As such, the title presents another paradox. The mime creates expression, while the literary text, though reduced to stage directions, suggests visual images. The predominance of acting is tightened in the subtitle, *A Mime for One Player*. While the title stands out as the emblem of visual language, the speechless mime enacts a kind of minimalist pantomime.[31] Its heightened visibility pays homage to the Greek etymology of *theatron*, which refers to a place where one goes "to see" a drama, that is to say, something acted out.[32] Both words are anchored to the visual, which still is the primary metaphor of Western ontology. But the default of visibility recurs in Beckett's plays. Hamm is blind, and so is Pozzo the second time he appears on stage, where characters fall asleep. Were Godot to show up, would anyone notice him?

At the far corner of a road that probably leads back toward the wasteland, the purposeless action of playing with hats as well as with names has curtailed the concept of mimesis as purposeful action.[33] Although Vladimir and Estragon keep talking to each other from beginning to end, their exchanges remain inconsequential, and the text uses intelligence to unhinge itself:

ESTRAGON: Use your intelligence, can't you?
(*Vladimir uses his intelligence.*)
VLADIMIR (*finally*): I remain in the dark. (12a)

VLADIMIR: What is terrible is to *have* thought.
ESTRAGON: But did that ever happen to us? . . .

VLADIMIR: We must have thought a little.
ESTRAGON: At the very beginning. (41a)

The implication is that "waiting" has consumed thought, much as existence has worn out ambition.

VLADIMIR: You should have been a poet.
ESTRAGON: I was. (*Gestures toward his rags.*) Isn't that obvious? (9)

The drawn-out wait has depleted the tramps' intellectual capital, and their pantomimic sense of humor voices spiritual impoverishment.

Because Gogo and Didi do not recognize that the spot where they stand is the same as that of the night before, the inference is that any stretch of any unused road can become a place of waiting.[34] This kind of logistics is symbolic of a mental no less than of a physical condition. While waiting, the road turns into a cul-de-sac where Gogo and Didi have been roaming around long before the curtain goes up.

In the Beckettian practice of theatrical performance, Clov kills a flea on stage and promises to kill a rat somewhere else. Nell dies during the performance, and Nagg no longer answers from his ashbin.[35] Speech is useless and characters talk bits of dialogue just because they are on stage.[36] Hamm and Clov wait for something to begin, and they make up things; they wait for something to end and make up things as well. The closed space of the theater is the only one in which depleted human existence is still bearable. If deeds on stage are not tragic in the traditional sense, the slow consumption of human consciousness is. Emphasis is placed on improvisation, which reduces speech as meaning to speech as presence. In a world of uncertainties, language utters the last sign of human activity before defaulting in silence. Some have been telling us that there is nothing outside the text, but Beckett has shown us that there is not much inside it, either. Yet he tried to stop the downfall of neither textuality nor theatricality.[37] The ensuing failure turned out to be productive, for it spearheaded the transition from the modernist end to the postmodern dead end.

To illustrate such a transition, I want to relate *waiting*, which precedes and follows the staging time, to the stretched-out *end* of *Endgame*. Verb and noun merge into what could be construed as "waiting for the end," which paraphrases much of what happens in both plays. Inanity is lodged indoors in *Endgame,* a sheltered space that recalls T. S. Eliot's lines:

> Waiting, waiting, always waiting.
> I think this house *means* to keep us waiting
>
> (T. S. Eliot, *The Family Reunion*, scene 2)

The title's *game* takes the plot out of any direct representation of live events. The grand narrative of cause and effect has yielded to a scene that hardly calls for playfulness. The formal mechanism of the game becomes "content" inasmuch as the deadlock exhausts the players. On stage, they execute their final move without ending their agony. Performance enacts the title but fails to make the move that would terminate *Endgame*. Appropriately, Stanley Cavell's essay on Beckett, "Ending the Waiting Game," bears a title that interprets a play (*Waiting for Godot*) through the language of another title (*Endgame*). Commentary falls back on Beckettian language: "God must repent once more—not indeed by destroying, nor again by sending salvation, but by doing nothing more: by repenting precisely all repentance. Above all by stopping waiting. We waited for him and we were left waiting; now he waits for us and we keep him waiting. But that is vengeance, the game nobody can win, because nobody can end."[38] Since there is no specific goal (hope, anguish), waiting justifies action for action's sake.

As a temporal concept, waiting is inexhaustible, and the challenge is to make it bearable. With conviction, Didi pauses: "We have kept our appointment and that's an end to that. We are not saints, but we have kept our appointment. How many people can boast as much?" (51a). The answers is revealing:

ESTRAGON: Billions.
VLADIMIR: You think so?
ESTRAGON: I don't know.
VLADIMIR: You may be right. (51a)

It does not take the faith of a saint to wait. Without Godot, Didi recognizes that we could be bored to death: "And we'll be alone once more, in the midst of nothingness" (52). Were Godot to show up, however, the action would either end or turn into a miracle play. The very fact that Didi and Gogo are tramps turns the tragic into the tragicomic, which may be another reason why God goes by the name of Godot.[39] By the roadside, the two tramps improvise,[40] talk, argue, and move in circles; neither miracle nor rebellion can change their dim condition.

Delay becomes the destiny of Gogo and Didi; it waits them out. In the place where people move because they are going somewhere, the two tramps relapse into verbal games that slow down thinking itself. They walk nowhere in the same place. Like the title, the text suspends time between desire and fulfillment. While *Waiting for Godot* implies the possibility that something might begin, *Endgame* enacts the opposite action of an ending that fails to execute its own terminality. Both are plays of impasse in which characters face the major task of killing time; much of the action—or lack of it—is about strategies of deferral that toy with the end no less than with endlessness. Hamm is stuck in a wheelchair, Nell dies during the performance, Nagg no longer answers from his ashbin,[41] and Clov cannot go anywhere because he sees destruction outside.[42] Speech is useless and characters talk because that is the very last thing they can do.

Hamm and Clov make things up while they wait for something to begin. By affecting language and performance, the first half of the play's one-word title, *End*, takes up a temporal condition. Whereas "waiting" is endless because its object fails to show up, "end" suggests a terminal point where the characters seem to be speaking from the beyond. The title qualifies the end as a place of activity where the classical movement toward resolution is delayed.[43] In Hamm's words, "The end is in the beginning and yet you go on."[44] The other half of the title, *Game*, refers to a reality where rule and order are as essential as they are inconsequential. Let us not forget that the original French title, *Fin de partie*, plays up Beckett's ironic approach to tragic outcomes through the lighthearted perspective of a game of chess. Like the title, the play does not probe into why such a doomsday reality has come about. In a way, "waiting" and "end" complement each other by encompassing vast expanses of time. Verb and noun merge into what could be "waiting for the end," which describes much of what happens in *Endgame* and *Waiting for Godot*. In this sense, we can agree with Wolfgang Iser, who writes that Beckett's titles "open up horizons of human endings."[45] Theatricality tests the lowest level of human expression, where emphasis falls on speech as presence rather than speech as meaning. The object of *Endgame* is just as vague as that of *Waiting for Godot*. In a Kafkaesque turn, causes do not link up to their effects, and characters face the major task of killing time.

On Beckett's stage, performance fails failure, just as the text enacts the title without making the last move, which would end the game. At the end of play, therefore, we must reread the title, *Endgame*, as a contraction in which the last move becomes itself a strategy for circumventing the end in favor of one more move. But how effective can that last move be?

In as stationary a play as *Endgame*,[46] centaur-like characters trust bicycles to carry on a bygone familiarity with movement, the only true measure of human living:

> CLOV: There are no more bicycle-wheels.
> HAMM: What have you done with your bicycle?
> CLOV: I never had a bicycle. (8)

Later, the best that Hamm can do is tell us about a wheelchair, even though he favors "big wheels. Bicycle wheels!" (25).[47] Bicycle-less, the road turns into a useless topos. If wheels made a major contribution to the rise of civilization, the Beckettian enclave is the final way station on the road to cultural breakdown. Whether their names are Murphy, Molloy, or Malone, cyclists' physical condition deteriorates quickly,[48] and Beckett is caught between dramatic motion and intellectual idleness, the "healthy" bicycle and the "deadly" ashbin.

Action in *Waiting for Godot* unfolds along the perimeter of the stage, which is what one would expect from such marginal figures as our tramps. Only when Pozzo appears with Lucky on a long leash does the action move toward the center, where Lucky delivers a monologue that laments the agony of speech. While speaking, he holds two pieces of luggage that do not touch the ground, as if to remind the audience that he stands in a place of transit. His words make it clear that language itself has become a metaphorical vehicle: "For reasons unknown but time will tell" (45a). In the second act, all four characters fall to the ground and remain silent in the middle of the stage, as if to give visual presence to the imminent demise of theatricality. Emphasis on silent action brings out the "surface depth" of Beckettian dramas, an oxymoron that is at once visual and acoustical. Somehow the demotion of spoken language is offset by a greater trust in body language. The director Herbert Blau, better known as an academic writer and a theorist of theater, points out that Beckett followed in the wake of Joyce's Stephen Hero, who called for "an art of gesture" that spurred the director to stretch the opening sequence of *Endgame* to fifteen minutes of silent mime.[49] Of course, silence spearheaded the break down of theatricality, until Eugene Ionesco linked the demise of dialogue to the moans and groans of a deaf mute orator in *The Chairs*.[50]

To shed some light on the absurdity of waiting on an abandoned road, we ought to consider a character who moves through the maze-like space of Beckett's *Fizzles:* "Instead of turning left a little further on he turns right again. And see how now again, as he expected, he turns left at last."[51] By contrast, the later *Texts for Nothing* takes up movement with an apparent sense of purpose: "There's a way out there, there's a way somewhere, then all would be said, it would be the first step on the long travelable road, destination tomb, to be trod without a word."[52] To recapitulate is to go nowhere. If travelers do not know where they want to go, the road cannot lead them there; the beginning has fallen out of sight and the end is elusive. From stage to page, we get closer to Beckett's penchant for depicting puny movements. Either memorable or prosaic, human deeds exhaust themselves in the mechanics of physical motion. Words describe the stripped-down posture of one's upright stance. By the roadside, waiting scales back "reasonable expectations" because any turn adds to circular aimlessness. This is an introduction to Beckett's systematic decentering of the action.

The road is a theatrical dead end where action has ceased and narrative expectations have been shattered. In the playwright's own words, "There is nothing but what is said. Beyond what is said there is nothing."[53] There is nowhere for Didi and Gogo to go, so why should Godot rush to get there? What we have, Shira Wolosky remarks, is "a radical de-figuration of a whole tradition of literary journeys."[54] In fact, the peripheral country road is a place where waiting exemplifies a purgatorial condition, which echoes Dante's presence in Beckett's writings. "Waiting" points toward a no-man's-land where Gogo and Didi expect that Godot, should he show up, will make decisions. While waiting, however, no "cleansing" takes place. Didi and Gogo do not try to turn "waiting" into "searching" under the aegis of the purgatorial law of *contrappasso,* which makes sinners expiate by doing the opposite of their sin. In purgatory, salvation is delayed, and so is departure on the country road,[55] where procrastination is self-fulfilling rather than instrumental.

Since Beckett's writings water down political and theological issues, his dominant theme is that of regressive evolution,[56] which draws another parallel with Dante. At the bottom of hell, the greatest sinner is Satan, whose treason has reduced him to sheer matter in a glacial underworld where he remains speechless because sounds freeze in his mouth. In Beckett's work, loss of speech also follows loss of humanity, which becomes as heavy as the earth itself by the time we find Winnie buried in the ground in *Happy Days.*

The metaphysical place of choice for waiting would be limbo, where neither damnation nor redemption takes place. It is there that Dante and Virgil meet Homer, Ovid, Horace, and Lucan:

> They welcomed me as one of their own group,
> So that I numbered sixth among such minds.
>
> (*Inferno* IV, lines 101–2)

Dante is the sixth among the great poets of antiquity in limbo, whereas Beckett is the last modernist to disclaim poetic glory before Roland Barthes and Michel Foucault would dismiss the very idea of the writer as a unique individual entitled to undersign authoritative texts. Along the perimeter of "Limbese," one of Beckett's outstanding neologisms, Mr. Rooney points out that the meaningless routine of bureaucratic work demonstrates "what it means to be buried alive, if only from ten to five" in the radio play *All That Fall*. Not even a "fully certified death can take the place of that."[57] Human demise can be natural as well as self-induced. The inference is that Beckett's limbo is close to hell, where sinners carry the burden of their flawed humanity for eternity. The theatrical action suggests no more than an improbable miracle from a lesser deity whose name suggests a reinscription of the theological name-concept.[58] In Beckett's words, "Limbese" does not call for speech because it does not need a story; he exists in the pit of his "inexistence."[59]

In the novel form of subhuman existence, in *Malone Dies*, Malone "lived in a kind of coma," which could be considered as a more secular, if not clinical, form of "Limbese." For him, the decline of consciousness "was never any great loss."[60] Language echoes posthumousness when Malone describes his condition through an old verb, "to coffin."[61] While echoing Joyce's "coffined thoughts" (*Ulysses*, 9:352), "to coffin" starts the process of one's downfall early in life. By the end of *Waiting for Godot*, everyone will have seen how much of life has been "corpsed" (30), to use another neologism very much in tune with Beckett's penchant for the necrological. The disappearance of "what" and "why," so well phrased in a title such as *How It Is*, does not deny the staging of human presence. Beckett proved that artistic expression could endure beyond the spent ashes of a defunct culture. At the threshold of idleness, waiting allows us to exist without either having or wanting. Questions and answers are gone, ideologies have waned, but existence still goes on under the guise of verbal and physical deeds that turn waiting into its own object. Alain Robbe-Grillet put it better than most when he wrote that waiting "does not possess, as waiting, the slightest stage value. It is neither a hope, nor an anguish, nor even a despair. It is barely an alibi."[62] In Beckett's hands, the barely valuable became theatrically invaluable.

At an authorial level, "waiting" spelled out a mode of production that led Beckett to write *Worstward Ho,* a neologism that points to the worst, which, late in his life, suggested artistic and physical death. Yet the expectation of the worst did not extinguish the determination to push on, which has been described as the Beckettian imperative.[63] The text opens and closes with the preposition "on." It stands as an exhortation, spurring on the act of writing, no matter what. In this sense it points back to the Victorian orthodoxy of progress, which exploited the trope of onwardness.[64] In the title, such an impetus is carried on by *Ho,* a word-sound that rallies us to action. The first page of *Worstward Ho* foregrounds goals: "On. Say on. Be said on. Somehow / on. Till nohow on. Said nohow on." Saying "on" again and again is self-energizing, but only to a point. Beckett would never want to be carried away. "On" defies inanity, but it does not find its own object; there is no endpoint to it.[65]

Waiting for Godot has spawned countless imitations, parodies, and transformations. In 1950 Paul Tillich published a book of sermons and entitled one of them "Waiting." The opening paragraph describes our relation with God as one of waiting, which "means *not* having and having at the same time. For we have not what we wait for; or, as the apostle says, if we hope for what we do *not* see, we *then* wait for it." The sermon ends with a recognition: "Our time is a time of waiting; waiting is its special destiny. And every time is a time of waiting, waiting for the breaking in of eternity. All time runs forward. All time, both in history and in personal life, is expectation. Time itself is waiting, waiting not for another time, but for that which is eternal." Waiting is the natural condition of humankind, whether or not we turn to religion. Tillich concedes that "it is not easy to endure this not having God, this waiting for God," whose time must be delayed simply because it is eternal: "I think of the theologian who does not wait for God, because he possesses Him, enclosed within a doctrine. I think of the Biblical student who does not wait for God, because he possesses Him, enclosed in a book. I think of the churchman who does not wait for God, because he possesses Him, enclosed in an institution."[66] This statement gives us a better understanding of why two tramps represent the dispossessed. Without books to read or institutions to which they might turn, they can raise the issue of faith in what we do not have, do not see, and do not know. As the philosopher sets the human time of history against eternity, so does the playwright set hopelessness against the cyclical time of natural growth, which yields new leaves on the tree during the second half of *Waiting for Godot*.

Commenting on *Malone Dies*, Maurice Blanchot writes that the "*vagabond* is nothing more than a *moribund*." This image, which also applies to *Waiting for Godot*, takes us to Blanchot's *L'attente l'oubli* (*Awaiting Oblivion*). Published in 1962, this text asks questions on how to deal with what seems to have become a universal condition.

> In waiting, he could ask no questions about waiting. What was he waiting for, why was he waiting, what is there to await in waiting?
> Waiting fulfilled by waiting, fulfilled/disappointed by waiting . . .
> To know how to wait, like a knowledge that could be given only through waiting, provided that one could know how to wait.[67]

The road turns back to the selfsame place; for what counts in life no less than on the stage is to be somewhere because of the simple fact that one exists. Likewise, the existence of titles leads Blanchot to ask, "What can this title designate, if in any case the one writing is already no longer Beckett but the demand that led him outside of himself?" The title thus points to an existence "lived under the threat of the impersonal."[68]

Threats added up, until they defined a condition of being in the Beckettian follow-up, *The Writing of the Disaster*, in which Blanchot gave a postmodern slant to hopelessness. The title entitles us to enter a world "where power does not reign—nor initiative, nor the cutting edge of a decision—there, dying is living. Dying is the passivity of life." We endure "by waiting, by awaiting a misfortune" yet to come. Like Beckett, Blanchot believes that questions weaken the semantics of language: "The disaster does not put me into question, but annuls the question, makes it disappear—as if along with the question, 'I' too disappeared in the disaster which never appears."[69] This statement downgrades the role of the subject and describes what the title of Peter Brook's reflections on the theater calls the empty space, where despair takes on the faces of Gogo, Didi, and Willie Loman.[70]

As tramps, Didi and Gogo talk past each other, and proximity separates as much as it unites them. They are alone together, and their relationship entails alienation and dialogism, both of which concern the philosopher Martin Buber. Through a cluster of titles that give full exposure to human exchanges, Buber makes transitive what Beckett keeps intransitive.[71] Published in 1947, *Between Man and Man* asserts the idea that "the basic movement of the life of dialogue is the turning towards the other." Beckett uses dialogue to wear out life, and Buber warns that he "who wishes to speak with men without speaking with God is not fulfilled; but the word of him who wishes to speak with God without speaking with men goes astray."[72] Gogo and Didi are waiting for some deity. That is why they are there, even though Godot never enters their dialogue.

Buber's goal is to fill the "betweenness" of human relationships: "Only man with man is a completely outlined form. Consider man with man, and you see human life, dynamic, twofold, the giver and the receiver, he who does and he who endures, the attacking force and the defending force, the nature which investigates and the nature which supplies information, the request begged and granted—and always both together showing forth man."[73] *I and Thou*, the most popular of dialogic titles, begins by considering man's twofold world as what he calls "primary words," which "do not signify things"; instead, "they intimate relations." One primary word is the plural combination *I-Thou*, whereby "all real living is meeting."[74] Once it is linked to meeting, waiting marks a temporal stage in a story with a hopeful outcome. God will appear: "Meeting with God does not come to man in order that he may concern himself with God, but in order that he may confirm that there is meaning in the world." Waiting for Godot, instead, is to linger in meaninglessness. Conversely, Buber suggests that "he who goes on a mission has always God before him: the truer the fulfillment the stronger and more constant His nearness."[75] What for Buber is a promise turns out to be an abjection for Beckett. In a way, Gogo and Didi embody the negative of I-Thou. The performative relationship is there, but ontological exchanges are inconsequential.

Moving from ideas to art, Buber wrote a play, *Elijah*, knew actors and directors, and believed that "drama is pure dialogue."[76] Commenting on the Italian actress Eleonora Duse, Buber considered her talent synthetic, a term by which he meant that she was able to translate the archetypal forms of the cultural ethos into physical gestures. By contrast, "the word is never something for and in itself but only comes to completed reality through being received."[77] For Buber, the word "moves *between beings*." The upshot is that "two men never mean the same things by the words that they use, that there is, therefore, no pure replay, that at each point of the conversation, therefore, understanding and misunderstanding are interwoven—from which comes then the interplay of openness and closedness, expression and reserve." The breakdown of relationships in speech steers readers toward Beckett, who would agree with Buber that "the strength of the actor is the gesture."[78] Gestures are the most that Gogo and Didi act out on stage.

Roland Barthes has indexed waiting as *attendre* in *A Lover's Discourse*. The psychological scene of waiting is pinned to "an arrival, a return, a promised sign. This can be futile, or immensely pathetic ... I have no sense of *proportions*."[79] Lack of proportion probably entails anxiety about self-control. The scene of waiting is similar to that of *Waiting for Godot*, which also combines the futile with the pathetic. The analogy gains strength when Barthes proceeds to describe the "[s]cenography of waiting: I organize it, manipulate it, cut out a portion of time in which I shall mime the loss of the loved object and provoke all the effects of a minor mourning. This is then acted out as a play."[80] This description could be read as a stage direction in Beckett's play. The prologue describes delay "as yet only a mathematical, computable entity (I look at my watch several times)." The chronological measure draws a line between a specific event with "real" people and the "generic" waiting of Didi and Gogo, who linger in a timeless state of being.

Act II of Barthes's *A Lover's Discourse* involves recriminations against the beloved's lack of punctuality. In Act III abandonment sets in; one can wait by the telephone idly, because "waiting is an enchantment." Yet, what kind of magic is at stake here? The Barthean lover finds himself "with nothing to do, punctual, even ahead of time"; he is *the one who waits*. By contrast, *to make someone wait* is the "pastime of humanity." To illustrate the permanent condition of waiting, Barthes refers to a mandarin who falls in love with a courtesan. She asks him to wait one hundred nights sitting on a stool. The mandarin waits for ninety-nine nights; then he stands up, "puts his stool under his arm," and goes away.[81] Waiting is an acceptable test, but the mandarin decides that there are limits. She is not worth the wait because she betrayed love when she made an unloving request. In this case, waiting leads to a revelation.

A similar process of self-discovery is absent in those who are dominated by relations of power. The two tramps do not question Godot; but does Godot fail to show up because he has lost his power? Beckett's "waiting" seems to point toward the waiting for the return of the absent gods, a trope central to both Judaism and Christianity. One awaits the coming of the Messiah, and the other waits for the second coming.[82] Otherwise, as Edmond Jabès put it, it would be the case that "everything was in the wait for Nothing, and Nothing preceded our wait. . . . The question creates. The answer kills." It is indeed possible that "God died of His premature answer."[83] Has Godot learned that lesson? Would Didi, Gogo, or anyone else deserve a better reply? Perhaps the freedom of waiting without worrying about Godot could be our greatest victory.

2

Asked who Godot is, Beckett answered that he did not know; otherwise he would have told us. We should believe him because, had he known, he would have stopped writing. But writing kept on speaking for him, and *Texts for Nothing* refers to a voice that will "always speak, of things that don't exist, or only exist elsewhere, if you like, if you must, if that may be called existing." These words describe the existential condition that binds Didi to Gogo and Beckett to each one of us. "Elsewhere" is the great illusion, and the road, which takes us from here to elsewhere, does not warrant hope: "What more is it waiting for now, when there's no doubt left, no choice left?"[84]

When all is said, who is Godot? For sure, he is as intransitive as the gerund that precedes his name. Perhaps the two tramps see in him a witness, a metaphysical Thou whose failure to appear leads them to accept the fact that nothing is all we have. This kind of desolate awareness is the necessary measure of our being "here," which is where the wait is real. Gogo and Didi are beyond asking and denying. Yet the title makes *us* ask, makes *us* test the indicative through the conditional; why, for what, for whom should we be waiting? In the process of taking up this challenge, we make the wait our own. Could a title be more provocative?

Beyond waiting, what remains is a barren field of un-worded language and de-created objects. Amid characters without authors, titles without texts, and plays without plots, the last thing left for the title to do is un-title itself. With Beckett, however, un-wording and un-titling took up the rest of his life.

8

The Dustbin of Titles: From "The Literature of
Exhaustion" to "The Literature of Replenishment"

> As for the dustbins of history themselves, they are not so much full
> of events or outdated ideologies as of present events . . .
> transformed into crushed residues, into a charnel-house of images.
> —JEAN BAUDRILLARD

In 1922, T. S. Eliot enclosed the modern topography of the Western experience within *The Waste Land*. At its edge, Borges, a modernist ahead of his fellow modernists, wrote a short story whose title, "The Nothingness of Personality," breached modernist fragmentation. Still in 1922, the Argentinean writer paved the way for Beckett, Pessoa, and Blanchot, when he wrote:

> I want to tear down the exceptional preeminence now generally awarded to the self. . . . I propose to prove that a personality is a mirage maintained by conceit and custom, without metaphysical foundation or visceral reality. I want to apply to literature the consequences that issue from these premises.[1]

Well ahead of his time, Borges outlived what would become the modernist aftermath.

After 1922, modernism piled debris throughout the wasteland before reaching the postmodern periphery. Robert Langbaum put it better than most when he wrote that, while Eliot portrays the breakdown of our civilization, "Beckett portrays the period after the wreck," and, I would add, right before the postmoderns began to vandalize, counterfeit, recycle, parody, and rearrange the wreckage. In fact, it could be said that many of Beckett's plays are set in the wasteland. *Waiting for Godot* takes place by an abandoned country road with only a bare tree, *Happy Days* on an expanse of scorched grass, and *Endgame* in a room where one hears reports about a lifeless gray sky. Civilization has been destroyed, and nature has dried up.[2] Characters are stationary because there is nowhere to go, and titles tell the story of an epoch-making downturn.

Ironically, Beckett never led textuality to extinguish itself in nothingness. At the end of the modernist trajectory, he left a trail of terminal reductions that find expression in a title as concisely emblematic as *Lessness*.[3] It acts out the "principle of parsimony," which is otherwise associated with the idea that less is more. A title as well as a kind of "ideological imperative,"[4] *Lessness* highlights a feature of Beckett's poetics that relishes equations between humankind and "a speck in the void" or a "little bit of grit."[5] Such a reductionist mindset was abroad by the middle of the twentieth century. E. M. Cioran insists that Beckett coined the term *lessness* and considered the German equivalent *Losigkeit*. Having found inadequate translations in the French *sans* and *moindre*, Cioran went back to the Latin *sine*, which inspired him to coin *sinéité*. Yet translations remained unsatisfactory, and *lessness* best expressed the inexhaustible "mixture of privation and infinity."[6] In Beckett's work, nothingness amounted to something—not much, of course, but enough to bypass extinction and thrive on belatedness,[7] which made the shift from modernist decline to postmodern exhaustion almost seamless.

If modernism did not end, neither could postmodernism. Rather than *another* end, such as *fin de siècle*, autumn, or wanings of sorts, postmodernism marks not a stage in but the dead end of the Western tradition. At the threshold of utter negativity, Eliot introduced much Beckettian inanity:

> I could not
> Speak, and my eyes failed, I was neither
> Living nor dead, and I knew nothing
>
> (*The Waste Land*, 38–40)

With a view to the evolution from modernist fragmentation to postmodern refuse, Eliot played a role at once introductory and directional. As early as 1909 he wrote verses that paved the way for the modernist downturn.

> The charm of vacant lots!
> The helpless fields that lie.
> Sinister, sterile and blind –

> Entreat the eye and rack the mind,
> Demand your pity.
> With ashes and tins in piles,
> Shattered bricks and tiles
> And the débris of a city
>
> (*Second Caprice in North Cambridge*)[8]

Even before the start of World War I, the debris of an exhausted culture began to pile up:

> There is no end, but addition: the trailing
> Consequence of further days and hours,
> While emotion takes to itself the emotionless
> Years of living among the breakage
> Of what was believed in as the most reliable—
> And therefore the fittest for renunciation.
>
> (*Four Quartets, The Dry Salvages*, lines 55–60)

Because it sustains accumulation without spurring progress, addition fosters repetition, which indulges in descriptive lists, indexes, and catalogues.

With a eye to the mounting ascendancy of description over narration in the arts at the turn of the twentieth century, I would like to place Eliot's "addition" midway between the "bibelot" of French narrativity—from Balzac's *Le Cousin Pons* (1847) and Huysmans's *A rebours* (1881) to Proust's *A la recherché du temps perdue* (1913–22)—and Andy Warhol's "serialization." It suffices to add that the "combines" of Robert Rauschenberg inventoried the "bibelot" of junkyards the world over. Bibelots were knickknacks, curiosities, collectibles, and antiques that began to crowd narratives, not as details that enhanced storytelling but as signposts—Gertrude Stein's tender buttons—of a material culture independent of the Aristotelian mimesis of "men in action." The world of objects began to take on a life of its own. Since superfluousness unifies the world of bibelots, Janell Watson has examined the cumulative descriptiveness that absorbed so many writers throughout the century.[9] It was therefore predictable that accumulation would get out of hand and turn into debris, waste, and refuse. Even though its evidence surrounded Eliot on all sides, it was too daunting for him to confront it. He knew that the answer would test the range of tradition and the resources of individual talent.

Instead of generating new life, Eliot's lines rearranged the remains of lives past. The "failed" expectation of nothingness led him to exploit minimal forms of artistic exhaustion. The fragmented "many" had the best of the "one," and it has been the business of postmodernism to make "less" break down into myriad bits and pieces.[10] Jacques Barzun's words about decadence resonate: "The forms of art as of life seem exhausted, the stages of development have been run through. Institutions function painfully. Repetition and frustration are the intolerable result."[11]

John Barth's paradigmatic title, "The Literature of Exhaustion," published in 1967, popularized the idea that the "exhaustion of certain possibilities" need not be a source of despair as long as one plays up the "used-upness" of literary forms. The title, therefore, states a dominant condition. Literature has been worn out, even though parody and permutation can help us to keep on writing.[12] The O.E.D. tells us that exhaustion describes "the action or process of consuming or using up completely." As a transitional state, it is degenerative, but it is not terminal. Since it borders on the shift from physiology to pathology, exhaustion raises questions: how long can it go on before turning into either death or health? Instead of daring the unknown future, much art feeds on the saturation of what already exists. Amid layers of literary references, Barth writes that Borges plays up rereading: "A remarkable and original work of literature, the implicit theme of which is the difficulty, perhaps the unnecessity, of writing original works of literature. His artistic victory, if you like, is that he confronts an intellectual dead end and employs it against itself to accomplish new human work."[13] The mind preys on its own cultural decline[14] to justify activities that have made exhaustion prolific.[15] Perhaps the highest compliment Barth has paid to Borges is that he is "a technically up-to-date artist" who magnifies the "used-upness of certain forms of the felt exhaustion." Barth addresses concerns about the decay of matter vis-à-vis the growing popularity of manner. Hence he asks whether exhaustion applies to the tradition of rebellions or whether all those rebellions have exhausted tradition itself.

In a later essay, entitled "The Literature of Replenishment" (1979), Barth tells us that exhaustion yielded derivative forms of writing: "It is easier and more sociable to talk technique than it is to make art." As a result, "artistic conventions are liable to be retired, subverted, transcended, transformed, or even deployed against themselves." To avoid his own authorial demise, the American writer explains that he never meant to say that fiction is kaput. In fact, explicators, annotators, and allusion chasers set out "to mediate between the text and the reader." Postmodern writing is a kind of "pallid, last-ditch decadence, of no more than minor symptomatic interest."[16] Once it is assumed that everything has been written, emphasis falls on technique. Again, editing takes precedence over inventing.[17] The postmoderns favor recycling the incomplete, the overfull, and the improbable.[18] Exhaustion can foster scriptural practice in the intransitive province of the has-been, where the dead end of history has turned out to be a bottomless horn of plenty.

Barth is well aware that the postmodern tendency is to "write a fiction that is more and more about itself and its processes, less and less about objective reality and life in the world."[19] The exhaustion of ideological choices gave rise to techniques that have produced a derivative universe of bits and pieces. Having lost its teleological linearity, history has enriched its reservoir of available forms. Amid the referential culture of postmodernism, how favorable can any beginning be amid future-pasts, tainted restorations, disjunctions of all kinds, and posthumous echoes after the end of art? The utopian has yielded to the ruinous, which testifies to the disintegration of the past as well as to its endurance into the future. Wedged at the boundary between old and new, the ruinous resists "scraping" and "reinscription" alike. Paradoxically, used-upness has replenished exhaustion much as it has exhausted replenishment. We have not succumbed to the contradiction, but we have not been able to overcome it either. Across the arts, we have endured exhaustion by resorting to fragmentation and reduction, if not outright annihilation.

1

Looking back at eventful moments in the history of theatrical representation, Borges tried to visualize the instant when Aeschylus introduced a second character on stage; unity became plurality, and discourse proliferated to infinity. A prophetic spectator would have seen that a crowd of characters would follow in their footsteps: Hamlet and Faust and Segismundo and Macbeth and Peer Gynt and others our eyes cannot yet discern.[20] Two millennia after Aeschylus, Pirandello zeroed in on the crisis of playwrights no longer at ease with strong-willed characters. After him, Beckett took up the very demise of theatricality.[21] He contributed to the downfall of mimesis, the exhaustion of historical fulfillment, and the radical critique of humanist progress, which bent along a curve that favored backtracking. As a result, the endpoint turned into a circular cul-de-sac. Annihilation failed to reach its endpoint, and Beckett made nothingness prolific through techniques of stylistic and conceptual procrastination. What are we to gather from this?

Some of the answers can be found in Beckett's titles. Negativity becomes biological in *I Gave Up Before Birth* (Fizzle 4), a title that links the act of will to prebirth memory: "I gave up before birth, it is not possible otherwise, but birth there had to be, it was he, I was inside, that's how I see it . . . it was he who had a life, I didn't have a life, a life not worth having, because of me, he'll do himself to death. . . . He'll rot, I won't rot, there will be nothing of him left but bones, I'll be inside, nothing left but dust, I'll be inside."[22] This is yet another step toward the unpresentable, and the title suggests that language has stopped naming things and people. Accordingly, *Not I* (staged in September 1972, published in 1973) precedes I, who cannot avoid birth. The denial of identity is pinned to birth, which amounts to "just the birth cry to get her going." In a Beckettian sense, the title is hollowed out; the negative particle takes the identity of *I* out of existence. The nameless female speaker is identified through the female voice that plays the part, which is limited to the mouth alone. Without the rest of the body, Mouth cannot act. Instead, it narrates a mutilated story in which the speaking voice is a synecdoche of both I and Not I. From a narrative point of view, the titological ambiguity of the first person introduces an autobiography that, spoken in the third person, denies the first person. The title thus stands out as the *J'accuse* of a human condition that has led Mouth to confess that she has "no idea of what she was saying." She knows only that, perhaps twice a year, her mouth starts to speak, releasing an unbearable buzzing that she can neither explain nor understand: "now can't stop . . . can't stop the stream . . . and the whole brain begging . . . something begging in the brain . . . begging the mouth to stop." Toward the very end, however, the body seems to recover its limbs: "sitting and staring at her hand . . . there in her lap . . . palm upward . . . suddenly saw it wet . . . the palm . . . tears presumably . . . sat and watched them dry."[23] This image tells us that Mouth is a whole person sitting on a chair. But the audience cannot see her because only the mouth is illuminated on stage. From the one to the many, his later play, *What Where,* introduces four characters and a voice on stage. But only the voice reaches the end, which closes with an utterance at once spaceless and meaningless: "Make sense who may, I switch off!"[24]

Whereas utopian discourse thrives on the connectedness of language, Michel Foucault writes that heterotopias "desiccate speech, stop words in their tracks, contest the very possibility of language at its source; they dissolve our myths and sterilize the lyricism of our sentences."[25] Sterility is a word that captures the broader condition of Beckett's world, which is dominated by dead-end roads, rooms surrounded by a world of debris, dark stages about to disappear in shadow, and people sick, blind, deformed, and half-buried in urns, ashbins, or dirt. It is a world without a future, and it is up to the reader-spectator to fill in the gap between *I* and *Not I*, which spurs the playwright to vacillate between leaving out and not bringing in.[26] Rhetorically speaking, it has been argued that Mouth enforces the rhetoric of the "what-not."[27] It is a rhetoric of saying by not saying, which confirms that Beckett is prone to leaving out: physically, conceptually, scenically, and titologically. First and foremost, *Not I* is a title that points to the disintegration of meaning.

One more step, and we come to *Breath* (completed in 1966, published in 1969). In the key of Beckettian negativity, the last thing to do is to take a final *breath*, which is title, text, and performance. As such, breath refers to the physiology of life; in fact, it stands for life itself. The first breath begins life and the last ends it. Between these two points, breathing keeps us alive. Yet Beckett uses the noun *breath*, not the gerund *breathing*. Unlike the action of waiting, which allows Didi and Gogo to delay, the single breath is the first and the last. The noun makes no room for temporal expansion. Theatrically speaking, one ought to expect the kind of representation that has been reduced to a single fleeting moment. Because there is nothing else to say, the last breath exhales a voiceless speech that suggests an invisible presence.

The title is the play, and stage directions point to the last remnants of the mechanics of life. Accordingly, the opening cry is meant to yield a "slow increase of light for about ten seconds." After a lapse of five seconds, what follows is "expiration and slow decrease of light together reaching minimum together in about ten seconds." The cries must be identical; they record "the instant of recorded vagitus," which refers to the beginning of life. The human being who inhales and exhales is an infant who, born amid rubbish, takes a deep breath and does not let the sin of being born endure. E. M. Cioran believes that, as "we come closer to the Unbreathable," the only task left for man to perform is "unmaking" and "decreating." In *The Trouble with Being Born*, a titological commentary on *Breath*, the recurrent phrase "ever since I was born" becomes "unendurable."[28] If modernism announced the end of history, could postmodernism view the future as other than the very last gasp of the Western tradition?

In the theater of modernism, Beckett's *Breath* was the final curtain call for theatricality as we knew it. The idea of ontological progress had turned on itself, and failure acted out linguistic as well as physical dismemberment.[29]

In fact, much of Beckett's theatrical aesthetics pits action based on gestures without words against action based on words without gestures, especially the radio plays—from *Happy Days* to *Krapp's Last Tape*. Both undermine the presence of actors inasmuch as theatrical "mimesis" dematerializes under the protocol of what Martin Puchner has called "modernist anti-theatricalism."[30] Human presence breaks down into a limbless trunk (*Happy Days*), a mouth (*Not I*), or heads sticking out of urns (*Play*) and ashbins (*Endgame*). Beckett reduced single figures to their essential bareness in much the same way that Alberto Giacometti sculpted noses, heads, and legs before reducing the whole body to a skeletal presence. Giacometti, who designed the tree for the 1961 Paris production of *Waiting for Godot* (Fig. 12), also believed that failure is an artistic task: "The more you fail, the more successful you are."[31] Failure entails the denial of physical integrity, and what is left is a ghostly presence somehow equidistant from life and death.

However fragmented, theatricality remains anchored to human subjects. We can understand why Beckett found in Giacometti a lifelong friend and an artist equally committed to the representation of human figures. Alone at the center of the dehumanized space of *Endgame*, Hamm sits blindly, very much like some of the seated figures that Giacometti painted a few years before the

FIG. 12 Giacometti, *Annette*, "Portrait of Annette," 1950. © 2007 Artists Rights Society (ARS), New York / ADAGP, Paris.

play was staged. Images such as *Annette: Portrait of the Artist's Wife* (1954) embody human presence at the center of utter isolation. To borrow from Beckett, Giacometti's group of standing figures on the large bronze base known as *The Forest* (Figs. 13 and 14) ends up "never seeing never hearing one another. Never touching."³² In small spaces, sculptor and writer represent man's alienated condition in the starkest possible terms. For Sartre, who also befriended the sculptor, the space of traditional art is crowded with "too much." In Giacometti's group figures, one of which is buried up to his chest, space eats everything away because it "is a cancer on being."³³

The same can be said of Beckett's plays and prose, which present plenty of unhealthy people who tend to be autistic (Krapp), homicidal (Lemuel), sadistic (Hamm), and infanticidal (Rooney). Their illnesses betray their "hellish" state of being.³⁴ It seems that language, expression, and humanity have been revoked, and that what is left is the "thereness" of inert physicality. Beckett describes these bodies as "short of being" in *The Lost Ones*, where there are no names, no voices, and no stories.³⁵ Even the last bastion of human presence, the aimless gerund "waiting," has been stilled beyond the last shreds of language itself. One of those shreds is *Texts for Nothing*, a title that introduces a fragmentary reflection at the border of nothingness: "I'd like to be sure I left no stone unturned before reporting me missing and giving up."

FIG. 13 Giacometti, *The Forest, Seven Figures and a Head*, 1950. Kunsthaus, Zurich. © 2007 Artists Rights Society (ARS), New York / ADAGP, Paris.

Discourse steadily outlines the anatomy of nothingness: "I am far from that heap of flesh, rind, bones and bristles."[36] It is as if Beckett were uttering posthumous words from the "other side."[37] Beckett's late *How It Is* also begins in the mode of a final demise: "My life last state last version ill-said ill-heard ill-recaptured ill-murmured in the mud brief movements of the lower face losses everywhere." At the lowest level of a worm's-eye point of view, where we remember that the unnamable called himself "Worm," the "tongue gets clogged with mud."[38] The mud, voice, presence, and breath merge into shapes and gestures bound to solidify themselves into clay silhouettes, very much like Giacometti's bronze figures. Beckett hears "something dripping" (50) in his head, and Giacometti lets bronze drip, like melting wax, on the bones of human skeletons. Beckett's own tall, bony, gaunt figure could have been a model for a Giacometti figure.[39]

In 1949 Beckett wrote that his friend Bram van Velde had "gone" abstract because he no longer had a reality to paint. Like Kandinsky, Beckett asked

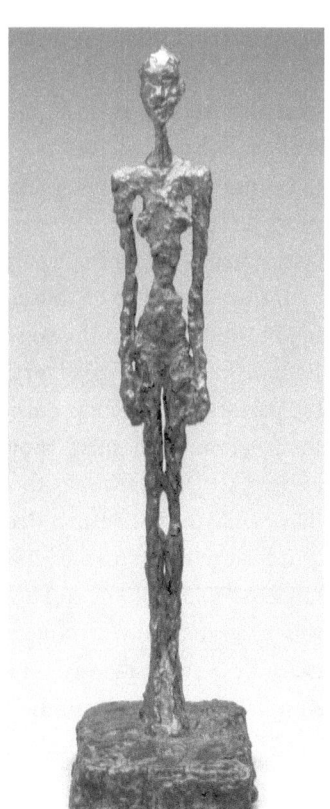

FIG. 14 Giacometti, *Femme debout* (*Standing Woman*), detail, 1956. Yale University Art Gallery, New Haven. Gift of Susan Morse Hilles. © 2007 Artists Rights Society (ARS), New York / ADAGP, Paris.

himself, "what is left of representation if the essence of the object is to disrobe itself of representation?"[40] The question, of course, was redundant, because most of Beckett's oeuvre is about "disrobing" by means of reduction and abstraction: "I have freed myself from certain formal concepts. Perhaps, like the composer Schoenberg or the painter Kandinsky, I have turned toward an abstract language."[41] In *Endgame,* the game of chess eliminates pieces from the board.[42] The same happens to characters on stage. Blindness moves Hamm to relinquish objects one after another, until there are neither biscuits nor painkillers to give away. Once Beckett staged *Breath,* many believed that theatricality had terminated itself once and for all. Yet Beckett considers abstraction a deficiency, and a title such as *Lessness* involves the unraveling of language in "blank planes sheer white eye calm," until "long last all gone from mind." As every figure disappears into lessness, what remains is a never-ending erasure.[43]

There is little doubt that we are bordering on the paradox of what has been called the end of art. Everyone has predicted it, but no one has acted in a way consistent with what "the end" calls for. At the edge of literary and theatrical disappearance, Beckett did not stop; at the edge of pictorial abstraction, Mondrian and Kandinsky did not quit either. Why? Prediction was everyone's business, but no one was willing to take the last step and fade into the sunset. Whereas the prefix *ri-* in *rinascita* (renaissance, rebirth) assumes the recovery of the distant past, the prefix *post-* in postmodernism upholds the continuity of the immediate past.

If the past was to be cancelled, then an altogether new future would spring up. But it did not. At the edge, everybody stopped and began to look around. Rather than forge ahead, artists and writers turned backward and revisited the past from unusual points of view. Instead of taking a decisive step toward the new, the modernists moved sideways toward the dead end of postmodernism, which gave the pathological a new lease on life. Some would suggest that, while the modernist Beckett ended up with nothingness, the postmoderns have gone no further. Italo Calvino put a cosmic spin on minimal expectations: "Everything space and time contains is no more than that little that was generated from nothingness, the little that is and that might very well not be, or be even smaller, even more meager and perishable."[44] This "little" is not so much physical as grammatical.

While the prose piece *The End* concedes that Beckett has told a story without "the courage to end or the strength to go on,"[45] a title such as *Texts for Nothing* proves that nothing itself can be quite a lot. Just as words gain meaning through associations with other words,[46] so do Beckett's titles gain semantic depth as they relate to one another. Thus *Texts for Nothing* links up to *The Lost Ones* and to *Lessness* in a kind of diminutive crescendo amid the ashes of worn-out signifieds.[47]

Beckett's titles often rely on diminuendos to introduce textual variations that stem from self-defeating efforts.[48] The musical analogy steers us toward John Cage, who toyed with minimal forms of musical composition. In "Cheap Imitation," Cage writes, "there are no climaxes, no harmonies, no counterpoints in which to hide one's lack of devotion"[49]—a Beckettian phrasing indeed! In spirit no less than in form, *Texts for Nothing* so echoes Cage's "Lecture on Nothing" (1949) that Vladimir could have spoken the opening phrases: "I am here, and there is nothing to say. If among you are those who wish to get somewhere, let them leave at any moment. What we require is silence; but what silence requires is that I go on talking . . . I have nothing to say and I am saying it and that is poetry as I need it." Repetition is as insistent as in Beckett's dialogues: "More and more I have the feeling that we are getting nowhere. Slowly as the talk goes on we are getting nowhere."[50]

Written ten years later, the title of Cage's "Lecture on Something" (1959) suggests minimal improvement: "This is a talk about something and naturally also a talk about nothing. About how something and nothing are not opposed to each other but meet each other to keep on going."[51] This passage could be part of *Waiting for Godot,* especially when we read, some pages later, that "the grand thing about the human mind is that it can turn its own tables and see meaninglessness as ultimate meaning." Cage wrote this piece for unfortunate human beings—"lame, blind, stupid, schizoid, or poverty-stricken"—as marginal as Beckett's tramps.[52]

Beckett knew that he was testing language no less than thought, writing in *The Unnamable,* "But what then is the subject? . . . Bah, any old pronoun will do, provided one sees through it. Matter of habit."[53] The subject of *The Unnamable* is either eliminated or left unmentioned. In fact, it is a voice without a body. Beyond it, Beckett borders on "inexistence," which occurs when the words slow down and "the subject dies before it comes to the verb." The rhetorical device of posing questions for which there are no answers still allows writing to unfold. And unfold it does, through the verbal forms of "unquestioning" and "unbelieving." As we shift from title to text, we are not encouraged to raise the most "unnamable" of questions: "Why?" Instead of probing into metaphysical matters of first causes or Promethean will, Beckett takes existence as is, which is just about the worst thing humankind could be burdened with. The inference is that the title points to the death of the author and of textuality.[54]

2

One way to accommodate the demise of any linear future was to revisit the past in the mode of what Robert Cowley calls the counterfactual history of "what if?" This is the title of a collection of essays that considers what the Western tradition would have been[55] "had a Locrian horseman ridden down Socrates that late November afternoon" of 424 B.C. at Delium.[56] Things might have been different, Borges imagined, if two afternoons were erased from history, "that of the hemlock, that of the Cross." The conditional tense adds virtual grounds to the concluded past, which has become a hypothetical future-past. The title of Borges's *Things That Might Have Been* lets the past offer alternatives that Octavio Paz anchors to the postmodern "twilight of the future."[57] Nowadays the issue is not what happened in history but what we can do with it as a subject of artistic fiction. Anyone can partake of the ongoing process of literary construction and deconstruction, because anachronism has set it free. Fiction bridges spatial and temporal gaps, favoring synchronicity over sequence. Wallace Stevens spelled out the overarching principle: "The final belief is to believe in fiction, which you know to be a fiction, there being nothing else. The exquisite truth is to know that it is a fiction and that you believe in it willingly."[58] To maintain some kind of loose and yet inclusive unity, artists assembled composite forms of art that recycled bits and pieces of the past. Artificial arrangement displaced mimetic representation. At the dawn of the twentieth century, the production of art that quoted art moved to center stage, where the artistic product encompassed parts large and small from unlikely sources. Anomaly as variety and plurality as accumulation fostered techniques of assemblage, which best describes much of this age of pluralism after relativism. The art of assemblage can pillage fiction and reality as well as normality and abnormality by means of pastiche, installation, happening, collage, and bricolage.[59]

Pastiche, which makes something new out of old stuff, derives from the Italian *pasticcio*, which describes a hodgepodge of meat, eggs, vegetables, and other variable ingredients. As a genre of painting, the dictionary definition of *pasticcio* refers to a *pittore eclettico che dipinge con tecniche e stili diversi*, an eclectic painter who resorts to diverse techniques and styles (especially those of the great masters).⁶⁰ In modernist literature, Joyce called the corrected galleys of his master novel "mosaics," an assemblage-based technique that turned him into a "scissors and paste man."⁶¹ Materials taken from other texts were rearranged in *Finnigans Wake*.⁶² In our own time, Carlo Gadda popularized *pasticcio* in a title that spells out the word itself (in the Roman dialect), *Quer pasticciaccio brutto de Via Merulana* (*That Awful Mess on Via Merulana*, 1975). The novel is famous for its mixture of different languages: learned, common, popular, and hybrid lexicons that echo Pulci,⁶³ Folengo, and Rabelais.⁶⁴

Eclecticism so attracted Calvino that he quoted Gadda at the beginning of his study on the diversity of human beings: "Who are we, who is each one of us, if not a *combinatoria* of experiences, information, books we have read, things imagined? Each life is an encyclopedia, a library, an inventory of objects, a series of styles, and everything can be constantly shuffled and reordered in every way conceivable."⁶⁵ Combinatorial techniques fall back on macaronic literature and the classical no less than on the medieval tradition of *centoni*, poems constructed with pieces—usually one hundred (*cento*)— that poets borrowed from other poets. In his commentary on the unity of *Don Quixote*, Vladimir Nabokov uses the image of a "meat pie" that mixes together heterogeneous ingredients.⁶⁶

Umberto Eco put his own approach to pastiche in the form of reminiscences: "I was beginning to write those parodies and pastiches that later would become *Diario minimo*. Influenced by what? Perhaps the strongest influence there was Proust's *Pastiches et mélanges,* so much so that when *Diario minimo* came out in French I chose the title *Pastiches et postiches*. But I recall that when I later published *Diario minimo,* in 1963, I thought of giving it a title that alluded to a title of Vittorini's, *Piccola borghesia,* except that I would have liked to change the title to *Piccola Borges-ia*. The point of this, then, is to explain how a network of influences and echoes began to come into play."⁶⁷ In an equally lighthearted vein, Arthur C. Danto has coined the portmanteau term "artphilohistocritisophory" to describe the collaborative effort of "art makers, art historians, teachers, philosophers, and critics of art" who are "interlocked in one another's activities."⁶⁸ Rolling together gastronomy with scholarship, a recent text has offered the following recipe: "Modernism is about finding out how much you can get away with leaving out. Postmodernism is about how much you can get away with putting in."⁶⁹ Considering the ingredients, the overstuffed menu of present-day pastiches has been palatable beyond expectations.⁷⁰

Playfulness belies the unnerving complexity of a culture in which referentiality absorbs mimesis and irony borders on the ridiculous. For Jacques Derrida, every linguistic or nonlinguistic sign "can be *cited,* put between quotation marks; in so doing it can break with every given context, engendering an infinity of new contexts."[71] In fact, he "can do nothing more than cite."[72] If grammatology is the theory of writing as citation, pastiche is its technique, which often consists of parasitic *grafting.* Classical citations spur the progress of history, whereas postmodern quotations recycle the has-been.[73] Complacency has led many to utter: "I quote, therefore I am"; misquoting, however, makes the postmoderns at heart feel even better.

3

Assemblage recycles what is there instead of daring the new. It was thus inevitable that the "practice" of art about art would run out of steam. To the postmodern, even the "torn" piece is a fragment on its way to becoming either refuse or ruin. In Yves Bonnefoy's poem, *L'imperfection est la cime* (*Imperfection Is the Summit*), the title makes it desirable to equate imperfection with destruction:

> There was this:
> You had to destroy, destroy, destroy.
> There was this:
> Salvation is only found at such a price.
>
> You had to
> Ruin the naked face that rises in the marble,
> Hammer at every beauty every form,
>
> Love perfection because it is the threshold
> But deny it once known, once dead forget it,
>
> Imperfection is the summit.[74]

In the arts at large, twentieth-century New York became what Paris had been a century earlier. The Triestine art dealer Leo Castelli understood all that and opened shop in Manhattan. Mindful of Julius II's patronage of the "divine" Raphael and Michelangelo, the patron-businessman found his own blue-collar divinities: Robert Rauschenberg and Jasper Johns. New York, of course, was not Rome. Elitism had to give way to more democratic, though not populist, stands. Cunningly as well as ostentatiously, Andy Warhol scaled down matters of privileged inheritance to the practical level of popular culture and artistic production: "You look around and see what the second-rate artists are doing, and then you do the same thing, but better."[75] Such a commonsense paradigm allowed artists to feel at ease in the imperfect world of everyday reality, where second-rate models of imitation made emulation more feasible.

The imperfect moment, the imperfect gesture, and the imperfect deed led Wallace Stevens to write:

> Perhaps there are times of inherent excellence,
>
> As when the cock crows on the left and all
> Is well, incalculable balances,
> At which a kind of Swiss perfection comes
>
> And a familiar music of the machine
> Sets up its Schwärmerei, not balances
> That we achieve but balances that happen.[76]

"Perhaps" is conditional as well as retrospective; the inference is that times of inherent excellence are long gone. Knowledge draws sustenance from forecasts about a future language of particles,[77] semantic negativity, and epistemological nihilism.[78] To borrow from Jean Baudrillard, people "are subletting the leftovers of the strong ideas of the beginning of the century. Perhaps a culture is obliged to go through a process of garbage disposal."[79] From textual narrative to urban sanitation, we are asked to "imagine entire towns put together not from the waste of what has already served a purpose" but of things that were waste "from the outset."[80] Debris and ruins became highly metaphorical once they crossed paths with the ruinous architectures of discourse, tradition, and authority.

Once Borges conceded that memory itself had become "a garbage heap,"[81] the stage was set for the proliferation of refuse. A titological development could be traced from Eliot's *The Waste Land* to A. R. Ammons's *Garbage* (1993), a title that introduces urban sanitation:

> Garbage has to be the poem of our time because
> Garbage is spiritual, believable enough.[82]

Marginality has been moving toward center stage:

> And garbage keep alive, offering to the gods
> Of garbage, of retribution, of realistic
>
> Expectation, the deities of unpleasant
> Necessities: refined, young earthworms ... (8)

Refuse generates its own mythology of hellish deities who preside over necessity rather than vision. In a world where health has yielded to sickness, the American poet rephrased Eliot's "future futureless":

> I have seen the future; it just went by, put
> Away: it advertises strokes, hip replacements,
>
> Insulin shots, sphygmomanometers or digital
> Punches: there is an end to delays and
>
> Remedies, regimens, and rehabs; another
> Pathology interrupts following on pathology. (46)

Pathology is physical as well as intellectual, and the poet finds that writing itself generates garbage:

> A waste of words, a flattened-down, smoothed-
> over mesa of styrofoam verbiage; since words were
>
> introduced here things have gone poorly for the
> planet: it's been between words and rivers ... (74)

In the dead end, refuse is bound to engulf us. The wasteland and the dead end outline a nightmarish landscape in which garbage does not go away. Instead, it piles up things no less than titles. We may have reached a point where the junkyard is everyone's backyard, which is gaining on the front lawn.

What is happening now is that we are rescuing to the life of art what reality has relegated to the dumpster. The used up is being recycled beyond used-upness itself. The result is sometimes funny, sometimes ironic, and often mesmerizing. To keep our critical bearings, the opening statement of as emblematic a critical title as *Rubbish* is worth quoting: "Most of us have been at a gallery exhibition where someone is heard to remark, 'That artwork is a piece of garbage.' The remark is a metaphor—and a verdict. But in the late twentieth century it increasingly became possible to make the same remark and to mean it literally. Garbage art—pieces of colorful, creative eclecticism and beauty constructed out of what would otherwise have been thrown away—is today the forefront of the avant-garde art world."[83] Indeed, a whole literature about refuse has developed. There is "Garbage Land," and lifetimes spent in the pursuit of "Garbology," which has spawned the "Archaeology of Garbage." The rhetoric of excess went over the top when Larry Fuentes created a fantastic collage of "found garbage" that appeared on the front cover of *National Geographic*. Even as distinguished a publisher as Harry H. Abrams has printed a volume called *Recycled, Reseen: Folk Art from the Global Scrap Heap* for the Museum of International Folk Art in Santa Fe.

I would suggest that *The Waste Land* stands in equipoise with *Garbage*. One lays out the modernist framework, and the other fills it up with postmodern contents. "Post," after all, tells us that time has had "plenty of time" to amass garbage. The current preference for ashbins, junkyards, and dumpsters also tells us that "land" defines a cityscape filled with refuse—industrial no less than artistic. The past has been revisited in different ways. Each time, memory has filled the distance between tradition and individual talent with the ruinous aftermath of modern representations, their modernist wreckage, and postmodern rearrangements. As a result, *Garbage* takes up physical as well as ideological refuse. The closing lines set the Renaissance inheritance against its belated disintegration:

  Nonrepresentation is a representation
Of nonrepresentation: things are awash in

Ideality: ideal meaninglessness, ideal absurdity,
Ideal ideals: we want to know the reality of

These perfectly, ideally, as themselves: poems
That give up the ideal of making sense do not

Give up the ideal of not making sense: nom de
Plumage best feathers a nest egg, ivory doorknob. (89)

While much of the scaffolding of Western culture has collapsed, negativity feeds on itself. As we all know, garbage has piled up on both coasts of the Atlantic Ocean, a condition that offers graphic evidence of the common heritage that binds London and Dublin to Boston and New York.

In the matter of postmodern spaces, the title of Calvino's *Invisible Cities* conjures up geographies of the mind in which the nightmarish overshadows the laudatory. Beyond the wasteland, Calvino ventures into enclaves lost to dehumanized conditions of life. One tale raises the problem, fabulous in the story but apparent in our midst, of what to do with waste. The more talent makes new materials in Leonia, the more rubbish resists "fermentations and combustions. Heaps of leftovers surround the city on every side, like a chain of mountains."[84] Geography has become mental; its territory begins and ends within the printed pages of ominous forecasts. The natural image is at once plausible and haunting. From textual narratives to urban sanitation, the disposal of waste has tested human ingenuity.

Ruins are a presence, but waste is a problem. Both are the aftermath of technological processes that we cannot quite control. Loss of control dates to the aftermath of World War II, when the poetry of Czselaw Milosz revealed a petrified reality of destruction around a library in Warsaw (1941). The title of his poem, *A Book in the Ruins* (1941), draws together literature, refuse, and ruins:

> Pages of books lying
> Scattered at your feet are like fern-leaves hiding
> A moldy skeleton, or else fossils
> Whitened by the secrets of Jurassic shells.
> A remnant life so ancient and unknown
> Compels a scientist, tilting a stone
> Into the light, to wonder. He can't know
> Whether it is some dead epoch's shadow
> Or a living form.[85]

Much debris accumulated, and measures were taken for recycling the incomplete and the overfull. The war ended, but the refuse endured, especially in the hearts and minds of those who experienced, or were told about, carpet-bombing and nuclear explosions.

The culture of postmodernism has withstood a maelstrom of world conflicts and political terrorism.[86] All have affected our living space, where compression into the "dead end" has forced everything to mix with, or crush into, everything else. The grand narrative has crumbled into a heap of ruins, and we often look back on the second millennium from a posthumous point of view that favors ruins over foundations.

Walter Benjamin linked the ruinous to the very unfolding of human experience when he identified Paul Klee's *Angelus Novus* with the angel of history. After the ruins of World War I and before the even worse devastations of World War II, the destructive storm of progress propelled the angel "into the future to which his back is turned, while the pile of debris before him grows skyward."[87] The angel could barely keep a step ahead of the cultural debris of a spent tradition. Benjamin made that prediction before taking his own life as the Nazis invaded France. After his death by the Spanish border, the Holocaust, atomic explosions, and genocide have tested the idea of progress as a process of amelioration.

Benjamin's reference to the debris of human experience about to overtake the angel of history was symbolic of modernist horrors, which eventually gave way to parodies in the postmodern cul-de-sac. The very idea of the angel as a carrier of providential narratives has lost credibility. For Joyce, history is a nightmare; for E. M. Cioran, even the rare periods of serenity are a "brilliant nightmare." The overarching lesson teaches us that, "like tragedy, history resolves nothing, because there is nothing to resolve. It is always by failure that we study the future."[88] Lack of resolution cannot but foster the proliferation of debris. For Giorgio Agamben, "the angel of history, whose wings became caught in the storm of progress, and the angel of aesthetics, who stares in an a-temporal dimension at the ruins of the past, are inseparable."[89] It would seem that the historical experience of the past several decades has proved him right. We are making the ruinous so familiar that, when terrorism strikes, we almost take it in stride. We simulate ruinous anomalies while reality delivers deadly blows that produce real ruins. What else could we expect in the dead end of history?

At present, nuclear waste has become the subject of literary meditations as well as a problem for big business. The central metaphor of waste takes us to Don DeLillo's *Underworld* (1997), in which Jesse Detwiler, a waste trader, believes that garbage compels people to deal with it by mastering organization, science, and technology.[90] Nowadays, nuclear waste disposal firms can "pick up waste anywhere in the world, ship it to Kazakhstan, put it in the ground and vaporize it." Within the broader sweep of history, refuse thrives on the "twin-theme" of weapons and waste, which is "the secret history, the underhistory, the way archaeologists dig out the history of earlier cultures." Hence "the fusion of two streams of history, weapons and waste."[91]

The wasteland did not end modernism; instead, it expanded into postmodernism. If modernism was born as a wasteland that announced the end of history, could postmodernism not look just as wasteful? At once psychological and epistemological, such an impasse has made ruins ever more relevant to our experience of art, which has taken in the waste of industrialization as well as the debris of consumerism. This also means that the symbolism of the junkyard relishes the past and accepts the future only insofar as it will replenish junkyard "holdings" with ruins in the making. Nowadays, waste has become a form of production, and society finds it ever more difficult to get rid of all that it throws away. Ruins take up space, and waste pollutes the environment, engulfing rural and urban areas alike.

Needless to say, manmade wastage as ruin abounds in our global culture of ideological diversity, economic excess, and political terrorism. After the 1996 explosion of bombs in London's Docklands and the Oklahoma City bombing, the threat of terrorism made new demands on urban planning, which called for the creation of "security" architecture. Those events were preambles to the suicide mission that leveled the Twin Towers of the World Trade Center in New York City. For Jean Baudrillard, the Twin Towers ended the competitive dialogue among skyscrapers. By projecting "the idea of the model that they are one for the other," the Twin Towers exemplified "a vertigo of duplication." In his own "Cloning Story," Baudrillard writes, "The clone is the first born from a single cell of a single individual, his 'father,' the sole progenitor, of which he would be the exact replica, the perfect twin, the double." When the double materializes, "it signifies imminent death."[92] Superstition adds that, should we ever cross paths with someone who looks exactly like us, we would be staring at death. Since they were built, therefore, the two skyscrapers faced each other's death, which came to be on September 11, 2001. It is a matter of bitter irony that, for different reasons, Minoru Yamasaki has seen two of his major projects destroyed. One, the Pruitt-Igoe Public Housing Project, marked the beginning of postmodernism when it was blown up at 3:32 P.M. on July 15, 1972.[93] Did the Twin Towers mark its end, or the beginning of something else?

Baudrillard has made the connection between waste and belatedness central to what he calls "garbage-can sociology." Concern with the excesses of consumption has led him to consider waste "a kind of madness, of insanity, of instinctual dysfunction."[94] All that remains to be done is to play with "the vestiges of what has been destroyed. This is why we are 'post': history has stopped, one is in a kind of post-history which is without meaning."[95] The idea of a posthistory without meaning takes us to the denial of ideology as well as of aesthetics, which foregrounds a dreadful hypothesis. Since we have become accomplished at deconstructing beginning, end, and much of everything in between, we must ask: what are we to expect from an aftermath

FIG. 15   The Destruction of the Pruitt-Igoe Public Housing Project in Saint Louis, 1972. *The Saint Louis Dispatch.*

FIG. 16   The Destruction of the World Trade Center, September 11, 2001. *The New York Daily News.*

littered with so much debris? Yet reality itself denies utter skepticism. Urban nightmares have become matters of everyday life, but our postindustrial culture has shown resilience. So far, it can rebuild faster than anyone can destroy. Even the immense debris in the Lower West Side of Manhattan has been cleared, and reconstruction is under way. It seems that, for the time being, "postness" is all that we have, and the next section of this study will show that much is being made of it.

Once historical continuities turned into a disjointed array of materials, reality was crowded with broken images, which made birth itself unimaginable.[96] Having lost semantic integrity, the old and the new have been reused and misused. The wasteland is closing in on us, and neither Eliot nor Baudrillard has offered leads that may steer us out of it. The best they could do was to make our posthistorical condition somewhat bearable, first by using myth to offer relief and then by using simulation to provide distractions.

4

In the realm of everyday superficiality, Michelangelo Pistoletto went to work under the aegis of *arte povera* (poor art). By combining the plaster cast of a classical Venus with a heap of rags, Pistoletto gave us *Venere degli stracci* (*Venus of the Rags,* 1967) (Fig. 17). The title is parodic, for it turns the classical goddess into the deity of refuse. To Robert Rauschenberg's utmost satisfaction, this multimedia ensemble pits the artistic against the conceptual. To begin with, the classical nude is a plaster reproduction that viewers see from the back. Its whiteness clashes with the multicolored pile of worn-out clothes. The "ruined" or "used-up" clothes refer to the immediate past. The statue, by contrast, seems to have walked a long way out of antiquity before reaching a pile of rags with which she might cover herself. Conversely, one could look at the pile of rags as the debris of history about to overtake the "classical" angel of history. Ambiguity is pervasive.

The coexistence of as material a reality as rags with an artificial plaster cast of a classical statue may appear frivolous at first. Yet it is as representative a hybrid as one could find for illustrating a paradigm shift in the aesthetics of the West, which finally traded mimesis for simulation. In this study, which takes us from dawn to decadence, simulation, either overtly or covertly, has been there throughout. At dawn it played a minor role vis-à-vis mimesis. At dusk the relationship has been reversed, and simulation has become predominant.

Amid texts that bear kindred titles, it suffices to mention the sixteenth-century *Apologia della menzogna* (*The Apology of Deception*) by Giuseppe Battista, who maintains that "even though things disparage the lie, the lie is to be found in everything."[97] To appear and to hide mean to feign and to counterfeit, which are grammatical variants of simulation. The paradigmatic title for postmoderns is Torquato Accetto's *Della dissimulazione onesta* (1641): "Dissimulation is a practice which aims at hiding things as they are. One simulates that which is not; just as one dissimulates that which is."[98] Of course, what was marginal during the Renaissance was bound to become central thereafter.

Centuries later, Oscar Wilde's *Decay of Lying* did a lot to popularize the idea that nature imitates art, before Giorgio Manganelli followed suit and wrote *La letteratura come menzogna* (*Literature as Deception*). For the Italian writer, "the literary work is an artifice," which contains, "ad infinitum, other artifacts."[99] A character in Italo Calvino's *If on a Winter's Night a Traveler* imagines a literature made entirely of "false attributions, of imitations and counterfeits and pastiches." In a faraway country, "everything that can be falsified has been falsified: paintings in Museums, gold ingots, bus tickets." From prediction to practice, "mystification for mystification's sake" has become ever more popular.[100]

FIG. 17   Michelangelo Pistoletto, *Venere degli stracci* (*Venus of the Rags*), 1967. Hirshhorn Museum and Sculpture Garden, Smithsonian Institution, Joseph H. Hirshorn Bequest Fund, 1999. Washington, D.C.

Baudrillard, the master topographer of the postmodern *Simulacra and Simulation,* echoes this thought: "To dissimulate is to feign to have what one has. To simulate is to feign to have what one hasn't. One implies a presence, the other an absence."[101] Beyond the demise of the Aristotelian mimesis of reality, Baudrillard calls "simulacra" those art forms that represent previous art forms. Lodged as they are in archives, museums, libraries, and computer stations, simulacra take it for granted that artifice is an integral component of any definition of reality. Artifice "is in no way concerned with what *generates,* merely with what *alters,* reality. Artifice is the power of illusion."[102] In fact, "Things disappear through proliferation or contamination, by becoming saturated or transparent, because of extenuation or extermination, or as a result of the epidemic of simulation, as a result of their transfer into the secondary existence of simulation."[103] Since simulation gives meaning to "represented" reality, the effect is one of ontological ambivalence.[104] The real no longer is as real as it used to be.[105]

Although it may be difficult to see what will come out of the debris of the wasteland after *The Waste Land,* the fact is that postmodernism has gained a position of social and cultural prominence. The present state of experimentation is not one that we can compare directly to previous turning points along the cyclic recurrence of classical and romantic, or renaissance and baroque. At the end of the twentieth century, Jean Baudrillard began to realize that the modernist endpoint had been expanding right under his feet. In fact, he understood that the endpoint had become a curve that twisted itself into a circular loop in which everything is tossed around. The French sociologist has thus asked us to visualize the postmodern dead end as a "concave" cul-de-sac where things neither stop nor vanish.[106] Instead, they circulate. As A. R. Ammons puts it:

> I look for the way
> Things will turn
> Out spiraling from a center
>
> For that point in the periphery where
> Salience bends into curve
> And all saliences bend to the same angle of
>
> Curve and curve becomes curve, one curve, the whole curve[107]

For a while now, cultural developments have been thriving on the retrospective grounds of the familiar future-past, which has recycled writing under the aegis of the "always-already." The decline of the West has turned back on itself, so that plots, themes, and motifs mix everything with everything else.

A title such as *The Illusion of the End* (1994) is most appropriate for a book in which Baudrillard insists that the end is elusive: "We shall not be spared the worst—that is, *History will not come to an end*—since the leftovers, all the leftovers—the Church, communism, ethnic groups, conflicts, ideologies—are indefinitely recyclable.... History has only wrenched itself from cyclical time to fall into the order of the recyclable." In the Euclidean space of history, "the shortest path between two points is the straight line." In our non-Euclidean *fin de siècle,* space is a curvature that "unfailingly deflects all trajectories." Anachronistic forms are ready to reemerge, "intact and timeless, like the viruses deep in the body." It seems that the gravitational time-space of history is as curved as cosmic space: "By this retroversion of history to infinity, this hyperbolic curvature, the century itself is escaping its end."[108] Ontological and teleological questions about "why" and "what" have made room for procedural matters about "how" to take advantage of circularity by rearranging and recycling whatever was shored up in the postmodern dead end.

Since it does not lead to disappearance, Baudrillard goes on, circularity fosters a dispersal that bounces back once it hits the curved perimeter: "Nothing (not even God) now disappears by coming to an end, by dying. Instead, things disappear through proliferation or contamination."[109] If we take modernism as the culmination of the Western tradition, it follows that postmodernism describes its aftermath, which thrives on retention as well as on regression. Paradoxically, the prefix *post-* in postmodernism is introductory rather than conclusive. By signaling that something "followed" modernism, *post-* suggests an end that failed to materialize. It is there that procrastination makes the best of exhaustion and replenishment. As a result, belatedness has gained a life-giving permanence, for we live in the postmodern *dead end* after the modernist *end.*[110]

5

To quote a popular title, Robert Hughes's *The Shock of the New* (1981) brings to the fore twentieth-century artists who have revisited the past from unusual points of view. For Hughes, much of the new is shocking because it has turned the future into hybrid rearrangements of the past, and the last chapter of the book is appropriately entitled "The Future That Was." Since the future already has a history, the challenge of the new does not probe the limits of the unknown. Instead, it resorts to stylistic manipulations that give a new look to what surrounds us. Hughes complains that, by 1975, "all the isms were wasms."[111] However exhausted, the "wasms" are still with us, and they consist of exhausted aftermaths. The twentieth century dawned under the auspices of an entrenched dedication to the heritage of Naturalism and the Victorian age. What followed, however, was a precipitous dive into shallow waters, where the injuries of World War I did not heal and rescue was not attempted. Out to sea, modernism hung for dear life to the floating debris of the prefix *post-*, which, as postmodernism, rode the waves at the periphery of everything: undrowned, undead, and yet bound to remain a mass of wreckage far from any shore.

Whereas the Renaissance invented the future as a utopian vision of the present, we now invent the future as a parodic variant of the past. We have increased the output of studies on the subject of futurity, but in the strange guise of a snake that bites its own tail.[112] The "failed" end has yielded its aftermath. Circularity has rearranged literary and artistic leftovers in the heterogeneous world of kitsch, pop art, and their afterglow.[113] In other words, circularity has energized circulation, which Borges lodged in the inclusive spaces of libraries and archives. The humanist *studiolo*, an intimate little room, has given way to the library of Babel, whose geometric chambers have multiplied to the point of containing the universe itself.

POSTMODERN

9

"La biblioteca de Babel":
The Archititle in a Library of Titles

Is there a narrative beyond the Archive? Do archival fictions give
way to new kinds of narratives that announce a new masterstory?
—ROBERTO GONZÁLES ECHEVARRÍA

Between Callimachus in Alexandria and Borges in Buenos Aires, writers, librarians, and writer-librarians took books out to the desert with Jerome, on windy highland roads with Don Quixote, and into long winter nights with Calvino and his "traveling" readership. Since the invention of printing, book knowledge has gravitated around a walled-in universe of written sources and literary references. A single bookshelf makes it possible for writers and readers to undertake the longest journeys out in space and back in time without leaving the comfort of their study. The great explorers of the Renaissance were Petrarch and Erasmus no less than Columbus and Magellan. It is perhaps ironic that Fernando Colón, Columbus's illegitimate son, became a librarian in Seville, where his own library numbered sixteen thousand volumes. His goal was to assemble all the texts ever published inside and outside Christendom, so that the library's expansion would be commensurate with that of Charles V's vast empire. The older Colón's reading of maps stood next to the younger Colón's maps of reading.[1] The collection of books has so stretched the perimeter of the library that the world of books has taken in much of reality itself. Nowadays, literary maps of the imagination are sheltered within the pages of books that at once rely on the comfort of precedent and offer the challenge of novelty.

There is little doubt that the library embodies a recurrent theme that has contributed to the emergence of what Gérard Genette has called *architexts*. A case in point is Torquato Tasso's *Jerusalem Delivered,* which recalls the *Aeneid,* which recalls the *Odyssey*, which recalls the *Iliad*. The Christian epic divulges a kind of generic memory that profiles architexts.[2] Put differently, José Ortega y Gasset wrote in his *Meditations on Don Quixote* (1914) that every epoch contains palimpsests of the *Iliad*, just as *Don Quixote* is embedded in every novel. Texts such as the *Odyssey* and *Don Quixote* are synoptic nutshells of literary production.[3] I submit that the same could be said about titles whose significance and influence allow us to call them "archititles."

The year 1922 was eventful for the novelist (Joyce) and the poet (Eliot), as well as for the philosopher, Ludwig Wittgenstein. His *Tractatus-Logico-Philosophicus* left no doubt that "the limits of my language means the limits of my world." Language does not comment on reality; instead, reality itself has been absorbed by language, which "is not contiguous with anything else."[4] In the physical form of printed pages, reality is contained in the library, the repository of recorded language. By combining antithetical structures, Borges created a postmodern archititle when he wrote "La biblioteca de Babel" (1941), which stacked up bricks and books in one of the most emblematic spaces of contemporary epistemology. In order to accommodate scriptural forms of human expression, "The Library of Babel" consists of endless aisles that house tomes whose contents fill to capacity a book-bound enclave where understanding the unknown and discovering the new have given way to the logistics of an indexical approach to knowledge. Rooms cluster into hexagons that multiply throughout. At the end of a canyon-like corridor, a mirror "faithfully duplicates all appearances." The literary builder has imagined ways of incorporating bookstores, catalogues, indexes, *Wunderkammern, studiolis,* and manuscripts in a library as immense as the universe itself.

At the heart of "The Library of Babel" there exists a mythical connection between the library, where books and languages are ordered, and the Tower of Babel, where linguistic confusion and intellectual disorder reign supreme. On pictorial grounds, the assonance between Babel and Babylon is rooted in myth, for both are architectural wonders. As the queen city of Mesopotamia, Babylon was one of the seven wonders of the world. Unlike the other six, however, Babylon quickly reached the legendary status of a fabulous place; people talked about it but did not necessarily visit it. However real in time and space, Babylon could have been one of Calvino's invisible cities of the imagination. Its architectural and botanical marvels began to decline when it was destroyed by the Persian king Darius. Nevertheless, it recovered and grew into a commercial center that was conquered two centuries later by Alexander the Great, who died there on June 13, 33 B.C. Among its ruins, only a little hamlet was left standing; its name was Babil. At the southern edge of the city stood the temple of Marduk. The traditional location of the Tower of Babel was near this temple, and Nimrod was in charge of its construction.

Pieter Brueghel the Elder painted two versions of the tower, *The Small Tower* (1554–55) and *The Big Tower* (1563–64) (Figs. 18 and 19). The basic round plan with arches follows the design of the Colosseum. The gigantic space occupied by the Roman stadium was the obvious model for the equally gigantic tower. Destruction at the top does not affect the rest of the bastion, which is anchored solidly to the ground. The tower seems to be perfectly integrated into the city and its workforce. In a version by another Flemish artist, the *Tower of Babel* (1587) (Fig. 20), the tower is set in an urban enclave, and only the very top shows damage. A fourth illustration, by Frans Francken at the beginning of the seventeenth century (Fig. 21), puts the tower in the distant background, while a group of architects explains construction plans to Nimrod. Since the tower is already damaged, the inference is that punishment has already been delivered; yet construction goes on, because human will and technological knowledge have been preserved.[5]

All of these images of the Tower of Babel pay homage to destruction as well as to resistance. Although the top has suffered damage, much of what has been constructed still stands. The technological know-how has not been lost, and symbolism is somehow split between ruins and shelter. The vertical tower was conceived in a spirit of unrestrained ambition, which tested the limitations that God, Nature, Fate, and Fortune had placed on human ingenuity. The tower's "incomplete" height upheld a physical measure of human pride, and the ruined top warned of the punishment that would follow defiance. At a more constructive level, the library lays out the horizontal space of the inventory, which is conceived in a spirit of conservation. This odd juxtaposition brings up a significant aspect of modern culture. While the mythical tower sets up a bird's-eye point of view on the outside world, the historical library shields the products of human ingenuity from external threats. For the longest time, libraries were birthplaces not of invention but of conservation; they treasured "the written" by insulating intellectual accomplishments from the disturbances of life in the making.

An ideal list of a library's VIPs would include Socrates, Augustine, Petrarch, Montaigne, Flaubert, Eliot, and Borges, to name just a few. The Tower of Babel, by contrast, would give precedence to Faust and Frankenstein, with Paul Valéry shuttling between the two. Having tested myth and experience alike, these characters tell us that the human task is to test the range of learning

FIG. 18 Pieter Brueghel the Elder, *The Small Tower*, 1563. Kunsthistorisches Museum, Vienna.

FIG. 19 Pieter Brueghel the Elder, *The Big Tower*, 1568. Museum Boymans van Beuningen, Rotterdam.

FIG. 20   Lucas van Valckenborgh, *The Tower of Babel*, 1594. Louvre, Paris.

FIG. 21   Frans Francken II, *The Construction of the Tower of Babel*, 1620. Museo de Santa Cruz, Toledo, Spain.

and the possibilities of invention. If mimesis fosters an imagistic imagination,[6] the library falls back on a linguistic imagination that favors rhetorical constructions.[7]

In myth, the Tower of Babel crumbled, and some believe this was good, because its fall allowed the vitality of different cultures to thrive. For Umberto Eco, "the 'Babel' effect"[8] renders words unstable and sources ex-centric. Likewise, the dictionary tells us that *babélien, babélique, babéliser, debabélisation* are linguistic markers that spell out confusion.[9] From the space of paper to that of myth, Eco imagines a conversation that takes place between the banks of the Tigris and the Euphrates rivers, where the future of computer languages is discussed. Egyptians and Chaldeans are mentioned as being on the cusp of breakthroughs. Nimrod, however, prefers "a dwarf-writer, an African Pygmy as modified in Sidon. You know what those Phoenicians are like, they copy everything from the Egyptians, and then they miniaturize." Mythology has gone futuristic without giving up its constituent features. The markers of technology, variety, and anomaly (dwarf, miniature) are operative even among those who use "an Apple Nominator from Eden Valley." Uruk believes that the creation of a new language every day will generate confusion. Nimrod replies, "Don't worry. It could never happen here. Not in Babel."[10] Among the postmoderns, nobody tells us much about action inside the library, although Jonathan Swift reported that, as far back as 1697, a Babel-like brawl erupted between books on ancient wisdom and books on modern knowledge. At the end of the address of "The Bookseller to the Reader," Swift wrote that, whenever Virgil is mentioned, we are not to understand the "Person of a famous Poet, call'd by that Name, but only certain Sheets of Paper, bound up in Leather, containing in Print, the Works of the said Poet." Is it possible that nothing else is going on in the Library of Babel?

Babel-like cacophonies alert Borges to the fact that "[t]he dictionary is based on the hypothesis—obviously an unproven one—that languages are made up of equivalent synonyms." In a way, dictionaries are "Babelic" antidotes, which were found to be ineffective long before the postmoderns began to relish irregularities of all sorts. Semantics confirms that library and Babel are incompatible nouns, much as etymology points to the dual nature of the word *library*. The Greek *bibliotheke* emphasizes the building, whereas the Latin *libraria* stresses the books. In a chapter entitled "De bibliothecis," Isidore of Seville, the medieval guardian of etymologies, writes: "Library, *bibliotheca*, is a word of Greek origin: the term derives from the fact books are kept there. We can translate: *biblion*, of books; *theke*, depository."[11] Of course, Borges was particularly concerned with the logistics of the library as *bibliotheke*.

Logistics aside, the library triggers processes of selection that create ontological models and stylistic paradigms. In other words, authority is to be found in the library itself, for it is there that the obsolete and the topical shine forth.[12] The outcome is that the aftermath of master stories resists oblivion but cannot reverse exhaustion. In the universe of our contemporary culture, inversions have had a field day. Any long novel is to the short prose of "The Library of Babel" as a microscopic cell is to the macroscopic design. Both project reality beyond the humanist inheritance of visual clarity and narrative linearity. Ontological markers have collapsed, tomes contain illegible scribbles, and the letters printed on the spines of books neither form titles nor indicate "what the pages will say."[13] Borges combines antithetical structures by stacking up bricks and books in a space at once instructive and deceptive. Borges's title, therefore, pivots on an anomaly, and this chapter will take up anomalies that derive from archival technologies, linguistic incommunicability, the scriptural activity of writing as writing, and what Jacques Derrida considers the two meanings of the archive-library: commencement and commandment.

1

"The Library of Babel" is a title whose reach vies with that of *The Waste Land* inasmuch as it encompasses the human universe. Whereas Eliot highlights the downfall of civilization, Borges reconstructs it as an immense library,[14] which has turned the Babelic curse of human disorder into an architectural universe where more time is spent in the classification of ideas than in the pursuit of knowledge. Nowadays, the bibliographer often outshines the writer, an outcome that has led Borges to parody intellectual pride: "Man, the imperfect librarian, may be the product of chance or of malevolent demiurgi; the universe, with its elegant endowment of shelves, of enigmatical volumes, of inexhaustible stairways for the traveler and latrines for the seated librarian, can only be the work of a god" (52). Babel and the library accommodate a human-made reality built on the assumption that art thrives on its own artifacts.

The *studiolo* of fifteenth-century humanists was a Ptolemaic place of individual betterment, but the Library of Babel is a post-Copernican architecture of eccentric displacements:[15] "I know of districts in which the young men prostrate themselves before books and kiss their pages in a barbarous manner, but they do not know how to decipher a single letter. . . . Perhaps my old age and fearfulness deceive me, but I suspect that the human species—the unique species—is about to be extinguished, but the Library will endure: illuminated, solitary, infinite, perfectly motionless, equipped with precious volumes, useless, incorruptible, secret" (58). Human nature has grown ever more bibliographical, and the library has become the source as well as the depository of questionable productivity. What this means is that the library seems to be charged with preserving the cultural decline of its context. Like nature, human artifacts cannot escape decay. Unlike the Tower of Babel, however, the library shelters the deterioration of order. For Debra A. Castillo, "the gathering and classification of ideas takes the place of real thought" in the library.[16]

Believing as he does that "God is an intelligible sphere, whose center is everywhere and whose circumference is nowhere," Borges applies the geometric metaphor to his own literary universe: "The Library is a sphere whose exact center is any one of its hexagons and whose circumference is inaccessible."[17] This multilayered analogy gives the library a parodic range. Theology illuminates order as cosmos, whereas technology churns out discord as chaos. We have invented the "contradictory Library," which contains the best topography of hell and the worst of heaven. Stacked horizontally, books are Daedalian markers of progress; stacked on top of one another, they create a "vertical wilderness" that defies heavenly heights.[18]

After the fall of the Argentinean dictator Juan Peron, Borges was appointed director of the National Library, and he never relinquished the belief that the library is the locus of literary epistemology and spiritual bliss. In fact, as he wrote in the poem *The Gifts,* he "Always imagined Paradise / to be a sort of library." To give a sense of what paradise meant to Borges, we ought to consider how he addressed his fellow poet and librarian, Leopoldo Lugones: "Leaving behind the babble of the plaza, I enter the Library. I feel, almost physically, the gravitation of the books, the enveloping serenity of order, time magically desiccated and preserved."[19] The transition from life to art is like the transition from the babble of the street to the quiet of the library, where Lugones reads his friend's book in their literary haven of choice. What life wrongs, art makes right; and what death takes away, the library preserves in a place where people have become literary images stamped in the writer's memory.

The mythical Babel shouldered human defiance, whereas the library stores books so that we may preserve the earthly continuity that binds us to the past. This discord troubled Borges, and a title such as *The Wall and the Book* magnifies the correlation between bricks and books by pointing to a legendary emperor, Shih Huang Ti, who built a wall to keep out strangers. To avoid critical comparisons, he also ordered that all books be burned, so that he alone would be center and circumference, memory and presence, of his empire.[20] Just as guardians stand at the gates of heaven, *The Guardian of the Books* oversees a Borgesian milieu where "eternal laws" secure "the concord of the orb." This vision is remembered, not seen:

> These things or the memory of them are in the books
> Which I guard in the tower.

The guardian of the tower is a more humble incarnation of the emperor himself:

> My name is Hsiang, I am he who guards the books,
> Which are perhaps the last ones to remain,
> Because we know nothing of the Empire
> And the Son of Heaven,
> There they are on the high shelves,
> Near and far at the same time,
> Secret and visible like the stars.
> There they are, the gardens, the temples.[21]

The humanist impulse to assign human laws to nature has failed, and the only choice left is to equate reality with the library itself. In 1962 W. H. Auden reiterated the fundamental dichotomy:

> In
> Speech, if true, true deeds begin.
>
> If not, there's International Babel,
> In which murders
> Are sanitary measures.[22]

At this point, the library is inhospitable as well as unintelligible.[23]

The expansion of the archetypal Babel finds a postmodern equivalent in the cartographic extension of what Borges himself calls Miranda's map. *A Universal History of Infamy* describes an empire that is "of the same scale as the Empire."[24] Actually, Borges refers to J. A. Suarez Miranda's *Travels of Praiseworthy Men* (1658). Having attributed Miranda's story to Borges, Jean Baudrillard opens his own paradigmatic text, *Simulacra and Simulation,* by creating a third stage of representation where the map "engenders the territory."[25] Literary maps are larger than their geographical counterparts, and cartographic representations are better known than the original places. In an essay entitled "On the Impossibility of Drawing a Map of the Empire on a Scale of 1 to 1," Umberto Eco finds some maps absurd. His final corollary states: "Every 1:1 map of the empire decrees the end of the empire as such and therefore is the map of a territory that is not an empire."[26] Beyond questions of imitation, parody, and duplication, the anomalous realm of hyperreality is one where displacement has traded the real for representations of it.

Borges himself located Stevenson's *New Arabian Nights* in London, which is a London similar to Baghdad—not the Baghdad of reality, but the Baghdad of *The Thousand and One Nights.* Borges's own Buenos Aires is "as unreal as his Babylons and Ninevehs. Those cities are metaphors, nightmares, syllogisms. What is that metaphor saying, what is that dream dreaming? Another dream named Borges."[27] In his probing inquiry into the literature of South American foundations, Octavio Paz writes that "reality recognizes itself in the imaginings of poets—and poets recognize their imaginings in reality. Our dreams are waiting for us around the corner."[28] We can find plenty of Londons-that-look-like-Baghdads in the library, where discrepancies between reality and printed representations of it are to be resolved in favor of the latter.[29]

A recent book by Thomas L. Friedman tells us that, because of globalization, the world is flat. While Friedman has undone Columbus, cartography takes over in the "flat" world of Saul Steinberg, whose map of New York contains streets that are as close to the Hudson River as the Hudson is to the Pacific Ocean (Fig. 22). To borrow from Arthur C. Danto, New York occupies "the center of the world."[30] Lawrence Ferlinghetti has updated the postmodern "mapping" of simulated reality by way of a technique that has pinned his poetic topography to

> a Rand McNally globe
> with compass roses looking like real islands
> and trees towers telephones

bridges bedsprings rivers

...

And the whole scene turning and turning
through the soundless wingless air
like some huge store-window carrousel
with a Special Clearance Sale of Famous Masterpieces
Including one replica of Rodin's Thinker with hand and chin
pondering the insoluble problem
next to one bronze head of Albert Einstein

...

next to a cardboard Lincoln Memorial
with Lincoln inside
pondering the insoluble problem
next to a painting of Washington Crossing the Delaware
standing in the boat against Navy regulations.[31]

Beyond questions of duplication, displacement has traded the real for representations of it. The spatial world of printed matter offers sources and

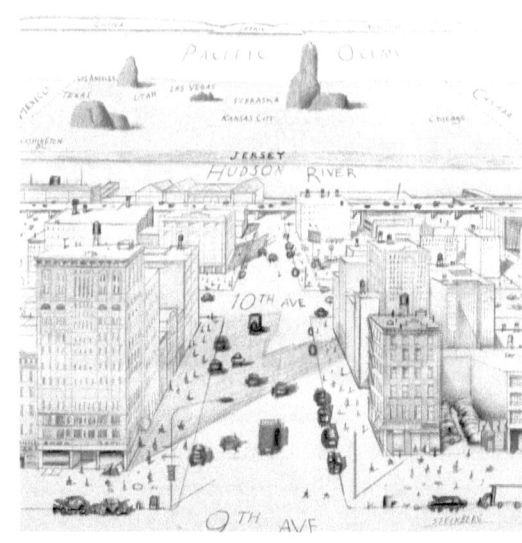

FIG. 22 Saul Steinberg, *A View of the World from 9th Ave.* Cover drawing for *The New Yorker*, March 29, 1976. © 1976 The Saul Steinberg Foundation / Artists Rights Society (ARS), New York.

models of representation—maps, indexes, catalogues, libraries, archives—that have developed their own archaeology. Recently, manuscripts of Johann Sebastian Bach and Louisa May Alcott have been recovered in those very libraries where they had been catalogued and yet lost in the first place.

As Galileo predicted in the seventeenth century, every book ever written is the product of different combinations of the letters of the alphabet, which contains all the words of all the books ever to be published. Borges has warned that books remain "the great memory of all centuries," and that their function is irreplaceable. Therefore, "if books disappear, surely history would disappear, and man would also disappear."[32] The disappearance of books will entail the disappearance of human experience. At the fabulistic level, Isaac Bashevis Singer imagines that the last little demon has nothing left to eat but books. Once he devours the last letter of the last page, the universe itself will be totally consumed.[33] The inference is that creation itself is literary to begin with. Mallarmé may have been the first to foresee such an outcome, and Borges put it in anecdotal form when he proposed that the universe amounts to a single book. In the Borgesian library, people exist in the form of tomes that are stacked in the most immense of humanity's cenotaphs. The writing of books about other books carries out the ritual of translating ashes into ashes. In a world drawn on the map of literature, exploration equates typography with topography. The introductory epigraph of Umberto Eco's *The Name of the Rose* reads, "Naturally, a manuscript," which means that the "natural" mode of book production is "obviously" typographical.[34] By drawing on Thomas Aquinas, Bernard of Cluny, Rabelais, Manzoni, Doyle, Joyce, Borges, and others,[35] *The Name of the Rose* turns into a miniature library of elitist quotations, and the jacket of the Italian edition confirms that "this text is a textile of other texts, a 'whodunit' of quotations, a book built of books."[36]

A book lover and an admirer of Borges, Umberto Eco gives the priestly guardian of the medieval abbey of Melk (Austria) the highly referential name of Jorge de Burgos. An inquisitor before the onset of the Inquisition, he hides books and hurts people who read them. The very idea of the library has been turned upside down: "The good of a book lies in its being read. A book is made up of signs that speak of other signs, which in turn speak of things. Without an eye to read them, a book contains signs that produce no concepts; therefore it is dumb. This library was perhaps born to save the books it houses, but now it lives to bury them."[37] If that were not enough, fire destroys the library, an outcome that ought to trigger thoughts about the fragility of knowledge. If we lose the texts, are we going to lose knowledge altogether? The last page of the novel describes the ruins of a "library made up of fragments, quotations, unfinished sentences, amputated stumps of books.... The more I reread this list the more I am convinced it is the result of chance and contains no message."[38] The burned-out library has caught up with burned-out language. One may wonder whether sentences are unfinished because of the fire or because somebody wrote them that way. The belief that history is at once purposeful and progressive has collapsed.

Outside the library, the bibliographical mindset creates compatible enclaves. In *The Island of the Day Before,* Eco presents a character, Roberto della Griva, who is "shipwrecked and cast up upon a deserted ship."[39] Convention has it that one is shipwrecked from ship to shore. Roberto, however, is "the only man in human memory" to have been shipwrecked from ship to ship. Once he climbs aboard the deserted *Daphne,* Roberto starts to write as soon as he finds "pen and paper in the captain's quarters."[40] Survival has spurred scriptural deeds that turn the ship into a *studiolo*. The abandoned *Daphne* becomes a "Theater of Memory."[41] The library can be shipwrecked, but it is never lost. Babel has become ubiquitous; it could not be otherwise, because the library contains the universe. By the postmodern seashore, textuality engulfs us, and we often come ashore to find once again the books from which we have been trying to sail away.

In the end, the narrator concedes that he could not have produced a novel "except by making a palimpsest of a rediscovered manuscript." Roberto imitates Don Quixote: "The young Roberto spent his time without friends, daydreaming of distant lands as he wandered, bored, through the vineyards, or of falconry if he was hunting swallows, or combating dragons as he played with his dogs, or hidden treasures as he explored the rooms of their little castle or fort, as it could also be called. His mind was inspired to wander thus by the dusty volumes of romances and chivalric poems he found in the south tower" (21). References are made to Cervantes on matters of lost pages that the writer extracted "from a miscellany of other defaced and faded manuscripts." The parody of the chivalric masterwork is apparent. Were Roberto to dive into the sea to reach shore, he would drown, because he cannot swim. Just as Don Quixote cannot survive madness, Roberto cannot survive nature; neither one can adjust to life as it is. Construction and destruction converge in the thematics of the Library of Babel, where we get lost only to find ourselves shipwrecked over and over again. Whether a tower or a shipwreck, the "place" is Babelic, and therefore contaminated by the linguistic viruses of irregular languages and anomalous narratives. Although *écriture* will go on because the possibility of writing "variations" is inexhaustible, we move amid the uncertainties of a cultural space where each interpretation is "reversible, and susceptible to continual modifications."[42] Because its very definition is relative, selection has become regressive: from sense and communication to nonsense and incommunicability.

We no longer need to reach up toward the empty heavens of discredited gods, because the progress of humankind has created its own earthly mythologies. The library outlasted Babel, but the Babelic has presided over the disintegration of the library, not as an architectural bastion but as an ontological structure. In his study of genesis, which he considers the vital core of the dichotomy of unity and multiplicity, Michel Serres also has gone back to Babel, the mythical archetype of linguistic diversity: "We are this tatter of languages fringed with murmuring. A tower plus noise, a system plus *noise*, tremendous architecture of walls, plus wailing walls where the moans, groans, and weeping can cleave the stone already loose. Then, we understand. History begins."[43] But it begins for the worse. Standing as we do at its tail end, we might as well agree with Joyce that we are rummaging amid the moans and groans of an endless nightmare. The Babelic mode has broken down the plurality of voices into fragmentary forms of writing as production. The selective filter of memory no longer sorts out the exemplary from the incomprehensible; nor can we assume that libraries preserve the best that human ingenuity has created. The time has come to concede that the map, the index, the catalogue, and the archive preserve the normal and the abnormal, the legible and the illegible—in other words, whatever is produced.[44]

Borges describes the Library of Babel as limitless and periodic. "If an eternal voyager were to traverse it in any direction, he would find, after many centuries, that the same volumes are repeated in the same disorder (which, repeated, would constitute an order: Order itself)" (58). Since the library includes reality at large, it is becoming ever more difficult to distinguish museums and reading rooms from junkyards and dumpsters. Thresholds have collapsed, and the very idea of a "selective" inventory of reality is now considered to be discriminatory, because it upholds "abusive" concepts of authorship, narrative preferences, and intellectual elitism.

Very much in the Babelic mode, much linguistic experimentation consists of nonsense, and its literary by-products have invaded libraries the world over. In France, experimentation clustered around the French-based Oulipo Laboratory. In its second manifesto, François Caradec calls attention to a field of verbal oddities: "The creative effort in these works is principally brought to bear on the formal aspects of literature: alphabetical, consonantal, vocalic, syllabic, constraints, structures, or programmes. On the other hand, *semantic* aspects were not dealt with, meaning having been left to the discretion of each author and excluded from our structural preoccupations." Questions of semantics and ideology aside, the focus is on the viability of literary means of expression that become progressively unintelligible. Jacques Jouet forsakes human discourse and chooses to write in great-ape language:

> Zor hoden tanda
> Kagoda bolgani
> Rak gom tand-panda[45]

Raymond Queneau wrote *Exercices de style* (two editions, 1947 and 1973). The title echoes ancient manuals of rhetoric. As such, the exercises are procedural rather than teleological, and they apply to banal and eccentric subjects. Each exercise bears a title. "Notations" points to short, informal notes of unusual derivation, whereas "En partie double" is centered on duplication and bifurcation—*autobus* and *véhicule de transports*. The exercises include rhetorical tropes, parodies of literary genres, and prosaic discourses. Queneau shows that rhetoric works its way into everything.[46] Thus he breaks language down into groups of two, three, four, and five letters: "Jo un ve ur mi rs su di ap rl te la rm fo rr." Illegibility shifts to *Hellenismes:* "Dans un hyperautobus plein de petrolonautes, je fus martyr de ce microrama en une chronie de metaffluence." Playfully, pig Latin comes to the fore: "Sol erat in regionem zenithi et calor atmospheri magnissima. Senatus populusque parisiensis sudebant. Autobi passebant completi." Next, experimentation turns to letter groups that are altogether incomprehensible: "Ed on to ay rd wa id sm yo da he nt ar re."[47] Even the alphabet, the last bastion of regularity and universalism, bears the signs of amputations, implants, overgrowths, and displacements. Langage cannot be pronounced, and *écriture* brings forth letters meant to fail meaning and reading alike.

Linguistically speaking, nonsense edges on the pathological in Edward Lear's *The Yonghy Bonghy-Bo*, Lewis Carroll's language of Wonderland, and Alfred Jarry's pataphysics. Eccentric and delightful, these languages have no consistent word-meaning correspondences; they spell out the science of nonsense by means of words that utter other words for the sake of it.[48] The Babelic indicates gaps in our systems of order, and it is in those gaps that nonsense, as the negative language of common sense, finds a parallel in illegible vocabularies. The punitive Babel of too many languages has yielded a cacophony in the echoing chambers of postmodernism, and I am afraid that the library of nonsense shelters texts for which no Rosetta stone will ever be found. By comparison, Dan Brown's *The Da Vinci Code* is but a prelapsarian game for the simple at heart.[49]

Much as the gigantic and the miniature exceed the normal in the realm of sight, so do double sense and nonsense undermine the grammatical in the realm of language; one stands between categories and the other makes them inaccessible. "The world lifted out of history has only itself as recourse. The word," Susan Stewart writes, "becomes its own last resort. And this is the beginning of nonsense: language lifted out of context, language turning on itself."[50] Whether we think of linguistic reversals or of textual fragmentation, it is clear that we have entered a self-referential world of etymological duplicity, grammatical displacements, and semantic disarray. To borrow from the 1997 Nobel lecture by the playwright Dario Fo, this downturn has generated the "rambling nonsense-speech of the *grammelot*."[51] On Babelic grounds, such linguistic disarray is bound to erode narrativity, all to the advantage of techniques that favor means over ends and fragments over wholes.[52] For many, the *fragment* is a disappointing genre, but the only honest one.[53]

Among sinners against language, moderns, modernists, and postmoderns would confess to tautological abuses. Art has traded the language of human commerce for that of art alone. Logology, which upholds the metaphysical clarity of knowledge, has degenerated into logomachy, which dictionaries define as a war of words having little to do with reality. For Kenneth Burke, logomachy toys with unity because it relies on "stylistic subterfuges for representing real divisions in terms that deny division." Tautology puts forth the meta-language of a "Speech-of-speech-of-speeches" (*Dialectician's Prayer*).[54] Borges writes, "Ontological markers have defaulted and tomes bear illegible scribbles in the Borgesian Library of Babel, where the letters printed on the spine of books neither form titles nor give any suggestion of 'what the pages will say'" (52). Only decoders can try to identify so many languages in the universe of books, which is made up "of the letters MCV, perversely repeated from the first line to the last. Another (very much consulted in this area) is a mere labyrinth of letters. . . . This much is already known: for every sensible line of straightforward statement, there are leagues of senseless cacophonies, verbal jumbles and incoherences. (I know of an uncouth region whose librarians repudiate the vain and superstitious custom of finding a meaning in books" (53). We move in a printed world where Borges turns on himself as he confronts the unruly logistics of knowledge. As he writes elsewhere, "The impious maintain that nonsense is normal in the Library and that the reasonable (and even humble and pure coherence) is an almost miraculous exception. . . . The best volume of the many exagons under my administration is entitled *The Combed Thunderclap* and another *The Plaster Cramp* and another *Axaxaxax mlo*." Books are printed in "a Samoyedic Lithuanian dialect of Guarani, with classical Arabic inflections" (57, 54). Markers such as "etymology," "normality," and "coherence" call to mind the traditional reliance on narrativity. In fact, they summon forth their opposites: illegibility, exception, and obscurity (58).

Steve McCaffery has denounced grammar as a "[r]epressive mechanism designed to regulate the free flow of language. Imposing its constraints upon non-gravitational circulation, it realizes a centered (and centralized) meaning through a specific mode of temporalization."[55] The last section of his book is entitled "Lasworda," an incomprehensible noun drawn from Old English: "Fram dam ongeat cnihtum scufan mid motan in scynscada aenigne hetelic weard fela heahfaestne fleon lastworda."[56] Obscurity and disintegration are central to *Theory of Sediment*, which begins with legible words and quickly veers toward illegibility.

Franz Kafka describes the Tower of Babel through the verb *pappeln*, which means "to chatter" or to "talk nonsense." (*Description of a Struggle*). Likewise, *babblen* (to babble) derives from the name of the tower.[57] To talk nonsense in a library is to deny its traditional mission, which is to preserve signs of human communication. To capture the inevitability of the Babelic condition, Kafka's parables are instructive: "If it had been possible to build the Tower of Babel without ascending it, the work would have been permitted." Inasmuch as it tests superior powers, the mastery (not only the construction) of verticality cannot be tolerated. *The Pit of Babel* turns things around: "What are you building?—I want to dig a subterranean passage. Some progress must be made. My station up there is much too high. We are digging the pit of Babel." From the prehistorical myth to the posthistorical antimyth, "digging the pit" entails the construction of an antitower that stands as a symbol of antiknowledge. From top to bottom, Babel probably would look like one of Piranesi's prisons. While the Italian engraving shows instruments of torture at the bottom, the interior of Kafka's Babel is a library with a printing press, which itself delivers punishment. Of course, titles strengthen the parallel; the *Prisons (Carceri d'invenzione)* foreshadows *The Penal Colony*.

Babel was, after all, a technological feat. Technology by definition catapults progress beyond its latest accomplishment. From this point of view, Borges's title spells out a fundamental tension in Western culture. While *Babel* tests *homo faber*, *Library* shelters *homo sapiens*. The challenge is to reconcile the storage of philosophical inheritance, which tends to be retrospective, with the challenge of technological invention, which is progressive. Kafka's "The City Coat of Arms" is a very short story that focuses on a double undertaking; one is the building of the Tower of Babel and the other is the construction of a city for the workers who have been assigned to construct the tower. It is clear to everyone that the tower's completion may take generations.[58] At this point, a fundamental disjunction between things and words emerges. This dualism has opened a gap that has spawned disruptions between the "utopia" of narrative linearity and the "heterotopia" of nonsensical discourse.

The building site turns out to be a place of linguistic, social, and economic discord. The people in charge are "[t]roubled less about the tower than the construction of a city for the workmen. Every nationality wanted the finest quarters for itself, and this gave rise to disputes, which developed into bloody conflicts. These conflicts never came to an end." As generations came and went, "[t]echnical skill increased and with it occasion for conflict. To this must be added that the second or third generation had already recognized the senselessness of building a heaven-reaching tower; but by that time everybody was too deeply involved to leave the city."[59] The long-term curse is technology. Under the philosophical rubric of "thinking," Ludwig Wittgenstein asked: "Could a machine think?—Could it be in pain?—Well, is the human body to be called such a machine? It surely comes as close as possible to being such a machine."[60] A student of the human condition, Hannah Arendt identifies *homo faber* with labor at a time when technology pervades all aspects of a material culture that has taken in the majority of humankind: "Productivity and creativity, which were to become the highest ideals and even the idols of the modern age in its initial stages, are inherent standards of *homo faber*."[61] Since the progress of technology is endless by definition, it follows that human beings define themselves as workers and toolmakers. To work is to be human, but Arendt is worried about the prominent role that labor and production play in defining man as an *animal laborans*. If *humanism* is consciousness that somehow accounts for causes and effects, Arendt is concerned about the ruptures between the human as a reality and humanism as a philosophy. I am afraid that, on the grounds of Borges's library, such ruptures probably took place a long time ago, and nothing more than testimonial traces are left.

Because mimesis refers to sources embedded in art, the only alternative to the end of ideological writing is writing itself.[62] The boundaries between writers, translators, librarians, and bibliographers have collapsed. The active subject is not the uniquely talented writer-creator but the writer-writer. Short types of fiction have become so short that the act of writing is inscribed in the title of Salvador Elizondo's *El Grafógrafo* (*The Graphographer*):

> I write. I write that I am writing. Mentally I see myself writing that I am writing and I can also see myself seeing that I am writing. I remember writing and also seeing myself writing. And I see myself remembering that I see myself writing and I remember seeing myself remembering that I was writing and I write seeing myself write that I remember having seen myself write that I saw myself writing that I was writing. I can also imagine myself writing that I had already written that I would imagine myself writing that I had written that I was imagining myself writing that I see myself writing that I am writing.[63]

This is a diagram of the literary intake meant to spur the production of "writing." Since the whole passage alternates "write" and "see," textuality tself is about the multiplication of printed paper by means of graphic acts. In the world of the graphographer, being and doing do not exceed a reality in which the writer exists because he sees himself writing. Inside the library, creative writers have been losing ground to graphographers (students of graphic signs), lexicographers (compilers of dictionary lists), and bibliographers, whose literary output is akin to a machine-like routine.

The mechanics of scriptural codes make it clear that although meaning may be in disarray, the practice of writing remains intact. In Georges Perec's words: "To write: to try meticulously to retain something, to cause something to survive; to wrest a few precise scraps from the void as it grows, to leave somewhere a furrow, a trace, a mark or a few signs." The traces of "new" writing have become the only form of writing possible when history has nowhere to go. Perec overshadows grammatical meaning in favor of scriptural practice:

> I write . . .
> I write: I write . . .
> I write: 'I write . . .'

> I write that I write . . .
> etc.
>
> I write: I trace words on a page.
> Letter by letter, a text forms, affirms itself, is confirmed, is frozen, is fixed.
> . . .
> I write: I inhabit my sheet of paper, I invest it, I travel across it.

A few pages later, he spells out the writer's task: "I simply cling on to these activities of withdrawal: tidying, sorting, setting in order. At these moments I dream of a work surface that is *virgo intacta:* everything in its place, nothing superfluous, nothing sticking out, all the pencils well sharpened (but why have several pencils? I can see six merely at a glance)." The writer is identified with his scriptural instruments.[64]

This posture has precedents. Calvino writes that one of the first to consider "the instruments and actions of his own work as its true subject" was the thirteenth-century poet Guido Cavalcanti, who wrote a sonnet in which pens speak in the first person.

> We are the sad, dismayed pens,
> the scissors and the sorrowing knife.[65]

While Bettino da Trizzo praised the new way—*nuovo modo*—of making books in abundance ("far libri in abondantia"), stylish *maniere* met the challenge and the Petrarchan carried the day. Throughout the sixteenth century, the bulk of printed materials made it possible for books to circulate within a universe of their own. We edge on language as performance, a development that led John Shearman to generalize about "a silver-tongued language of articulate, if unnatural, beauty."[66]

Lexical oddities find pictorial equivalents. Arcimboldo painted *The Librarian* as a human bust constructed with books (Fig. 23). The librarian *is* what he *does*. At first, the anthropomorphic guise—or disguise—mixes old and new by flaunting elegant bookmarks. Although painted less than a century after the invention of the printing press, this picture foreshadows the ascendancy of the book as ornament over the book as knowledge. As a form of ornamentation, eccentricity got the best of clarity, and language itself became a field of bizarre anamorphoses and semantic reversals.

Among literary places of learning, Anton Francesco Doni's *Libraria* (1550) contains tomes with illegible words, implausible languages, invented authors, paradoxical entries, and absurd titles that spell out the delights of simulation. If we were to find a place of work for Arcimboldo's librarian, Doni would welcome him in his library, where one confronts entries on nonsense in books where writing is reduced to "a grammatical struggle" (*la zuffa della grammatica*)—and a "loot of words"—(*il bottino di vocaboli*). Books contain a "deluge of words" that make odd combinations "without falling outside the alphabet." Words grow on other words amid a plethora of printed authors who willfully construct "labyrinths of errors."[67] The transitive language of human exchange is set against the printed signs of writers who indulge in grammatical aberrations.[68] Reality itself is viewed as an alphabetical world that can disregard truth altogether. If one were to open some of the older volumes in Arcimboldo's portrait, we would find Marot's *poèmes-rebus*, whose linguistic mixtures were meant to confuse the keenest eyes.

In the writer's own description of his craft in the prologue to his master work, Cervantes has just completed his endeavor; except for the preface,

FIG. 23 Giuseppe Arcimboldo, *The Librarian*, c. 1566. Skoklosters Slott, Balsta, Sweden.

which leads him to an impasse. There are moments of indecision: "Many times I took up my pen to write it, and many times I put it down, not knowing what to say." The pen sketches out the very rhythm of the thinking process. The act of writing falters at first, and then stops altogether "[w]ith the paper before me, my pen in my ear, my elbow on the desk and my hand on my cheek, thinking what to write." The mind is idle, and the pen seems to be posted by its source of motion; lodged between brain and ear, it stands as a graphic organ ready to register the thinking process. As if held hostage to the entrapments of learning, the pen waits, ready to shift from behind the ear (perception) to a hand still weighed down by indecision (expression). Cervantes is lost in doubt.

Once technique prevails over ideology, the instruments of art begin to play a significant role in the creative process. The painter-poet Bronzino wrote an emblematic poem on the paintbrush, *Del pennello:*

> Because of this I was forced to judge
> The paintbrush, which I did, and which I will
> Praise if it is worthy of praise ...
> Who cannot enjoy to reason
> Of the things which can be done by this paintbrush
> Which is born of pig tail or horse hair?[69]

The personal takes second place to the professional, and rivalry is pinned to mastering the instruments of production. The last line focuses on the physical characteristics of the paintbrush. The inference is that the artistic autonomy of the medium gained grounds throughout the twentieth century, when Jasper Johns turned a *Savarin* can with paintbrushes into a pictorial subject (1977) (Fig. 24).

From the pictorial to the scriptural, words are title, text, and self-reflective subject matter in Jean-Paul Sartre's *Les mots* (1964). Authorship itself merges with printed language: "I, twenty-five volumes, eighteen thousand pages of text, three hundred engravings, including a portrait of the author. My bones are made of leather and card-board, my parchment-skinned flesh smells of glue and mushrooms, I sit in state through a hundred thirty pounds of paper, thoroughly at ease. I am reborn, I at last become a whole man, thinking, talking, singing, thundering, a man who asserts himself with the peremptory inertia of matter."[70] Sartre thinks of books as the bricks of an anthropomorphic architecture that could be paired with the Arcimboldesque librarian.

Let us not forget that during the 1960s and 1970s structuralism and post-structuralism traded the concepts of *auteur* and *oeuvre* for those of *scripteur* and *écriture*. The exchange contributed to the demise of authorship,[71] which was predicated on the belief that the very idea of selection implies the abusive power of individual creativity and intellectual elitism. To overcome these traditional "evils," the library's inventory must be "unselective." One way of achieving this is to take in everything. The lineage of urinals and Brillo boxes peaked when vacuum cleaners and beer cans entered the museum, while Peanuts, Superman, and other comic strips crowded neighborhood reading rooms and art galleries. Libraries and museums have made room for artifacts that justify the modern penchant for depthless vacuity.[72]

Since it contains the whole of reality for better or worse, the library has not stopped its intake of printed materials, which technology has increased exponentially. Content aside, the production of books has favored an indexical approach to knowledge.[73] Gustave Flaubert visited museums in order to crowd his literary milieus with catalogues of things. His *Dictionnaire des idées reçues* describes a culture of things that stand for themselves. It suffices to mention that texts such as *Bouvard and Pécuchet* paved the way for postmodern narratives in which description as enumeration and writing as copying have become predominant.[74] If the pursuit of knowledge has waned, its classification thrives, all to the advantage of archival expertise.

FIG. 24 Jasper Johns, Installation view of the exhibition "Jasper Johns: A Retrospective." The Museum of Modern Art, New York. October 15, 1996 through January 21, 1997. © Jasper Johns/Licensed by VAGA, New York.

In 1998 Martha Cooley published *The Archivist*, a title that gives a human face to Babelic maintenance. The assumption is that literature can regenerate itself by taking advantage of what the library has to offer, and the opening paragraph is emblematic of the "connectedness" that ties the postmodern to the modernist: "With little effort, anything can be shown to connect with anything else: existence is infinitely cross-referenced. And everything has more than one definition. A cat is a mammal, a narcissist, a companion, a riddle. I have been reading T. S. Eliot again, the nice hardback edition of his poems that Roberta gave me before she left. I'd almost forgotten how heady Eliot is, how much thinking he crowds into 'Four Quartets.'"[75] The library as index opens up a horizontal plain field whose grounds are transhistorical. For anyone who has accepted the idea that literary production is derivative, the library is the source of all the resources ever needed to keep writing incessant. Different expressions of human ingenuity are pitted against one another. Even the encyclopedia, the book that contains all the letters of all the words ever published, is described as illusory in the preface to the second part of *Ficciones*.[76] Vitality has given way to exhaustion, which neither begins nor terminates anything. Because it is a late condition, somebody else has to take responsibility for having started the downfall of art and letters somewhere upstream. While early instigators such as Nietzsche had something to do with it, the modernists, Martin Heidegger, and their cohorts were more directly involved. Postmodernism did not drive the last nail into the coffin of the Western tradition; instead, it exhumed the dead at the periphery of the wasteland and recycled their remains. Part and parcel of the postmodern inventory of history is a recurrent sense of ending that favors sunset over sunrise. Actually, we can look on postmodernism as a label that has established a posthumous point of view on our age. Who, therefore, will name the last book? Will it be Jorge de Burgos? Historians would warn us that books contain post-Babelic tales about conflicts between the constructive fabric of meaningful language and the deconstructive debris of meaningless nonsense. In Borges's "contradictory Library,"[77] the scriptural has offset the mimetic.

If it is true that Babelic libraries have inspired many to doubt that the order of the catalogue allows us to distinguish between poets and fools,[78] some have raised questions in the archive, where new narratives have failed to yield master stories.[79] In fact, museums, libraries, and art dealers have inventoried much of what writers, painters, sculptors, and architects salvaged from the debris of artistic and technological waste. Andy Warhol was the first to understand that the museum as warehouse can house technological no less than artistic products. Warhol's passion for storing commercial jars, cans, and trinkets stands out as a variation of what popular culture has marketed under the aegis of art as merchandise. Invention has come to terms with inventory. In the cul-de-sac of such a crowded wasteland, progress has waned and sequence has dwindled into variations of the "recycled."

It is easy in hindsight to make the connection. If it was easy for Arcimboldo to build a librarian out of a stack of books, it was inevitable, at a time when Robert Rauschenberg worked his way through dumpsters in order to produce "combines," that someone would transform the library into a junkyard. The title of George Herms's 1960 sculpture-combine *The Librarian* (Fig. 25) echoes Arcimboldo and gives a full measure of the shift from the anthropomorphism of a technological portrait to the assemblage of the material objects—a wood box, newspaper, brass, books, and a painted stool—that make up what looks like a very dysfunctional library. It is a ruinous image of books left unread for ages, as if to symbolize the obsolete condition of intellectual endeavors.

FIG. 25   George Herms, *The Librarian*, 1960. Norton Simon Museum, Pasadena, California. Gift of Molly Barnes.

Amid such debris, sanitation may offer valid reasons for evacuating the library of nonsense, where knowledge as refuse has become a compelling metaphor in the title of Ammons's *Garbage:*

> I punched
>
> out Garbage at the library and four titles
> swept the screen, only one, Garbage Feed,
>
> seeming worth going on to; and that was about
> feeding swine right: so I punched Garbage Disposal
>
> and the screen came blank—nothing! All those
> titles, row on row, of western goodies, mostly
>
> worse than junk, but not a word on Disposal.[80]

A writer and an artist, Robert Smithson goes so far as to tell us that his drawing, *A Heap of Language* (Fig. 26), "is built, not written": "In the illusory babels of language, an artist might advance specifically to get lost, and to intoxicate himself in dizzying syntaxes, seeking odd intersections of meaning, strange corridors of history, unexpected echoes, unknown humors, or voids of knowledge."[81] A mound of spent words has replaced bricks and books.

Although paradise may not be a library, the lines of our librarian of choice, Borges, are both instructive and admonitory:

> Every single thing becomes a word
> in a language that Someone or Something, night and day,

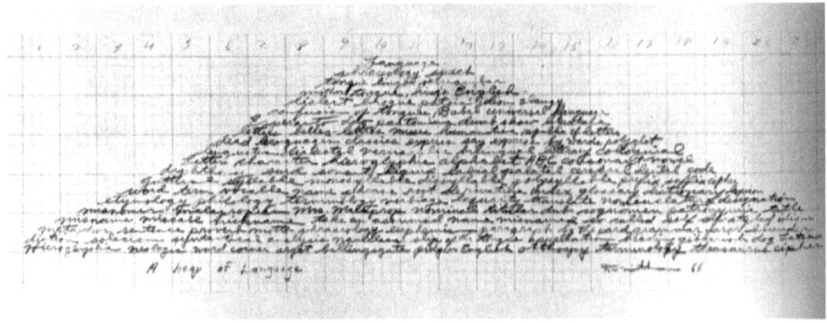

FIG. 26 Robert Smithson, *A Heap of Language*, 1966. John Weber Gallery, New York. © Estate of Robert Smithson / Licensed by VAGA, New York.

writes down in a never-ending scribble,
which is the history of the world, embracing

Rome, Carthage, you, me, everyone,
my life, which I do not understand, this anguish
of being enigma, accident, and puzzle,
and all the discordant languages of Babel.[82]

If "Borges and I" at times are one, Jorge de Burgos could never claim to be Jorge Luis Borges. Perhaps this denial is a measure of what still keeps us human. Let us hope that the distinction will hold; otherwise, we will have to write the inventory of our deconstruction of everything. While Jorge de Burgos punishes those who read books, many a modern critic has been no kinder to those who have written those books. Death sentences have been pronounced left and right. After the nineteenth-century announcement of the death of God, twentieth-century literati upheld the idea that the author was just as dead. In the cul-de-sac of postmodernism, the cosmic order of the library coexists with the chaotic disorder of Babel, and the Borgesian archititle has captured the twin dynamics of such a divided experience.[83]

In 1942 Borges created a character, Funes the Memorious, who, while incapable of groundbreaking "platonic ideas," was able to memorize all the details of life: "In the overly replete world of Funes there were nothing but details, almost contiguous details."[84] I would like to suggest that Funes opened the way for postmodernism by immersing himself in the retrospective universe of minutia that crowded the mind with bits and pieces of the past. Funes's eccentric condition was due to a fall from his horse. Half a century later, Yambo, a character created by Umberto Eco, also endures a pathological condition. Because of amnesia, he can remember all the things he "read in a book somewhere, or was told, but not the things associated with [his] direct experience." He knows that Napoleon was defeated at Waterloo, but he cannot remember his mother's name.[85] Yambo's mental landscape is one in which the initial identification is with "Arthur Gordon Pym" (3). His memory, in fact, "is made of paper" (73). The reconstruction of "book identity" leads Yambo to the attic, where prints, magazines, photos, newspapers, and other memorabilia gradually allow him to reconstruct his past: "Had I tried to remake myself completely among those pages, I would have become Funes the Memorious, I would have relived moment by moment all the years of my childhood, every leaf I heard rustling in the night, every whiff of coffee in the morning" (154). Like Funes, Yambo is anchored to what has happened, which makes him incapable of dealing with the future. At ease in the enclosed world of his library, Yambo has "a studio full of old books." He is "an antiquarian book dealer," and a "tireless reader" with "an iron memory" (16). Literary knowledge lets him be acquainted with Julius Caesar, but it does not tell him what he "should do" (29).

If history is a nightmare from which the modernist Joyce is trying to awaken, the postmodern Eco confirms that "history is a blood-drenched enigma" (65). The illustrated novel closes with an ominous image. As he looks up, Yambo cannot help asking, "Why is the sun turning black?" (449). The future is unwelcome because it is bound to yield more tragedies. If dawn is darkened, how will the oncoming daylight end up? Beyond the ominous threat of natural phenomena, the human mind has found safety in the familiar universe of paper memory. Its vanishing point is Borgesian, and it inspires Eco's deathbed vision: "I saw the center of my Aleph from which shone forth not the infinite world, but the jumbled notebook of my memories" (421). Semantics takes us back to etymology. The word *library* derives from the Latin *liber*, which is akin to *libertas*, liberty. As a body of knowledge, books can set us free of ignorance and bestow wisdom. By the same token, understanding may or may not spur action. The postmoderns give us little reason for hope.

Textuality has woven a tangled web of contradictory discourses, discontinuous narratives, endless variations, and uncertain boundaries.[86] Complexity is ever more threatening because there is no escape from the library, which some consider the producer as well as the repository of knowledge. Indeed, as Borges has been telling us for a long time, the book is the library, and the library is the universe; its origins are scriptural and its form is printed. Once the pursuit of the new slowed down at the threshold of modernism, belatedness bested invention. Novelty relapsed, and the arts at large sped up an indexical approach to reality. Nowadays, more time is spent in the classification of inherited ideas than in the pursuit of groundbreaking knowledge. The libraries of Rabelais and Cervantes still offered a way out, but that of Borges does not; and the books shelved in it are ever more illegible.

In a kind of circular paradox, we seem to have been caught between Babel and Chaos. Unquestionably, it is a testing time; could things get any worse? Might things get better? Is it fair to assume that Babel has gotten the best of the library? The title of this chapter emphasizes the inventory as the emblematic document of postmodern art; it lists, copies, and counterfeits.

Like libraries and museums, the inventory does not create. In the spirit of the inventory, Borges designs the library as a mechanism based on the addition of exagonal units. Their repetitive accumulation ultimately takes in the universe; sameness stretches out but does not entail transformation. Ontological dilemmas are there to stay. In the meantime, life goes on; and so do the "technologies" of literature. The Library of Babel proves that language has fulfilled a dehumanizing role inasmuch as the written is no longer readable.

Maurice Blanchot is categorical: "The book is the *a priori* of knowledge. We would know nothing if there did not always exist in advance the impersonal memory of the book and, more essentially, the prior disposition to write and to read contained in every book and affirming itself only in the book."[87]

2

In the thematics of memory and the archive, Jacques Derrida has focused on the etymology of *arkhe*, which entails two different meanings. One is *commencement*, which refers to where things begin. The other is *commandment*, which gives the power of enforcement to the beginning.[88] The dualism of commencement and commandment is not as circumscribed as it would appear at first. The French philosopher has already told us that there is always a beginning before the beginning, and the French sociologist Jean Baudrillard has added that the end is endless because the endpoint has turned into a curve. As a result, there are several commencements and just as many commandments. The archive shelters plural memories, which, as Derrida himself recognizes, are "not easy to archive."

Equally problematic is Derrida's concern with the gathering function of the archive, which he relates to the "power of consignation." While assigning residence, consignation executes the more important task of articulating the "unity of an ideal configuration. In an archive, there should not be any absolute dissociation, any heterogeneity or *secret* which could separate (*secernere*), form partition, in an absolute manner. The archontic principle of the archive is also a principle of consignation, that is, of gathering together."[89] The master deconstructivist looks around and tries to find a common thread, but Borges would remind him that it is too late. We have killed the Minotaur, and there is no point in waiting for Godot. Confusion is all we have, and artists such as Robert Rauschenberg and Jean Tinguely have proposed that the disorder of reality ought to be reflected in any form of human organization, so much so that the architect Frank Gehry considers chaos a main component of democracy. To this extent, the postmodern emphasis on heterogeneous accumulations is better represented by the dumpster and the junkyard. The original has been traded for the leftover. Put in mythical terms, the other Babel no less than the anti-Babel were never located too far from the original tower.

Historians would add that, whereas the Homeric tales gave a kind of foundational unity to Mediterranean culture, no authoritative text mapped out the emergence of Atlantic cultures. In his study of Seville and the Atlantic, Pierre Chaunu tells us that the mercantile port city produced *libros de registros* of the *Casa de la Contractatión*, whose output gave rise to the statistical history of the Atlantic.[90] An expert on myth and the archive in South American literature, Roberto Gonzáles Echevarría writes that the archive is at once capacious and incomplete; it can include and classify the universe, but it also echoes the enclosed space of the prison and the negative condition of death. The archive does not let us leap toward eternity.[91] Instead, it contains eternity within Borges's Library of Babel, which is as infinite and as deadly as the silent and inhuman universe.

The mounting predominance of English and the technologies of globalism are bound to yield a post-Babelic uniformity that might be just as dreadful.[92] Derrida would have considered this outcome inevitable, because "what is no longer archived in the same way is no longer lived in the same way."[93] Insofar as humankind is concerned, the Library of Babel contains eternity. Logistics aside, it seems to me that the symbolism of the ruinous Babel has come full circle, for the artifact has finally caught up with its agents: the giants that built it (commencement) and the divinity that destroyed it (commandment). What survived was the technology of the mythical structure. It survived the giants and somehow fell into the hands of man the builder, who has found that "building" puts him in command. But this does not mean that the library has lost its Babelic liabilities.

At once architectural, ontological, and functional, the library has multiplied beyond the pyramids, it has expanded in excess of pagan temples, and it is more ecumenical than religious buildings. The Babelic mode has broken down the plurality of voices, and writing as production cannot sort out the exemplary from the incomprehensible. Inside the library, Geoffrey Hartman's righteous comment echoes throughout: "How thoroughly the human condition is a verbal condition!"[94] Ontological dilemmas, then, are here to stay, at least for the time being. Construction may have stalled, but deconstructive rereadings and misreadings have been piling up for a long time. However identified with parasitism, plagiarism, and counterfeiting, derivative structures have filled the stockyards of literary reproductions. For better or worse, archititles have sustained "continuities," whether they be called picaresque, quixotic, or something else.

10

Cervantine First Pages:
The Inadequacies of Retitling

> The subject of poetics is *transtextuality,* or the textual transcendence of the text.
> —GÉRARD GENETTE

After the turn of the twentieth century, Miguel de Unamuno and Jorge Luis Borges exhausted the lexicon of chivalric tales in the referential universe of literary stories about literary stories—authored, attributed, or authorless. In the archival universe of literature, the written condition of humankind has entitled quixotic titles to exploit commitments to referentiality. Rereading upholds the resilience of textual appropriations that preceded Cervantes and worked their way through Franz Kafka, Carlos Fuentes, and Robert Coover. As such, referentiality fosters circulation, which tends to cluster around mythical themes, master plots, and modes of expression that are both cumulative and recurrent. They all weave intertextual grids whose underpinnings thrive on variations of the chivalric, the picaresque, the quixotic, and so on. We confront a type of literature that is heavily memorial. Speaking for all of them, Robert Coover calls on the Spanish master to take stock of our contemporary culture: "But, *don* Miguel, the optimism, the innocence, the aura of possibility you experienced have been largely drained away, and the universe is closing in on us again. Like you, we, too, seem to be standing at the end of one age and on the threshold of another. We, too, have been brought into a blind alley by the critics and analysts; we, too, suffer from a 'literature of exhaustion.'"[1]

In the literary cul-de-sac, exhaustion has found a new resilience, convincing many a postmodern to trust procrastination. The world of narrativity thrives on the storytelling continuity of tale after tale, which have traded the unique for the derivative. Put briefly, we have moved from the modernist axiom "less is more" to the postmodern preference for "more is not less" and "more is more, is more."[2] The result has been the proliferation of illegitimate pirating, parasitic hybrids, creative transformations, and more.[3] Whatever the label of choice, we have entered a realm where titles quote other titles, texts draw on other texts, and authorship is either lost or counterfeited in the shuffle.[4]

If the Renaissance pushed forward by looking backward, modernity has moved sideways while looking around. On old and new continents alike, the present-past of modernism has moved ahead toward the future-past of postmodernism. The "new" literature is littered with the markers of postchivalric textuality. Quixotic titles point to a "transtextual" field in which authoritative commentaries on Don Quixote's paperbound journey have given way to experiments in self-fulfilling anachronism.[5] Insofar as Don Quixote is concerned, the modernist Unamuno is convinced that he is a better commentator than Cervantes by the sheer force of literary competence and spiritual superiority. The postmodern Borges gives a different reading of the quixotic text at a time when it is legitimate to create fictional cohorts who pretend to write new books by rereading old ones.

Having found the alleged Ur-manuscript by the Arabic chronicler Cide Hamete Benengeli in an old shop, Cervantes had the Arabic text translated into Spanish as *Historia de Don Quijote de La Mancha*. Expectations of chivalric distinction come to the fore when fiction became metafiction in Cervantes's title *El ingenioso hidalgo Don Quijote de la Mancha*. Vis-à-vis the Arabic *historia*, the Cervantine title tells us that we may be dealing with the same protagonist, but not necessarily with the same personality. Questions arise from the two titles: how *ingenioso* was Don Quixote in the Arabic text, and how much did he change because of transcriptions and translations? Has *ingenioso* turned the chronological account of a *historia verdadera* into the heroic narrative of a novel? But then again, how truthful were *comedias verdaderas* at that time? Dictionaries (Covarrubias, Corominas) inform us that *ingenioso* means clever, inventive, and prone to tell stories—*talento para contar historias divertidas, talento para inventar cosas*. Roberto Gonzáles Echevarría has translated *ingenioso* as witty in the sense of inventive to an almost pathological degree.[6] The dictionary of the Spanish Royal Academy identifies *ingenioso* with the tendency toward "prompt and effortless discourse and invention." The inference is that *ingenioso* fosters the ability for "making up things." By bordering on falsehood, *ingenioso* makes the title as allusive and elusive as the chapter titles.[7] *Ingenioso* also qualifies "invention," which shapes the generative impulse of *ingenio*.[8] During the golden age, mental *ingenio* and manual *invención* qualified two moments of artistic production.

Cervantes's title certainly provides a focus for the text by intensifying an otherwise gray story. But what is the price for such intensification? Is too much of the story left out? In terms of characterization, *ingenioso* spells out the "creational" impulse that brings the *hidalgo* to life. As Stephen Gilman has written, the title presents us "not with a story but with a living person."[9] Vis-à-vis humanist titles, *ingenioso* highlights the scriptural thinness of *I libri della famiglia* and *Il libro de Cortegiano*, whose titles are willfully rooted in the intellectual fiction of "the book." By testing Aristotle's juxtaposition between the historical and the poetic, *ingenioso* parodied the *libros de caballerías* and was itself parodied by Alessandro Tassoni's early Cervantine variation, *La secchia rapita* (*The Stolen Bucket*) at a time when *Stultifera Navis* (Brant's *The Ship of Fools*), *Lo spaccio della bestia trionfante* (Bruno's *The Expulsion of the Triumphant Beast*), and *Moriae Encomium* (Erasmus's *The Praise of Folly*) brought to the fore uncanonical titles that exposed social abnormalities.[10] Whereas Juan de Valdés, Saint Theresa, and Saint Ignatius of Loyola read chivalrous fictions without losing their sanity, Don Quixote went mad because he so misread chivalric romances that he attempted the final translation of chivalric reading into novelistic living; *ingenioso* drew the line between them, and the title failed to bridge the gap. The Italian humanists did not allow their classical dreams outside *studioli* and *accademie*, and Machiavelli never thought of having his prince walk the streets of Florence dressed in a Roman toga. But humanism gave way to the Baroque when Don Quixote "incarnated" his chivalric stories by sallying forth in beaten-up armor down the roads of La Mancha.

Chivalric journeys unfolded along literary paths that did not pretend to exceed the boundaries of the library-*studiolo*, a room at once secretive and revelatory where reading led Don Quixote to confuse reality with literature. Although the priest found very few books "that did not deserve punishment by fire,"[11] one can only guess how many windmills the knight dreamed of charging as he reread verses in the familiar landscape of Ariosto's *Orlando furioso*. Hoping that he would forget tales of old that cast long shadows on life in the making, friends and relatives denied the *hidalgo* access to his beloved study. The title is fixed on Don Quixote, but the text also refers to Quexada and Quijano; the upshot of the onomastic confusion is that the narrative tests the concepts of beginning and end. Does the novel take its start with Quexada? Does it end with Don Quixote? After all, the title has replaced a lifetime *historia* for a particular stage of the *hidalgo*'s life. Quexada faced a momentous choice. Either he would forget chivalric tales or he would try to live them out on the planes of Castile. The time had come to "incarnate" fictional reading in live action; Quexada was on his way to becoming Don Quixote. Once he was deprived of his beloved library, the sedentary Quexada so took to heart the chivalric stories he had read that he chose to live them out in the streets. *Ingenioso* discharged physical deeds on the plains of La Mancha, where Quexada went mad and became Don Quixote. Eventually Quexada regained his sanity, cast off *valer* (to be worthwhile) for *ser* (to exist), renamed himself Don Quixano el Bueno, and passed away peacefully. The titological *ingenioso* aptly describes the chivalric randomness of Ariosto's endless adventures. But the title offers no indication of Cervantes's eventful shift from romance to the novel.

We have already seen that, for Claudio Guillén, *La vida de Lazarillo de Tormes y sus fortunas y adversidades* is the first title that met the novelistic challenge of shaping not mere episodes but an entire *vida* of picaresque trials and tribulations. By contrast, Cervantes's title centers on an aging gentleman whose uneventful life becomes noteworthy only when mental illness spurs him to enact chivalric deeds. Especially in Spain, humanist legacies (via Sannazaro and Castiglione) stood against Erasmian clashes (via Juan Lopez de Hoyos, Cervantes's tutor) between wisdom and folly. Reality robbed Quixote of his imagination. As Carlos Fuentes puts it, "Quixote can no longer imagine."[12]

Like Don Quixote, *ingenioso* remains extraneous to the introduction as well as to the conclusion of the novel. While it highlights what the author sets out to reject, *ingenioso* ignores what the knight seems to endorse. *Ingenioso* thus sets up the dualism of sanity and insanity alongside the analogous dualism of title and antititle. In fact, we could suggest that the text about Don Quijano survives the title about Don Quixote, which is what Cervantes intends to do in the introduction. Yet how many readers would care to read a book because it is about Don Quijano? At best, title and narrative are at odds; at worst the title is inadequate to introduce significant aspects of the text that neither begin nor end with Don Quixote. The final page loops back toward Cide Hamete Benengeli, the Arabic chronicler who is presented as the original author of the quixotic tale. His pen speaks the last words of the book long after not only he but the narrator, the second author, and the illustrator have given versions of the duel between Don Quixote and the Basque. Such complexity applies to characters, authors, and plots as well as to a cluster of literary forms that make up a book of chivalric adventures meant to discredit the literature of pernicious romances.

Don Quixote's preliminary task is to repudiate Don Quijano, who nevertheless precedes and outlasts the mad *hidalgo*. Just as the book with windmills and basins cancels out the one with giants and helmets, Don Quixote and Don Quijano live by denying each other. If that were not enough, how does Sancho's appearance affect the concept of protagonist? Sancho brought to the fore a popular culture that set the title's poetics, which is pinned to the imitation of romances, next to the text's prosaics, which took notice of humble enclaves where young rogues grew to adulthood in the name of survival rather than adventure. The title shows its flagrant inadequacies, not only vis-à-vis chivalric anachronisms but especially with regard to the emergent realism of popular culture. Once Sancho enters the narrative, the title becomes a synecdoche for a larger text that it can no longer handle. The Cervantine narrative can contain both, but the title cannot.

For Don Quixote, the very concept of individual authorship gave way to a wholehearted trust in the narrative map of adventurous stories. While negotiations take place between the time when the text is written and that of the latest rereading, the gap between these two moments points to cultural sedimentation, which is bound to change the way books are read, plays are staged, and audiences respond to both. Much "rethinking" goes into our approach to older texts. In a seminal essay of 1908, Pirandello noted that the act of publication transfers textuality to the reader, whose active reading may exceed what the author had in mind: "Actually, we reach a point where we express better in our own words what the author has expressed poorly or has not expressed at all. Indeed we find in a book what in reality is not there; in other words, we succeed where the author has failed."[13] Belatedness affords insights and makes room for commentary. Because of the sheer unfolding of human experiences, we bring to the artwork a body of knowledge that was not available to the artist. Yet the thesis that we can succeed where the original artist has failed puts the very status of authorship in jeopardy. I trust that Pirandello neither foresaw nor favored such an outcome. Nevertheless, he must have suspected that, just as Cervantes could not help creating the Cervantine, he would not stop the emergence of the Pirandellian; rereading and misreading were but immediate measures of widespread success.

1

Almost a decade passed between the publication of part 1 and part 2 of the Spanish masterpiece. The impostor Alonso Fernandez de Avellaneda took advantage of this and published a derivative text, which treated Don Quixote and Sancho so ineptly that Harry Levin felt compelled to retitle those figures "à la Pirandello, *Two Characters in Flight from an Author*."[14] Just as there are characters in search of authors and authors in search of characters, so there are texts in search of rereadings that probe this side of renewal and the other side of obsolescence. Cervantes thus anticipated the Pirandellian challenge: is it possible to represent a character by rejecting it? Can art thrive on its own undoing? Early in the story, the priest burns all translations in Quijano's library because they could not be "as good as the original." For that very reason, what credence could readers give to Spanish translations of Arabic manuscripts? Cervantes seems to be in league with his reader as a commentator upon narrative inauthenticity. While a forgotten manuscript downgraded Cervantes's originality, an impostor urged the writing of the second part of the novel, which was cut "from the same cloth as the first" and did nothing but present "the knight at greater length" (470).

Cervantes thrived on literary legacies. His masterpiece points to missing pages, unreliable translations of Arabic manuscripts, forgeries, detours, and endless interruptions. In the final speech to the dead *hidalgo* the "speaking" pen utters the words, "Only we are at one, despite that fictitious and Tordillescan scribe who has dared, and may dare again, to pen the deeds of my valorous knight" (940). To avoid illegitimate spin-offs, friends request a certificate of death for Don Quixano the Good. As we all know, that last request went unheeded. Necrology was no match for posthumous revivals.

Regardless of Arabic chroniclers and Castilian novelists, or of manuscripts lost and found, Unamuno never wavered in his belief that Don Quixote had sprung up from the roots of the Spanish soul. In 1905 he published *Vida de Don Quijote y Sancho según Miguel de Cervantes Saavedra explicada y comentada por Miguel de Unamuno*, which was translated as *The Life of Don Quixote and Sancho According to Miguel de Cervantes Saavedra, Explained and Commented on by Miguel de Unamuno*.[15] The title begins with *vida*, which is not geared to the chronology of biographical fortunes or autobiographical adversities of a "realistic" character such as Lazarillo; instead, *vida* deliberately refers to the life of fictional characters. With an eye to the development of Western literature, the titological difference between the picaresque and the

Unamunian *vida* highlights nothing less than an early instance of the forthcoming paradigm shift from mimesis to simulation.

By pairing Don Quixote with Sancho Panza, Unamuno's title introduces a narrative in which insanity and common sense validate and discredit each other. For Unamuno, Don Quixote berated Sancho Panza's "sublime heroism": "Cunning was malicious Cervantes in twisting Sancho's intentions and shuffling his purposes that the noble squire has gotten an ummerited reputation, from which we Quixotists will redeem him, I trust, since a good Quixotist has to be a Sanchopanzist as well" (462). The emergence of an appreciable reputation for Sancho was such that it generated Sanchiopanzism, which led Unamuno to propose a new assessment of the squire:

> For if Don Quixote was enamoured of Dulcinea, Sancho was no less so, with the difference that the master quit his house for love of glory and his servant did so for pay; but the servant began to get a taste for glory, and in the end he was, in the heart of him, and though he would have denied it, one of the most unmercenary men the world has ever known. And by the time Don Quixote died, grown sane again, cured of his madness for glory, Sancho had gone mad, raving mad, mad for glory; and while the hidalgo was cursing books of chivalry the good squire begged him, with tears in his eyes, not to die, but to go on living so they might sally forth along the roads in search of adventure. (462)

Sancho embodies the material world of empirical necessities as a counterweight to his master's idealism. In the end, however, he is "bequixotized" (132).

Eventually, insane Don Quixote and sane Don Quijano die, but Sancho sallies forth in his master's armor. The title implies a synthesis that lets the squire grow to a point where he exchanges pay for glory. In this way Unamuno works his way out of Cervantes's dead end:

> Inasmuch as Cervantes did not dare kill Sancho, still less bury him, many people assume that Sancho never died, and even that he is immortal. When we least expect it, we will see him sally forth, mounted on Rocinante, who did not die either, and he will be wearing his master's armor, cut down to size by the blacksmith at El Toboso. Sancho will take to the road again to continue Don Quixote's glorious work, so that Quixotism may triumph for once and all time on this earth. (462)

Perhaps Unamuno's retitling links up to "a mythology, all the more needed in these days, when we are creating the myth of the democratic Spanish republic of workers of all classes" (441). In each epoch, "the hero who is needed appears ... and every hero other than the one needed must end in wretchedness or oblivion, in the galleys or the lunatic-asylum, even perhaps on the scaffold" (342).

If seventeenth-century idealism rests with Don Quixote, its twentieth-century counterpart belongs to Sancho Panza. The title seems to assert some sort of equivalence between master and servant, which leans toward the representation of life-size individuals. Once he wears Don Quixote's helmet, would Sancho Panza turn his gaze toward the future? What does the future have in store for him? Don Quixote despised social mediocrity. Like his master, Sancho was bound to cross paths with common people whose human condition moved Unamuno to write *The Tragic Sense of Life in Men and Nations*. Long after Spain had been "the head and front of the Counter-Reformation," a "de-essentializing" of Catholicism ensued. For Unamuno, "the ideal of an eternal, ultra-terrestrial life" gave way to "the ideal of progress, of reason, of science, or, rather, of Science with the capital letter."[16]

A "descriptive" plot lays the groundwork for "interpretative" rereadings that led the Basque writer to draw a distinction between Cervantism and Quixotism: "Everything depends on separating Cervantes from *Don Quixote*, and substituting the sacred legion of Quixotists for the plague of Cervantophiles or Cervantists. We are as short on Quixotism as we are long on Cervantism" (454). The inference is that Quixotism entails continuous rewriting, and Unamuno's title validates a philosophical axiom: "We should pay more attention to being fathers of our future than to being sons of our past" (99). The rewriting of the windmill episode gives the full measure of change. Don Quixote's giants, in fact, have become locomotives, dynamos, steamships, and automobiles. "But the battered Don Quixote will go on living, because he sought health within himself and dared to charge the windmills" (58).

For Don Quixote, the crown makes the king, and Unamuno believes that Sancho, just by wearing the knight's armor, can "continue Don Quixote's glorious work, so that Quixotism may triumph for once and all time on this earth" (462). Sancho will continue the knight's adventures, but his motivation is altogether different. Trusting logic, Sancho Panza believes that "we all mean the same thing when we use the same words." To approach the present as present, and to read language by relying on common sense, is to read like Sancho, who is blessed with a literal sense of life that is immune to idealism and insanity alike. Trusting faith, Don Quixote "knew that with identical words we usually manage to say totally opposite things." While instigating individualism, diversity makes understanding possible: "If my neighbor understood from what he says the same things I understand, his words would not enrich my spirit nor would mine enrich his. If my neighbor is merely another me, what good is he to me?"[17] Cervantes would have dismissed as "too ingenious" the possibility that Quixotism could ever yield to Sanchopanzism. Is it the case that he can play a more prominent role because the world has changed for the better or for the worse? What will happen to the soul of Spain once Sancho Panza takes over for his master? Is his Spain just as terrestrial, or will he redefine Spanish idealism?

Unamuno for good reason pretends to know more than Cervantes insofar as textuality is concerned. In the 1928 preface to the third edition of his book, Unamuno answered a query from an English translator, "I believe that Cide Hamete Benengeli was no Arab but a Jew, a Moroccan Jew, and that he did not make up the story either. In any case, this Arabic text of Cide Hamete Benengeli is in my possession . . . in this text I have discovered that as regards the passage cited by Professor Earle it was Cervantes who misread the text, so that my interpretation, and not his, is the faithful one" (7). To substantiate his claim, Unamuno informs us that he has read the Arabic text in the original. In other words, he did all by himself what Cervantes accomplished with the help of translators. While drawing on previous sources, Unamuno's rereading probes untapped levels of meaning. Confidence thrives on its own dynamics: "Since when is the author of a book the person to understand it best?" (449). Is it possible that Unamuno is trying to secure greater authority by drawing a deeper gap between the two texts? Textuality is open-ended, and Unamuno concedes, "I do not pretend to discover the meaning Cervantes aimed to impart to his work, but only the meaning which I myself give it" (4).

The shift from Don Quixote to Sancho involves the epoch-making transition from chivalric romances to realistic novels. It was inevitable that Unamuno would detect "the element of the picaresque" in the womb of Quixotism (366) before paying homage to the heritage of nineteenth-century Realism and Naturalism. For Unamuno, Don Quixote and Sancho "were born so that Cervantes might relate their lives and I explain and comment upon them" (324). Unamuno's reassessment of Cervantine priorities is spelled out in the title of his rewriting. While the title's *comentada* upgraded the Renaissance practice of commentaries, *explicada* asserted independent judgment, which would eventually translate the chivalric into the bourgeois—Dulcinea del Toboso into Emma Bovary. We border here on the world of metaliterature.

As the structural and semantic pivot of Unamuno's title, *según* (according to) is revolutionary, for it forces title and text to keep pace with cultural changes. Beyond the urbane practice of commentaries, *según* became an agonistic wager that eroded the stability of authorship once it made Cervantes's commentary still relevant but no longer exclusive. The transfer of characters from one text to another provides an apt illustration for the coexistence of titles and "figures on loan." The borrowing, however, can only occur when the literary reality is malleable enough to allow the shift. Theodore Ziolkowski reminds us that such a development calls for "frangibility," which can be effective only when one world breaks apart in order that the figure may enter another world.[18] I suspect that such open grounds, so familiar to novelistic wonderers, would be hard to find in the world of the epic. And I would suggest that, with regard to Unamuno's title, *según* stands out as the sharp plough blade that cuts through the frangibility of novelistic textuality. Such a reconfiguration of authors, commentators, and characters opened the floodgate of interpretation by trading the certain for the relative. The Basque writer built his rereading on the belief that "everything is clearly relative; but is not relativity itself also relative?" (129). As a literary device, relativity unsettles time and space, much as *según* entails a chronological shift from the original text to the later commentary. As ingeniously as the chivalric knight, Unamuno, Borges, and their postmodern cohorts have played up belatedness with a passion.[19]

At both ends of the title's *según,* Cervantes and Unamuno stand in a relationship that fosters change and preserves continuity by unlocking authorship to the future: "What do I care what Cervantes did or did not mean to put into that book or what he actually did put into it? The living part of it for me is whatever I discover in it."[20] Commentary takes center stage on the assumption that readers are familiar with *Don Quixote.* In fact, each generation has "added something to this Don Quixote" (451), who has been made to do and say things he never said or did in the Cervantine text. Because of countless additions, "Don Quixote is immensely superior to Cervantes. . . . For if Cervantes was his father, his mother was the country and people in which he lived and from which Cervantes derived his being" (455). While writing about the experience of writing, Unamuno gives literary form to a narrative in which Don Quixote outclasses Cervantes and any other writer who would ever try to "pen him again."[21] For Unamuno, Cervantes interfered with Don Quixote's true intentions. In a Pirandellian turn of mind, it seems that characters exist independently of writers. *Según* strings out many voices, several blueprints, diverse beginnings, illegitimate detours, longed-for sequels, and innumerable translations. A more appropriate title for Unamuno's work would be *The Life of Don Quixote and Sancho According to Miguel de Unamuno*.

In our own days, fabulators of Quixotism have grown to believe that every novelist who writes in Spanish is a variant of Avellaneda,[22] that is to say, a commentator as well as an impostor. These are instances of "rewording," a term that George Steiner borrowed from the linguist Roman Jakobson and applied to literature: "The same original text is often translated by several contemporary and subsequent translators, and that such a sequence of alternative versions is an act of reciprocal, cumulative criticism and correction."[23] *Según* confirms that commentaries were on their way to becoming as significant as textuality itself. There is a point where Unamuno, as he reflects on his quixotic rereading, turns traditional relationships upside down: "The characters are real, it is they who are the authentic beings, and they make use of the person who seems to be of flesh and blood in order to assume form and being in the eyes of men" (323). The radical inference is that characters are real and writers are fictional: "Far from Cervantes being their creator, it is they who created Cervantes" (430).

Back in 1925, Unamuno understood that every translation in effect is "a new and original work.... Does a song not sound the same when played on the violin, the flute, the harp, the bassoon?"[24] Actually, it would be disastrous for Quixotism if the original manuscript of *Don Quixote* turned out to be "in the handwriting of Cervantes."[25] While it could be debated whether bibliographical findings ought to be welcome, *según* would keep the latest writer clear of previous commentators. Ultimately, there is always a later *Don Quixote*, "replete with traces of 'previous' handwritings,"[26] and *según* is there to assert difference and secure the proliferation of rewriting through the revolving door of metaliterary beginnings: "The truth is that any gate serves as a sally port upon the world, and when one is bent on some great purpose there is no need to hesitate in choosing the gate from which to start.... Does not this sally recall the one made by that other knight, of Christ's Militia, Inigo de Loyola?" (32). Actually, the saint's life, by Pedro de Ribadeneira, was one of the books in Don Quixano's library, where temporality was pitted against timelessness. While it makes the title neither dogmatic nor obsolete, *según* sharpens cultural gaps and turns referentiality into a form of active anachronism. Having chosen the very word *anacronismo* to describe Unamuno's commentary on the quixotic text,[27] Borges qualifies his own literary endeavors as "exercises in anachronism."[28] Since any reading of any published book is anachronistic vis-à-vis the time of the original writing, the title becomes an instrument of transfer that keeps textuality at once open and topical.

Like Unamuno, Borges finds that the "deeper theme" of the master novel is "the friendship between Don Quixote and Sancho Panza."[29] Like Unamuno, he reads Cervantes's title vis-à-vis the literature that followed it:

> Let us take the title of one of the most famous books in the world, *Historia del ingenioso hidalgo Don Quijote de la Mancha*. The word *hidalgo* has today a peculiar dignity all its own, yet when Cervantes wrote it, the word *hidalgo* meant "a country gentleman." As for the name "Quixote," it was meant to be a rather ridiculous word, like the names of many of the characters in Dickens: Pickwick, Swiveller, Chuzzlewit, Twist, Squears, Quilp, and so on. And then you have "La Mancha," which now sounds noble in Castilian to us, but when Cervantes wrote it down, he intended it to sound perhaps (I ask the apology of any resident of that city who may be here) as if he had written "Don Quixote of Kansas City." You see how those words have changed, how they have been ennobled. You see a strange fact: that because the old soldier Miguel de Cervantes poked mild fun at La Mancha, now "La Mancha" is one of the everlasting words of literature.[30]

Let us not forget that the prologue to Cervantes's novel takes for granted that authority is based on that "long catalogue of authors." I bet that many a postmodern would let Don Quixote spend the rest of his days in his library, where he would die peacefully in the hope of embarking on one more adventure. Borges says as much when he lets Don Quixote get rid of authorial supports:

> Of that gentleman with the sallow, dry complexion
> and knightly disposition, they conjecture
> that, always on the edge of an adventure,
> he never actually left his library.
> The precise chronicle of his campaigning
> and all its tragicomical reversals
> was dreamed by him and not by Cervantes
> and is no more than a record of his dreaming.

In the closed world of the library, dialogues between texts foster recurrence and thrive on their own dynamics. In 1939 Borges's metaliterary title *When Fiction Lives in Fiction* confirmed that fictions can fictionalize textuality as well as authorship. Having understood that narrativity belongs to whomever claims it, Borges invented Pierre Menard, who enforced a literary technique based on "deliberate anachronism and erroneous attribution." Whereas Don Quixote acted out glosses, annotations, commentaries, spin-offs, rereadings, and misreadings, Pierre Menard stayed put because bibliography built his literary persona in the library itself. The *hidalgo* took it on the road; his postmodern heir browsed card catalogues.

Menard considers *Don Quixote* an open text that one can reread without changing a single word.[31] In fact, he does not set out "to compose another *Quixote*—which is easy—but *the Quixote itself.*" His goal is to reread the book through "the experiences of Pierre Menard," who intends to produce "a few pages that would coincide—word for word and line for line—with those of Miguel de Cervantes."[32] First we look at reality through the eyes of Don Quixote; then we look at the *hidalgo* through the eyes of Unamuno. Finally, Borges centers on the manipulation of authorship in *Pierre Menard, autor del Quijote (Pierre Menard, Author of the Quixote)*. *Según* opened a titological Pandora's box; the time had come for titles to introduce metanarratives written in the mode of "according to."

Whereas Unamuno rewrites the quixotic text in his own identifiable style, Borges rewrites it as an exact copy of Cervantes's text. Because difference is a matter of internal content rather than external style, the text bears no evidence of Menard's "intervention." Can one claim authorship without rewriting? Is Borges advancing an ontological dilemma or is he introducing a literary practice? Is he making fun of both? Subject, point of view, and context change the moment books are published, and Borges concedes that "scribes take a secret oath to alter, omit, and interpolate. *Indirect* falsehood is also practiced."[33] In fact, the overlooked goal of the Menard "affair" is to "play an impersonal joke . . . for the sheer fun of it." The story is a "bit of a hoax," but many people in Buenos Aires and two literary men "took the whole thing seriously."[34] In a way, the title enables Menard to make an authorial claim that is implied but not stated in Unamuno's title. Moderns and postmoderns alike have tampered with the quixotic title, and the questions Michel Foucault asks in his essay on the death of the author bear directly on the Borgesian title: "Who is the real author? Have we proofs of his authenticity and originality?"[35] At once daring and outrageous, these claims lead readers to seek out some "unburied truth" whereby Cervantes himself might turn out to be another impostor.

At first Menard plunges himself back into the seventeenth century to achieve identification with the spirit of the age, which demands that he must "[k]now Spanish well, to re-embrace the Catholic faith, to fight against Moors and Turks, to forget European history between 1602 and 1918, and to be Miguel de Cervantes." His rewriting, however, ought to be as contemporary to the twentieth century as Cervantes's was to the seventeenth. Because of contextual changes, one can read the same text differently: "History, *mother* of truth; the idea is astounding. Menard, a contemporary of William James, does not define history as an investigation of reality, but as its origin. Historical truth, for him, is not what took place; it is what we think took place."[36] To a twentieth-century reader, history is a matter of opinion, which makes historical "truth" circumstantial rather than obsolete. The difference between presentation and reception measures intellectual development. For an idea of what "truth" means in today's world, here is E. M. Cioran on the subject of real and ordinary truth: "Our only choice is between irrespirable truths and salutary frauds. The truths that allow of no existence alone deserve the name of truths." They are inhuman because "no one can do without props disguised as slogans or as gods."[37] The postmodern writer appropriates the past by "rereading" it as a "combinatory" bricolage of possible variations.

Unlike Unamuno, whose comments cover the entire text of *Don Quixote*, Menard's rewriting is limited to "the ninth and thirty-eighth chapters of the first part of *Don Quixote* and a fragment of chapter twenty-two." We have fewer than three chapters out of 126 (52 in Part I and 74 in Part II). Such a disparity has been pinned to the difference between the truth of correspondence, which is linked to reality, and the truth of coherence, which is linked to textuality. Examples of this "correspondence" are Marguerite Yourcenar's *Hadrian's Memoirs* and Manuel Mujica Lainez's *Bomarzo*. In the case of Unamuno and Borges, however, the distinction applies to "coherence" only. Quite correctly, Linda Hutcheon writes that "if the archive is composed of texts, it is open to all kinds of use and abuse,"[38] whether it is a matter of rereading or misreading. Yet the reduction of textuality over textuality itself exposes the factual inadequacy of Borges's title, which refers to only a fragment of the Cervantine narrative.

Reduction, of course, is typical of Borges's approach to literature. As early as 1935 he reduced "a person's entire life to two or three scenes" in *A Universal History of Infamy*.[39] The preliminary notes to Borges's *Cuentos Breves y*

Extraordinarios (*Extraordinary Tales*, 1967) explain that "the anecdote, the parable, and the narrative have all been welcome, on the condition that they be brief."[40] Instead of trusting a narrative line, Borges relies on synoptic phrases that exemplify a theory of key-passages.[41]

Having written *A Universal History of Infamy*, why did Borges not instruct Menard to write *A Universal History of Chivalry*? Out of the exhausted romances of chivalry, the Spanish master created the novel's novel, whereas Borges could not write a novel because he had problems with the size no less than with the ideology of linear narratives. The prefatory statement to *Ficciones* calls for brevity: "A laborious and impoverishing waste—that is what the composition of long books is: the expansion to five hundred pages of an idea whose perfect oral exposition takes a few minutes. A better procedure is to imagine that these books already exist and to offer a resume, a commentary.... I have preferred writing notes about imaginary books."[42] Notes on imaginary texts single out narratives that have been either overused or used up. The inference is that all texts have been read, reread, and misread; all myths, legends, and plots have been recycled. Since he manages to stay always one step ahead of any last rewriting, Borges believes that what remains to be done is to keep on rewriting with different intonations books that already have been written.

Because he found it impossible to handle the novel form, Borges imagined that someone else had already written the book he wanted to write, so that he could comment on it by way of "notes upon imaginary books."[43] Borges never felt compelled either to write or to read a novel: "I'm fond of short stories, but I'm far too lazy for novel writing. I'd get tired of the whole thing after writing ten or fifteen pages."[44] For Borges, reduction favors craftsmanship over ideology: "A philosophical doctrine begins as a plausible description of the universe; with the passage of the years it became a mere chapter—if not a paragraph or a name—in the history of philosophy."[45] The inference is that readers pay more attention to chosen parts than to entire texts.[46] Like wine, textuality ages by distilling prolixity into a more concentrated "essence." But there are limits to both laziness and concentration. Can one rewrite such a long novel as *Don Quixote* by relying on exclusion more than inclusion? How much should one quote in order to make a case for the entire work?

Returning to Menard's selection of Cervantes's text, the ninth chapter of the masterwork takes us back to the duel between Don Quixote and the Basque, which stalls because some pages of the manuscript are missing. The narrator blames the "first author" for the loss, which harks back to the moment when Cervantes found the Arabic manuscript amid a bunch of parchment papers. A translator identified the writer as Cide Hamete Benengeli, who should "be praised not for what he writes, but for what he has refrained from writing" (46). Could one say the same about Menard? The title's irony is that the character outshines the writer. Readers know Don Quixote but ignore Pierre Menard, whose puny achievements have turned him into an author in search of a character who might give him the sort of recognition he never enjoyed on his own. His bibliographical *vida* can claim different translations of a single sonnet published twice. Another entry is about a philological fragment by Novalis that outlines the theme of *total* identification with a specific author. Also listed are texts that place Don Quixote on Wall Street.[47] Since his biography is entirely book-bound, Menard's profile is as derivative as Borges's own.

In the virtual reality of Tlön, Borges writes, the dominant opinion in matters of literature "is that everything is the work of a single author. As a result, books are rarely signed. The concept of plagiarism does not exist because all books are the work of one writer, who is timeless and anonymous."[48]

> No one can write a book. Since
> Before a book can really be
> It needs the dawn, the dusk, centuries,
> Arms, and the binding and sundering sea.

Even Ariosto dreamed: "Again the dreams that had been dreamt."[49] In Cervantes's case,

> To get rid of or to mitigate the cruel
> weight of reality, he hid his head in dream.
> The magic past of Roland and the cycles
> of Ancient Britain warmed him, made him welcome.
> ...
> Suddenly, plunging deep in a dream of his own,
> he came on Sancho and Don Quixote, riding.[50]

If plagiarism does not exist and Shakespeare can be anybody, then we can understand why some have grown tired of asking, "Who is the author?" If the world is a replica of the book, it is no wonder that Maurice Blanchot considers Borges's *Fictions* and *Artifacts* as the "frankest titles an author can give to his works,"[51] even though some believe that rewriting "does not claim to produce *anything*."[52] As an instance of "maximal imitation," Menard's *Don Quixote* achieves its radical transformation in the reader's mind.[53] While failing from a scriptural point of view, Borges's title may succeed psychologically.

The assets and liabilities of rereading à la Menard entail no visible rewriting. His project is "[c]omplex in the extreme and futile from the outset. He dedicated his conscience and nightly studies to the repetition of a pre-existing book in a foreign tongue. The number of rough drafts kept on increasing; he tenaciously made corrections and tore up thousands of manuscript pages. He did not permit them to be examined, and he took great care that they would not survive him. It is in vain that I have tried to reconstruct them."[54] Menard let no one examine his pages for the obvious reason that no one would have recognized them as his. Hence the question: Menard certainly reread, but did he rewrite? What does rewriting consist of when there is no textual difference between the written and the rewritten? It would seem that identity between writing and rewriting stands against difference between reading and rereading.[55] Borges himself finds such a juxtaposition troublesome: "I have thought that it is legitimate to consider the 'final' *Don Quixote* as a kind of palimpsest, in which should appear traces—tenuous but not undecipherable—of the 'previous' handwriting of our friend. Unfortunately, only a second Pierre Menard, inverting the work of the former, could exhume and resuscitate these Troys."[56] However unwittingly, any new reading overlays the text with new interpretations. Anybody can reread and rewrite the Spanish text as long as he or she approaches it from a point of view that is somewhat different from the original. Menard reads texts, translates them, and makes them up; his task is to alter univocal meanings.

Assuming as he did that translation is a matter less of accuracy than of transformation, Borges, who had not mastered Greek, found an unlimited number of possible rereadings in the Homeric text. Spanish texts, however, presented a challenge. Borges could have reread *Don Quixote* in his own person, so that one's Castilian would have been adapted to the other's Argentinean. But Borges, who was as well versed in Spanish as Cervantes, could not reread the quixotic text as creatively as the French-speaking Menard did.[57] In the prologue to *Ficciones*, Borges writes that his collection of stories is a "diagram" of his mental history.[58] Textuality rests on continuity "in the manner of," or "in contrast to," previous literary models:

Let others boast of pages they have written,
I take pride in those I have read.[59]

Much of Borges's literary activity translates "their" writing into "his" reading, which assumes that "quotations are all we have now. As a matter of fact, language is a system of quotations."[60] We now live in a culture where each reading is a bifurcation: "Whenever I read myself I suppose I am also changing what I wrote, since I read it with different experiences."[61] We also know that Borges reread the quixotic text several times. Having written a detailed analysis of the last chapter in 1946, Borges pitted the knight's death against the immortality of Don Quixote, "who is not a fiction, neither by Cervantes nor by ourselves."[62] Although a variable feature of textuality, reading has become a primary aspect of artistic creation.

Borges's approach to Cervantes's masterpiece is even more elusive in his short piece "A Problem," which replaces alternate authorships with problematic rewritings. What if Don Quixote were to discover, "after one of his many combats, that he has killed a man. At that point the fragment ends; the problem is to guess how Don Quixote would react."[63] The title proposes a textual dilemma that suggests an altogether different reading. Borges was not alone in exploiting hypothetical narratives about the past as it might have happened. Writers such as Carlos Fuentes and Manuel Mujica Lainez have combined the mythical method with side shadowing, which has allowed them to conjecture the ghostly presence of might-have-beens in *Terra Nostra* and *Bomarzo*.[64] Indeed, the narrative "as if" of virtual history favors mosaic-like arrangements by means of collage and pastiche, which take place here and now.[65]

Secure in his world of books and confident about his talents, Borges could have written the story in his own name, *Jorge Luis Borges, autor del Quijote,* but he did not. Instead, he created a virtual "other" before fictionalizing himself: "The world, unfortunately, is real; I, unfortunately, am Borges."[66] Perhaps we are someone else's dream: "You are dreaming me. No, I'm wrong. I am dreaming you."[67] If "Borges and I" are not one in the *ficción* about the writer and the person, why should the author of *Ficciones* and that of each *ficción* be the same? Can the same question be asked about characters? I suspect that Don Quixote would agree with Paul Valéry's Faust, who voiced the inevitable complaint: "They have written so much about me that I no longer know who I am." But the rest of the world knows who Don Quixote is. By the turn of the third millennium, the knight has journeyed all the way to the Americas, where his deeds of old still inspire writers the world over to write *según*.⁶⁸ The artist has turned into a skillful practitioner, and John Barth adds that Borges's "*ficciones* are not only footnotes to imaginary texts, but postscripts to the real corpus of literature."⁶⁹

Individual talent still thrives on clever approaches to the inherited world of artistic forms. In the dead end of postmodernism, the intransitive has become productive, because the end is not a point but a cul-de-sac where everything bounces back into new combinations. Nowadays, histories and stories cannot but make directional adjustments from linear progress to repetitive curves.⁷⁰ Since it is highly fictive, the postmodern cul-de-sac has not ceased to welcome quixotic narratives that have dispersed authorship amid writers who are yet to tire of explaining the master text "according to"— *según*—individual variations.

2

Because it oscillates between the literary and the metaliterary, the transformational semantics of *según* takes us back to Pirandello's *in cerca*, which also encompasses different concepts of authorship. *In cerca* and *según* uphold the resilience of the text while authors are lost, recovered, downgraded, refused, or counterfeited. In other words, *in cerca* and *según* remind us of modes of representation that transcend the individual writer who created them. The implication is that the twentieth-century universe of textuality multiplies itself along the ebb and flow of a handful of master plots. Along with the recurrence of mythical variations, even universal history consists of "different intonations" that writers have given to a few metaphors.⁷¹ Of course, different intonations are interpretative, and interpretation plays up difference. Stories go forth about travelers who have crossed literary thresholds only to meet a Menard after Pierre Menard, who is not alone in trying to explain a story *según*. Will the time come when a latter-day Pierre Menard will rewrite the Borgesian title because that is the only thing worth rewriting? Will future Menards give us pages without letters and titles without texts? It is now up to their kin to let *écriture* go on because the combinatorial range of writing not only is limitless; it is the only thing left. Linear narratives of the novelistic kind have become suspect, and scholarship has played up the ascendancy of honest fragments over illusory wholes.⁷² A postmodern before postmodernism, Borges already has come back from wherever his heirs have been trying to go.

From characterization to authorship, Cervantine titles foreground the inadequacies of titles. Menard is not much of an author, Don Quixote is not the only character, and the genre rests on the quicksand of an uncomfortable blend of novelistic and chivalric, that is to say, the hopeful and the nostalgic. Because it best enforces transtextual changes, *según*—like *in cerca*—tells us that writers come and go, but stories can linger as long as we narrate them according to . . .

11

The Picaresque and the Quixotic: An Adventure in Titology

> So what, after three centuries, has happened to adventure, the first great theme of the novel? Has it become its own parody? What does that mean? That the path of the novel winds up in a paradox?
> —MILAN KUNDERA

After chapters on individual titles and titological clusters, this chapter will trace an overview—what the historian Fernand Braudel would call a *longue durée*—meant to illustrate the way titology can contribute to, and draw from, thematics. Because of the outreach of certain titles, rereading and rewriting have generated thematic modes of expression in literature as well as in the arts. We can say that titles exist in relation to other titles, and my chapters on Cervantes and Joyce have made a case for the reciprocity of thematics and titology.[1]

The title *Narrative as Theme* introduces Gerald Prince's reflections on thematics, which "expresses a relation of being about."[2] The "aboutness" of this chapter centers on the picaresque, a titological hybrid that has drawn together character (*pícaro*) and title (*Guzman de Alfarache*, popularly known as *El Pícaro*) in a generic mode of literary expression that has contributed to the development of Western literature *from* dawn *to* decadence. Linked to the birth of the novel, the picaresque focused on the materialistic everydayness of a lowbrow humanity that gained prominence during the Industrial Revolution, which saw the vindication of human rights and social responsibility as well as the consolidation of democratic ideals.

The universe of titology is interactive, and what Chapter 2 of this volume shares with the other chapters is the theme of the journey. From the pastoral to the chivalric, adventurous quests have turned out to be as heterogeneous as the novel itself. It is time to let titles chase, echo, test, and renew one another.

Thus I will pit knights and squires who journeyed after fame and honor against resourceful scoundrels in search of better luck—the narrative of chivalric knighthood mixed with popular tales of destitute roguishness. Both made promises that were either kept or betrayed. Across geographical boundaries, social thresholds, and literary conventions, adventure has made room for the recurrence and transformation of titles as they crossed, clashed, and coiled in the cul-de-sac of postmodernism. Because of its diachronic range, the picaresque can offer points of entry into the study of literary history no less than the history of ideas.[3]

1

In the title *Lazarillo de Tormes y sus fortunas y adversidades, fortunas* stands out as a semantic hybrid that entails favorable as well as adversarial deeds. Resilience activated the itinerant geography of the picaresque, which covered Castile at first and then the rest of Spain before crossing the Atlantic Ocean in the path of the Spanish Conquest. Lázaro's toilsome *adversidades* act out an autobiographical narrative that opens with a reference to Lázaro's father, Tomé. From beginning to end, Tormes reminds the *pícaro*-turned-town crier of his father's criminal conduct. In the village of Tejares, Tomé stole grain, confessed his guilt, was convicted, and went to prison, which he left only upon volunteering in the service of a knight who undertook a military adventure that led him to fight the Moors. If theft entailed punishment, it was a forced honor that led Tomé to die "like a loyal servant."[4] Whether they were crusaders, mercenaries, or volunteers, the foot soldiers who did the loyal serving and the honorable dying ventured forth because they had no better alternative. They served knights, whose praiseworthy adventures paid homage to the kind of aristocratic gallantry that found its way into the literature of medieval romances. But clearly the knight's choice was the squire's obligation. While the *conquistadores*, Cortés and Pizarro, sailed westward to exploit the riches of the American Indies, Tomé's knight went south for the glory of Christendom. Tucked into the very beginning of the novel, the "soldier's tale" tells us much about a society that, though engaged in building the largest Western empire since Rome, still appreciated chivalric adventures.

Although the political leadership was more interested in strategies of colonial expansion and mercantile acquisitions, the anachronistic nostalgia for chivalric adventures in the cultural landscape of the Renaissance cannot be underestimated. Jacques Le Goff tells us that medieval man lived in "a constant anachronism,"[5] obsessed as he was with attributing to the ancients medieval modes of behavior. Anachronism pointed the other way when Don Quixote tried to impose the medieval on the Renaissance. As we saw in the previous chapter, Cervantes's title, *El ingenioso hidalgo Don Quijote de la Mancha*, pivots on *ingenioso*, which enacts the thematics of an eccentric journey whose retrospective outreach let the Moorish *Arabian Nights* coexist with the Christian *Amadís de Gaula*, the prototypical chivalric text that grew from four to twelve books by the middle of the sixteenth century. Both thrived in the multilayered culture of Spain, where adventure inspired the aristocratic and militaristic *libros de caballerías* as well as their parodic counterparts, the picaresque and Moorish novels.[6] At long last, Castile, the land of medieval castles, took notice of a new adventurer who, under the power of dire necessity, journeyed along the river Tormes from destitute Tejares to academic Salamanca. Once he reached mercantile Toledo, Lázaro made choices that exceeded survival in a tale about the underbelly, not the shining armor, of Renaissance society.[7] To draw an introductory line of development, I call attention to W. P. Ker's *Epic and Romance*, a title that associates the epic with the heroic, romance with the chivalric, and the novel with the popular.[8] This tripartite division applies to predominant estates: military for the epic, courtly for the chivalric, and mercantile for the bourgeois.

Since knights required squires, the chivalric highbrow and the popular lowbrow were tied at the navel. Such a coexistence explains why the title of this chapter centers on the picaresque and why it considers the quixotic its dialogic kin. The third chapter of *Lazarillo de Tormes* tested titological *adversidades* to the point of tragedy, once the *escudero*, an impoverished member of the low-ranking nobility, took the aristocratic code of moral superiority and material affluence to the Toledan enclave of Lázaro's indigence. Sartorial details of chivalry—cloak and sword—camouflage his shameful poverty. When action is called for, he parades to church because prayers are free of charge. Otherwise, his lack of picaresque resourcefulness feeds a starvation diet. At lunchtime, however, the *escudero* never fails to go out into the street, where, pretending to have just finished a meal, he picks "his teeth which had nothing stuck between them" (59). His empty gesture is full of foreboding. Like Don Quixote, the *escudero* has no future. The picaresque "trial" causes him to fade out of existence.

As authoritative a voice in the theory of narrativity as Mikhail Bakhtin's tells us that "the idea of testing the hero, of testing his discourse, may very well be the most fundamental organizing idea of the novel."[9] By introducing the notion of a trial, "testing" made it possible for adventure to discredit the hero, an outcome so revolutionary that it set the novel apart from the epic. Adventure avoided neither picaresque criminality nor Cervantine insanity, and Lázaro's parental heritage of petty theft was typical of lowbrow titles, from *La Celestina* and *La pícara Justina* to *Rinconete y Cortadillo*. Unheroic onomastics reversed the idealism of titles such as *The Prince* or *The Courtier,* much as Tormes and Tejares were but insignificant dots on a map that flaunted a titology of memorable sites, from Petrarch's *Africa* to Sannazaro's *Arcadia*. Although such titles as Ronsard's *Franciade* and More's *Utopia* upheld timeless ideals during eras that were neither epic nor utopian, the picaresque brought to the fore social pathologies that were abroad in Spain, where the imperial golden age could not afford its own splendor. By 1600 Charles V's disastrous economic policies plunged many a member of the middle class and the lower nobility into impoverishment. Lázaro's long-term goal, by contrast, was to move from outside vagrancy to inside employment. Thus he set out to turn *adversidades* into a propitious quest that led him to land the job of town crier (*pregonero*), the lowest rank in the local bureaucracy.

At the start of his picaresque quest in Salamanca, Lázaro served a blind beggar who, once the stream of alms slowed to a trickle because the boy was cheating him, decided to move to Toledo. In the city of commercial and religious exchange, adventure was scaled down to chasing after people who were good only because they owned "the goods." It is the good-hearted archpriest of Toledo who helps Lázaro secure the job of town crier and marry the priest's own mistress. Chivalric tales demanded that love be the engine of quests after Angelica or Dulcinea del Toboso. In downtown Toledo, however, the bliss of marital exclusivity did not stop Lázaro's wife from spending evenings next door. Shunned by his neighbors as a cuckold, Lázaro did not spend the lonely evenings reading chivalric tales. Instead, he embarked on a future-oriented education that provided legal protection once a superior authority (Vuestra Merced) asked him to answer rumors about his *ménage-à-trois*. Rather than deny the charge, Lázaro developed a strategy of collective guilt that denounced secular as well as ecclesiastical authorities. Whereas romances were conceived as literary fictions that perpetuated their fictitiousness, charges of moral misconduct in a society steeped in juridical rhetoric brought to life the picaresque novel. Roberto Gonzáles Echevarría reminds us that legal writings deal with legitimacy and transgression, and people at the margins of society are disproportionately liable to criminal entanglements.[10]

Punishment opens and closes the picaresque narrative. Tomé's "soldier's tale" comes back in the prologue. Written years later, it ends with an indictment, but it also tells us that Lazarillo, having become familiar with Cicero and Livy, projects his father's military worthiness onto himself. Writing has given the town crier the newfound "desire for praise" (23) that motivates valorous soldiers who reach the top of the scaling-ladder. Indeed, the thieving beggar has become an educated writer who tests the establishment by means of a literary weapon bound to be a liability for the abuser no less than the abused. Comic episodes in the opening chapters might entertain superficial readers, but the less than comic critique that follows led vigilant authorities to include *Lazarillo de Tormes* in the Index of forbidden books. Under such censorious conditions, how adventurous could a novel be? Caution is not typical of adventure tales, but it is typical of picaresque stories that warn about impending threats. Chivalric adventure is about courage and victory; its picaresque counterpart is about expedient ways of setting ethical judgment against questionable deeds that often lead to failure. Guzmán de Alfarache wrote his story in the galleys; its author, Mateo Alemán, also spent time in prison, a place all too familiar to Cervantes himself.

By the time *Guzmán de Alfarache* was published in 1599, the picaresque narrator had taken a moralistic stand: "Can't you think it an honor that your horses should be as fat as their skins can hold ... while the poor fall down at your gate for want of food?" Twelve times longer than its concise precursor, Alemán's narrative combined adventures with moral commentaries that voiced the dictates of the Counter-Reformation. The social satire and stylistic chiaroscuro of Lázaro's denunciatory posture lost their bite and gave way to Guzmán's duplicitous role as an unrepentant outsider and self-righteous insider. Textuality became ever more referential, until the *pícaro* turned into a busybody in Vicente Espinel's *Marcos de Obregón*. Never-ending adventures across the European continent catapulted the picaresque from the street to the library, where it joined forces with the chivalric.

However repetitive, the picaresque did depict the less than adventurous lives of ordinary folks. Onomastic titles revealed novelistic plots tied to the protagonist's deeds and misdeeds. By the turn of the nineteenth century, castles and forests had given way to marketplaces and tenement houses. Titles like *Oliver Twist* translated the picaresque into the realistic, which left little room for adventure once Charles Dickens reduced the concept of education to "nothing but Facts" in the opening statement of *Hard Times*. Very much like Lázaro, Josiah Bounderby is "errand-boy, vagabond, labourer, porter, clerk, chief manager, small partner." While Lázaro was given away by his mother, Josiah was left with his grandmother, who "was the wickedest and the worst old woman that ever lived." Harry Levin reminds us that, "etymologically, realism is thing-ism." The adjective *real* derives from the Latin *res*, whose context is real estate.[11] How adventurous could "a man of realities" be? That question applies to the whole nineteenth century, when life came to terms with prosaic existence on a scale hitherto unimaginable.

After the French Revolution, a new familiarity with ideological touchstones (liberty, equality, fraternity) spawned ambitions that mixed the empirical with the ideological, and *Great Expectations* described Pip's state of mind. The protagonist is parentless, and he names himself after misreading his parents' name; Philip Pirrip becomes Pip. Reversal is contained in Pip's name, which is a palindrome.[12] Since the name is composed of three letters, adventure cannot go very far. Pip's future is tied to repetition. In spite of hard times, he nurtures hopes that update Lázaro's ambitious plans. Both depend so heavily on patronage that material advantage entails moral degradation. In the world of everyday life, journeys are shortened because they have to deal with concerns extraneous to chivalric narratives. Whereas Walter Scott upheld the ethics of chivalry in his novelistic plots about heroes who ventured forth in the name of love and honor, Dickens populated urban enclaves with people in pursuit of material goods, often as rather picaresque characters who tested their wits at the boundary between the lawful and the lawless.

Dickens's titles stand shoulder to shoulder with those of Honoré de Balzac, who also translated the chivalric into the realistic in his preface to *The Human Comedy*. To begin with, errant journeys obey chance, which is "the greatest novelist in the world." Balzac's world is that of French society. As its self-appointed "secretary," Balzac set out to write a history of social manners. Self-confident to a fault, he saw himself as the "painter of human types, the narrator of the dramas of intimate life, the archaeologist of social property, the namer of professions, the registrar of good and ill." After the great expectations raised by the Revolution and the Napoleonic age, *Illusions perdues* spelled out disillusionment because of the decline of bourgeois ideals and the progressive capitalization of society and literature alike. Asked to define fame, the publisher Dauriat answers, twelve thousand francs' worth of newspaper articles. Interestingly, *Illusions perdues* begins with the image of the printing press, which sets up comparisons between the little village of Angoulême and the city of Paris. Some of the differences are defined through technological advancement. "Although its paper-making industry kept it in contact with

Parisian typography," the provincial town still used "wooden presses." Printing there "was behind the time."[13] The printing press fostered business ventures that considered romances sources of potential income. Ideology was reduced to a commodity, and the alternative to disappointment was resignation.

Illusions perdues is a post-Napoleonic title about youths determined to construct a better *avenir*. As in the picaresque, onomastics betrays social ambitions inasmuch as the proper name becomes a marketable asset. Much as Tormes remains a liability for Lázaro, Lucien's onomastics stands out as a valuable commodity, should he succeed in appropriating his mother's aristocratic name, Rubempré, through a royal ordinance.[14] *Illusions* inspires the Rubempré cycle by making Lucien's experiences universal. It is in this sense that Proust read lost illusions as the lessons of experience. Along the broader perimeter of nineteenth-century narrativity, *lost* implies disappointments that qualify the protagonist's "failure" for Balzac and his defeat for Verga.

The time had come for titles to showcase the lower classes not only as individuals but also as groups. Jules Michelet offers a memorable description of the lower classes on the eve of the Revolution: "Masses until now immobile, ignorant, who, like the bottom of the Ocean, had never been able to hear storms, classes neither the Fronde nor the Revocation had stirred, this time raised their heads, asked about the public affairs."[15] Balzac counted between three and five thousand social types in his novels. Interestingly enough, he portrayed the way of life of French society by finding a collective model in the chivalric narratives of Walter Scott.

The shift from individuals to groups gained strength in *Les Paysans* (*The Peasants*, 1845). The title is ironic, for it acknowledges the growth of the peasant class as a danger, which shapes a comparison between the noble castle and the ignoble cottage. In fact, Balzac writes, "The peasant has the same instinct for his abode that the animal has for his den or his burrow, and that instinct was much in evidence in all the arrangements of the hovel."[16] The study "of the question of pauperism" presumes that the "peasant may lead a good life or a bad life, according to your way of looking at it; he goes as he came, in rags, and you in fine linen!" (119). Here, education echoes picaresque teachings: "The shrewd way is to keep close to the rich, there's always crumbs under their tables. That's what I call a fine education and a solid one" (120). The priest, Brossette, stands with the rich: "'Madame la comtesse,' said the curé, 'in this commune we have none but voluntary misery. Monsieur le comte means well; but we have to do with people of no religion, who have but a single thought; to live at your expense'" (107). The churchman describes the poor as parasites, and Balzac's title presents a peasant point of view that serves to set up a critical perspective on both the middle class and the aristocracy in postrevolutionary France. The title, therefore, needs qualifications, because the programmatic preface to *The Human Comedy* and the textual narrative turn out to be quite unsympathetic to the rise of the peasants:

> This essentially unsocial element, created by the Revolution, will some day absorb the middle classes, just as the middle classes have destroyed the nobility. Lifted above the law by its own insignificance, this Robespierre with one head and twenty million arms is at work perpetually; coaching in country districts, entrenched in the municipal councils, under arms in the national guard in every canton in France,—one result of the year 1830, which failed to remember that Napoleon preferred the chances of defeat to the danger of arming the masses. (4)

Apart from the socially conscious Victor Hugo and the overtly revolutionary Karl Marx, the rise of the working classes was widely feared on the European continent in spite of egalitarian proclamations in France, Manzoni's Christian pietism in Italy,[17] and revolutionary Marxism from England to Russia.

In 1922, the year *Ulysses* and *The Waste Land* were published, José Ortega y Gasset published *España invertebrata* (*Invertebrate Spain*), a title whose anatomical qualifier is overtly negative, pointing as it does to a major structural deficiency. Spain is personalized as the social body; an old metaphor served the modern writer in highlighting the unwillingness on the part of the lower classes to be led by a superior minority. As a result, Spain could not support itself because it was caught in the midst of an extreme case of historical "invertebration." Ortega y Gasset never doubted that "without a minority to act on a collective mass, and a mass which knew how to accept the influence of the minority, there would be no functional society."[18] The anatomical deficiency degenerated into a social pathology, with disastrous consequences.

In 1930 Ortega y Gasset published *The Revolt of the Masses*. In this work Balzac's peasants have joined forces with the rest of the lower classes. Together, they are unhinging the traditional order of society, and Ortega y Gasset's opening statement spells out an ominous prophecy: "There is one fact which, whether for good or ill, is of utmost importance in the public life of Europe at the present moment. This fact is the accession of the masses to complete social power. As the masses, by definition, neither should nor can direct their own personal existence, and still less rule society in general, this fact means that actually Europe is suffering from the greatest crisis that can afflict peoples, nations, and civilisation."[19] While a title such as *The Waste Land* suggests that Eliot gave up on the future of Western culture in 1922, Ortega y Gasset's title suggests radical change in the future of Western society. The book ends with a probing question: "What are the radical defects from which modern European culture suffers? For it is evident that in the long run the form of humanity dominant at the present day has its origin in these defects."[20] A couple of years later, civil war broke out in Spain between Communists and General Franco's fascist-royalists. Revolutions and revolts gave a social twist to the range and role of adventure. Escapist fictions had to confront the political ills of society, which meant that windmills and dragons had to be fought at the center rather than at the periphery. Quests for the Holy Grail were overshadowed by manifestoes that called for civic action in city streets rather than faraway forests. Adventure came to terms with labor conditions as well as with social mobility and class discrimination.

Much as it dealt with determinism before Darwin, the novel also took up class struggle before Marx. Industrialization and the rise of socialist ideologies created challenges that tested the very possibility of adventure. Could adventure consist of labor power and be reconciled with productivity on the assembly line? On closely related matters of clock-paced time in the age of mechanical reproduction, could adventure be relevant to people who dreaded anything extraordinary? How adventurous could a bureaucrat be? Literary criticism has taken up the prosaic nature of human existence in Michel de Certeau's *The Practice of Everyday Life*, a title that pays homage to "the ordinary man."[21] For the longest time, Certeau writes, the individual of mediocre qualities has fallen outside the grand narrative of outstanding deeds. Could adventure adjust to the practice of everyday life without undermining itself? By and large, adventure challenges the expected and courts the unorthodox. As a folkloristic, social, and economic mythology, picaresque adventurism still exists in the world outside the library, where it can serve the broader concerns of popular culture, social justice, and criticism of established narratives.

At the boundary between the picaresque and the popular, Sancho Panza, Don Quixote's squire, set the imitation of romances next to the prosaic. We saw in the previous chapter that, by the turn of the twentieth century, Unamuno had given Sancho titological stature and narrative prominence. His title, *The Life of Don Quixote and Sancho According to Miguel de Cervantes*

Saavedra Explained and Commented on by Miguel de Unamuno, makes it clear that the time had come for Sancho to emerge, if not as a hero, at least as a protagonist who would pitch the popular against the chivalric. Having understood that the future belonged to some variant of the lowbrow Sancho Panza, Unamuno's retitling of the Cervantine masterwork reflected mounting concerns. Sancho was bound to cross paths with people who confronted industrialization in an era when José Ortega y Gasset worried about the ascendancy of mechanization over civilization, whose technological growth disturbed Edmund Husserl, absorbed Martin Heidegger, and urged Herbert Marcuse to predict that technological rationality would generate the One-Dimensional Man. Indeed, literature took notice of humble enclaves where young rogues grew to adulthood in the name of survival. For them, adventure was a lifetime endeavor meant to bestow social stature and material substance on "the myth of the democratic Spanish republic of workers of all classes."[22] Would Sancho play a more prominent role because the world was changing for the better or for the worse? Had Spain become more secular?

2

Cervantes's titological *ingenioso* is focused on Don Quixote, whose deeds lose steam rather quickly, so much so that the writer felt compelled to introduce Sancho Panza, a unique squire bound to survive his master and play a major role after Quixote's death. Yet the title, *El ingenioso hidalgo Don Quijote de la Mancha* (*The Ingenious Knight Don Quixote de la Mancha*) failed to keep up with the text, which entailed a ten-year hiatus between the first and the second parts. This fact is quite relevant to my thematic focus on the picaresque, which obviously favors the pedestrian squire over the adventurous knight. While Sancho describes his master as "a raving lunatic," a sonnet appended to the end of Part I presents "the simplest squire the world has ever seen." But Cervantes had seen much more of the world than Sancho had. How could a writer who had endured slavery and imprisonment, and achieved military glory at the battle of Lepanto in 1571, be reconciled with the creation of common folks bound to play a more prominent role in society without exceeding their ordinariness? Once victory was followed by the disaster of the Armada in 1588, a title such as *Sueños*, by Francisco de Quevedo, turned dreams of grandeur into a national nightmare. Estranged from a leadership bent on chasing imperial dreams, much of society thrived on the coexistence of acceptance and refusal—*engaño* and *desengaño*. National bankruptcy was declared in 1595, and post-Armada Spain nurtured literary forms of despair. Américo Castro calls attention to the following facts in his overview of Spanish civilization:

> At the climax of its imperial moment, the Spanish state went bankrupt several times. The emperor Charles V had to delay his return to Spain several months, after his dramatic abdication in 1554, because he lacked funds to pay the people of his household; for the same reason it was necessary for him to postpone the funeral of his mother, Joan the Mad. In the seventeenth century King Philip IV, monarch of two worlds, once had difficulty getting the meals of the day prepared in the royal palace.[23]

Spain could conquer, but governing was an altogether different matter. By the end of the sixteenth century, the glory of Charles V had faded into a royal twilight. Five years later, Cervantes published his book.

Weary of tradition and originality alike, Cervantes wove quixotic deeds into layers of the old that offered him an image he could not find in life. Rogues, knights, squires, and modest country gentlemen aside, the shapelessness of existence resisted anachronistic quests that shifted in and out of "quoted" narratives. After a few sallies, Sancho's appearance set up a kind of "dialogic protagonism" that kept chivalric clichés at bay but could not conceal signs of exhaustion. Sancho left home and family to follow Don Quixote. Like the people at the inn, he had been told enough about chivalry to find it attractive. Although he emerged as the survivor, could Sancho be the alternative to the old world of knighthood? Could a writer create a plain man out of a reality dominated by *parecer* and illusory *figuras*? Cervantes must have foreseen the possibility of fathering a book with a protagonist of strictly human dimensions. After a long and difficult pause, he was urged on by the impostor Avellaneda to write the second part of his master novel, in which Don Quixote is ever more deeply influenced by written stories. Don Quijano ran out of life, and Sancho eventually refused to grow cabbages again. As promised, the writer did expose chivalry, even though he could not bring himself to give ideological depth to the raw reality. Depictions of "low life" gained little strength beyond the comic, the compassionate, and the extravagant. Along Mediterranean shores, interest in the whole social spectrum stopped short of democratic concerns, let alone outright reform.

At once parodic and humorous, *Don Quixote* became a boundary text that pointed toward the past because the present had little to offer. Cervantes foresaw the possibility of stretching episodes into whole lives, but he did not create a protagonist who would carry out that project. Instead, he resorted to a *given* character, a subtext, and a stated goal that widened the gap between history and adventure. In this sense, *ingenioso* is an "exclusive" marker that dismisses anything either normal or collective. Yet Cervantes could not help writing a narrative that is socially, generically, and historically inconclusive. In its chivalric mode, adventure provides distraction, but not change; and Cervantes could not fail to realize that he was yet to father a character free of quixotic insanity in a present-oriented work. He could not let characters guided by utopian dreams of old travel those time-bound roads of life so familiar to humankind at large.

A ray of hope filtered in when Don Diego de Miranda, who studied Latin and Greek for six years at Salamanca, brought to the novel an educated gentleman holding promises for the future. Unfortunately, he "soaked in poetry" and spent whole days in his criticism of ancient authors, with little regard for "modern writers in the vernacular."[24] Once again "reading" prevailed over "doing." At the outer margins of art, much sustenance was given to the modern novel. In that no-man's-land between literary and extraliterary genres, Cervantes could unearth no more than chivalric vestiges. By definition, a no-man's-land lies at the periphery, where sociocultural forms must emerge if the artist is to draw an image out of them. Chivalric tales aside, the novel voiced the frustrations of the déclassé members of the middle class. In a country highly suspicious of novelty, Cervantes did not create an exemplary character capable of carrying the future.

For Victor Brombert, nineteenth- and twentieth-century literature is "crowded with weak, ineffectual, pale, humiliated, self-doubting, inept, occasionally abject characters." They all embody the antihero, who emerges in cultures that are ready to confront alternatives because they already have presented heroes.[25] Such alternatives were sporadic during the Renaissance but multiplied with the advent of the Industrial Revolution. Antiheroes brought to the fore the decline of the novelistic protagonist, whose responsibilities for much class exploitation disturbed Georg Lukács, the dean of Marxist criticism, who felt uncomfortable with such titles as *The Idiot, The Hollow Men*, and *Notes from the Underground*. One way or another, these titles spell out human pathologies above and below ground. With regard to Robert Musil's *The Man Without Qualities*, Lukács refers to the passage in which Ulrich, when asked what he would do if he were in God's place, replies that he would feel compelled to abolish reality. For any red-blooded Marxist, that would be just a tad too much to take! Indeed, I wonder what socially minded critics such as Frederic Jameson and Terry Eagleton would say about adventure vis-à-vis industrialization. The inference is that a *pícaro* would be a Marxist in feeling but not necessarily in deed, because rogues have a hard time picking up working habits at once legal and efficient. Lazarillo did, but most *pícaros* did not.

George Lukács would argue that self-consciousness offers an alternative to his idea of an integrated civilization, which occurs when the starry sky is the map of all possible paths. "Everything in such ages is new and yet familiar, full of adventure." These are times when the soul "lives through adventure, but it does not know the real torment of seeking and the real danger of finding. . . . Such an age is the age of the epic."[26] In the world of the epic, adventure is safe, because it enacts *nostos* through a journey of exile and return that tests order without seeking change. The known ontology of remembrance reigns supreme in the world of the epic, which does not condone forgetfulness. *The Odyssey* is as resonant a title as myth itself. By the turn of the nineteenth century, such titles as *Le Père Goriot* and *Oliver Twist* confronted readers with altogether "new" characters. Each one of them spoke to a readership whose socioeconomics was specific rather than universal. The postepic novel is open-ended, and conscious of the heterogeneous plurality of languages.[27] If the epic tends to pursue life as essence, the novel pursues life as existence, which demands that the adventurous make room for the routine.

Here we come to an impasse. While agreeing with Mikhail Bakhtin that the epic excludes adventure as an event that will test the hero by producing unexpected results, Lukács points out that the novel, by exploiting the activism of trials and errors, tends to be progressive.[28] Only that "biological and sociological life has a profound tendency to remain within its own immanence; men want only to live, structures want to remain intact."[29] Here is where picaresque ambition comes to terms with life as it is, which limits the potential for change to what is circumstantially possible.[30] The implication is that adventure can defy both dogmatism and relativism as long as it dwells in choice, does not ignore circumstance, and pays due attention to need. Adventure is there to tell us that millstones grind prosaic life much as windmills flag out cultural inadequacies that force "hesitant heroes" to become even more gregarious in the world of daily transactions.[31] Scholarly studies of Thomas Mann's picaresque Felix Krull highlight shallowness, which tends to merge the individual with the dominant class, an outcome that first inspired Lazarillo de Tormes and then curbed his best instincts. Thomas Mann himself could take just so much shallowness. Thus he devised a strategy of "regression full of novelty," which turned Felix Krull into a Hermes-like figure that trusted classical mythology to make the present at least more bearable.[32] The anachronistic receded into the archetypal.

3

Adventure tales are woven into the fabric of Western narrativity, not only around the Mediterranean Sea but east and west of the Atlantic Ocean as well. Ironically, the age of discovery produced less literature about its pathbreaking adventures than retrospective literature in the pastoral, epic, and chivalric modes. Many a writer ignored the discovery of the Americas. Even the letters of the Spanish emperor Charles V rarely mention his vast holdings overseas. The Indies were conquered, colonized, and exploited, but they were far from the center of cultural conversation. On the other side of the Atlantic, the conquistadors probed the unknown with their feet. The conquered territories, however, were filled with the familiar items of Castilian language and Christian religion, unsolicited gifts for which the natives had to pay dearly.

The *picaro*'s toilsome adventures started in Tormes and ended in South America, where Concolorcorvo (Alonso Carrio de la Vandera) published *El Lazarillo: A Guide for Inexperienced Travelers Between Buenos Aires and Lima* (1775–76), in which the resourceful rogue becomes a guide.[33] The spatial and thematic range of American Indian texts almost coincided with "epics of losers" such as Ercilla's *Araucana*. Mateo Alemán also migrated to the Indies, where the popularity of *Guzmán de Alfarache* played a role in the "archival" colonization of the Americas. Intellectually speaking, explorations were so retrospective that the *Historia verdadera de la conquista de la Nueva España* (1632), what Alejo Carpentier considers the "only honest-to-goodness book of chivalry that has ever been written,"[34] recorded the amazement that Bernal Díaz del Castillo and his soldiers felt, as they rode into Mexico City, at the sight of towers and buildings that resembled the architecture described in the chivalric legend of Amadís de Gaula. Barbara Fuchs opens her remarkable study of European and New World identities with an epigraph that describes a 1570 pageant in Cuzco, Peru:

> As Viceroy Francisco de Toledo makes his formal entrance into the city, he is greeted with elaborate pageantry. In the main square, once site of the Inca festivals, a Moorish castle and an enchanted wood have been erected for the celebration. The mock-Moors emerge from the castle to capture young women at a fountain, only to be pursued by valiant Christian knights, who engage them in fierce mock combat. The conquistadors play "themselves." The Moors are played by the Indians.[35]

The Mediterranean script produced the American event, much as characters of the European reconquest, the Moors, were equated with native Indians in the case of the American conquest. From folklore to literature, such transfers yielded an array of imitations and counterfeits.[36]

The irony, however, is that Spanish authorities resisted the export of romances. Why? Perhaps because they could have stirred dreams of empowerment among the oppressed. Spanish authorities rationalized censorship because the overt fictional nature of romances could train native readers to assume that all written texts, included sacred ones, were equally fictional, and thus entertaining rather than instructive. In a document dated 1536 and addressed to Antonio de Mendoza, viceroy of New Spain, Empress Isabella wrote, "Some days ago the Emperor ruled that no Romance Books of profane matter and fables be sent to those lands, lest the Indians who know how to read give themselves over to them, abandoning books of good and healthy doctrine."[37] Although Erasmian humanists began to criticize chivalric romances as early as the 1520s, metropolitan concerns found their way into the colonies because Spain's claim to the New World masked colonialism under the cloak of religion. The *conquista*, in fact, was legitimized by a pontifical grant that required the Christianization of the natives.[38] Picaresque adventures trained the American natives to assimilate models of hopelessness that poor Spaniards had known all along. As a troublesome undertaking, picaresque adventure carried a negative gene whose range was ubiquitous. At a time when imperial power shifted from military conquest to commercial trade and from the aristocracy to the middle class, Bartolomé de Las Casas, Juan Luis Vives, and Furió Ceriol began to denounce imperialistic practices.[39]

What was atypical during the Renaissance became typical in the literature of the twentieth century on old and new continents alike. In our own time, Carlos Fuentes, so thoroughly familiar with the titological geography of quixotic deeds, has bridged the oceanic gap in his gargantuan narrative

Terra Nostra (1975). While retaining the Italianate etymology, the title of this *novela total* claims native ownership against colonialism. The narrative begins with chaos in 1999 Paris and works its way back to Brant's "Ship of Fools," which made it to the New World behind the ships of the *conquistadores:* "Campanella was the navigator, Erasmus the cartographer, Thomas More the lookout, and the ghost of Hieronymus Bosch lurked somewhere in the hold."[40] The politics of colonialism aside, art had a future in the Americas, where it landed some of the best minds of the time. The brain drain had begun!

Of course, foolishness sounded a warning about the reliability of European models, and Fuentes concedes that the new world turned out to be "a transposition of the historic past into a future that will have no history." The narrative is grounded in the archival, and thus horizontal, universe of literariness. In the "already-always" of a bookish world, characters can be granted extended leases on life because their existence is scriptural. Thus Guzman added new layers to his original identity by becoming one facet of Philip II's prismatic huntsman. Produced by the spirit of commerce and imperialism, he found the time to massacre Belgian heretics and Mexican Atzecs, on the assumption that several lives are necessary to fulfill a personality. Archival sources play up a bibliophiliac condition whereby textuality makes "new" what already is old![41] By the turn of the third millennium, colonial voices of exclusion have been waning, and Carlos Fuentes believes that "the Atlantic is not an abyss but a bridge."[42]

It has been asked whether a move beyond the archive would bring about the end of narrative or the beginning of a new narrative.[43] *Lazarillo de Tormes* moved beyond the archive, proposed a new narrative, but did not replace archival entries. Eventually it found its way among them because society itself was not ready to bring forth a new adventurer. An expert on historical incongruities, Claudio Guillén writes that to contradict is "to offer a problem-solving model" that can be transformative.[44] Lázaro's self-consciousness, however, does not lead to radical change. That last step was beyond the anonymous *converso* as well as beyond Cervantes and the culture of the Renaissance. It is here that I return to Mikhail Bakhtin and the revolutionary aspect of the novel. Revolutionary vis-à-vis the epic, yes, but only partially so in regard to the novel's long-term potential. Indeed, the revolutionary potential was there, but the picaresque was not transformational enough, because society itself was not ready to take sharp turns. Instead, it was ready to absorb Lazarillo, who let it happen because no better choice was available to him.

Like the chivalric, the picaresque ended up favoring distraction instead of commitment and sympathy rather than reform. What ensued was a successful vogue, which, like its chivalric kin, appeased vast majorities whose role in society was to remain peripheral. Lázaro's unique pathbreaking experience was short-lived. As a mode of expression, the picaresque gave precedence to manner over matter, and stylization prospered far beyond the age of discovery.

We live at a time when the multilayered reality of rereading finds its line of descent in the complex perspectivism of quixotic adventurism. The ingenious way of foregrounding the coexistence of criticism and self-criticism brought to the fore the modernity of Cervantes's critique of reading, which anticipated the mounting dialogue between literature and criticism among the postmoderns. Nowadays, the writer's vulnerability is commensurate with the reader's empowerment. Cervantes assumed as much when he called on the idle reader (*desocupado lector*) to construct meaning by parting company with those who were enjoying the reading of chivalric romances.

I would like to think that Cervantes entrusted the reader with the ultimate translation of art into reality. Such a precedent should stand out among contemporary readers who want a better idea of where they are going. Especially after the turn of the third millennium, it is time to challenge the popularity of the chivalric, which has always belonged to the archive. Dante knew this. At the end of the Middle Ages, he denounced the corrupt world of knights and ladies and had Paolo and Francesca, the adulterous readers of the *libro galeotto*, killed. Two centuries later, Cervantes knew that Dante had failed, because he himself was seduced by the literature of romance, which he set out to dismiss regardless of printing presses in Barcelona that poured out chivalric texts.[45] Although he subjected Don Quixote first to madness and then to outright rejection, Cervantes created the most beloved of all *hidalgos*. His feats were physically awkward, socially innocuous, and, given his insanity, beyond the reach of the legal system.

While the chivalrous epic of the Middle Ages had become an empty shell, the entertainment literature of the romance endured.[46] Nurtured on tales of chivalry, Don Quixote set out to change the real world. Yet the real world did not change, and the *hidalgo* did not mind, because his deeds were not meant to exceed the space and time of their own performance. Cervantes introduced Don Quixote as an old man who did not even make it to the end of the narrative. So what could he say about the future? Cervantes did not create a new character because society was not ready to inspire it. Neither the quixotic nor the picaresque were ready to dare the future; but they were all too prone to linger on in the aftermath of texts that began to represent the way things were.

To move outside the archive, we ought to trust adventure to take us beyond the demise of authority, the default of the author, the unreliability of language, and the breakdown of exploratory ideologies. A world without human adventures may do justice to reality, but what does it do to us and our humanity, if not our humanism? Unless we want to venture from the archaeology of knowledge to the necrological refuse of art after the end of art, we can no longer go on cherishing Don Quixote and roaming around the back allies of belatedness. Novelistic grounds, Carlos Fuentes writes, accommodate "all the things that history either did not mention, did not remember, or suddenly stopped imagining."[47] Things not mentioned refer to the world of ordinary people that novelistic narratives have either ignored or relegated to the margins. Even Lazarillo de Tormes finally settled down at a point where the novel downgraded its premises and betrayed its promises.

The death of humanism as a progressive ideology steered modern writers toward an obsessive concern with the mechanics of literary fiction. Much as Wallace Stevens proclaimed that the subject of a poem is poetry itself, even summary readings of Italo Calvino and John Barth would surmise that the subject of prose narrative is narrativity itself. And narrativity has relied on myth since time immemorial. The resilience of myth at the end of literature makes a case for posthumousness, much as any rejection of the novel ought to give us pause about the priorities of the postmodern mindset. I would like to believe that adventure should hold some promise of novelty and distinction. In that spirit, the anonymous *pícaro* invented the most revolutionary of literary genres because his welfare was at stake in real life.

Whereas the disintegration of cultural values was typical of the first generation of modernists (Joyce, Proust, Mann), a later generation, writers from William Faulkner to Saul Bellow opted for a painful recovery of the sense of life, which Ignazio Silone rooted in a rebirth-conversion that R. W. B. Lewis called "companionship," the very value that Lazarillo had to give up in order to accelerate his social ascent. Companionship entails sharing, a sharing of pain and of bread (*cum* panis), which are two basic ingredients of picaresque adventurism as well as of Silone's *Pane e vino* (*Bread and Wine*, 1937). Silone's title plays up the symbolism of a sacramental meal that makes the quest for brotherhood wholesome. Picaresque adventure thus traded roguishness for secular variants of saintliness that emphasized hope, after Silone's *Fontamara*

(1933 in German, 1934 in English and Italian) had denounced the despair of a little town in the Abruzzi region of central Italy in the grip of Fascism.

Fascism also moved Carlo Levi to present the wasteland of an abandoned humanity in *Cristo si è fermato a Eboli* (*Christ Stopped at Eboli*). While the text was written in 1943–44, the title points back to 1935, when the writer, a combative antifascist, was exiled in the southern region of Lucania. The geographical landmark is deliberately polemical, presenting as it does a place "without comfort or solace, where the peasant lives out his motionless civilization of barren poverty in the presence of death."[48] In 1935 Levi was transferred from the small village of Grassano to the even smaller Gagliano, another godforsaken place isolated from the rest of the world. The little town of Eboli is located south of Salerno, where road and railway made a stop to let unfortunate souls off so they could begin the hard climb eastward toward the mountainous hinterland. For a Jewish medical doctor from Turin, the capital city of Piedmont at the foothills of the Alps was indeed another world, geographically, socially, linguistically, economically, and culturally. It was so far from civilization that even the locals knew it. Their sense of exclusion had found expression in the phrase that inspires the book's title, which warns, by way of a hyperbolic metaphor, that even Christ would not care to go beyond Eboli.

Amid rugged hills and arid highlands, indigence was such that desperate people lived in villages that had been ignored by invaders and compatriots alike. If Christ did not care about those places, why should anyone else? As a geographical marker in the minor key of the picaresque *Tormes,* Eboli was an unknown place where folks struggled day in and day out against cruel forms of depravation. Levi's title gives us a geographical sense of the extent to which the journey, even as an ordinary undertaking meant to sustain life, excluded so many whose socioeconomic conditions never rose to the level of daring such a move. All of this is suggested in Levi's title, which pits the geography of Eboli against the theology of Christ. The two coincide in the notion of an ecumenical fellowship. Shortly before Beckett wrote about the failed visitation of an improbable Godot in France, Levi gave us a title in which the godly visitation is denied altogether in southern Italy. No one in Gagliano is waiting for any deity, because everyone knows that no one ever planned to go there, at least not voluntarily. Eboli is the fork that sorts out Christians from non-Christians. In the language of the dejected ones, *Cristiani* are human beings who have been visited by Christ and can anticipate some kind of bearable survival. Beyond Eboli, however, even Lazarus would stir envy, because survival itself has bottomed out at unthinkable depths.

Levi's title sets up the physical and spiritual posts of the narrative; the space between is filled with the author's unwanted visitation. Politics forced him to bring history to a place that never had one. History thrives on grounds that have something to offer to those who act it out through deeds that have a material, intellectual, and spiritual basis. In the mountains beyond Eboli, those grounds and those motivations have never been allowed to take root and become valuable. Beyond Eboli, one finds only survival at its most elementary. Beyond Eboli, Carlo Levi was forced to venture on a journey of discovery that made the primitive contemporary. His title tells us that there are places where geography has curbed—if not excluded—the dynamics of social progress.

In this sense Gagliano is the geographical kin of Aci Trezza, the fishing village on the eastern coast of Sicily where Verga set the would-be series of novels that took the collective title *romanzi della fame*—novels of hunger that followed in the path of what Benedetto Croce has called the picaresque *epica della fame* (epic of hunger). By exploiting the thematics of indigence, such narratives brought to the fore *Il ciclo dei vinti* (*The Cycles of the Defeated Ones*). Inland, Verga highlighted the reality-based poetics of *verismo*, which drew from foreign and indigenous traditions alike. In the novella entitled *Rosso Malpelo* (in the collection *Vita dei campi*, 1880), he depicted a meanspirited character whose odds of survival were less than "picaresque." The nickname *Malpelo* means "bad hair," and *rosso*, red, is a sign of evil in some parts of Sicily. The title spells out the youth's fate: "He was called Malpelo because he had red hair; and he had red hair because he was a mean and bad boy, who promised to turn into a first-rate scoundrel. So everybody at the red-sand quarry called him Malpelo; and even his mother, having always heard him called by that name, had almost forgotten his real one."[49] The picaresque imagery of rat, snake, and wolf gains strength in the modern narrative. While Malpelo's father dies like a rat (*sorcio*) when an avalanche of red sand buries him, his crippled companion is called *Ranocchio*—little frog. Quite Darwinian at heart, Verga's environment leaves no room for complexity. Malpelo is an underdog who, having suffered abuses, has become abusive himself.[50] Even the poor can be despicable, and Malpelo is so bad that his place of work takes his name: *la cava di Malpelo*—the quarry of Malpelo. At the end of the story, he disappears into a mine.

Carlo Levi realized that the vanquished had been able to stay alive even though Christ had abandoned them. Beyond Eboli, peasants are *non-Cristiani*:

We're not human beings; we're not thought of as men but simply as beasts, mere creatures of the wild. They at least live for better or for worse, like angels or demons, in a world of their own, while we have to submit to the world of Christians, beyond the horizon, to carry its weight and to stand comparison with it. But the phrase has a much deeper meaning and, as is the way of symbols, this is the literal one. Christ did stop at Eboli, where the road and the railway leave the coast of Salerno and turn into the desolate reaches of Lucania. (3)

The opening sentence of the first chapter, a single page that could be taken as the titological subtitle-preface, states that 1935 was one of those "years of war and of what men call History" (3). The war in question was the Ethiopian campaign, which, together with the Spanish Civil War, turned out to be a dress rehearsal for World War II. The subtitle, *The Story of a Year,* describes the year when history wrote a hyperbolic tale of pseudoheroic imperialism, which had no effect whatsoever on a strata of the population on the Italian mainland that was as destitute as the lands that the Fascists occupied overseas. The irony is that it took Fascist arrogance to expose Levi to a humanity that his Piedmontese monarchy kept unknown to most Italians, by chance as well as by choice.

4

During the second half of the twentieth century, much effort has gone into forms of literary expression that traded Eboli and Aci Trezza for Calvino's *Invisible Cities,* the mimesis of existence in the marketplace of Gagliano for secretive rereadings in the library of Melk. Memory got the best of reality also in Umberto Eco's *Island of the Day Before,* on which we can land just by opening the book. These titles tell us that time is as anachronistic as the places are anatopistic; everything happens on the page.

Should we want "living" to reclaim some priority over "reading," we'd better concede that much of literature is not necessarily progressive. To stop other writers from writing more quixotic deeds, the priest requested a death certificate, which did not stop the proliferation of quixotic sequels. Even Cervantes's prologue assumes that authority is based on a "long catalogue of authors" whose artifacts are stored in the library, which creates stylistic paradigms as well as ontological models. At its most constructive, the novel contributes to discovery. When the novel fails to move toward uncharted territories, then it falls outside its own historical progress. For Milan Kundera, a novelistic adventure consists of "a luminously causal chain of acts." Luminosity, however, has been lost because quixotic and picaresque narratives reversed causality and took referential detours.[51]

In his masterly study *The Novel According to Cervantes,* Stephen Gilman pivots the chivalric on adventure and experience, the zenith and nadir of novelistic narrativity. From Cervantes to Fuentes, novelistic plots have always been problematic. Yet Gilman detects a development. The novel steadily curbs adventure in its preference for experience, with the result that the plot slows down. The dynamics of the quest give way to the restrictions of the plague with Camus and of inanity with Sartre. Appropriately, Gilman quotes Sartre's *La Nausée (Nausea):* "I have never had adventures. Things have happened to me, events, incidents, anything you like. But no adventures."[52]

It is thus clear why postmodernism—pathological, escapist, and retrospective—has drawn so much from Cervantes, who left a novelistic heritage framed by the pages and pens of a library at once physical and mental. If mimesis fosters visual imagination, the library trusts a linguistic imagination of unlimited resources. Yet we cannot have an adventurer committed to the future as long as society looks backward and does not tire of moving in circles. The archival popularity of Sheherazade, Don Quixote, and Pierre Menard is symptomatic of derivative preferences in the drawn-out aftermath of postmodernism. Among referential preferences, Jean-François Lyotard has pinned the failure of narrativity to the metanarrative of its "great hero, its great dangers, its great voyages, its great goals."[53] This list includes all of the ingredients that make up adventurous plots in the epic and chivalric modes.

For a breath of unrecycled air, let us walk outside the archive, where we might cross paths with a restless rogue who is looking over his shoulder. Let's give Lazarillo a better, not just a second, chance, and our own odds will be vastly improved. Beyond the comfort of referential tales, we should start believing that adventure can put exhaustion on trial and drive terminality out of sight. Nowadays, such an opportunity could be groundbreaking.

12

Se una notte d'inverno un viaggiatore:
Et cetera, Et cetera

> We can easily imagine a culture where discourse would circulate without any need for an author.
> —MICHEL FOUCAULT

In the preface to *Historia universal de la infamia* (*A Universal History of Iniquity*, 1935), Jorge Luis Borges lists a story entitled *Etcetera*, which includes six short extracts that are derived from Burton, Swedenborg, and the *Arabian Nights*.[1] Borges also refers to three basic stories that have been retold throughout the ages: the tale of Troy, the tale of Ulysses, and the tale of Jesus.[2] It would not be too difficult for readers to come up with their own variations of recurring stories. Indeed, it would seem that the unexpected has yielded to the predictable. One might ask: does "etcetera" affect referentiality no less than titological redundance? Is Borges undermining his own authority by resorting to a title that stifles novelty?

As we have seen in the previous chapters, the thematics of picaresque and quixotic narratives rest on the resilience of repetition in variation, which must pay equal attention to the dynamics of "sameness" and "diversity," that is, tradition and innovation. Themes are based on constants that update themselves to remain relevant. With time, constants—variously called myths, legends, archetypes, tales, and so on—so gained range and resonance that they exist quite independently of specific bards-speakers-artists. Nowadays, the thematics of the "quixotic" entails images and deeds that have become entrenched in the readership, to the point that we could almost take them for granted. It no longer needs repeating that quixotic windmills can be warring giants. Familiarity makes references superfluous, and Graham Greene has called on readers to draw parodic implications between Don Quixote and

Monsignor Quixote, the old steed Rocinance and a FIAT SEAT (the priest's old clunker). Their proximity is such that the bishop takes time to wonder: how could Father Quixote "be descended from a fictional character?"[3]

Language has earmarked recurrent phrases like "as we know," "it is common knowledge," and "as the old saying goes." Another linguistic equivalent of etcetera is Barthes's *on le sait,* which "ascribes to current opinion" and recovers to the present the weight of layered traces.[4] Since it is not meant to be groundbreaking, Steve McCaffery defines etcetera as "again and again. And so on. And so forth. And back again. And once more. And one more time. Again and again and through and through. Over and over again and again."[5] Literary practice yields the repetitive etceteras of fictions about fictions.[6] Amid a textual universe of insatiable rereadings, etcetera pillages the literary heritage, proves that derivative forms of expression will not go away,[7] and prospers wherever change is slow. Conservative and cohesive cultures are full of etcetera, whereas the opposite is true wherever revolution and radicalism have effected transformations.

Because Western civilization had reached the point of exhaustion, the culture of modernism could count on a number of etceteras. Notwithstanding the rejection of etceteras by such revolutionary movements as Dada and Futurism, most educated people knew what W. B. Yeats meant when he wrote that "the center does not hold." We know it just as well, even without having read what Rudolph Arnheim and Georges Poulet have written on the power of the center and the metamorphoses of the circle. In the culture of postmodernism, which thrives on aftermaths, dead ends, procrastination, and belatedness, etcetera has expanded its range no less than its depth.

Cervantine or otherwise, much postmodern writing flows through recurrent plots that are highly derivative. As an author without "an iota of inspiration," Georges Perec confesses that he developed a passion for "accumulation, saturation, imitation, quotation, translation and automatisation,"[8] which describe literary techniques in the mode of etcetera. Folklore and mythology aside, literature itself thrives on its own recurring plots and characters. As Milan Kundera put it, "all of History is merely the story of a few characters" who have traversed Europe's centuries.[9] They have become so familiar that readers and writers can spin stories under the aegis of etcetera. Nowadays, we can dispense with authorship because we have reached the point where the "death of the author" has given way to the proliferation of the "literature machine," which has given a technological slant to the serialization of etceteras.

Literary borrowing rests on the premise that much of what has been written is so familiar that reiteration is unnecessary.[10] From prose to poetry, e. e. cummings describes the way his family confronted the theme of war:

> My sweet old etcetera
> Aunt Lucy during the recent
>
> War could and did tell you just
> What everybody was fighting
>
> For,

While his sister Isabel made ear warmers:

> Etcetera wristers etcetera, my
> Mother hoped that
>
> I would die etcetera
> Bravely

Quietly, the poet himself lingers:

> In the deep mud et
>
> Cetera
> (dreaming,
> et
> cetera, of
> Your smile
> Eyes knees and of your Etcetera)[11]

War is normalized through repetitive deeds that etcetera has made routine. As a mode of production, etcetera stems from the Latinate *et cetera*, which becomes adverbial whenever the Anglicized noun means "and so on, and so forth." In the form of "always-already," etcetera entails a self-propelling momentum that ties reliance on the past to predictability about the future. Amid a culture of disjunctions, etcetera is conjunctive.

The range of etcetera as a mode of production that spurs repetition affects literature as well as the arts; it is central to poetics no less than to aesthetics. Cases in point are Constantin Brancusi's *Endless Column* (Fig. 27) and Arata

Isozaki's *Art Tower Mito* (Fig. 28). These vertical forms are as easily augmentable as the horizontal soup cans and Coca-Cola bottles that multiply in the "serial" paintings of Andy Warhol, who links etcetera to the world of ordinary objects (Fig. 29). His artifacts have turned the painter's studio into the polymath's factory, where techniques based on multiplication echo the technologies of the assembly line. At the crossroads where the industrial meets with the aesthetic, etcetera thrives amid those cultures that are either unwilling to move or incapable of moving beyond the status quo.

In the age of mechanical reproduction, etcetera gives priority to the produced over the producer. In 1934, Walter Benjamin foreshadowed postmodern developments when he wrote, "As writing gains in breadth what it loses in depth . . . the reader is at all times ready to become a writer, that is, a describer, but also a prescriber." As technical precedents, Benjamin cites medieval engravings and etchings as well as nineteenth-century lithographs and photographs. But he also maintains that "the whole sphere of authenticity is outside technical—and, of course, not only technical—reproducibility."[12] The aura of authenticity has been overshadowed by the productivity of

FIG. 27 Constantin Brancusi, *Endless Column*, 1937–38. Târgu-Jiu, Romania.

FIG. 28 Arata Isozaki, *Art Tower Mito*, 1988–90. Mito, Ibaraki, Japan.

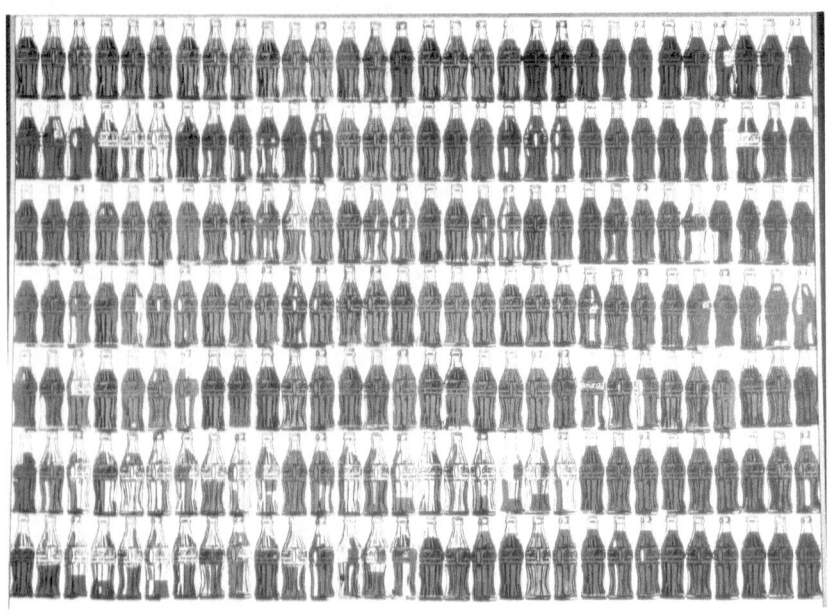

FIG. 29 Andy Warhol, *210 Coca-Cola Bottles*, 1962. Synthetic polymer paint and silkscreen ink on canvas. © 2007 Andy Warhol Foundation for the Visual Arts / Artists Rights Society (ARS), New York.

technology, much as the prestige of authorship has been degraded by the output of reproductions. Half a century later Michel Foucault drew our attention to the emergence of the "regular" over the "original": "It is not legitimate, then, to demand, point-blank, of the texts that one is studying their title to originality."[13] Since it takes advantage of what already is there as well as of what already has been successful, etcetera reassures us that literature trusts continuity, even though it does not guarantee progress.

The postmodern reliance on the "rhetoric of etcetera" tells us that much culture is performative rather than groundbreaking. For Ross Chambers, the etcetera principle tells us that "no context is ever the whole context." Ultimately, "the etcetera being inexhaustible—going too far can never go far enough."[14] Yet, etcetera does go far enough to privilege the technological over the unique and readership over authorship. In this chapter, the etcetera mode of literary production first centers on the author's reliance on the recycling of the already written, and then moves on to show how the already written calls on the author to relinquish authorship. As a result, the educated reader becomes a kind of functional author who activates textuality by trusting his or her own talent for adding etceteras to known plots.

In his postscript to *The Name of the Rose,* Eco insists that "[b]ooks always speak of books, and every story tells a story that has already been told. Homer knew this, and Ariosto knew this, not to mention Rabelais and Cervantes. My story, then, could only begin with the discovered manuscript, and even this would be (naturally) a quotation."[15] Once literature began "to write itself," rereading expanded its perimeter and multiplied the potential for interpretation. So much so that even Eco recognized that "the rights of the interpreters have been overstressed." Although "a text can have many senses," it cannot "have every sense."[16] The very title of Eco's book, *The Limits of Interpretation,* takes up the excesses of reader-reception theory. The question is: how inclusive should the "open" text be? Intertextual spin-offs have added up. As he delivered the Norton Lectures at Harvard University a few years after Italo Calvino's death, Eco opened *Six Walks in the Fictional Woods* with a warning: "One might think that my book was a response to Calvino's novel."[17] The novel in question is *Se una notte d'inverno un viaggiatore* (1979), and it is worth noting that Calvino himself would have delivered the Norton Lectures, had he not died two months earlier. Independently, therefore, the two men took up related matters that led to a textual dialogue between dark nights and fictional woods in the spirit of much postmodern narrativity, which tends to stay within the familiar boundaries of referentiality.

This chapter takes titology to explore the ideological as well as the technological aspects of the poetics of etcetera by focusing on Calvino's *If on a Winter's Night a Traveler* (1981). In his critical essays, Calvino takes up the challenge of "writing apocryphal novels, which I imagine to have been written by an author who is not me and who does not exist." He has carried out this undertaking in the novel "about the pleasure of reading novels. The protagonist is the reader. Because of no fault of his own, he tried for ten times to start to read a book that he could finish reading it. Thus he has written the beginning of ten imaginary novels."[18] I contend that such beginnings lay the grounds for the almost authorless writing of ten etceteras.

1

In the postmodern dead end, narrativity has strengthened the belief that the proliferation of tale after tale empowers readers to recite familiar stories. Calvino's *If on a Winter's Night* singles out a young woman who is "a passionate admirer, et cetera, et cetera, of the productive writer and loathed the tormented one.... Or else: The same, replacing, et cetera."[19] Preference is given to the writer who imitates imitations. The eye alone can acknowledge the extent to which "the work will keep on being born, judged, destroyed, and renovated." Originality is so derivative that many have been looking at authorship as a passive instrument of "writing." What is essential is the eye that reads, and what "will disappear will be the figure of the author, this personage to whom we attribute functions that are not of his competence."[20]

The title's opening *If* foregrounds the conditional mode, which introduces a dependent clause that fails to qualify a thesis because the main clause is missing. The title is as open and incomplete as the text that follows. By creating uncertain conditions of time and space, *If* calls into question the subject, whose identity is unknown in the title and whose role is indeterminate in the text. Within the context of what George Steiner calls the "darkened" grammar of reality, *If* expresses an attempt to escape "the despotism of fact,"[21] at least on a cold winter night. A wager on the uncertainties that affect year-round narratives, *If* has become ever more significant in the literature and philosophy of postmodernism.

Given that many books encourage reading as rereading,[22] the inference is that whatever readers may want to write on their own includes the evaluation of titles: "Having rapidly glanced over the titles of the volumes displayed in the bookshop, you have turned toward a stack of *If on a winter's night a traveler* fresh off the press, you have grasped a copy, and you have carried it to the cashier so that your right to own it can be established" (6). If the universe is but an immense library or a well-stocked bookstore, the very idea of traveling can be pinned to literary journeys from cover to cover. The anonymous traveler has little to fear from the rigors of winter, because his/her journey wavers between the library and the bookstore.[23] Although we have been warned that all these memories, all these archives, all this documentation may not give birth to a single idea,[24] they do facilitate literary output. In fact, artistic developments by means of either addition or assemblage have led Calvino to comment on "multiplicity": "Who are we, who is each one of us, if not a combinatoria of experiences, information, books we have read, things imagined? Each life is an encyclopedia, a library, an inventory of objects, a series of styles, and everything can be constantly shuffled and reordered in every way conceivable."[25] This is an anthropomorphic diagram of the scriptural apparatus; its autonomy, its functions, and the literary intake that is necessary to spur production.

Calvino insists that books preserve the past "as if in geological layers of silent words," such that "our civilization is based on the multiplicity of books; one can find the truth only by chasing it from one volume to another volume." Because the same truth inspires a plurality of books, originality is weakened by its very multiplicity. Such a loss, however, is no longer significant in an age when the *plurileggibilità della realtà* (the multireadability of reality) is a fact "outside which any other reality cannot even be approached."[26] The text becomes the place where derivative writings are combined and contested.[27] Multiplicity works its way into *Il libro, I libri* (*The Book, the Books*, 1984), a title that spells out the inclusive readability of literary texts. The result is that the author is the "instrument of something that writes itself independently from him." What survives is the "modern *scriptor*," whose hand, "detached from any voice, born by a pure gesture of inscription (and not of expression), traces a field without origin—or at least with no origin but language itself."[28] Truth is stratified according to principles of accumulation rather than transformation; in other words, it is an etcetera rather than either a birth or a rebirth.

For Calvino, one multireadable novel that thrives on layered rereadings is *Don Quixote*. Having tried "to recover myth outside the books," the *hidalgo* crosses paths with common sense, everyday toils, and the religious dictates of the Counter-Reformation on a journey that tries to rescue chivalric etceteras of old.[29] Journeymen, as we all know, are recurrent in Western literature, and

Calvino has paid attention to the traveler who is about to embark on a quest in Franz Kafka's *Der Kübelreiter* (*The Knight of the Bucket*). This is a story in which the writer "wanted to tell us that going out to look for a bit of coal on a cold wartime night changes the mere swinging of an empty bucket into the quest of a knight-errant."[30] As we saw in the previous chapters, the theme of lives changed by the books of romance started with Paolo and Francesca, peaked in Don Quixote, and returned with Emma Bovary.[31]

Since recurrence applies to plots as well as to images, there are metaphors such as time and river, life and dreams, sleep and death, eyes and stars, women and flowers, that appear everywhere in the universe of literature,[32] promoting invention through the suffixal mode of derivative "isms" and "esques." Calvino describes the "romanzo elevato all'ennesima potenza" (the novel elevated to the nth degree) as a hyper-novel in which different narrators would tell many stories.[33] To implement such a plan, authorship becomes apocryphal, and the novelistic structure of *If on a Winter's Night* calls on readers to try their own hands at spin-offs: "For some time now, every novel I began writing is exhausted shortly after the beginning, as if I had already said everything I have to say. I have had the idea of writing a novel composed only of beginnings of novels" (197). By beginning with a sentence that does not end, the title introduces a traveler who can start an indefinite number of journeys on the assumption that narrativity is bound to pursue "the possibilities implicit in its own material." Like the traveler, readers read ten beginnings that they may expand into full plots. Calvino challenges readers to write etceteras that involve different modes (detective, revolutionary, parodic) and contexts (American, Hispanic, Russian, Japanese). On the trail of improbable journeys, emphasis is placed more on memory than on invention, and we end up with a list of books that begin and end with the very first line, "If on a winter's night a traveler."[34]

The hypothetical *If* has novelistic precedents. The journeyman, in fact, shows up in the opening sentence of *The Castle of Crossed Destinies:* "In the midst of a thick forest, there was a castle that gave shelter to all travelers overtaken by night on their journey: lords and ladies, royalty and their retinue, humble wayfarers."[35] In the castle, *he* and *we* can play cards and mix texts no less than titles. In the shuffle, one might suggest this: "If on a winter's night a traveler happens to venture into a dark forest, he had better know where to take shelter." Of course, danger is a rhetorical device, because the author can recombine available materials by moving in a space at once safe and familiar.[36] By keeping previous readings in mind, readers are expected to give "currency" to the technology that makes the rearrangement of texts possible.[37] Actually, "all of literature is implicit in language and . . . literature itself is merely the permutation of a finite set of elements and functions." A book that consists of ten beginnings can offer unlimited choices, because each "beginning develops in very different ways from a common nucleus."[38] The conditional "if" stands out as the introductory wager of possible variations for a text in the making, a critical term that challenges progress as well as closure. We can draw the hypothetical title and the virtual plot together on the belief that circulation will have the best of influence in the productive mode of etcetera.[39]

Although the end of the road remains unknown, *If* qualifies traveling conditions that are unfavorable only from a meteorological point of view. The potential beginning of yet another quest entitles all journeymen to challenge safe expectations. If all else fails on a winter's night, Calvino's fellow travelers can still journey across literary topographies littered with footprints familiar to the genre of romance.[40] Yet one may still wonder: does writing boil down to mere plot combinations?

Because "combinatorial" etceteras are virtually unlimited, many a postmodern has drawn from "potential literature," which clustered around Raymond Queneau and the Oulipo group, whose mission was to push the limits of language. Calvino belonged to it, and one of his pieces bears the title *How I Wrote One of My Books*. It "quotes" Raymond Roussel's *How I Wrote Certain of My Books* and takes up scriptural "possibilities":

> The author manages to write only the beginnings of novels
> The reader manages to read only the beginnings of novels
> The author does not manage to write a complete novel
> The reader does not manage to read a complete novel
>
> The reader does not find the solution of his problems with the author
> The complete book is perhaps made up only of beginnings.[41]

Writers and readers share assets and liabilities. Anyone can start a novel, and the equation between writer and reader means that either one can author beginnings. Novelistic experiments with beginnings and fragmentary texts were under way. In 1979 Giorgio Manganelli published *Centuria*, a book that contains one hundred very short novels. The title is taken from the Roman military formation of one hundred soldiers and also from the one hundred *novelle* of the *Decameron*, which was translated into French as *Cents nouvelles*.[42] Calvino admired *Centuria* and wrote an introduction to the French translation. In a lighthearted vein, he also worried that his forthcoming ten beginnings would hardly offset one hundred one-page novels.

On matters of content, Calvino warns that the reader of *If on a Winter's Night* should not "expect anything in particular from this particular book. You're the sort of person who, on principle, no longer expects anything of anything" (4). The repetition of forms has eaten away at the originality of content. While the title allows readers to add their own twists and turns to stories that everybody knows, the text makes an introductory statement of unyielding nihilism. What the reader reads and writes can be entertaining, even though, philosophically speaking, it is of little consequence. The inference is that books treasure a universe of communal tales that do not exceed the self-gratifying circumference of literature itself. That said, the introductory *incipit* can link up to a universe of familiar narratives that afford countless possibilities. After all, why seek out paths of discovery when we can draw from a stockpile of forms that can be recycled with ease? "Every time I sit down here I read, 'It was a dark and stormy night.'" The impersonality of that *incipit* makes readers share in a forthcoming journey "from the time and space of here and now to the time and space of the written word. I feel the thrill of a beginning that can be followed by multiple developments, inexhaustibly" (176–77). The conditional title opens up to the possible text; we have entered the world of the virtually scriptural.

Like Borges, Calvino does not trust himself to sustain drawn-out narratives, nor does he believe that his readers can do so. Such a condition of "impaired" narrativity breaks down inclusive forms of knowledge: "I dream of immense cosmologies, sagas, and epics all reduced to the dimensions of an epigram."[43] To a considerable extent, loss of narrativity entails loss of personality, which is conducive to loss of language. The critique of mimesis becomes radical: "Will I ever be able to say, 'Today it writes,' just like 'Today it rains,' 'Today it is windy'? Only when it will come natural to me to use the verb 'write' in the impersonal form will I be able to hope that through me is expressed something less limited than the personality of an individual" (176). As a mode of expression, etcetera has empowered the verb "to write" to dispense with unique individuals, who have given way to "writerly" subjects. Calvino echoes a widespread belief when he states that the book "should be simply the equivalent of the unwritten world translated into writing" (171). Tradition has it that writing, as a Godlike gesture, constitutes an authorial prerogative that yields Godlike creations. At the postmodern crossroads, however, God has become Godot, who failed to appear. Cultural prerogatives have lost their exclusivity, and contributions to the written universe have become both anonymous and unpretentious.

Anonymity cancels names as well as personalities, and Calvino writes that he is "made of ink and periods and commas" (190–91). Others perceive him as "nothing but an impersonal graphic energy." The scriptural act becomes the most autobiographical of fingerprints, yet it is meant to bear no name. In an introduction to a show of Saul Steinberg, who arranged the instruments of painting in *Summer Table* (1982, Fig. 30), Calvino writes that visual images are geometric "anatomies" that transform the world "into line."[44] In Steinberg's own words, "biography gets confused with calligraphy. One's life is a form of calligraphy—blunt, brush, etc."[45] The paintbrush and the pen stand on their own as subjects in the first person, while the hand that moves them is an instrument that facilitates execution. In the same spirit, Michel Foucault describes the book as a box of tools with punctuation and letters.[46]

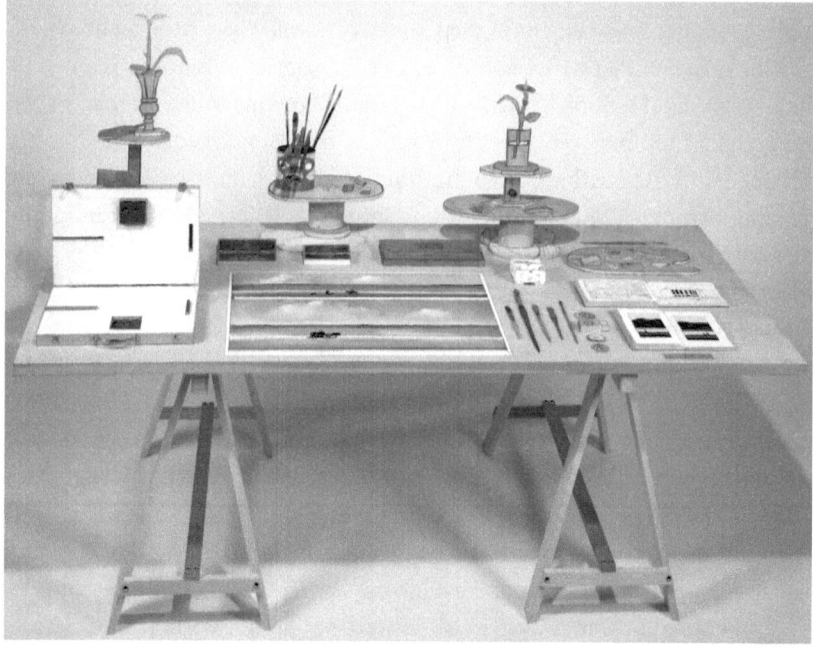

FIG. 30 Saul Steinberg, *Summer Table*, 1981. Mixed media collage on wood, 57 × 80 × 36 inches. Private collection. © The Saul Steinberg Foundation / Artists Rights Society (ARS), New York.

By pointing to a poetics that can thrive on technical virtuosity alone,[47] the instruments of artistic practice carry out the protocol of art regardless of specific users. We are dealing here with automatic technologies of literary expression at a time when the idea that spearheads art is technology itself. Bill Brown, a scholar interested in the sense of things, has imagined "a kind of cultural and literary history emanating from the typewriter, the fountain pen, the light bulb—component parts of the physical support for modern literary production."[48]

The "mechanization" of the writing subject in *If on a Winter's Night* is so drastic that Silas Flannery wishes to become "a hand, a severed hand that grasps a pen and writes. . . . Who would move this hand? The anonymous throng? The spirit of the times? The collective unconscious?" The hand takes on a life of its own, moved as it is by a mysterious impulse to "transmit the writable that waits to be written, the tellable that nobody tells" (171). At best, the "anonymous editor" becomes a fragment of the "illegible world, without center, without ego, without I" (180). The denial of ontology has been offset by the resilience of technology. Wolfgang Iser has studied the reader's reception of literary texts, and Calvino has gone a step further by focusing on the reader's involvement in their construction. If the writer is but a hand that holds a pen that writes about writing, the subject of mimesis is a pair of hands that hold a book which is being read: "Looking at the woman in the deck chair, I felt the need to write 'from life,' that is, to write not her but her reading, to write anything at all, but thinking that it must pass through her reading" (171–72). Whatever the variations, the basic fact is that art and technology have merged as never before.

We might venture to guess that Calvino's book would be a best-seller in Borges's Tlön, a place where the elimination of individualism has created a world that is "a heterogeneous series of independent acts." Even language boils down to "impersonal verbs."[49] Once writing becomes its own scriptural subject, what disappears is the figure of the author. To sharpen literary understanding, readers are urged to ask: Who is telling the story? Where does it begin? Calvino spurs them to explore their potential as writers,[50] should they care to do so "independently of the personality of the author."[51] A title such as *Beyond the Author* confirms Calvino's belief that authorship spurs self-effacement: "How well could I write if I were not there! I wish that my person did not stand as an inconvenient screen between the white sheet of paper and the brewing world of words and stories which take shape and vanish without anybody writing them."[52] This statement transforms the author into a

Se una notte d'inverno un viaggiatore 275

"facilitator" who reorders the experiences of life in such a way that readers can turn into writers on the assumption that "[e]ach life is an encyclopedia, a library, an inventory of objects, a series of styles, and everything can be constantly shuffled and reordered in every way conceivable."[53] Textuality belongs to the reader, and a knowledgeable humanity will realize that the author is "a machine and will know how such a machine works."[54] While machines maximize the production of "impersonal" etceteras, technology minimizes authorship.[55] For Calvino, the key word is "editor," and his task is to edit a collection of tales that consist of either one sentence or a single line.[56]

In a note at the end of *The Castle of Crossed Destinies,* Calvino considers the idea of a third part based on "comic strips" about "gangsters, terrified women, spacecrafts, vamps, war in the air, mad scientists."[57] At best, readers can find in this open-ended project the beginnings of their own narrative etceteras. It is for this reason that Calvino goes back to the last *canto* of *Orlando furioso,* where Ariosto introduces the poem's courtly readers; their journey begins where the poet's ends.[58] By way of paraphrase, Ariosto's "Tale of Astolfo on the Moon" deals with a poet who lives at the center of the planet.[59] There he will "tell us whether it is true that the Moon contains the universal rhyme-list of words and things." It is from that "arid sphere that every discourse and every poem sets forth; and every journey through forests, battles, treasures, banquets, bedchambers, brings us back here, to the center of an empty horizon."[60] Earth and moon are wastelands that only literary skills can make prolific. In the spirit of the chivalric *errare,* whose defining quality is "errant movement,"[61] the verb "to err" means both to wander and to divert. It is no accident that Calvino's essay on the subject is entitled "The Structure of *Orlando furioso,*" a literary work "which, while refusing to begin and to end," can generate countless tales.[62]

With regard to a winter's night, *errare* could be the verb of the main clause, for it tells us about a traveler who wanders somewhere in a literary world where *errare* draws together character and writer by departing from the conventions of travel literature. Ariosto himself concedes that he knows no more than his audience:

Se le sapete voi così come io?
(Do you who know them better for than I?)
(Ariosto, *Orlando Furioso* xi. 5. 3–4).

Thus he makes a pre-Calvinian statement:

> Di queste, qual si vuol, la vera sia:
> (Here are the variations; choose your own.)
>
> (xxix. 7. 7)

Borges also goes back to Ariosto when he formulates a literary hypothesis:

> No one can truly write a book. To be
> Ingenuous, a book must comprehend
> The different suns at daybreak and day's end,
> Arms, epochs, and the binding, rending sea.
> So Ariosto thought, but yielded to
> The lazy pleasure that he found in journeys
> Through marble columns and black pines—returning
> To ancient dreams, dreaming them anew.[63]

The book uses available plots to execute its own scriptural practice, which turns into the anonymous agent of literary etceteras that raise a potential question: how "open" can an "open work" be? Again, Ariosto offers precedents for the modern writer inasmuch as Calvino "narrates" Ariosto by reflecting on a chivalric situation: "A study which I would like to have carried out, and which, if I do not manage it, someone else can do in my place, concerns this situation: a seashore or riverbank, a person on the bank, a boat a little way off, bringing news of an encounter which will initiate the new adventure."[64] Here are the ingredients of literary productivity. Once the world of ideological signifiers crumbles, the traveler becomes an Ariostesque journeyman who no longer worries about finding the Holy Grail. The world of *poemi cavallereschi* offered Calvino such a wealth of etceteras that he felt compelled to ask, "Do we still need to write novels?" His own answer involved a shift in genre as well as in medium, for he had grown to believe that cinema, journalism, and sociological essays could better express the cultural problems of our time. Those who insist in writing novels to compete with movies are doomed to failure.[65]

Let us not forget that Calvino's novel consists of beginnings that rest on narrative constants: "A story could end only in two ways: having passed all the tests, the hero and the heroine married, or else they died. The ultimate meaning to which all stories refer has two faces: the continuity of life, the inevitability of death." Continuity links one narrative to another: "You stop for a moment to reflect on these words. Then, in a flash, you decide you want to marry Ludmilla." Reading makes of the world of literature a place where readers join in the matrimonial act of reading: "A great double bed receives your parallel readings" (260). Ludmilla "closes her book, turns off her light, puts her head back against the pillow, and says, 'Turn off your light, too. Aren't you tired of reading'?" But "you," that is to say, each one of us, answers: "Just a moment, I've almost finished *If on a winter's night a traveler* by Italo Calvino" (260). At that point, art remains art, and the double bed invites compatible readings. Ludmilla's marriage has taken place in an archive-library where novelistic *incipits* open adventurous paths for people who have just married into the world of literature.

In his own winter's night, Calvino's hypothetical *If* unhinges journeys of fact and myth alike.[66] Once the end loses its teleological role, narrativity makes it possible for the writer to exhaust every novel "shortly after the beginning" (197). The contiguity of books generates a contagious energy that is unique to written words. Maurice Blanchot puts things in perspective: "A book is a Book when it does not reflect someone who might have made it and when it is as unsullied by his name and as detached from his existence as it is from the reader's."[67] Textuality traces a field without origin. As a result, Calvino's new novel is readable "independently of what you expect of the author" (9). The authorial voice yields to the impersonal pronoun: "Saying not 'I think' but 'it thinks'" (176). Ultimately, "the book should be the equivalent of the unwritten world translated into writing" (171). By shifting authorship toward a traveler, the writer has accepted the idea that a winter's night somehow will write itself by trusting the scriptural resilience of etcetera, a concept that already has traveled the routes of literary geographies.

At that point, etcetera comprises both redundancy and contradiction. Calvino seems to have taken an escapist stand vis-à-vis the "weight, the inertia, the opacity of the world,"[68] which also reflects his political estrangement from the Communist Party. As a young man in Fascist Italy, Calvino noted that one "writes fables in periods of oppression. When a man cannot give clear form to his thinking, he expresses it in fables."[69] In times of freedom, he can "move on to other things."[70] Freedom returned after the fall of Fascism, but Calvino, though some of his essays kept a sociopolitical slant, seemed to favor inconsequential *raccontini*—very short stories. He held fast to his lifelong interest in fantastic and comical deformations of reality, which probably was not any more real than the world of his beloved fairy tales.

Politics aside, Calvino's literary ideology was rooted in learned scholarship and intellectual elitism. He did not endorse popular culture because he believed that to set "the literature of the people" as the universal standard is to take a step backward: "Literature is not school. Literature must presuppose a public that is more cultured, and *more cultured than the writer himself.* Whether or not such a public exists is unimportant. The writer addresses a reader who knows more about it than he does. . . . Literature has no choice but to raise the stakes."[71] Like Borges, Eco, and Barth, Calvino writes texts for literary, not just literate, readers. This view of art is as selective in the culture of postmodernism as the one professed by Eliot, Joyce, and Pound in modernist culture. In this sense, etcetera does not thrive at street corners, where it would represent the everyday routines of existence. Instead, we can rest assured that Calvino's traveler has left a sheltered port for another sheltered port: "What harbor can receive you more securely than a great library? Certainly there is one in the city from which you set out and to which you have returned after circling the world from book to book" (253). On a winter's night, the traveler might think of Odyssean or Dantean journeys. It is just as feasible that Robert Frost would urge him to remember that he has more mundane, but no less literary, promises to keep. He will not doubt that all paths are book-born and book-bound, because, Calvino goes on, he is moving in "a particular world, that of the written word."[72]

In the world of books, Calvino's *If* comes back as the hypothesis of writing not a single book but "a whole library," which reassures him that whatever he writes will be "integrated, contradicted, balanced, amplified, buried by the hundreds of volumes that remain" to be written (182). If such a book could be written, what would its title be? Perhaps it could be a transtextual etcetera that would echo titles old and new, the transparent eye that reflects the whole universe of literature. In fact, Calvino treats title and text as prologues, a technique that is also at the core of Macedonio Fernández's *Museo de la novela de la eterna* (1982), which lists fifty-six prologues that favor digressions and interruptions: "I must go on writing prologues just as long as I don't get carried away and try to prologue *them* . . . and just as long as I do not permit my novel the folly of prologuing itself . . . just as I assure you as I'm doing now that I am on the trail of the autoprologue which would satisfy the ambition of all prologues." Ironically, the prologue is self-fulfilling rather than introductory, and the goal is to create an "anticipatory literature of prologuing."[73] But how far can these "beginnings" go? Can there be a text less likely to fail a title's expectations than the story of an uncertain journey that is undertaken on a winter's night for no apparent reason?

A popular way of keeping the practice of writing alive is to let etcetera represent variations of what happened in the mode of "as if." Robert Coover begins *Pinocchio in Venice* with Calvinian titles in mind: "On a winter evening of the year 19—, after arduous travels across two continents and as many centuries, pursued by harsh weather . . ." Roberto Cotroneo published the parodic *Se una mattina d'estate un bambino* (*If on a Summer Morning a Child*). Indeed, history can be arranged as it might have happened. For Calvino, *If* warrants and unsettles an array of narratives that rest on verbal forms such as "what seems," "might be," or "could seem." Throughout, alternate readings are called for, and the conditional mode spells out a sense of uncertainty that is at once linguistic and literary.

A knowledgeable humanity, Calvino writes with conviction, will realize that the author is "a machine and will know how such a machine works."[74] Progress in cybernetics will give us "the true literary machine," which will "produce avant-garde work to free its circuits." In fact, nothing prevents us from "foreseeing a literature machine" that at a certain point starts to propose new ways of writing, turning its own codes completely upside down."[75] For Calvino, writing is an autonomous realm where letters refer to epistles as well as to "alphabetical letters, the atoms of which the written universe is made," and to "the phenomenon of literature itself, the third main sense of our word *letters*."[76] Literature is a lexicon with a propensity for spin-offs.

For a while now, the "literature machine" has been churning out story after story. Death threats have given birth to storytelling, which has always been life-giving. These days, the "literariness of literature" entitles everybody to rewrite everything ever written.[77] The world of the library is one in which stories are there for the taking. Beyond the mortality of individual authors, Umberto Eco insists that "stories often write themselves, and go where they want to go." In fact, every text "is a lay machine asking the reader to do some of its work."[78] Texts and titles alike ask us to be activated, and open texts have spurred a literary production that eventually led the reader to get rid of the author in order to rely on the "literature machine" alone.

2

John Barth rescues characters (Harrison Mack, Jerome Bray, Todd Andrews) from earlier narratives in *Chimera*, and then mentions some kind of computerized machine: "Once a number of works by a particular author were fed into it, it could compose hypothetical new works in that author's manner."[79]

Evidently, Pierre Menard has gone technological, for the machine can rewrite earlier texts faster if not better.

Barth's *Countdown: Once upon a Time* contains stories that weave a dialogue with *If on a Winter's Night a Traveler* through a common task that is central to the structure and meaning of etcetera: how can we start a story, and how can we keep it up? The Italian writer offers ten beginnings, while his American counterpart goes further, believing that:

> *Any line at all*
> ... can start a story.... Throw me a line. Any line at all.[80]

Any line from any tale can start a new tale. The "once upon a time" opening refers to a world of preexistent texts that are set at a distance from, but still available to, the reader-narrator. For Barth, the successful repetitiveness of "tales within tales" is conducive to the writing of "[a]nother story about a writer writing a story! Another regressus ad infinitum! The very word etcetera edges on redundancy when it is written as 'etcetcetcetcetc.'"[81] Spelling stretches etcetera into a typographical lettering at once extravagant and familiar. Instead of explaining, we can assume; and one of the scriptural signs of such an acknowledgment is etcetera, which empowers writers to take shortcuts on the assumption that the general readership is acquainted with the subject at hand. One of Barth's characters feels that "the body which he inhabited—the only one et cetera—was et cetera. The idea of et cetera."[82] Identity itself is based on the inheritance of the typical over the unique.

The literary universe of endless rereading keeps the world of fiction alive, and the last chapter of *On with the Story* takes us from "once upon a time" to the "once upon another time" of "tales unended, unmiddled, unbegun." Like Calvino's *If*, Barth's "once upon a Time" sets the narrative free from the constraints of linear time, making it possible to find "just the closing words of some story and not even in complete sentences: *Bosnia, Haiti, Rwanda, The web of the world*. Rest of the page blank." Blank pages are there for readers to fill with stories about places that books can make attractive once again. For Barth, these bits and pieces call on grammar to make adjustments: "No end-stops in *their* love-story; only semicolons, suspension points." Yet there are "narrative options still unforeclosed, other story worldlines wormholing through the multiverse."[83] On balance, a title such as *On with the Story* plays up the resilience of inheritance. It is the known world of fairy tales heard, recited, and read over and over again.

Se una notte d'inverno un viaggiatore   281

The roots of etcetera are very deep indeed! In fact, recurrence sets etcetera against the mythical figure of Echo, which also expands, repeats, and multiplies. Together, they have carried on reiteration for the longest time. John Hollander warns us that, as a literary metaphor, echo affects theories of consciousness, intention, and the hermeneutics of overhearing.[84] In a figurative sense, "echoing" reverberations can make room for parody, mockery, allusion, and quotation. Barth himself gives a rereading of Echo in the story by the same title: "What she gives back as another's speech may be entire misrepresentation." Moreover, "Echo never, as popularly held, repeats all, like gossip or mirror. She edits, heightens, mutes, turns others' words to her end."[85] By way of fictions appended to other fictions, etcetera resorts to combinatorial techniques that favor "*how* write instead of *why* write."[86] Narration must go on if we are to make it through the night by reciting an etcetera's worth of titles.

Etcetera has come a long way from quixotic spin-offs. While machines maximize the production of "impersonal" etceteras, technology minimizes authorship. Even etcetera tells us that ideology has reached its endpoint, where technology has taken over. However serious the humanist crisis might be, the progress of technology has not let up. Assembly lines carry on regardless of doomsday predictions. If intellectual life has waned and much of the biological health of the planet is going up in smoke, technology will give us spare parts for everything that is left behind. Typewriters, shorthand, and computer programs have altered material conditions and intellectual mindsets to an extent that it should give us pause. It seems to me that the Agora and the Forum have surrendered first to Flint and then to Silicone Valley. It may not be accidental that critical parlance has coined the term "literature machine" at a time when higher forms of technological efficiency have changed the "written object" as well as the "writing subject."

The artist echoed the writer when Andy Warhol wrote that he wanted "to be a machine." In the assembly line of his Factory, serialization satisfied his need to admire "boring things." Because he liked "things to be exactly the same over and over again," Warhol stretched his visual etceteras from seductive smiles to Coke bottles. In the postmodern mode of etcetera, he also stretched his mundane notoriety, and John Updike reminds us that, whereas each one of us will be famous for fifteen minutes, Andy Warhol's "fifteen minutes are still stretching."[87] Visually, Saul Steinberg stretched serialization of people and letters under the banner of etcetera, which led Roland Barthes to write, in a short comment entitled "Etc.," that there is no etcetera "in nature, which says everything." Only man has the power to restrict meaning to three short letters, etc. Because the word of Steinberg is not natural, "it is full of etc.," which is "repeated and reverberated (répété, réverbéré).[88]

For less than fifteen minutes, an array of minor Warhols and Menards can claim authorship, at least according to the terms of the "literature machine." I would suggest that Pierre Menard is anyone who, having bought a book, signs and dates it. This common practice makes the book anachronistic vis-à-vis the day of completion no less than the day of publication. Such inevitable displacements are fortunate inasmuch as they are conducive to interpretation. While the signature inscribes material ownership, the reader also "authors" the book by signing his or her name on the title page. Such an authoritative act cannot but foster "strong readings." It suffices to add that literary "transfers" affect readers as well as editors and translators. The librarian D. F. McKenzie believes that we have come full circle: "From a defense of authorial meaning, on the grounds that it is in some measure recoverable, to a recognition that, for better or worse, readers inevitably make their own meanings."[89]

As a result, everyone can be, at least wishfully, a Pierre Menard, that is to say, everybody and anybody. In the spirit of etcetera, I would like to add my own authorial *incipit*; it stems from age-old misreadings and does not expect to find a place in any archive worthy of its name:

> If, on a spring morning a traveler, tired of sailing to Byzantium by way of either Ithaca or Ravenna, should decide to venture forth, he had better do it after having thrown the map of *nostos* overboard. Let him journey as Odysseus and Aeneas never did. Without probing into motives, let him sail forth like Christopher Columbus, who, moved by greed and favored by luck, discovered a new continent while looking for an old one. Let us encourage our wayward journeyman to leave all books ashore if only to avoid landing on the island of the day before. Since one can never exhaust the future-past of libraries, we might as well move on just because the anxiety of the new and life untamed push us to dare through, if not beyond, book covers.

Depending on their ingenuity, readers on a winter's night can indent this paragraph and have a text; without indenting it, they can have a short story. By so doing, they would make Calvino happy, keep themselves in Borges's good stead, and avoid a collision with someone else's unauthored shipwreck.

Se una notte d'inverno un viaggiatore 283

Dark nights need not be part of the winter of our discontent, if we can only settle with the idea that we can expand literature to the nth degree whenever we write about places we have discovered one more time in literary maps of the imagination.

Borges ends his story "Everything and Nothing" by letting Shakespeare tell God in the day of final recognition: "'I who have been so many men in vain want to be one and myself.' The voice of the Lord answered from a whirlwind: 'Neither am I anyone; I have dreamt the world as you dreamt your work, my Shakespeare, and among the forms in my dream are you, who like myself are many and no one."[90] Shakespeare was Godlike because he was everyone and no one. Nowadays, instead, the collective expansion of the "I" into the anonymous and collective "we-as-everyone" has marked a development at once inevitable and problematic, one that borders on Borges's own dilemma about the wisdom of pushing the resilience of order and the potential of disorder.

Of course, etceteras belong to human constructs that demand stability and continuity. The realm of etcetera curbs progress and fosters variations of what already is there. What is "there" is all that a culture has institutionalized by means of a "coded" body of referential markers. Barthes writes forcefully that a text does not consist of a line of words "but of a multi-dimensional space in which are married and contested several writings, none of which is original: the text is a fabric of quotations, resulting from a thousand sources of culture."[91] Such a wealth of sources affords reliability because the world of etcetera is set in the archive, the library, and the museum. Perhaps it would be fair to guess that the literature machine has been churning out the inevitable; it may be the case that postmodernism is but an etcetera to modernism.

13

After the End of Art:
The Obituary of Titles

> In the world of Letters as a whole, we are witnessing the
> capitulation of the Word which, curiously enough, is even more
> exhausted than we are. Let us follow the descending curve of its
> vitality, surrender to its degree of overwork and decrepitude,
> espouse the process of its agony.
> —E. M. CIORAN

In spite of an apparent loss of clarity, "unauthored" writing has expanded its outreach among the postmoderns. The literature machine has found in etcetera a mode of literary production that favors the transfer of narrative points of view. It is not by accident that the "growth" of the reader as the "functional" author of familiar plots has entailed the parallel decline of the traditional concept of individual authorship. This development has led Warren Motte to ask: "Does *not* having written a book perhaps suffice, in itself, to distinguish a man?"[1] The answer involves negative modes of expression that absorbed many a writer during the second half of the twentieth century—from Beckett to Blanchot.

Linearity marked the progress of Western culture from the Renaissance to modernism, after which a kind of regressive circularity has taken us from the modernist end to the postmodern dead end. I believe that such a state of "terminality" is best expressed through the title of a critical book, for it is criticism that has created, after John Barth's "The Literature of Exhaustion" and "The Literature of Replenishment," concepts as resonant as Jean Baudrillard's "illusion of the end" or Jean-François Lyotard's "post-modern condition."

In *After the Death of Art: Contemporary Art and the Pale of History* (1997), the philosopher and art critic Arthur C. Danto acknowledges that "the great master narratives which first defined traditional art, and then modernist art, have not only come to an end, but contemporary art no longer allows itself to be represented by master narratives at all." The title centers on the paradox of life after death. Yet death is artistic, not physical, which means that we are facing the aftermath of predictions that have turned out to be incorrect. Master narratives may have become obsolete (neoconservatives' protests to the contrary notwithstanding). But contemporary art has survived the death of art; however exhausted, terminality still has a future. Amid such contradictions, titles resist foredoomed predictions and accept the survival of art even after its traditional structures have collapsed: "Ours is a moment, at least (and perhaps only) in art, of deep pluralism and total tolerance. Nothing is ruled out." In this "post-historical moment," elitism has come to terms with the unregulated inclusiveness of popular narratives.[2] Since the boundaries between artistic and material production have blurred to an unprecedented degree, much textuality is under attack. Authorship is slipping toward anonymity, and titles hold on to the last shreds of individualism. This chapter highlights the extent to which the most radical forms of textuality have affected titology.

1

At present, cultural boundaries have been shattered, and recycling has replaced rebirth. Ideologies have faded, whereas practice is thriving. To rephrase all this by recourse to titles about literary practice, I turn to Michel Butor's *How Some of My Books Wrote Themselves* (1935), which was followed in 1969 by Louis Aragon's *Je n'ai jamais appris à écrire ou Les incipit* (*I Never Learned to Write, or Incipits*) and, in 1978, by Renaud Camus's *How Some of My Books Wrote Me*.[3] These titles confirm that the role of the author has been restricted to overseeing the output of the literature machine, which trades the original for the copy because "it is easier to copy than to think, hence fashion." Plural and collective, fashion has led Wallace Stevens to warn that "a community of originals is not a community."[4] Such a troublesome concept fosters the idea that conformism has had the best of originality.

Once originality fell away, Andy Warhol made it clear that, for postmoderns at heart, production entails reproduction. Indeed, representations have become exponentially more fictional. To copy, therefore, is *to be* the books that are copied. Since the copyist "apes" without saying anything new,[5] we can turn to Butor's *Portrait de l'artiste en jeune singe* (*Portrait of the Artist as a Young Ape*, 1967), a title that set up an introductory equation between the human and the animal: "In Egypt, the god of writing, Thoth, was often portrayed as an ape."[6] From antiquity to the Renaissance, apes and parrots have symbolized pedestrian, if not outright parasitic, forms of imitation. To the extent that these texts spell out the translation-transformation of the artist into a primate, artistic practice has played up the zoo-semiotics of titles, and some would argued that Borges introduced the simian writer in *Pierre Menard autor del Quijote*.

Etymologically speaking, the Latin deity Ops fosters abundance, natural plenty, and material riches. His offspring was *copis* and then *copia*, which implied eloquent speech. During the Middle Ages, *copia* came to mean a copy produced by monastic amanuenses who dedicated their lives to the transcription of manuscripts.[7] At court, popes and humanists like Pius II and Erasmus contributed to a method of imitation that included earlier texts of authoritative writers.[8] Even Flaubert would agree that, nowadays, many are tempted to copy copyists such as Bouvard and Pécuchet, two indefatigable librarians who, having failed to gain knowledge in several fields, bought a double desk, mastered the instruments of writing, and spent the rest of their lives copying books. Bouvard and Pécuchet were but the scriptural embodiments of the literature machine; they never asked why. Instead, they settled on "what" to copy; and "what" was "whatever." Their admiration for any subject was the cause of great concern to William H. Gass, who considered the book an indictment of "our European pretensions to knowledge."[9] The more tolerant Calvino noted that the copyist lives "simultaneously in two temporal dimensions, that of reading and that of writing." At any time, the copyist can "write without the anguish of having the void open before his pen."[10] Since copying allows us to write without saying anything new, the copyist "apes" texts already written. The new vocation, therefore, is very old.

Do titles signal a privileged status that has become obsolete amid the Xerox culture of repetitions at once systematic and redundant? Walter Benjamin warned us against the excesses of mechanical reproduction, Warhol proved him right, and Theodore Ziolkowski reminds us that the University of California at Berkeley has established a Xerox Distinguished Professorship of Knowledge in the Haas School of Business.[11] Anyone somehow conversant with the concept of distinction amid the wished-for homogeneity that pop artists have flaunted in front of our eyes would find this entitlement quite undistinguished. The copy of a copy, and the representation of a representation, point to "disguised" varieties of the same. On and off campus, we probably live at the "Degree Xerox of value,"[12] where the title is bound to disappear together with authorial markers. Umberto Eco has coined the term *xerox-civiltà* (Xerox civilization) to describe the comforts of copying machines, all to the detriment of the author's copyrights.[13]

In postmodern culture, it is difficult to distinguish the original from the copy, which often edges on counterfeiting. Since it is impossible to re-create the past as it was, "faking" has been indexed into categories: the perverse, the legitimate, the innocent, and the experimental. In a strange way, faking a text highlights its resilience, and some have suggested that culture exists because people of letters are counterfeiters. Often enough, postmodern artists are uncertain whether they are misreading or plagiarizing; who is to say whether the final product is an original, a fraud, or a hybrid? Forgeries have created a cultural category called "spurious literature," which Hillel Schwartz has written about in *The Culture of the Copy: Striking Likenesses, Unreasonable Facsimiles*.[14] K. K. Ruthven suggests that concerns with imposture and identity should lead us to look at the relationship between genuine literature and literary forgeries less contemptuously than one would look at the dualism of Dr. Jekyll and Mr. Hyde.[15] Clearly, traditional notions of ethics and aesthetics are at risk.

Serialization has done a lot to discredit mimesis and originality alike. The more we copy, the further the copy is removed from the original; and the widening gap favors distortion. The potential of "cunning" simulations aside, there have been instances when writers have claimed authorship through denial. Ironically, *Why I Have Not Written Any of My Books* (1986) spells out Marcel Bénabou's resistance to driving the last nail into the coffin of literary deconstruction: "Great, however, was my consternation before those capable of producing works in quantity: the self-dispersion implicit in such behavior was revolting to me, and I could not personally see offering myself up in so many bits and pieces. In my eyes, conceiving of a book as an element in a series was practically akin to imposture." Bénabou is fully convinced that the world is full of plagiarists ready to steal even from the books he has not yet written.[16]

By emphasizing the futility of writing, plagiarism takes us beyond the threshold of serialization, reader-author transfers, and authorless writing. The concept of art as innovation has relapsed to the same degree that we have enhanced the technical aspects of literary production.[17] The mechanics of literature have so facilitated self-effacement that the title introduces an antitextual narrative. The best that Bénabou can do is to propose Scheherazade-like hypotheses about a writer struck with a curse:

> He knows that the end of his life will coincide with the end of one of his books (but of course he does not know which one). Accordingly, he has imposed upon himself the constraint of never bringing any of his literary projects to term. He throws himself only into inordinately ambitious undertakings, with the hope that, aided by weariness and discouragement, he will be unable to complete them. Each abandoned project maintains his chances of survival: hence he takes pleasure in multiplying his projects.[18]

Proliferation has been turned on its head, and the book's jacket ironically tells readers that "Bénabou knows the heroic joy of depriving critics of victims, the kindness of sparing the publisher decisions, and the public charity of leaving more room in book-store displays."

At the divide between improbability and exclusion, Bénabou writes *Dump This Book While You Still Can!* This title introduces a narrative that is "conditional, hypothetical," and potentially self-destructive.[19] What is printed, however, is a series of nonbeginnings that lead to a paradox: "Much as I have only ever written inconclusive fragments, I have never ceased to take myself for a maker of literature." In the aftermath of utter denial, Bénabou insists, "Writing that one would like to write is already writing. Writing that one cannot write is still writing. In this negative mode, the recognition of one's 'ineptitude for writing' would lead to the discovery that to be a writer one must understand the 'absence' of one's 'uncompleted works.'"[20] Around the outer curvature of the literary horizon, we have run out of new territories as well as of stable borders. The topographies of art have folded and refolded into rippled layers, all to the benefit of duplication. Rearrangement often thrives on mistranslations along such retitling lines as *Faust, Mon Faust, Doktor Faustus, The Bedside Faust, Neo-Faust,* and *Who the Fuck Is Faust?* Connectedness has generated a "literature in the second degree" that has now exploded.[21] For more than half a century now, we have cluttered the postmodern cul-de-sac with literary and artistic leftovers that have been rearranged in various combinations.[22] The philosopher E. M. Cioran adds that we have reached not the end of another cycle "but of all" cycles.[23] The rondure of the "already-always" has so bent time that we can look forward to an array of future-pasts.[24] In the postmodern dead end, the past has become its own future, a juxtaposition that has trapped us in a web of mystifying anachronisms. Even the end of art has turned out to be a metaphor for procrastination.

At the crossroads between modernism and postmodernism, Eliot ended *The Waste Land* with fragmentation ("Da") and Sanskrit, while Wittgenstein closed the *Tractatus Logico-Rhetoricus* by insisting that "what we cannot speak about we must pass over in silence."[25] In 1925 the Spanish philosopher and cultural historian José Ortega y Gasset wrote about the artistic tendency: "Toward the dehumanization of art; to an avoidance of living forms; to ensuring that a work of art should be nothing but a work of art . . . an art which makes no spiritual or transcendental claims whatsoever."[26] The autonomy of the artwork set off the decline of the humanist mindset. Half a century later, what Ortega y Gasset considered a negative development Foucault saw as positive, and he set out to disengage the representation of things, people, and events from the shackles of ideological frameworks. By highlighting ruptures and discontinuities, the French philosopher set the human apart from the humanist worldview.[27] Amid a culture in which the humanist has given way to the antihumanist, we trust neither titles nor entitlements.

We may have exhausted sounds, but we are still thriving on the echoing noiselessness of the "has been."[28] This terminal condition comes to the surface in books of criticism, and titles such as Ihab Hassan's *The Language of Silence* and George Steiner's *Language and Silence* equate the impending death of literature with voicelessness. Too many calls for silence, however, have breached silence itself. The disintegration of textuality has followed suit. Titles such as *The Death of the Novel* and "The Death of the Death of the Novel"[29] have become as emblematic as Leslie Fiedler's radical *What Was Literature* (1982). For Alvin Kernan, the death of literature "looks like the twilight of the gods to conservatives or the fall of the Bastille of high culture to radicals."[30]

From the literary to the literal, Mary Roach has entitled the last chapter of *Stiff: The Curious Lives of Human Cadavers* "Remains of the Author." The subject is the disposal of her own body for the greater good of scientific research. Pedagogy finds a way of making waste useful: "I will include a biographical note in my file for the students who dissect me (you can do this), so they can look down at my dilapidated hull and say, 'Hey, check this. I got that woman who wrote a book about cadavers.' And if there's any way I can arrange it, I'll make the thing wink."[31] The writer visualizes her own *postmortem* in a book about medical protocols that act out an anatomical dehumanization of people. Even the necrological can be funny, should the corpse's "winking" deliver the last joke. In the midst of postmodern necrologies, the drawn-out process of ending is the dominant mode of our time. The goal of art is to say "nothing" beyond what has already been said, and many believe that authorship has become a passive instrument of "writing."

In a critical essay entitled "The Death of the Author," Roland Barthes writes that Mallarmé was the first to tell us that it "is language which speaks, not the author." The inference was that writers should be sacrificed to writing, which amounts to nothing more than the aftermath of language emptied of content. Like an empty shell, language becomes a purely visual presence. "The Death of the Author" is a title that acknowledges the inevitable, which "is not merely an historical fact or an act of writing; it utterly transforms the modern text." In fact, "the birth of the reader must be at the cost of the death of the author," because one's vulnerability is commensurate with the other's empowerment. The aim is to undermine language as the medium behind which "the whole of History stands unified and complete in the manner of a Natural Order."[32]

On more step and Barthes describes writing as a ruinous undertaking: "To write by fragments: the fragments are then so many stones on the perimeter of a circle: I spread myself around: my whole little universe in crumbs." Having devalued the literary, Barthes reduces the scriptural to lines at the edge of the unwritten. On the last page of *Roland Barthes by Roland Barthes*, the writer "doodles" his way into "the signifier without the signified" only to raise an unanswerable question: "And afterward?"[33] The issue as whether it is possible to "[k]now at what moment the verb *to write* began to be used intransitively."[34] The "graphic" doodle suggests that intransitivity has shredded the remnants of writing at the edge of verbal and visual expressions (Fig. 31). Calvino would add that, as we witness the "disappearance of the 'I,' the primary subject of the verb 'to write,' so the ultimate object eludes us." Author and narrative fade away, but the vacuum that opens up "is inexhaustible in forms and meanings."[35]

The "innocent" letter, Barthes goes on, "if it is alone, is innocent: the fall begins when we align letters to make them into words."[36] We have reached a crossroads where we confront one of the most emblematic titles of postmodern disintegration, *Writing Degree Zero*, which describes the point at which the meaningful, linear continuity of classical language gives way to the isolation and discontinuity of modern words that have become ever more difficult to decipher. The demise of language entails that of grammar, and the

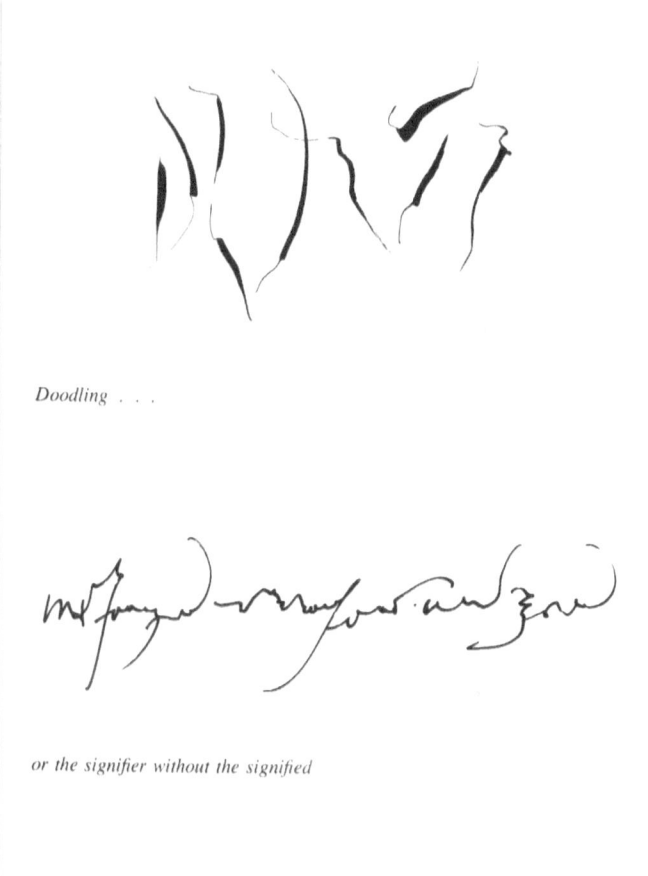

FIG. 31 Roland Barthes, "Doodling . . . or the signifier without the signified," 1972, from *Roland Barthes by Roland Barthes*, translated by Richard Howard. Translation copyright © 1977 by Farrar, Straus & Giroux, Inc. Reprinted by permission of Hill and Wang, a division of Farrar, Straus and Giroux, LLC.

"graphic" doodle suggests that what exists is nothing more than a graph in the graphographer's world. Beyond it, we may perceive echoes of Flaubert's older project to do "a book about nothing." At any rate, the descriptive has turned into the interrogative, and the explanatory into the problematic. Barthes's doodle is a scriptural sign that links up to André Masson's semiograms, which shatter the boundaries between writing and painting by falling back on Chinese ideograms. What Masson achieves is illegibility. The removal of writing from the image repertoire of legible communication gives the semiographer a chance to produce "the illegible."[37] I would like to draw a parallel between the philosopher and the artist. While Foucault's archaeology of knowledge seeks discontinuity, fragmentation, and autonomy, Barthes sees writing as an archaeology of meaningless presence, which has wiped out myth and history no less than scriptural and linguistic codes. What is left is the doodle and doodling, that is to say, the posthumous residues of textual contents lodged in *The Library of Babel*.

Postmodernism has relished forecasts about a future "language of particles,"[38] which play up the ascendancy of details over wholes.[39] Octavio Paz is convinced that between rupture and repetition there is nothing more than "_____."[40] The scriptural has exhausted itself in a dotted line that strings out the degree zero of presence as well as of expression. While A. R. Ammons lets poetry say that "Even nothing has a / rim around it, which makes it a / something," (*Glare*, lines 117–18), Jorie Graham's *The End of Beauty* introduces a collection of poems that include blanks and holes.[41] After all, the page is a blank space that writing as writing fills to capacity. The inference is that textuality has purged itself of scriptural contaminations that might point back to human references, especially the ghastly ghost of narrativity. The incredulous reader might ask: but where does the concept of textuality, with all its positives and negatives, come from, if not from human thought and human language? Personal reservations aside, we cannot bypass the titological inference. If textuality has been reduced to dots and doodles, titles seem to be the last scriptural survivors.

At this point, the disintegration of the scriptural crosses paths with the musical silences of John Cage and the "ripped" canvases of Lucio Fontana. They all would agree that the pen does not need the alphabet to make a mark, nor does the paintbrush need to "represent" anything to make a picture. While Mondrian and Kandinsky have made us familiar with "compositions" and "improvisations," the last shreds of names, words, and scriptural signs are about to disappear on the surface of Cy Twombly's *Untitled* canvases. The fading words that he paints and writes about the long-gone world of Valéry, as well as of Hero and Leander, are a kind of pictorial farewell to mythology, literature, and writing itself. In *Fifty Days at Iliam: House of Priam* (1978, Fig. 32), the fading word in the middle of the canvas is the name of Cassandra, the Trojan prophetess whose dire warnings faded in the wind as much as Twombly's letters are smeared out. In his comments on Twombly's *Works on Paper*, Barthes finds that the minimalist "graphism" of the word-name Virgil only "alludes to writing," which consists of what remains because the rest has been "*thrown away* as being of no use." What the gesture of writing transmits is "the memory of a defunct culture which has left no more than the trace of a few disappearing words."[42] Put otherwise, scribbles, scrapings, and blackboard rubbings border on the zero degree of adroitness in drawing and writing.[43]

Twombly's subtle calligraphy barely surfaces at the edge of childhood blackboards with signs traced and erased. Amid birthmarks and death whispers,[44] the fading words that he paints are a kind of farewell to writing as a technology of individual scripture with ink and pen. In a review of Twombly's

FIG. 32   Cy Twombly, *Fifty Days at Iliam: House of Priam*, 1978 (seventh of ten parts). The Philadelphia Museum of Art. Gift (by exchange) of Samuel S. White 3rd and Vera White, 1989.

1994 retrospective at the Museum of Modern Art, Jed Perl seems to round out my argument when, having described Twombly's "doodle of paint," he writes that "contemporary artists are intent on demonstrating that in the beginning and in the end there is nothing but the mark."[45] Scriptural and pictorial doodles merge together; and so does the terminal disintegration of language, inasmuch as the surfaces of Twombly's canvases accommodate hybrids of notebook pages, graffiti-scarred walls, chalkboards, blackboards, bulletin boards, and chaotic indexes of scriptural clutter.

Appropriately titled, *Letter of Resignation,* Twombly's series of thirty-eight drawings (done in Rome in 1967), show numbers better than alphabetical letters, except for stretching out the "m" consonant to the point of becoming a scriptural "sign" akin to Barthes's "doodle" (Fig. 33). In both instances the artist breaks boundaries and gives visual evidence to a pictorial presence that has either exceeded or survived linguistic codes meant to express meaning. The title, therefore, is a letter of resignation, thirty-eight pages long, from the conventions of *poesis* and *pictura* alike. Writing and painting merge into graphic images that are less than pictorial and more than scriptural. What gain expression are erasure and denial.

For Jasper Johns, what was left was to paint letters in *Gray Alphabets* (1956, Fig. 34), a title that wipes out grammar as much as mathematics in the canvases with painted numbers. We look at the debris of functional codes that have regulated human interactions for centuries. These artworks efface functional symbols of civilization, an outcome that is overtly polemical in Robert Rauschenberg's *Erasing a William de Kooning's Painting* (1953, Fig. 35). The title refers to a picture that consists of traces of ink and crayon on the paper of a real de Kooning work. The death of the author is carried out literally at

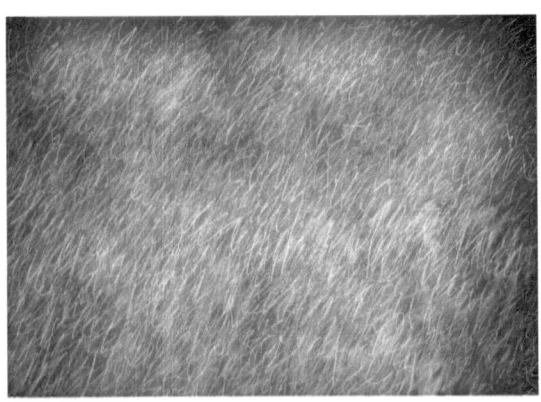

FIG. 33 Cy Twombly, Untitled. 1970. The Museum of Modern Art, New York. Acquired through the Lallie P. Bless Bequest and The Sidney and Harriet Janis Collection (both by exchange).

the objective (de Kooning) and at the subjective (Rauschenberg) levels. Likewise, Blanchot's *Le livre a venir* (*The Book to Come*) links the future of the book to the disappearance of literature, which has brought to the fore the death of the last writer.[46]

For Georges Perec, the only thing that one can still attempt is "to wrest a few precise scraps from the void as it grows, to leave somewhere a furrow, a trace, a mark or a few signs."[47] The idea of writing as ruinous debris has turned palimpsests on their heads. The traces that lie beneath new writing have become the only form of writing in a dead end where history has no place to go. If modernism was born as a wasteland that announced the end of history, could postmodernism view the future as other than the very last aftermath of the Western tradition? Postmodernism, in fact, draws sustenance from forecasting semantic negativity and epistemological nihilism.[48]

Among practitioners of posthumousness, nobody has written the last word, painted the last picture, and then quit for good. For Borges, such an outcome should have affected literature more than the visual arts: "I do not know whether music can give up hope in music, or marble in marble, but literature is an art that is able to foresee the moment when it will have grown

FIG. 34 Jasper Johns, *Gray Alphabet*, 1956. The Menil Collection, Houston. © Jasper Johns / Licensed by VAGA, New York.

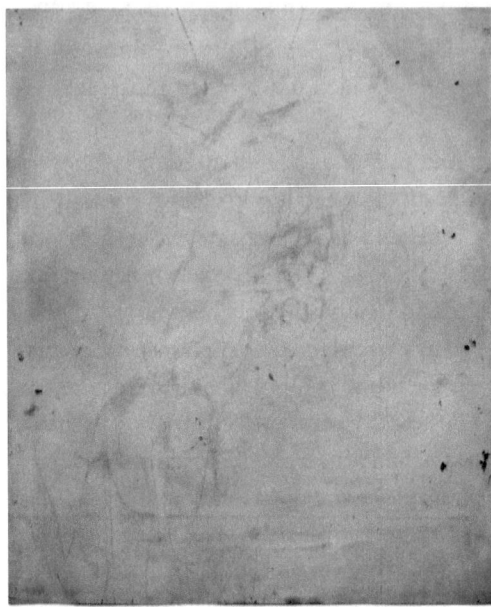

FIG. 35 Robert Rauschenberg, *Erased de Kooning Drawing*, 1953. San Francisco Museum of Modern Art. ©Robert Rauschenberg / Licensed by VAGA, New York.

silent, to scorn its own virtue, to become enamored with its own dissolution and to court its own death."[49] Many have uttered the death of art, and some have died; but the arts have survived. It has been the business of postmodernism to give the moribund a new lease on life, to make the pathological prolific, to stop the terminal at the edge of extinction, and to recycle death itself. In fact, necrologism is having not only a postmodern but a *postmortem* revival, and the title of a position paper by the architectural historian Charles Jencks reads: "Death for Rebirth."[50] In the dead end, what could rebirth entail?

Whether physiological or psychological, negativity finds immediate precedents at the end of the eighteenth century, when the "age of reason" turned toward unreason. Much art was accommodated in dungeons and mad houses, from Piranesi's *Prisons* to the Panopticon of the Bentham brothers. Francisco Goya put it in mythological terms and painted Saturn eating his own children. The reasonable and the unreasonable stared at each other. It suffices to add that the romantics made of illness an aesthetic condition. By the turn of the twentieth century, sickness had slipped into decadence. From sensitive individuals to working crowds, the industrial revolution, Darwinism, and Naturalism exposed the underpinnings of a social structure that starved the many and privileged the few. Idealistic frameworks crumbled, and materialistic counterparts offered alternatives that no longer could ignore "the reality of things." The physiological was downgraded into the pathological. Once antihumanist revisionism gained a solid footing, the rise of more earthbound ideologies—with Marxism at their forefront—took stock of the unfunctional, the unhealthy, and the outright abnormal aspects of the Western experience.

Michel Foucault took a radical stand: "The history of ideas, then, is the discipline of beginnings and ends, the description of obscure continuities and returns, the reconstitution of developments in the linear form of history... archaeological description is precisely such an abandonment of the history of ideas.... Archaeology is much more willing than the history of ideas to speak of discontinuities, ruptures, gaps." Statements of this sort discredited the linear cohesiveness of the grand narrative. In its place, Foucault promoted "cultural discourses"—such as the ones on the prison, the clinic, and madness—that followed their own autonomous paths. The goal was to approach human experience as it really happened instead of acquiescing to those who controlled the way stories were written, edited, and circulated. While producing a critique of linearity, Foucault found an alternative in the archaeologist, who "describes discourses as practices specified in the element of the archive." Because it is indexical, the archive preserves "discursive formations" without trying to normalize them; it lists but does not necessarily connect.[51] Antihumanist revisionism spurred unproportional approaches to established standards;[52] and earthbound concerns took up the unfunctional as well as the outright dysfunctional aspects of the human condition. Nowadays, the nonhuman and the posthuman have shattered the canonical signposts of the humanist heritage. Cosmos is yielding to chaos, which is proving to be not quite disorderly after all!

A variety of deconstructive impulses have spurred the postmoderns to delegitimize the world order of humanist elitism. Progress itself seems to have been exhausted, and enterprising people have no script to follow. The loss of prescriptive rules has entailed a commensurate loss of those linear threads that have woven master stories for millennia. It has been a loss for some and a gain for others. To be sure, the antihumanist point of view has sharpened everyone's critical acumen. Whether it be a theme, a motif, or a current, a new appreciation of the diversity of historical phenomena has enriched critical undertakings.

In the process, we have traded the anthropocentric for the anthropometric, which assumes that what is human is not necessarily connected to, or compatible with, the humanist. The defining feature of anthropometric thought is a bifurcation: the human no longer possesses an a priori connection to humanism.⁵³ Definitions of reality apart from humanity reveal one of the most problematic aspects of our culture. There is little doubt that the historian, as a storytelling subject who used to provide "narrative" interpretations of the past, has at last been cornered. The antihumanist critique of master narratives was long overdue, but what has taken their place? What is the human without the humanist? Language can spell the posthuman; but what kind of life is posthuman? Is language way ahead of us? Should we try to catch up to it? Perhaps we are beginning to realize that we have done a good job at deconstructing beginning, end, and much of everything in between; but what is there "after" everything?

2

In the broader context of the history of science, "everything" echoes the title of Bill Bryson's *A Short History of Nearly Everything*, which informs us that humankind has existed for only .0001 percent of the earth's history: "We are really at the beginning of it all. The trick, of course, is to make sure we never find the end. And that, almost certainly, will require a good deal more than lucky breaks."⁵⁴ In terms of historical time, we have outlived a slew of "renaissances." In terms of cosmic time, we are still struggling out of "naissance." How has it happened that, at the "dawn" of human time, we have managed to produce so much "decadence"?

Yet the very fact that we have overcome "falls" and endured "declines" should give us courage to keep on wrestling with anachronism as well as posthumousness. I would venture to say that Renaissance experimentalists were groundbreakers, but many of their postmodern heirs have become gravediggers. While it cannot be denied that gravediggers are fully employed, there are jobless groundbreakers who have not given up. Perhaps one reason is that they are not waiting for a Godot holier than any other Godot. Instead, they have ventured along an old dirt path, trying to catch up to Sisyphus and give him a hand in pushing the boulder of secular humanism in the hope that circularity in the dead end may eventually arrive at a crossroads.

In the circular dead end, the morgue is close to the delivery room. Between them, the waiting room of exhaustion and replenishment (as we have seen) thrives on procrastination, which mocks death and bypasses birth. In the cul-de-sac, everything feeds into the postmodern aftermath; even the obituary has a follow-up. And so does titology.

14
The Literature of Titles

We always write along the thread of Nothingness.
—EDMOND JABÈS

I would like to believe that titles have provided a point of entry for interpreting literary texts, from the Renaissance to postmodernism. As the *Ur* point in the nomenclature of titles, I like to turn to Petrarch, the first "modern man" even in matters of titology. In a letter dated April 27, 1374, he explained to a papal secretary that he was hunting down Cicero's *In Praise of Philosophy* because "the title excited" him. At the time, Petrarch was fully engaged in the recovery of classical texts wherever they had been buried and forgotten. Between digs and trips, his mind could not rest, and titles were palimpsests that created virtual texts. At once archaeological and potential, titles as themes began to create a mental library that fostered a kind of intercultural dialogue. Petrarch's search was as relentless as it was venturesome: "I promptly laid my hand on a book with that title—but it was the wrong book." The title is correct, but it introduces a different text from the one expected. Even before the invention of printing, titles were not protected by exclusivity; duplication had already begun to raise its ugly head! Thus Petrarch drew a titological lesson: "I tell you this to caution you against falling into my error, although I suspect that is impossible. When I read it and found nothing in it that the title promised, I blamed my own stupidity for what turned out to be someone else's mistake."[1] With time, the mistake would become a choice.

Moved less by ideological questions than by monetary considerations, the German writer Jean Paul maximized titles because he could not afford books. *The Invisible Lodge* (1793) contains a story, "The Contented Life of the Schoolmaster Wuz," about a character who went to book fairs, memorized every title, and wrote by hand a complete library of manuscripts that enriched his "handsome collection."² By the middle of the twentieth century, indigence had become irrelevant insofar as many writers had moved from the construction to the deconstruction of textuality.

The fragmentation of titles reflects the analogous disintegration of selfhood, which must be traced back to Beckett's mutilation of individuals, texts, and language. In his own words: "At the end of my work there's nothing but dust—the nameable. In the last book—*L'Innomable*—there's complete disintegration."³ The pronoun is negative in *Not I*, and the noun fails to name in *The Unnamable*, which is a title that cancels itself out. To borrow a mathematical metaphor that Robert Champigny used to describe the poetics of Beckett, "here is the zero place, now the zero moment, I the zero individual."⁴ Beckett seems to have pushed earlier lessons about the simplification of grammar toward their extreme conclusion. If Gertrude Stein was consumed by "the passion for the name of anything,"⁵ Beckett concluded that names describe nothing at all.

Yet Beckett could not stop writing, and the nameless first-person narrator of *The Unnamable* confesses that, even though he saw himself "slipping," he could not solve the final dilemma: "I can't go on, I'll go on."⁶ Beckett acknowledged that after 1950 he had become post-Beckett. Postness, however, did not dry out scriptural interest in the Irish playwright. In a long 1959 review of *The Unnamable*, Maurice Blanchot centered on the elusive "I" of the novels: "Who is doing the talking in Samuel Beckett's novels, who is this tireless 'I' constantly repeating what seems to be always the same thing?" Repetitiveness leads Blanchot to zero in on the essential literary quality of Beckett's writing. In spite of a lack of center, of a lack of beginning and end no less than of plot development, we have "a language that will never stop, that finds it intolerable to stop."⁷ There is no absolute silence; rather, silence keeps on resonating with words, however purposeless.

Circumstance and choice steadily purged textuality of traces that might point back to human references, especially the ghost of narrativity. The incredulous reader might ask: but where does the concept of textuality come from, if not from human thought and human language? Are we not left with the proverbial image of one who cut off his nose to spite his face? If textuality has been reduced to dots and doodles, titles seem to be the last literary survivors. They are informative as well as cognitive, because titology seems to have absorbed textuality.

What about titles that do not inspire texts at all? What is more provocative than a title without a text? Titles constitute the ultimate open-ended beginnings, that is to say, literary frames that can tell the least and suggest the most all at once; their potential is as boundless as that of empty pages, blank canvases, or musical scores. The mounting significance of titles over texts finally led Calvino to sound a warning at the very end of his book: "'But, look here, there's a misunderstanding,' you try to warn him. 'This isn't a book . . . these are only titles.'" Since the beginning of time, all texts boil down to a traveler who happens upon a crossroad where he is told a story about either "the continuity of life" or "the "inevitability of death."[8] That being the case, the title alone makes a difference, as Pierre Menard well understood.

1

My introductory metaphor maintains that seeds are foundational. Through time, origin and beginning build semantic layers that link up to matters of rebirth, renewal, and referentiality. In spite of detours and downturns, the wilderness of textuality expanded to the edge of modernism, where James Joyce brought to the fore the destructiveness of experimentalism when he foresaw the "abnihilisation of the etym." Paradoxically, the erosion of etymologies has been countered by the expansion of commentaries; and both have affected titles.

Stephen Dedalus, Leopold Bloom's younger acquaintance, weighed in on matters of titles when he, as a reader, expressed the belief that the title of a book should consist of letters only: "Have you read his F? O yes, but I prefer Q. Yes, but W is wonderful. O yes, W" (*Ulysses*, 1–3:14). Irony is at work here, but some sort of "minimalist" preference is at play as well. A later generation of writers took his recommendation seriously and produced titles in which words broke down into letters. Cases in point are Pynchon's *V*, Barthes's *S/Z*, Sollers's *Z*, and Updike's *S*. We move here in a scriptural world where typographical characters fail to construct words, sentences, and discourse; but they succeed in bringing to the fore the kind of experimentation that spurred Apollinaire and e. e. cummings to equate the ontological with the visual—even fractions thereof. Titology left no doubt that cultural exhaustion had taken a toll on narrativity, semantics, and etymology itself.

One more step, and titological conventions were uprooted. Our metaphor has it that the seed contains the tree. The working assumption is that the relationship is irreversibly linear. Yet we could not expect that the postmoderns would restrain themselves from unhinging traditional expectations. John

Ashbery's *Title Search* has turned referential markers into virtual plots that are meant to generate titles rather than texts:

> Voices of Spring. Vienna Bonbons.
> Morning Papers. Visiting Firemen. Mourning Polka.
> . . .
> In the Pound. The Artist's Life. On the Beautiful Blue Danube.
> Less Is Roar. The Bicyclist. The Father.

In five stanzas that cover barely a page, the poet highlights writing projects that could span lifetimes. Yet what is written down is neither titological nor textual but a hybrid equidistant from both.

Asked to provide a "clutch of titles" that Jane Hammond would illustrate by means of pictorial collages, Ashbery sent forty-four titles: "They had a special pathos for me in that they were gifts somebody else was going to unwrap and play with. I was supplying the wrapping paper and ribbon, which I hoped would be as bright as possible. In return, Jane would reward me and her other fans with a new set of worlds like Wallace Stevens's 'completely new set of objects.'"[9] Among Ashbery's titles are *The National Cigar Dormitory, Dumb Show, The Friendly Sea, Prevents Furring, No One Can Win at the Hurricane Bar, Pumpkin Soup II*. While recovering the traditional sequence, even Wallace Stevens lists the titles of his own poems to be:

> The Sonnet With The Diamond Ring
> The Large Blue Sonnet
> The Sonnet With Two Voices
> The Little Old Sonnet Carved in a Bottle[10]

Stored in the poet's *musée imaginaire*, these titles are apt to inspire everyone's imagery. But what we have are titles only.

In three poems that are part of *As We Know*, Ashbery seems to reverse the titological metaphor, for the titles are longer than the text. In one instance, the title is *The Cathedral*, which is followed by the textual

> Slated for demolition

Likewise, *I Had Thought Things Were Going Along Well* is followed by a text that answers:

But I am mistaken[11]

In an interview with David Lehman, Ashbery made statements that are central to any poetics of titles. Having acknowledged his penchant for borrowing titles such as *Civilixation and Its Discontents* on the assumption that instinct spurred him to make his home in someone else's nest, the poet writes:

> The title of a poem is really much more than the word title conventionally suggests; it's also the subject of the poem, implicitly, and sometimes contrary to one's impressions otherwise of the text. That's probably something that I originally got from reading Stevens. The title almost amounts to the "given" for me; it indicates a space in which I will work. In addition to introducing the poem, it introduces me to the poem.[12]

In the graveyard of meaning, what survives is the *will to write*, which endures because the self-consuming activity of annihilation has failed to wipe itself out of existence. Amid defunct meanings, Geoffrey Hartman writes that, "despite obsolete and atrophied words, and falsified, disputable, or undecidable meanings, the will to write persists."[13] And the will to write is bound to yield, rather than a universe of texts, a whole literature of titles.

2

Still on American ground, a title such as *Tales Within Tales Within Tales* highlights a framing device that is meant to produce endless multiplication, regardless of the subject matter. The technology of literature has become self-fulfilling. After all, the "literature machine" can yield no more than the mechanical output of its own productivity. By extension, John Barth's fabulistic title could be retitled *Once upon a Time There Was a Story That Began . . .* and so on. Wishful thinking does not relent, and the title "refers not to the subject or to the contents of the work but to the work itself."[14] For much of its long development, technology served ideology in the tradition of Western humanism. Today, antihumanist radicalism has made technology teleological. The title as text has collapsed structure and meaning together, and the novelist keeps on writing "another story about a writer writing a story!" Often, however, what is written is no more than a series of titles that contain potential texts.

Whether the symbolism is mythological or literary, we are bound to push the rock of narrativity up the mountain just to stay alive, for the world of literature is no less demanding than the world of experience. In the universe of Barth's has-been, the title "Life-Story" really means "Literature-Story," and its plot "may be imagined as consisting of a 'ground-situation' (Scheherazade desires not to die) focused and dramatized by a 'vehicle-situation' (Scheherazade beguiles the King with endless stories)."[15] Of course, the reference to Scheherazade takes us back to *The Arabian Nights*, which, together with *Orlando Furioso* and *Don Quixote*, constitutes the foundational trinity of postmodern titology. A literal translation of the Arabic collection is *The One Thousand and One Nights*, which made the "Oriental tale" popular through several editions—beginning with the 1704 French version by Galland. The title points toward a never-ending narrative.[16] The one tale beyond one thousand is teleological, so to speak; it starts another series of narratives, which reassure us that there will always be one more night. As we all know, storytelling saves Scheherazade as well as other narrators who can count on the same privilege. As notorious an expert on death and punishment as Michel Foucault confirms that "speaking so as not to die is a task undoubtedly as old as the world. The most fateful decisions are inevitably suspended during the course of a story."[17]

The numerical symbolism of life-threatening counts returns in the faraway land of Borges's Tlön, where the *Thousand and One Nights* contains a story of the *Arabian Nights* in which Scheherazade tells Shahryar a tale in which Scheherazade tells Shahryar a tale. The reference is false, and the counterfeit suggests that anybody can put a spin on earlier tales. Pausing on the title itself, Borges believes that "the word *thousand* is almost synonymous with *infinite*. To say *a thousand nights* is to say infinite nights, countless nights, endless nights."[18] Barth, who has given just as much thought to the same text, confirms that the odd story really means "plenty and then some."[19] The odd tale out starts the count all over again, so that the readable echoes what has already been read. The inference is that literary technique has taken on a life of its own. Narrativity can go on in the mind no less than on paper through a Scheherazadesworth of titles.

By way of either erasure or fragmentation, have we reached the point where titles without texts have made it possible to obliterate narrativity? Are we standing at the threshold of antititles? The question has merit, and it would be fair to revisit titles through the lens not of reader reception but of reader rejection.

Accordingly, we can read Calvino's *If on a Winter's Night a Traveler* as a text in which ten beginnings do not call for further meaning. After all, why would we want to do what the writer himself has been unwilling to do? We know that the seed contains the tree; why bother with growth from one to the other? It is time to look at seeds as beginnings in memoriam. In the postmodern cul-de-sac, even titology, has turned on itself.

In 1959, W. H. Auden wrote *T the Great*, a poem about a youngster:

Known among his kin as T,

A name, like those we never hear of,
Which nobody yet walked in fear of
. . .
Though T cannot win Clio's cup again,
From time to time the name crops up again[20]

How great can a youth be if the integrity of his own name has been tampered with? The name's letter describes a sense of wholeness at once deficient and contradictory. The title sets the loss of the onomastic noun against the exaggeration of the adjectival qualifier (*the Great*), which brings to the fore the general breakdown of names, words, and literary forms of expression.

Later in the twentieth century, the final words of Barth's tale *On with the Story* are "T-zero." They quote Calvino's *T con zero*, a title in which the letter T stands out as the fragment of a word about to disappear. Since it consists of a letter that is not a word and of a numerical sign that is not a number, Calvino's title could be read as "title without anything." Of course, the elimination of titles is but the flip side of the disappearance of texts. How far can reduction go? Inevitably, the postmodern dialogue among book titles has reached a ground zero common to the arts at large. In Harold Rosenberg's words, "painting divided by zero has, however, proved to equal infinity: art might be coming to an end but there has been no end to anti-art."[21]

Since zero fosters the idea of absolute emptiness,[22] John Barth spells out the demise of language as meaning and structure in a short story about exhaustion: "Plot and theme: notions vitiated by this hour of the world but as yet not successfully succeeded. Conflict, complication, no climax. The worst is to come. Everything leads to nothing: future tense; past tense; present tense. . . . Everything's been said already, over and over."[23] Under the aegis of nothingness, the last shreds of writing call for a title equally dehumanized and meaningless. Appropriately, Barth entitles a story "Title." It is a generic marker; instead of introducing a specific narrative, it spells out the possibility of bringing forth scriptural activity without starting a narrative, humanist, antihumanist, or otherwise. Scholars would call this "involution," which defines works that turn in upon themselves. An involuted sentence would read: "I am a sentence."[24] There is no transitive action because the title has no apparent purpose.[25] The transitive has become intransitive, and the scriptural is means and end. Title and text define their potential for self-reflexive forms of expression.

Narrativity has been worn out, and the title of Barth's "Title" has exhausted the teleological in the archaeological. For him, the only alternative to overused models is "silence. General anesthesia. Self-Extinction."[26] There was a time when writers wrote to express what they were. That "habit" has gone, and Maurice Blanchot believes that, now, "we are according to what we write."[27] Since we have decided to doodle ourselves away from writing while courting scriptural incomprehensibility, how can we know who we are? "Title," therefore, does not introduce a narrative but the mechanics of narrativity. Just like Jasper Johns's paintbrushes and Saul Steinberg's toolkit inventories, the instruments of storytelling act out their own technical condition, all to the heartfelt contentment of Roland Barthes, who feared oncoming disasters whenever alphabetical letters ganged up and formed words! It all goes to prove that the title can entitle a text without recourse to a meaningful discourse. We have reached the point where we can have titles that introduce their own grammatical anatomy. Like a pictorial still life, "Title" yields a text that spells out the title's own descriptiveness. Indeed, the first page is the whole book.

Nevertheless, even mathematics tells us that the terminal subtraction of the title from the text is not so terminal, if we only look at mathematics from a postmodern point of view that accounts for exhaustion no less than for replenishment. I cannot help but turn to the opening sentence of Robert Kaplan's *The Nothing That Is: A Natural History of Zero*, a title that consolidates literary and mathematical equivalences. Its opening sentence leaves no doubts: "If you look at zero you see nothing; but look through it and you will see the world. For zero brings into focus the great, organic sprawl of mathematics, and mathematics in turn the complex nature of things."[28] This statement suggests that the zero degree of titology could be, rather than an endpoint, a point of entry. And Barth's "Title" has inspired me to consider a titological analogy drawn once again from architecture.

3

As a native Roman, it would be easy for me to identify the frontispiece of literature with the façade of the Pantheon, which sheltered the Olympians in the uniform concord of a round temple. Inside, light comes in through a circular opening at the top of the spherical dome. It is the *oculus,* which lets in rain and snow, moonlight and sunshine, silence and sounds at the threshold between the natural and the artificial. The *oculus* is the still point through which we can look down on the ghosts of antiquity, the ritual altars of Christianity, the tomb of Raphael and that of the Savoia king Victor Emmanuel II.

Because it offers a panoptic overview of Roman history, the *oculus* takes me to "El Aleph," a short story by Jorge Luis Borges in which the universe funnels down to a corner of the cellar where the Aleph "is one of the points in space containing all points." It is the place where "all the places in the world are found, seen from every angle." The title's *Aleph* is the first letter of the Hebrew alphabet, which symbolizes the infinity of the divine in Kabalistic lore.[29] In the literary narrative, El Aleph, which measures two centimeters in diameter, contains "cosmic space" without "diminution."[30] For Borges, whose reality is book-bound, the world itself is mapped, not observed. His title, therefore, is the literary *oculus* that introduces a cartographic representation of the Library of Babel, which contains the manmade universe itself.

In the last page of this study, the titological journey seems to have run its course. *T con Zero* has given us the postmodern countdown of the signifier that has unsignified itself. By the turn of the third millennium, the term postmodernism seems to have lost its momentum. Marjorie Perloff asks, "How long, after all, can a discourse continue to be considered *post?*"[31] Having erased etymology and discredited semantics, we may have conquered the inadequacies of the word, but we are bound to lose the world if knowledge is reduced to technique. While technique can build a house of cards, architecture does not amount to a pile of bricks, and bricks do not exist to be stacked up so that we might call them buildings wherever we happen upon a pile.

"El Aleph" has taken us to a threshold where literature is at once palimpsest and panopticon, where the title is epigraph and epitaph, and where the first page is the last. As the *oculus* that opens into the universe of textuality, the title empowers us to write about everything. It is up to us to decide whether we will act upon our entitlement.

NOTES

Introduction

1. Quoted in *Latin-American Literature Today*, ed. Anne Fremantle (New York: New American Library, 1977), 135.
2. Quoted in Roger L. Williams, *The World of Napoleon III, 1851–1870* (New York: Free Press, 1957), 271.
3. Oscar Wilde reiterated: "The nineteenth century, as we know it, is largely an invention of Balzac. Our Luciens de Rubempré, our Rastignacs, and De Marsays made their first appearance on the stage of the *Comédie Humaine*. We are merely carrying out, with footnotes and unnecessary additions, the whim or fancy or creative vision of a great novelist." Oscar Wilde, *Intentions* (London: Methuen, 1921), 33.
4. Michael Seidel, "Running Titles," in *Second Thoughts: A Focus on Rereading*, ed. David Galef (Detroit: Wayne State University Press, 1998), 36. Seidel spells out the range of such terms: "Titles may seem by their nature anticipatory, a form of advertising, but when they are reread into the design or, indeed, into the historical place of the works they name, they are also recapitulative and reflective. Titles gather material already experienced and allow reading processes to begin anew at various points inside a work, before it, or even after it. Titles are at once hypothetical and revisionary. As part of a first reading, titles are apprehensive; as part of subsequent or retroactive readings they are comprehensive."
5. Appropriately, Gérard Genette has given the title *Seuils* to his book on the literary apparatus, which addresses the function of prefaces, subtitles, epigraphs, postscripts, annotations, and bibliographical notes. The book has been translated as *Paratexts: Thresholds of Interpretation* (Cambridge: Cambridge University Press, 1997). Genette refers to equivalents in Borges's "vestibule" and Philippe Lejeune's "fringe" (2). In *Palimpsests: Literature in the Second Degree* (Lincoln: University of Nebraska Press, 1997), Genette confirms that the paratext includes "a title, a subtitle, intertitles; prefaces, postfaces, notices, forewords, etc.; marginal, infrapaginal, terminal notes; epigraphs; illustrations; blurbs, book covers, dust jackets, and many other kinds of secondary signals, whether allographic or autographic" (3). See his "Introduction to the Paratext," *New Literary History* 22 (1991): 263–72.
6. In *On Romanticism* (New York: New York University Press, 1971), Donald Sutherland pointed out that "one could write an excellent history of literature by using only titles" (281). An early effort on the subject is Helen Gardner's "The Titles of Donne's Poems," in *Friendship's Garland: Essays Presented to Mario Praz on His Seventieth Birthday*, ed. Vittorio Gabrieli (Rome: Edizioni di Storia e Letteratura, 1966), 1:189–208.
7. John Hollander, *Vision and Resonance: Two Senses of Poetic Form* (New York: Oxford University Press, 1975), 213–14; Alastair Fowler, *Kinds of Literature: An Introduction to the Theory of Genres and Modes* (Cambridge: Harvard University Press, 1982), 92–98; Margherita Di Fazio Alberti, *Il titolo e la funzione paraletteraria* (Turin: Einaudi, 1984); John J. White, *Mythology in*

the Modern Novel: A Study of Prefigurative Techniques (Princeton: Princeton University Press, 1971), especially chapter 4; Wolfgang Karrer, "Titles and Mottoes as Intertextual Devices," in *Intertextuality*, ed. Heinrich F. Plett (Berlin: W. de Gruyter, 1991), 122–34. On classical precedents, see Mario Untersteiner, *Problemi di filologia filosofica* (Milan: Cisalpino-Goliardica, 1980), 3–13. For titles in the arts, see Jerrold Levison, "Titles," *Journal of Aesthetics and Art Criticism* 44 (1985): 29–39.

8. Helen Vendler, "Wallace Stevens," in *The Columbia History of American Poetry*, ed. Jay Parini and Brett Millier (New York: Columbia University Press, 1993), 381. To borrow from what William H. Gass writes about the preface, the title "should mean business, but it is not a reduction of its text to bite size." Gass, *A Temple of Texts: Essays* (New York: Knopf, 2006), 62.

9. An exception is the book-length study of the English poem by Anne Ferry, *The Title to the Poem* (Stanford: Stanford University Press, 1996), 279. Ferry also links the idea of titles as thresholds to the image of the door-room in "Frost's 'Obvious' Titles," in *Reading in an Age of Theory*, ed. Bridget Gelleert Lyons (New Brunswick: Rutgers University Press, 1997), 147–64. One of her reviewers warns us that the neglect of this topic appears unjustifiably frivolous; see Susan Ellenberg's review in *Comparative Literature* 51 (summer 1999): 263.

10. Harry Levin, "The Title as a Literary Genre," *Modern Language Review* 72 (1977): xxiii.

11. "In order to further structural analysis of the narrative," Barthes applied "microanalysis" to his masterly reading of Balzac's story "Sarrasine." He entitled his study *S/Z* because its dualistic structure set forth "a pluralistic criticism authorizing the interpretation of several meanings." See Barthes, *The Grain of the Voice: Interviews, 1962–1980* (Berkeley and Los Angeles: University of California Press, 1991), 107.

12. Ulrich Schneider's "Titles in *Dubliners*," in *Rejoycing: New Readings of Dubliners*, ed. Rosa M. Bosinelli and Harold F. Mosher (Lexington: University Press of Kentucky, 1998), 195–96, addresses the metaphors of a portal leading into a building, a menu at the entrance of an inn, and a mustard seed containing within it the whole plant.

13. Jacques Barzun, *From Dawn to Decadence: Five Hundred Years of Western Cultural Life, 1500 to the Present* (New York: HarperCollins, 2000), 718, 730.

14. Theodore Ziolkowski, the eminent literary thematologist, reminds us that the third or new humanism upheld the value of the classical tradition "as a bulwark against what many writers and thinkers regarded as the anarchy loosed upon the world as a result of spiritual, intellectual, and political upheavals of the early twentieth century—as their response, in short, to the cultural despair of the age." Ziolkowski, *The View from the Tower: Origins of an Anti-Modernist Image* (Princeton: Princeton University Press, 1998), xi–xii.

15. Stephen Greenblatt, *Renaissance Self-Fashioning from More to Shakespeare* (Chicago: University of Chicago Press, 1980), 174–75.

16. Gianni Vattimo, *The Transparent Society* (Baltimore: Johns Hopkins University Press, 1992), 1–2.

17. Almost half a century ago, Irving Howe asked, "How, come to think of it, do great cultural movements reach their end? It is a problem our literary historians have not sufficiently examined, perhaps because they find beginnings more glamorous." Howe, *Decline of the New* (New York: Harcourt Brace and World, 1963), 33. Preferences aside, I submit that beginning and ending foreshadow and fulfill one another.

18. Italo Calvino, *Numbers in the Dark and Other Stories* (New York: Random House, 1995), 266.

CHAPTER 1

1. George Steiner, *After Babel: Aspects of Language and Translation* (Oxford: Oxford University Press, 1975), 487.

2. Gérard Genette, "Structure and Function of Titles in Literature," *Critical Inquiry* 14 (1988): 699.

3. Carlo Hesse, "Books in Time," in *The Future of the Book*, ed. Geoffrey Nunberg (Berkeley and Los Angeles: University of California Press, 1996), 10.

4. Thomas M. Greene, *The Vulnerable Text: Essays on Renaissance Literature* (New York: Columbia University Press, 1986), 225; and David Quint, "Painful Memories: Aeneid 3 and the Problem of the Past," *Classical Journal* 78 (1982): 37.

5. Erwin Panofsky, *Meaning in the Visual Arts* (New York: Doubleday, 1955), 297–98; Gilbert Ryle, *The Concept of Mind* (London: Hutchinson, 1966), 255; Wolfgang Iser, *Spenser's Arcadia: The Interpretation of Fiction and History* (Berkeley and Los Angeles: University of California Press, 1980), 35.

6. Bruno Snell, *The Discovery of the Mind* (New York: Harper and Row, 1960), 281–82.

7. I draw here on J. Hillis Miller's *Topographies* (Stanford: Stanford University Press, 1995), especially 45.

8. Commenting on Virgil's fifth eclogue, Paul Alpers writes that "convening gives rise to convention." Alpers, "Convening and Convention in Pastoral Poetry," *New Literary History* 14 (1983): 279. See also Thomas M. Greene, "Spenser and the Epithalamic Convention," *Comparative Literature* 9 (1957): 219.

9. There is a published edition that gives the date as 1508. The work refers to a shepherd's exile caused by hungry wolves that have dispossessed him of land and belongings. The "escapist" genre functioned as a screen for mundane matters of possession and righteousness otherwise atypical of pastoralism.

10. For more on this, see E. Kegel-Brinkgreve, *The Echoing Woods: Bucolic Pastoral from Theocritus to Wordsworth* (Amsterdam: J. C. Gieben, 1990), 376–77.

11. I draw on Miller, *Topographies*, 6.

12. See E. A. Quain, "The Medieval Accessus ad Auctores," *Traditio* 3 (1945): 215–64. Gérard Genette adds that "the title page appeared only during the period 1475–1480," in "Structure and Function of Titles in Literature," 699.

13. Quoted in her "Introduction," in *Discussions of the Divine Comedy*, ed. Irma Brandeis (Boston: Beacon Press, 1961), 2.

14. Harry Levin, *The Myth of the Golden Age in the Renaissance* (Bloomington: Indiana University Press, 1969), 7.

15. See the conclusion of Maria Corti's long essay, "Le tre redazioni della 'Pastorale' di P. J. De Jennaro con un excursus sulle tre redazioni dell'Arcadia," *Giornale storico della letteratura italiana* 131 (1954): 350–51.

16. Annabel Patterson, *Pastoral and Ideology: Virgil to Valery* (Berkeley and Los Angeles: University of California Press, 1987), 26–27; Thomas M. Greene, *The Light in Troy: Imitation and Discovery in Renaissance Poetry* (New Haven: Yale University Press, 1982), 35–41; Joel Brink, "Simone Martini, Francesco Petrarca, and the Humanist Program of the Virgil's Frontespiece," *Medievalia* 3 (1977): 83–109. The illustration that Simone Martini painted for a Petrarchan manuscript of Virgil offers a visual parallel in which the central position held by Servius between bucolic Virgil and epic Aeneas highlights the centrality of the interpreter. The pastoral mode thus began to foreground quotations, references, and commentaries. Intertextuality spurred Virgil to move Greek culture toward Italy, while Petrarch and Simone Martini served as guides to the dawn of a new epoch.

17. I follow Roland Barthes, *New Critical Essays* (New York: Hill and Wang, 1980), 58–59. See also William J. Kennedy, *Jacopo Sannazaro and the Uses of Pastoral* (Hanover: University Press of New England, 1983), who writes: "The proper audience of the *Arcadia*, then, must bring to the text a double perspective allowing the pastoral tradition and the pastoral landscape to merge into one" (116).

18. Panofsky, *Meaning in the Visual Arts*, 297–98.

19. On the self-gratifying character of such a process, see Roland Barthes, *S/Z* (New York: Hill and Wang, 1974), 92–93. This quality also has been related to Epicureanism; see Thomas G. Rosenmayer, *The Green Cabinet: Theocritus and the European Pastoral Lyric* (Berkeley and Los Angeles: University of California Press, 1969), chapter 5; and Sukanta Chaudhuri, *Renaissance Pastoral and Its Developments* (Oxford: Oxford University Press, 1989), 3.

20. Sannazaro, *Arcadia and Piscatorial Eclogues,* trans. Ralph Nash (Detroit: Wayne State University Press, 1966), 72, hereafter cited parenthetically in the text. To set off Sannazaro's emphasis on symmetry, it is helpful to quote Anthony C. Antoniades's comments on Virgil's architectural frame of mind in the *Aeneid:* "Virgil gives us no clues as to his design conception of the outdoor spaces. He is certainly aware of the sublimity of absolute—of the circle, for instance, which helps him define regional areas (the 'region-entrance' to the infernal regions), and of the power of numbers. Yet he gives us no further hints as to the geometric forms of the man-made element of his landscape. He speaks of 'groves,' and 'small parks,' but gives no further clues in the *Aeneid*. We assume that his geometries must follow the utilitarian geometry of the particular agriculture, the distance between the trees so they can grow, the requirements of vegetation. We detect no linearity in his depictions, yet we imagine enclosures and large ceilings of trees through which we can meander with pleasure. His landscapes, even those that are apparently organized after the coming of man, are geometrically non-descript; we assume them to be in a 'free' interface with the absolutely natural." Antoniades, *Epic Space* (New York: Van Nostrand Reinhold, 1992), 91.

21. Leon Battista Alberti, *On the Art of Building* (Cambridge: MIT Press, 1987), 268–69.

22. Paul Alpers, "What Is Pastoral?" *Critical Inquiry* 8 (1982): 444, 457; Paul Alpers, "Empson on Pastoral," *New Literary History* 10 (1978): 101–24; Andrew Ettin, *Literature and the Pastoral* (New Haven: Yale University Press, 1984), 61.

23. Renato Poggioli, *The Oaten Flute: Essays on Pastoral Poetry and the Pastoral Ideal* (Cambridge: Harvard University Press, 1975), 20. Richard Cody, in *The Landscape of the Mind: Pastoralism and Platonic Theory in Tasso's Aminta and Shakespeare's Early Comedies* (Oxford: Oxford University Press, 1969), writes that "in the Italian Renaissance, in a Platonizing culture dominated by the courtly ethos, pastoralism becomes the temper of the aristocratic mind" (6).

24. Geoffrey H. Hartman, *The Fate of Reading and Other Essays* (Chicago: University of Chicago Press, 1975), 121. On the relation between Virgil and Sannazaro, see Ettore Paratore, *Antico e nuovo* (Caltanissetta: Sciascia, 1965), 213–42; Maria Corti, *Metodi e fantasmi* (Milan: Feltrinelli, 1969), 286.

25. For parallel matters of epic echoes from Virgil to Milton, see A. Bartlett Giamatti, *Exile and Change in Renaissance Literature* (New Haven: Yale University Press, 1984). Giamatti's conclusion about the epic sheds light on the pastoral as well: "Nothing is more traditional than the claim to be making an innovation.... One sense in which epics are literarily self-conscious is their view of themselves as inheritors and containers of previous epic literature" (6–7).

26. Thomas K. Hubbard, *The Pipes of Pan: Intertextuality and Literary Filiation in the Pastoral Tradition from Theocritus to Milton* (Ann Arbor: University of Michigan Press, 1998), 347–48.

27. See Leo Spitzer, "The 'Ode on a Grecian Urn,' or Content vs. Metagrammar," in *Essays on English and American Literature,* ed. Anna Hatcher (Princeton: Princeton University Press, 1962), 67–97; Murray Krieger, *Ekphrasis: The Illusion of the Natural Sign* (Baltimore: Johns Hopkins University Press, 1992), especially 6–8.

28. See James Heffernan, "Ekphrasis and Representation," *New Literary History* 22 (1991): 296.

29. Richard Brilliant, *My Laocoön: Alternative Claims in the Interpretation of Artworks* (Berkeley and Los Angeles: University of California Press, 2000), 74.

30. Francis Haskell, "Giorgione's *Concert Champêtre* and Its Admirers," in Haskell, *Past and Present in Art and Taste: Selected Essays* (New Haven: Yale University Press, 1987), 142.

31. Kenneth Clark, *Landscape into Art* (Boston: Beacon Press, 1969), 55. Annabel Patterson has applied Clark's title to a pastoral poem by Robert Burns; see her *Pastoral and Ideology,* 193.

32. Wilkins has updated, without claiming authorial rights, Frederick Hatt's magisterial *History of Italian Renaissance Art,* 5th ed. (New York: Harry N. Abrams, 2003), 635.

33. Clark, *Landscape into Art,* 58–59. Without providing explanations, Sidney Freedberg attributes the painting to Titian and calls it *Pastorale,* in his *Italian Painting, 1500 to 1600* (Baltimore: Pelican Books, 1974), 89; conversely, Frederick Hartt gives it to Giorgione as *Fête Champêtre,* in his *History of Italian Renaissance Art* (New York: Abrams, 1969), 531.

34. Erwin Panofsky might agree that even titology could fall under the rubric of *pseudomorphosis,* whereby images take on meanings not present in their precursors; see his *Studies in Iconology: Humanistic Themes in the Art of the Renaissance* (New York: Harper and Row, 1972), 71.

35. The nudes have been identified with poesia and art. See Patricia Egan, "Poesia and the *Fête Champêtre*," *Art Bulletin* 41 (1959): 303–13.

36. Charles Seigel, *Poetry and Myth in Ancient Pastoral: Essays on Theocritus and Virgil* (Princeton: Princeton University Press, 1981), 4; Peter M. Sacks, *The English Elegy: Studies in the Genre from Spenser to Yeats* (Baltimore: Johns Hopkins University Press, 1985), 2, 19.

37. Johan Joachim Winckelmann, *History of Ancient Art*, 4 vols. (New York: Frederick Ungar, 1968), 2:200.

38. John Hollander, *The Figure of Echo: A Mode of Allusion in Milton and After* (Berkeley and Los Angeles: University of California Press, 1981), 1–2.

39. See Jean Seznec, "Paul Claudel and the Sarcophagus of the Muses," in *Perspectives of Criticism*, ed. Harry Levin (Cambridge: Harvard University Press, 1950), 13.

40. In Poussin's *Et in Arcadia Ego*, warnings against the active life are explicit, for skulls and inscriptions on sarcophagi warn shepherds that all things must come to an end. Louis Marin reminds us that Poussin's "Et in Arcadia Ego" is an incomplete sentence, because it omits a proper name for the *ego*, which is typical of funerary poetry: "The fact that the *ego*'s name has disappeared makes *ego* a kind of 'floating signifier' waiting for its fulfillment by our reading." Because it is willfully indefinite, meaning adds to pastoral ambiguity. Marin, "Toward a Theory of Reading in the Visual Art: Poussin's *The Arcadian Shepherds*," in *The Reader in the Text: Essays on Audience and Interpretation*, ed. S. Suleiman and I. Crisman (Princeton: Princeton University Press, 1980), 321–22.

41. On the idea of reform, see the fundamental work of Gerhart B. Ladner, *The Idea of Reform: Its Impact on Christian Thought and Action in the Age of the Fathers* (Cambridge: Harvard University Press, 1959), 26. On the concept of "the dead who will bury the dead," I follow the provocative study, so relevant for the poetics of anachronism, by Jerome McGann, *The Beauty of Inflections: Literary Investigations in Historical Method and Theory* (Oxford: Oxford University Press, 1985), 110. On the self-renovating fertility of the sarcophagus-urn, see Murray Krieger's reflections on Keatsean imagery: "Keats's urn, a pure *ekphrasis*, is an object especially created to celebrate the teasing doctrine of circularity. If this doctrine is aesthetically complete in creating, through enforced chastity, a fruitful urn of the aesthetic sort out of the unfruitful urn of the empirically human sort, in its chaste circularity it touches the empirically human only fitfully." Krieger, *Ekphrasis*, 277–78.

42. Freedberg, *Italian Painting, 1500 to 1600*, 83–85.

43. See Ann Hollander, *Seeing Through Clothes* (New York: Viking Press, 1978), 163, 179.

44. Frank Kermode writes, "we are necessarily more involved with the living than with the dead, with what learning cherishes and interpretation refreshes rather than with mere remains." Kermode, *Forms of Attention* (Chicago: University of Chicago Press, 1985), 75.

45. On "customary time," see Michel Butor, *Inventory: Essays* (New York: Simon and Schuster, 1968), 32. On scenes of instruction, see the thought-provoking introduction and conclusion of Celeste Schenck's *Mourning and Panegyric: The Poetics of Pastoral Ceremony* (University Park: Pennsylvania State University Press, 1988), 1–4, 178–83.

46. Cesare Brandi, *Disegno della pittura italiana* (Turin: Einaudi, 1980), 288–89; David Rosand, *Painting in Cinquecento Venice: Titian, Veronese, Tintoretto* (New Haven: Yale University Press, 1982), 43. For Sidney Freedberg, "the sum of the effect of colours, lights, and textures that the painting emanates—its 'tonality'—is similarly not a record of a natural effect, but a pictorial idea." *Italian Painting, 1500 to 1600*, 82.

47. Nino Perrotta, *Music and Culture in Italy from the Middle Ages to the Baroque: A Collection of Essays* (Cambridge: Harvard University Press, 1984), 93.

48. Aristotle, *Politics*, ed. David Kent (New York: Oxford University Press, 1999), 135.

49. In the ekphrastic mode, emphasis has been placed on the *tono*, a pictorial term that subordinates line to volume while blending light with shadow. As a musical term, *tono* implies a sequence of notes bound together by a reciprocal convenience based on modulation. Within the tradition of *musica per immagini* before the turn of the fifteenth century, lyrical forms such as madrigals, *ballate, cacce*, the Venetian *giustiniana*, the Tuscan *lauda, frottola*, and *canzone* mixed

words with notes. See John Hollander, *Vision and Resonance: Two Senses of Poetic Form* (New York: Oxford University Press, 1975), 13; John Hollander, *The Untuning of the Sky: Ideas of Music in English Poetry, 1500–1700* (Princeton: Princeton University Press, 1961), 145–46; John Neubauer, *The Emancipation of Music from Language: Departure from Mimesis in Eighteenth-Century Aesthetics* (Princeton: Princeton University Press, 1986), 14; Claude Palisca, *Humanism in Italian Renaissance Musical Thought* (New Haven: Yale University Press, 1985), 371.

50. Giorgio Padoan, *La commedia rinascimentale veneta (1433–1565)* (Vicenza: Pozza, 1982), 46–49. For comments on Ruzante's theater, see Nancy Dersofi, *Arcadia and the Stage: An Introduction to the Dramatic Art of Angelo Beolco Called Ruzante* (Madrid: J. Porrua Turanzas, 1978); Linda Carroll, *Angelo Beolco (Il Ruzante)* (Boston: Twayne, 1990).

51. Poggioli, *Oaten Flute*, 2.

52. Walter Pater, *The Renaissance: Studies in Art and Poetry* (New York: Oxford University Press, 1985), xxxiii.

53. Pietro Bembo, *Gli Asolani*, trans. R. Gottfried (Bloomington: Indiana University Press, 1971), 34.

54. Michelangelo Muraro, "Giorgione e la civiltà delle ville venete," in Muraro, *Giorgione: Atti del Convegno Internazionale di Studi per il Quinto Centenario della Nascita* (Castelfranco Veneto, 1979), 174–76; and Paul H. Kaplan, "The Storm of War: The Paduan Key to Giorgione's 'Tempesta,'" *Art History* 9 (1986): 405–27.

55. *The Poetical Works of Robert Browning*, ed. George Robert Stange (Boston: Houghton Mifflin, 1974), 986.

56. Egan, "Poesia and the *Fête Champêtre*," 305.

CHAPTER 2

1. References are to *Lazarillo de Tormes and the Swindler: Two Spanish Picaresque Novels*, trans. Michael Alpert (New York: Penguin Books, 1986), hereafter cited parenthetically in the text. The occasional quotations in the original are from *Lazarillo de Tormes*, edited by Francisco Rico (Madrid: Catedra, 1989).

2. Marvin Carlson writes about the importance of names in drama: "In the highly concentrated narrative world of the drama, the names given to characters potentially provide powerful communicative device for the dramatist seeking to orient his audience as quickly as possible in his fictive world. Thus from the very beginnings of drama we may see working a variety of onomastic codes, differing from era to era, but always an important part of the general semiotic system of theatre." Carlson, *Theatre Semiotics: Signs of Life* (Bloomington: Indiana University Press, 1990), 26.

3. This chapter draws on my *At the Margins of the Renaissance: Lazarillo de Tormes and the Picaresque Art of Survival* (University Park: Pennsylvania State University Press, 2003).

4. Victor Brombert, *The Hidden Reader: Stendhal, Balzac, Hugo, Baudelaire, Flaubert* (Cambridge: Harvard University Press, 1988), 19.

5. Luis de León, *The Names of Christ* (New York: Paulist Press, 1984), 45.

6. Guzmán de Alfarache, *The Rogue, or the Life of Guzmán de Alfarache*, trans. James Mabbe (London: Constable, 1924), 2:33. And again in light of a proverb: "El nombre sigue a el hombre" (as is the man, so is his good name) (2:507). Later, Baltasar Gracian labeled *agudeza nominal* the art of literary name-play (*agudeza y arte de ingenio*).

7. I draw here on provocative studies on the relationship between name and person in Cervantine texts, namely, Leo Spitzer, "Zur Kunst Quevedos in seinem *Buscón*," translated as "Sobre el arte de Quevedo en el *Buscón*," in Gonzalo Sobejano, ed., *Francisco de Quevedo* (Madrid: Taurus, 1978), 142. In this connection, see Robert Louis Stevenson's "The Philosophy of Nomenclature," in Stevenson, *Lay Morals and Other Papers* (New York: Scribner, 1911), 145–50. See also Herman Iventosch, "Onomastic Invention in the *Buscón*," *Hispanic Review* 29 (1961): 15–32. On Cervantes, see Leo Spitzer's exemplary essay, "Linguistic Perspectivism in *Don Quijote*," in his *Linguistics and Literary History: Essays in Stylistics* (Princeton: Princeton University Press, 1970),

41–86. Commenting on Spitzer, Raimundo Lida, in "Estilistica, un estudio sobre Quevedo," *Sur* 4 (1931): 169, speaks of "creacion rabelaisiana de nombres propios" in the Spanish picaresque. Ernst Robert Curtius has sketched the sustained relevance of onomastics under the heading of "etymology as a category of thought," in his *European Literature and the Latin Middle Ages* (New York: Harper and Row, 1963), 495–500. See also Alastair Fowler's thoughtful comments on matters of generic names in general, and of authorial namelessness in particular, in *Kinds of Literature: An Introduction to the Theory of Genres and Modes* (Cambridge: Harvard University Press, 1982), 86.

8. On the genealogical imperative, see Patricia Drechsel Tobin, *Time and the Novel* (Princeton: Princeton University Press, 1978), especially 6–7.

9. Roland Barthes, *S/Z* (New York: Hill and Wang, 1974), 82–83.

10. Jordan Stump, *Naming and Unnaming: On Raymond Queneau* (Lincoln: University of Nebraska Press, 1998), 22. This is an inclusive and challenging study of the subject, with a comprehensive introduction and bibliography.

11. Américo Castro has highlighted the ordinary aspect of the epic *Poem of the Cid*, which "dissolves into a picture of everyday life. The Cid of the poem is the hero, who carries out marvelous enterprises and is, at the same time, the owner of some mills, which he exploits like any bourgeois tradesman." Castro, *An Idea of History: Selected Essays of Américo Castro*, ed. Stephen Gilman and Edmund L. King (Columbus: Ohio State University Press, 1977), 154.

12. Antonio Gramsci, *Quaderni dal carcere* (Turin: Einaudi, 1975), 2:1013 (my translation).

13. See the dictionary entries for *progreso, prosperar*, and *ser util* in Juan Corominas, *Diccionario crítico etimológico castellano y hispánico* (Madrid: Gredos, 1980), and in the *Diccionario de la lengua española*, published by the Real Academia Española (Madrid: Editorial Espasa Calpe, 2001).

14. I follow here Harry Sieber's study, *Language and Society in* La vida de Lazarillo de Tormes (Baltimore: Johns Hopkins University Press, 1978), 44.

15. I follow here the fine study of Balzac's language by Martin Kanes, *Balzac's Comedy of Words* (Princeton: Princeton University Press, 1975). Kanes refers to "germinating-words" (168–69) and "words-events" (171), which "focus more sharply than he might otherwise have done on basic themes and motifs, and above all to pinpoint the moment when they enter explicitly into the narration" (176).

16. Guzmán, *Life of Guzmán de Alfarache*, 3:152–54.

17. On this point, Roland Barthes writes that "the proper name is in a sense the linguistic form of reminiscence." Barthes, *New Critical Essays* (New York: Hill and Wang, 1980), 58–59.

18. See Luigi Sasso's recent study, *Il nome nella letteratura: L'interpretazione dei nomi negli scrittori italiani del medioevo* (Genoa: Marietta, 1990), 91–93.

19. On onomastics and mercantilism, see Benjamin Z. Kedar, *Merchants in Crisis: Genoese and Venetian Men of Affairs and the Fourteenth-Century Depression* (New Haven: Yale University Press, 1976), 103.

20. In his analysis of Poe's *The Facts in the Case of M. Valdemar*, Roland Barthes makes it clear that "a proper name must always be carefully examined, for it is, so to speak, the prince of signifiers; its connotations are rich, social, and symbolic." Barthes, *The Semiotic Challenge* (New York: Hill and Wang, 1988), 268. As background introduction, see Jean Starobinski, *Words upon Words: The Anagram of Ferdinand de Saussure* (New Haven: Yale University Press, 1979); and François Rigolot, *Poétique et Onomastique. L'example de la Renaissance* (Geneva: Droz, 1977), 22. Recently, Paul Barolsky has made a contribution to onomastics in the context of Vasari's *Lives*, in *Why Mona Lisa Smiles and Other Tales by Vasari* (University Park: Pennsylvania State University Press, 1992), especially 39–51. For a critical commentary on the Platonic theory of names, see Timothy M. S. Baxter, *The Cratylus: Plato's Critique of Naming* (Leiden: E. J. Brill, 1992). With an eye to Russian Formalism, Boris Tomashevsky writes: "A character is recognized by his *characteristics*. By characteristics we mean a system of motifs intimately related to a given person. More narrowly, characteristics are the motifs which define the psychology of the person, his 'character.' The simplest characteristic of a person is his name." Tomashevsky, "Thematics," in *Russian Formalist Criticism: Four Essays*, ed. and trans. Lee T. Lemon and Marion J. Reis (Lincoln: University of

Nebraska Press, 1965), 88. On Balzac's use of patronymics, see Michael Riffaterre, *Fictional Truth* (Baltimore: Johns Hopkins University Press, 1990), 33–35.

21. Leon Battista Alberti, *I libri della famiglia*, translated by Renée Watkins as *The Family in Renaissance Florence* (Columbia: University of South Carolina Press, 1969), 122.

22. On the onomastic subject and its bibliography, see A. D. Deyermond's brief essay, "Lazarus and Lazarillo," *Studies in Short Fiction* 2 (1964–65): 351–57. Philippe Bonnefis writes that "le nom rattache et detache dans le même temps," in "Scènes typiques avec legendes," in *La chose capitale*, ed. P. Bennefis and A. Buisine (Lille: Universite de Lille Press, 1981), 12. See also Michel Cavillac, *Gueux et merchands* (Bordeaux: Institut d'études iberiques et ibero-americaines de l'Université de Bordeaux, 1983), 38.

23. I take the term "abbreviated description" from Bertrand Russell, in his discussion of the theory of proper names in "On Denoting," in his *Problems in the Philosophy of Language* (New York: Holt, Rinehart and Winston, 1969), 174.

24. Claire A. Culleton suggests that proper names are outranked by charactonyms, in *Names and Naming in Joyce* (Madison: University of Wisconsin Press, 1994), 20–21. See also Michael Ragussis, *Acts of Naming: The Family Plot in Fiction* (New York: Oxford University Press, 1986), 38.

25. I refer to Bruce Wardropper's thoughtful essay, "The Strange Case of Lázaro Gonzalés Perez," *Modern Language Notes* 92 (1977): 203.

26. See Richard Bijornson, *The Picaresque Hero in European Fiction* (Madison: University of Wisconsin Press, 1977), 21.

27. William H. Gass, *Fiction and the Figures of Life* (New York: Knopf, 1970), 49.

28. Arnold Weinstein, *Fictions of the Self: 1550–1800* (Princeton: Princeton University Press, 1981), 21. This may be a case of what Jacques Derrida calls "phonetic writing" in *Of Grammatology* (Baltimore: Johns Hopkins University Press, 1998), 3.

29. Anne Cruz connects the leper to the *pícaro* through "a new literary archetype, one who replaces the leper in his ritual role as *pharmakos*, the perceived cause and effect of social malaise. The disappearance of the leper in society coincides with the emergence of the *pícaro* in part as a means of satisfying the social need for a new mythical scapegoat whose characteristics would contain the major ills seen to afflict sixteenth-century Spain. The *pícaro* thus assumes the position of a liminal entity, holding a symbolic value for society only so long as his role remains integral to the larger concerns of the dominant social group." Cruz, paper delivered at the Conference on Picaresque Marginality, Indiana University, Bloomington, spring 1992.

30. See Peter Burke, *The Historical Anthropology of Early Modern Italy* (New York: Cambridge University Press, 1987), 74; and Maurice Mohlo, *Introducción al pensamiento picaresco* (Salamanca: Anaya, 1972), 29–30. See also Alberto del Monte, *Itinerario del romanzo picaresco spagnolo* (Florence: Sansoni, 1957), 6. For linguistic comments, see Geoffrey Wagner, *On the Wisdom of Words* (Princeton: Princeton University Press, 1968), 186, 172.

31. In Luke (7:20) as well as in Matthew (11), Jean-Paul Sartre writes, Jesus insists on his criticism of the rich, who use law either to set up or to maintain structures of scarcity. Sartre, *Critique of Dialectical Reason: Theory of Practical Ensembles* (Oxford: Oxford University Press, 1976), 122–52.

32. Victor Garcia de la Concha confirms: "De boca del pueblo ha merecido tambien Lázaro el titulo 'de Tormes.'" De la Concha, *Nueva lectura del Lazarillo* (Madrid: Castalia, 1981), 261.

33. Américo Castro, introduction to *Lazarillo de Tormes*, ed. Everett W. Hesse and Harry F. Williams (Madison: University of Wisconsin Press, 1969), x.

34. For comments on first and later editions of the work, see Guillén, *Literature as System: Essays Toward the Theory of Literary History* (Princeton: Princeton University Press, 1971), 137–42.

35. Mikhail Bakhtin, *The Dialogic Imagination: Four Essays by M. M. Bakhtin* (Austin: University of Texas Press, 1981), 23.

36. José Antonio Maravall, *Teatro y literatura en la sociedad barroca* (Barcelona: Editorial Crítica, 1990), 156.

37. Boccaccio, *Decameron*, trans. Mark Musa and Peter Bondanella (New York: W. W. Norton, 1982), 97–110.

38. See my *The Cornucopian Mind and the Baroque Unity of the Arts* (University Park: Pennsylvania State University Press, 1990), 88–90; Guillén, *Literature as System*, 77–78.

39. For more general comments on this issue, see Kurt Heinzelman, *The Economics of the Imagination* (Amherst: University of Massachusetts Press, 1980), 25–26.

40. Paul Julian Smith articulates a critical stand in *Writing in the Margin: Spanish Literature of the Golden Age* (Oxford: Clarendon Press, 1988), 79.

41. *The Colloquies of Erasmus*, trans. Craig R. Thompson (Chicago: University of Chicago Press, 1965), 1:431.

42. I refer here to Hazard Adams's comments on this whole subject in his *Antithetical Essays in Literary Criticism and Liberal Education* (Tallahassee: Florida State University Press, 1990), 167–69. As to the clash between "power" in the *tratados* and "aestheticism" in the *prólogo*, Adams writes, "Every discourse striving for power must be opposed by a discourse struggling against its own tendency to invoke power criteria" (171).

43. Having taken up a crucial shift on matters of artistic creation, Michel Foucault believes that whereas art was meant to secure fame in the past, modern literary artifacts have claimed the right to kill their authors: "Where a work had the duty of creating immortality, it now attains the right to kill, to become the murderer of its author." Foucault, *Language, Counter-Memory, Practice: Selected Essays and Interviews* (Ithaca: Cornell University Press, 1977), 117.

44. In psychological terms, A. A. Parker makes the following comment on the more general character of picaresque dualism: "The *pícaro* is both a product of a particular social environment and, as an individual human being, an autonomous moral person." Parker, "The Psychology of the 'Pícaro' in 'El Buscon,'" *Modern Language Review* 42 (1947): 60.

45. *Colloquies of Erasmus*, 1:383–84. It is just as interesting that a Spanish translation of his colloquies was published in 1530, when the writing of the picaresque text was probably under way.

46. Gustave Flaubert, *Correspondances, 1830–1851*, ed. Jean Bruneau (Paris: Gallimard, 1973), 1:628, as translated by Eugenio Donato in his pertinent study, "The Crypt of Flaubert," in *Flaubert and Postmodernism*, ed. Naomi Schor and Henry F. Majewski (Lincoln: University of Nebraska Press, 1984), 44.

47. Stump, *Naming and Unnaming*, 1.

48. See Shoshana Felman, "Flaubert's Signature: The Legend of Saint Julian the Hospitable," in Schor and Majewski, *Flaubert and Postmodernism*, 68. See also Eugenio Donato, "Who Signs Flaubert?" *Modern Language Notes* 99 (1984): 726.

49. James D. Fernandez closes his study of autobiography in modern Spanish literature by stating, "We arrive to identity by subtraction. Autobiography. Autobio. Auto . . ." Fernandez, *Apology to Apostrophe: Autobiography and the Rhetoric of Self-Representation in Spain* (Durham: Duke University Press, 1992), 20.

50. See Alan Francis, *Picaresca, Decadencia, Historia* (Madrid: Gredos, 1978), 98.

51. Barthes, *S/Z*, 95, 40.

52. Stephen Greenblatt, "Racial Memory and Literary History," *PMLA* 116 (2001): 60–62.

53. I draw on Guillén's outstanding meditations on the picaresque in *Literature as System*, 156.

CHAPTER 3

1. I draw here on Michel Serres, *Hermes: Literature, Science, Philosophy* (Baltimore: Johns Hopkins University Press, 1982), 37.

2. *The Complete Essays of Montaigne*, trans. Donald Frame (Stanford: Stanford University Press, 1971), 736, hereafter cited parenthetically in the text. The French edition I have consulted is *Essais de Montaigne*, ed. Maurice Rat, 2 vols. (Paris: Editions Garnier Frères, 1962).

3. Floyd Gray, "Montaigne et Sebond: The Rhetoric of Paradox," *French Studies* 28 (1974): 143.

4. Theodor W. Adorno, *Notes to Literature*, ed. Rolf Tiedemann, trans. Shielly Weber Nicholsen, 2 vols. (New York: Columbia University Press, 1991), 1:10.

5. Francesco Guicciardini, *Maxims and Reflections*, ed. Nicolai Rubenstein, trans. Mario Domandi (Philadelphia: University of Pennsylvania Press, 1972), 59.

6. For criticism concerning the three editions and their arrangement, see Mario Fubini, *Studi sulla letteratura del Rinascimento* (Florence: Sansoni, 1948). See also Raffaele Spongano's critical edition of the *Ricordi* (Florence: Sansoni, 1951).

7. For examples of this type of literature, see Gene Brucker, ed., *Two Memoirs of Renaissance Florence* (New York: Harper and Row, 1967).

8. See Vittore Branca's preface to his edition of Morelli's *Ricordi* (Florence: Sansoni, 1955), 53–54.

9. See Nicolai Rubenstein's introduction to Guicciardini's *Maxims and Reflections*, 31.

10. Guicciardini, *Maxims and Reflections*, 71.

11. Jacob Zeitlin, in his introduction to *The Essays of Michel de Montaigne*, ed. Jacob Zeitlin (New York: Knopf, 1934), remarks that "for Montaigne the word *essay* itself had a more substantial force. To translate it into English one must frequently use the word *test* or *trial* in the sense of experiment" (1:lxvii). Erich Auerbach, in *Mimesis: The Representation of Reality in Western Literature* (Princeton: Princeton University Press, 1968), agrees that Montaigne's method is experimental: "Montaigne's apparently fanciful method is basically a strictly experimental method, the only method which conforms to such a subject" (292). For studies of the term *essai*, see E. V. Telle, "A propos du mot 'essai' chez Montaigne," *Bibliothèque d'Humanisme et Renaissance* 30 (1968): 225–41. For other sources of the term *essai*, see J. C. Dawson, "A Suggestion as to the Sources of Montaigne's Title: 'Essai,'" *Modern Language Notes* 51 (1936): 223–26. See also Hugo Friedrich, *Montaigne* (Berkeley and Los Angeles: University of California Press, 1991), 353–56.

12. Blaise Pascal, *Pensées: The Provincial Letters*, trans. W. F. Trotter (New York: Modern Library, 1941), 116.

13. John Donne, *Devotions* (Ann Arbor: University of Michigan Press, 1959), 23.

14. I refer here to the fine analysis by G. Douglas Atkins, *Estranging the Familiar: Toward a Revitalized Critical Writing* (Athens: University of Georgia Press, 1992), 6.

15. I draw on L. M. Patrick, *"Attic" and Baroque Prose Style* (Princeton: Princeton University Press, 1969), 6; Patrick is commenting here on Morris Croll's criticism. In addition to classical precedents, one should also consider the medieval traditions of *stilus humilis*, predominant in Bologna and northern Italy, and of the *stilus rhetoricus*, as popularized in the writings of Thomas of Padua and Pier delle Vigne. See Benjamin G. Kohl and Ronald G. Witt's introduction to *The Earthly Republic* (Philadelphia: University of Pennsylvania Press, 1978), 11.

16. Joan Webber, *The Eloquent "I": Style and Self in Seventeenth-Century Prose* (Madison: University of Wisconsin Press, 1968), 13.

17. Terence Cave, in *The Cornucopian Text: Problems of Writing in the French Renaissance* (Oxford: Clarendon Press, 1979), writes that the essays are centered on the interplay "between the desire for a fullness of experience said to be located outside language, and the contours (or detours) of a text which strives unremittingly to represent that fullness" (272).

18. Charles Baldwin, *Renaissance Theory and Practice* (New York: Columbia University Press, 1939), 232.

19. "This discontinuous aphoristic style," Northrop Frye writes, "has been in all ages and cultures the standard rhetoric of wisdom." Frye, *The Well-Tempered Critic* (Bloomington: Indiana University Press, 1963), 87.

20. John A. McCarthy, *Crossing Boundaries: A Theory and History of Essay Writing in German, 1680–1815* (Philadelphia: University of Pennsylvania Press, 1989), 59. See also Thomas Harrison, *Essayism: Conrad, Musil, and Pirandello* (Baltimore: Johns Hopkins University Press, 1992).

21. Montaigne would have applauded Marcel Proust's contention that readers "would not be my readers but readers of themselves, my book serving as a sort of magnifying glass." Proust, "The Past Recaptured," in *Remembrance of Things Past*, trans. F. A. Blossom (New York: Viking Press, 1984), 2:1113.

22. The humanist bestiary highlights the spider's geometric web in Alberti's *I libri della famiglia*, and the selective activities of bees in Castiglione's *Il libro del Cortegiano*. By the turn of

the seventeenth century, the ever-changing shapes of snails and snakes illustrated forms that did not conform to preconceived models.

23. Henri Focillon, *The Life of Forms* (New Haven: Yale University Press, 1942), 63.

24. First published in Giordano Bruno, *Opera latine conscripta*, ed. Tocco III (Florence, 1890), translated by Robert Klein as *Italian Art: Sources and Documents* (Englewood Cliffs, N.J.: Prentice-Hall, 1966), 187.

25. Giordano Bruno, *The Heroic Frenzies*, trans. Paul Memmo (Chapel Hill: University of North Carolina Press, 1964), 83.

26. Giambattista Marino, *Epistolario*, ed. A. Borzelli and F. Nicolini (Bari: Laterza, 1911), 2:55 (my translation).

27. Gary Saul Morson, *The Boundaries of Genre: Dostoevsky's Diary of a Writer and the Tradition of Literary Utopia* (Austin: University of Texas Press, 1981), 121.

28. Cave, *Cornucopian Text*, 333.

29. Samuel Taylor Coleridge, *The Philosophical Lectures*, ed. K. Coburn (New York: Philosophical Library, 1949), 344.

30. Northrop Frye, *Anatomy of Criticism* (Harmondsworth: Penguin Books, 1990), 223.

31. Ibid., 226.

32. In André Gide's introductory essay to *Montaigne: Selections from His Writings*, trans. John Florio (New York: Modern Library, 1964), 21 (Gide's introduction translated by Dorothy Bussy).

33. For inclusive treatments of the essay in its historical development, see Graham Good, *The Observing Self: Rediscovering the Essay* (London: Routledge, 1988).

34. I leave out the essays of Francis Bacon because they are structured by a scientific rigor that makes them less bounded than Montaigne's. On this subject I follow Peter Burgard, "Adorno, Goethe, and the Politics of the Essay," *Deutsche Vierteljahrsschrift fur Literaturwissenschaft und Geistesgeschichte* 66 (1992): especially 188–90.

35. Roland Barthes, *The Grain of the Voice: Interviews, 1962–1980* (Berkeley and Los Angeles: University of California Press, 1991), 26. For a concise yet comprehensive synopsis of the *essai* as it has been defined by scholars, see the foreword and appendix in Reda Bensmaia, *The Barthes Effect: The Essay as Reflective Text* (Minneapolis: University of Minnesota Press, 1987), viii–xxi, 95–103.

36. Susan Sontag, *Where the Stress Falls: Essays* (New York; Farrar, Straus and Giroux, 2001), 69.

37. Jorge Luis Borges "The Superstitious Ethics of the Reader," in Borges, *Jorge Luis Borges: Selected Non-Fictions*, ed. Eliot Weinberger, trans. Esther Allen, Suzanne Jill Levine, and Eliot Weinberger (New York: Viking Press, 1999), 54.

38. Borges, "The Homeric Versions," ibid., 69.

39. Borges, "Virgil, *The Aeneid*," ibid., 519.

40. Borges, "Superstitious Ethics of the Reader," 54.

41. George Steiner, *The Lessons of the Masters* (Cambridge: Harvard University Press, 2003), 33.

42. E. M. Cioran, *Drawn and Quartered* (New York: Arcade Publishing, 1998), 21–22.

43. Theodor Adorno, "The Essay as Form," published in *Noten zur Literatur* 1 in 1958; the English translation has appeared in *New German Critique* 32 (1984): 151–71.

44. For a comprehensive discussion of the essay from Goethe to Adorno, see Peter Burgard's preface to his *Idioms of Uncertainty: Goethe and the Essay* (University Park: Pennsylvania State University Press, 1992), especially 13–14.

CHAPTER 4

1. Quoted in Geoffrey H. Hartman, *Saving the Text: Literature, Derrida, Philosophy* (Baltimore: Johns Hopkins University Press, 1981), xv–xvi.

2. Octavio Paz, *The Other Voice: Essays on Modern Poetry* (New York: Harcourt Brace Jovanovich, 1990), 3.

3. Quoted in Leonard Diepeveen, *The Difficulties of Modernism* (London: Routledge, 2003), 87.

4. Pound considered Joyce the best novelist after Flaubert; see Pound's essay "James Joyce et Pécuchet," in *Pound/Joyce: The Letters of Ezra Pound to James Joyce, with Pound's Essays on Joyce*, ed. Forrest Read (New York: New Directions, 1967), 200–215 (letter written in 1922).

5. See Michael North, *Reading 1922: A Return to the Scene of the Modern* (Oxford: Oxford University Press, 1999).

6. Roland Barthes, *New Critical Essays* (New York: Hill and Wang, 1980), 58–59.

7. Jorge Luis Borges confessed in 1925 that he never "cleared a path through all seven hundred pages" of *Ulysses*, "a novel of cathedral-like grandeur." Having examined only "bits and pieces," he claimed knowledge of the whole text "with that bold and legitimate certainty with which we assert our knowledge of a city," even though we may not know all its streets. The Argentinean master of the shortest forms of prose fiction never doubted that the focused intensity of "deep readings" was preferable to textual prolixity. Borges, *Jorge Luis Borges: Selected Non-Fictions*, ed. Eliot Weinberger, trans. Esther Allen, Suzanne Jill Levine, and Eliot Weinberger (New York: Viking Press, 1999), 12–14.

8. James Joyce, *Ulysses: A Critical and Synoptic Edition*, ed. Hans Walter Gabler, 3 vols. (New York: Garland Publishing, 1984), 1-9:927–28, hereafter cited parenthetically in the text by volume, episode, and line numbers.

9. I borrow this concept from Italo Calvino's 1979 work, *If on a Winter's Night a Traveler* (New York: Harcourt Brace Jovanovich, 1981), 254.

10. Gérard Genette, *Paratexts: Thresholds of Interpretation* (Cambridge: Cambridge University Press, 1997), 409. This is the most extensive treatment of the classificatory aspects of titles. See also Claire O. Culleton, *Names and Naming in Joyce* (Madison: University of Wisconsin Press, 1994), 39. At the outset of this "critical" journey through the twists and turns of Joyce's complex title, let us remember that Mr. Valéry Larbaud found the key to *Ulysses* not in the door of textuality but on the cover. While Ezra Pound minimized Homeric references, Stuart Gilbert played them up. My approach takes the title as the key that opens the door to an assessment of the textual range and contextual depth of the titological cover.

11. Even Kevin Jackson has called for a "book-length" study of the title in *Invisible Forms: A Guide to Literary Curiosities* (New York: St. Martin's Press, 1999), xxi.

12. See Perry Meisel, *The Myth of the Modern: A Study in British Literature and Criticism After 1850* (New Haven: Yale University Press, 1987), 145. To date, Meisel's chapter remains the most provocative on matters of titology, which, however, are peripheral to his concerns.

13. See Hazard Adams, *Antithetical Essays in Literary Criticism and Liberal Education* (Tallahassee: Florida State University Press, 1990), 106, 134.

14. On the subject of Joyce's Roman heritage, see R. J. Schork, *Latin and Roman Culture in Joyce* (Gainesville: University Press of Florida, 1997). Yet no speculative references are made to the title of *Ulysses*.

15. R. J. Schork, *Greek and Hellenic Influences in Joyce* (Gainesville: University Press of Florida, 1998), 30.

16. In *Four Dubliners: Oscar Wilde, William Butler Yeats, James Joyce, Samuel Beckett* (New York: George Braziller, 1988), Richard Ellmann writes: "There is the title itself, so abrupt in its insistence on a mythical background, which however is never mentioned as it was in *A Portrait of the Artist*. The author's silence about it is intimidating, yet the relation to the *Odyssey* is problematic, and its intensity varies from chapter to chapter, or even from page to page. Joyce felt at liberty to deal with Homer as high-handedly as Virgil had done, keeping the basic typology but varying and omitting and adding as his own book required" (83–84).

17. J. Hillis Miller, *Topographies* (Stanford: Stanford University Press, 1995), 3.

18. Michael Longley, *Tuppenny Stung: Autobiographical Chapters* (Belfast: Lagan Press, 1994), 79.

19. On history and geography, see Edward Said, "History, Literature, and Geography," in Said, *Reflections on Exile and Other Essays* (Cambridge: Harvard University Press, 2000), 467.

20. John Freccero, *Dante: The Poetics of Conversion* (Cambridge: Harvard University Press, 1986), 138.

21. Ibid., 138–39.

22. I draw here on Carlos Fuentes's insights in *This I Believe: An A to Z of a Life* (New York: Random House, 2005), 204.

23. I draw on Clayton Koelb's provocative *Legendary Figures: Ancient History in Modern Novels* (Lincoln: University of Nebraska Press, 1998), 3.

24. Joyce, *Letters of James Joyce*, ed. Stuart Gilbert, 3 vols. (New York: Viking Press, 1957), 2:182.

25. I draw here on Jenny Straus Clay, "The Name of Odysseus," in her *Wrath of Athena: Gods and Men in the Odyssey* (Princeton: Princeton University Press, 1983), 54–64.

26. Likewise, Joyce's Shakespeare is no longer the Elizabethan bard but one who has been reread in terms of the nineteenth-century culture of the Victorian age, which the Irish writer identified—and quite critically so—with the British Empire. See M. Keith Booker, *Joyce, Bakhtin, and the Literary Tradition: Toward a Comparative Cultural Poetics* (Ann Arbor: University of Michigan Press, 1997), 3.

27. George Seferis, *George Seferis: Collected Poems, 1924–1955*, trans. and ed. Edmund Keeley and Philip Sherrard (Princeton: Princeton University Press, 1967), 425.

28. Booker separates Eliot's retrospective notion of the "mythical method" from Joyce's more progressive treatment of it. Booker, *Joyce, Bakhtin, and the Literary Tradition*, 19.

29. David Hayman, "Language of/as Gesture in Joyce," in *James Joyce: A Collection of Critical Essays*, ed. Mary T. Reynolds (Englewood Cliffs, N.J.: Prentice-Hall, 1993), especially 45–46.

30. See Michael Patrick Gillespie, "'In the Beginning Is the Void': Opening Lines and the Protocols of Reading," in *Pedagogy, Praxis, Ulysses: Using Joyce's Text to Transform the Classroom*, ed. Robert Newman (Ann Arbor: University of Michigan Press, 1996), 9–20. Fritz Senn synthesizes the opening paragraph: "One capsular reflection of the whole is this: that the novel, whose Latin title suggests a Greek hero based (as Joyce believed) on Semitic tales, begins like a play, with stage directions in the first paragraph and an opening speech by an Irish character whose language is English and who, with a flair for imitation, intones a sentence from the Latin Mass, which is in itself a translation of a Hebrew Psalm. The ethnological and literary multiplicity is already present, while on the surface of it we never for a moment leave a simple, realistic story." Senn, *Joyce's Dislocutions: Essays on Reading as Translation* (Baltimore: Johns Hopkins University Press, 1984), 125.

31. See Harry Levin, *James Joyce: A Critical Introduction* (Norfolk, Va.: New Directions, 1960), 29.

32. Leo Bersani, *The Culture of Redemption* (Cambridge: Harvard University Press, 1990), 156. Michael Seidel connects *Ulysses* to *Finnegans Wake* and refers to a "greeken hearted yude" (171), much as he finds a variant of Ulysses in "usylessly." See Seidel, "Running Titles," in *Second Thoughts: A Focus on Rereading*, ed. David Galef (Detroit: Wayne State University Press, 1998), 46.

33. As quoted in Richard Ellman, *James Joyce* (New York: Oxford University Press, 1959), 505.

34. Walter Benjamin, *The Origin of German Tragic Drama* (London: NLB, 1977), 178. Angus Fletcher closes his study of the subject by writing that allegory "allows for instruction, for rationalizing, for categorizing and codifying, for casting spells and expressing unbidden compulsions.... To conclude, allegories are the natural mirrors of ideology." Fletcher, *Allegory: The Theory of a Symbolic Mode* (Ithaca: Cornell University Press, 1970), 389. Obviously, such ideological mirrors have been cracked by modernism and postmodernism.

35. Fletcher writes that allegories "examine the philosophic, theological, or moral premises on which we act." Ibid., 153.

36. T. S. Eliot, "*Ulysses*, Order, and Myth," in *Forms of Modern Fiction: Essays in Honor of Joseph Warren Beach*, ed. William Van O'Connor (Minneapolis: University of Minnesota Press, 1948), 123.

37. On parodic implications, see Margaret Rose, *Parody: Ancient, Modern, and Post-Modern* (New York: Cambridge University Press, 1993).

38. See Alvin Kernan, *The Death of Literature* (New Haven: Yale University Press, 1990), 123–24.

39. I draw here on Daniel R. Schwarz's *Reading Joyce's Ulysses* (New York: St. Martin's Press, 1987), 18–21.

40. Umberto Eco, *Experiences in Translation* (Toronto: University of Toronto Press, 2000), 22.

41. See A. Walton Litz, "The Genre of Ulysses," in *The Theory of the Novel: New Essays*, ed. John Halperin (New York: Oxford University Press, 1974), 109–20.

42. See Eric Auerbach's essay "Odysseus' Scar," in his *Mimesis: The Representation of Reality in Western Literature* (Princeton: Princeton University Press, 1968), 3–23.

43. See Brook Thomas, *James Joyce's Ulysses: A Book of Many Happy Returns* (Baton Rouge: Louisiana State University Press, 1982), 123.

44. See Eric Gould, *Mythical Intentions in Modern Literature* (Princeton: Princeton University Press, 1981), 4, 141.

45. See Daniel P. Gunn, "The Name of Bloom," in *Joycean Occasions: Essays from the Milwaukee James Joyce Conference*, ed. J. Dunleavy, M. J. Friedman, and M. P. Gillespie (Newark: University of Delaware Press, 1987), 34–35.

46. See Genette *Paratexts*, 85.

47. Frank Kermode, *The Sense of an Ending: Studies in the Theory of Fiction* (New York: Oxford University Press, 1968), 58.

48. See Roland Barthes, *The Grain of Voice: Interviews, 1962–1980* (Berkeley and Los Angeles: University of California Press, 1991), 222–23.

49. As Michel Foucault comments, "the relation between Balzac's novels is not the same as that existing between Joyce's *Ulysses* and the *Odyssey*. The frontiers of a book are never clear-cut: beyond the title, the first lines, and the last full stop, beyond its internal configuration and its autonomous form, it is caught up in a system of references to other books, other texts, other sentences: it is a node with a network." Foucault, *The Archaeology of Knowledge and the Discourse on Language* (New York: Pantheon Books, 1972), 23.

50. Anthony Burgess, *Re Joyce* (New York: W. W. Norton, 2000), 85.

51. Georges Borach, "Conversations with James Joyce," in *Portraits of the Artist in Exile: Recollections of James Joyce by Europeans*, ed. Willard Potts (Seattle: University of Washington Press, 1979), 69–70.

52. I refer here to Carlo Ginzburg, *Wooden Eyes: Nine Reflections on Distance* (New York: Columbia University Press, 2001), 61.

53. Quoted in Ellmann, *James Joyce*, 521.

54. On matters of canonicity and creativity, Robert Alter, having highlighted the Joycean dualism of iconoclasm and hypertraditionalism, points out that the writer's encyclopedic reach "entails not only the exhaustive representation of a day in the life of an ordinary man but also a kind of grand recapitulation of three millennia of cultural history." Alter, *Canon and Creativity: Modern Writing and the Authority of Scripture* (New Haven: Yale University Press, 2000), 167.

55. While the genre included the epic as well as the comic novel and distortions thereof, the parallel between Ulysses and his modern counterpart is undeniable. Early, and not so early, reviews have stressed the "un-epic" lack of heroism, religion, and morality, not to mention meaning itself. See Thomas, *James Joyce's Ulysses*, 122.

56. In a single appraisal, Hugh Kenner describes Joyce's title as a metal plate (arguably not the most provocative of metaphors). The reference is to Bernini's colonnade in front of Saint Peter's. If we were to stand on a metal plate lodged in the pavement, we could see the rows of columns perfectly aligned. The inference is that the title sets up a similar alignment between the ancient and the modern text. See his *Joyce's Voices* (Berkeley and Los Angeles: University of California Press, 1978), 60.

57. See John J. White, *Mythology in the Modern Novel: A Study of Prefigurative Techniques* (Princeton: Princeton University Press, 1971).

58. James Joyce, *Finnegans Wake* (London: Faber and Faber, 1975), 107.

59. A recent essay worth citing is Friedhelm Rathjen, "On Translating Names, Titles, and Quotations," in *A Collideorscape of Joyce: Festschrift for Fritz Senn*, ed. Ruth Frehner and Ursula Zeller (Dublin: Lilliput Press, 1998), 407–26.

60. Perry Meisel writes: "The title is itself a signature for the Paterian recoil or reality of belatedness by which it responds to the will to modernity that it may seem only to reproduplicate. By virtue of a Latin rather than properly Greek title, the novel gives us a graphic clue for its programmatic failure to complete Eliot's 'parallel' even on its face. If *Ulysses*, as Eliot claims, is a mythic replication of *The Odyssey*, why, then, is the book not called *Odyseus?*" Meisel, *Myth of the*

Modern, 145. See also Tony Thwaites, *Joycean Temporalities: Debts, Promises, and Countersignatures* (Gainesville: University Press of Florida, 2001), 44–45.

61. Weldon Thornton warns us that *Ulysses* thrives on an array of references that are "continually intersecting, modifying, qualifying one another." Thornton, *Allusions in Ulysses: An Annotated List* (Chapel Hill: University of North Carolina Press, 1968), 4.

62. Campbell's statement is reprinted in the editor's foreword to *Mythic Worlds, Modern Words: On the Art of James Joyce*, ed. Edmund L. Epstein (New York: Harper Collins, 1993), vii.

63. Kevin J. H. Dettmar, *The Illicit Joyce of Postmodernism* (Madison: University of Wisconsin Press, 1996), 116–17.

64. See Francis Fergusson, *The Human Image in Dramatic Literature* (New York: Doubleday Anchor Books, 1957), 78.

65. Daniel Ferrier, "Characters in Ulysses: 'The Featureful Perfection of Imperfection,'" in *James Joyce: The Augmented Ninth*, ed. Bernard Benstock (Syracuse: Syracuse University Press, 1988), 149.

66. On Joyce's Dedalus in relation to Ovid, see Theodore Ziolkowski, *Ovid and the Moderns* (Ithaca: Cornell University Press, 2005), 33–35.

67. James Joyce, *A Portrait of the Artist as a Young Man* (New York: Penguin Books, 1978), 253, hereafter cited parenthetically in the text.

68. See David See, "Naming in Pynchon and Joyce," in *James Joyce: The Centennial Symposium*, ed. M. Beja, P. Herring, M. Harmon, and D. Norris (Urbana: University of Illinois Press, 1986), 47.

69. See Page duBois, *Trojan Horses: Saving the Classics from Conservatives* (New York: New York University Press, 2001), 11.

70. I follow here Michael Patrick Gillespie, *The Aesthetics of Chaos, Nonlinear Thinking, and Contemporary Literary Criticism* (Gainesville: University Press of Florida, 1996), 2, 106.

71. *The Modern Irish Writers: A Colder Eye* (New York: Penguin Books, 1984), 70–71.

72. See Alessandro Francini, "Joyce Stripped Naked in the Piazza," in Potts, *Portraits of the Artist in Exile*, 28.

73. W. B. Yeats, "Ireland and the Arts," in Yeats, *Essays and Introductions* (New York: Macmillan, 1961), 208.

74. I refer to Hugh Kenner's *Sinking Island: The Modern English Writers* (New York: Knopf, 1988), 3–4.

75. See Joyce, *James Joyce: Poesie e Prose*, ed. Franca Ruggieri (Milan: Mondadori, 2000), 523, 386, 390 (my translation).

76. I draw on the comprehensive essay by Peter A. Maguire, "*Finnegans Wake* and Irish Historical Memory," *Journal of Modern Literature* 22, no. 2 (1998–99): 293–327.

77. Katie Wales, *The Language of James Joyce* (New York: St. Martin's Press, 1992), 33.

78. Jorge Luis Borges, *Seven Nights* (New York: New Directions, 1984), 119.

79. Joyce quoted in W. B. Stanford, *The Ulysses Theme: A Study in the Adaptability of a Traditional Hero* (Ann Arbor: University of Michigan Press, 1968), 223.

80. Beryl Schlossman, *Joyce's Catholic Comedy of Language* (Madison: University of Wisconsin Press, 1985), 184–85.

81. Umberto Eco, *Umberto Eco on Literature* (New York: Harcourt, 2002), 97.

82. Leslie A. Fiedler, "To Whom Does Joyce Belong? *Ulysses* as Parody, Pop, and Porn," in *Light Rays: James Joyce and Modernism*, ed. Heyward Ehrlich (New York: New Horizon Press, 1984), 29, 34–35.

83. Hugh Kenner, *Flaubert, Joyce, and Beckett: The Stoic Comedians* (Boston: Beacon Press, 1962), 42.

84. See George Steiner, *After Babel: Aspects of Language and Translation* (Oxford: Oxford University Press, 1975), 447.

85. I draw here on Jean-François Lyotard, who insists that the title translation makes the name "shifty" and thus "equivocal." Lyotard, "Return upon the Return," in Lyotard, *Toward the Post-Modern* (Atlantic Highlands, N.J.: Humanities Press, 1993), 193.

86. George Lukács, *The Theory of the Novel* (Cambridge: MIT Press, 1971), 66.

87. See Joseph Farrell, *Vergil's Georgics and the Traditions of Ancient Epic: The Art of Allusion in Literary History* (New York: Oxford University Press, 1991), 17.

88. Senn, *Joyce's Dislocutions*, 202–6, 210. Senn writes that dislocution "could be used, after all, for redescribing or (Joyce's cue) 'transluding'" (FW 419.25) what was provisionally verbalized as metamorphoses, alienated readings, an auto-corrective urge, metastasis, the disrupted pattern principle, or polytropy.... It might even stand for all those effects that make us respond, spontaneously, with laughter" (211).

89. For more on this theme, see the fine essay by Reed Way Dasenbrock, "Constructing a Larger *Iliad*: Ezra Pound and the Vicissitudes of Epic," in *Epic and Epoch: Essays on the Interpretation and History of a Genre*, ed. Steven M. Oberhelman, Van Kelly, and Richard J. Golsan (Lubbock: Texas Tech University Press, 1994), 248–66.

90. Senn, *Joyce's Dislocutions*, x.

91. Joyce, *Finnegans Wake*, 185.

92. I draw on Robert Spoo, *James Joyce and the Language of History* (New York: Oxford University Press, 1994), 38.

93. For a fine essay on titles in *Dubliners*, see Ulrich Schneider, "Titles in *Dubliners*," in *ReJoycing: New Readings of Dubliners*, ed. Rosa Bosinelli and Harold F. Mosher (Lexington: University Press of Kentucky, 1998), especially 197.

94. Jeffrey Perl, *The Tradition of Return: The Implicit History of Modern Literature* (Princeton: Princeton University Press, 1984), 176, 282.

95. Joyce, *Letters of Joyce*, 1:193.

96. Ibid., 1:146–47.

97. Ibid., 2:167, 165.

98. On the Roman experience, see Giorgio Melchiori, ed., *Joyce in Rome* (Rome: Bulzoni, 1984).

99. Schork, *Latin and Roman Culture in Joyce*.

100. Joyce, *Finnegans Wake*, 271.

101. I draw on the introduction by Marjorie Howes and Derek Attridge to their collection of essays, *Semicolonial Joyce* (Cambridge: Cambridge University Press, 2000), 1–2.

102. See David Hayman, *Ulysses: The Mechanics of Meaning* (Madison: University of Wisconsin Press, 1982), 3.

103. Ellman, *James Joyce*, 252.

104. Quoted in Clive Hart, ed., *Conversations with James Joyce* (London: Millington, 1974), 74–75.

105. On the presence and influence of D'Annunzio in Joyce's writings, see the introductory essay by C. P. Curran, "Joyce's D'Annunzian Mask," in Curran, *James Joyce Remembered* (New York: Oxford University Press, 1968), 105–15.

106. In fact, it has been said that an entire era could be framed between two titles: *Madame Bovary* and *Il fuoco*. Michael Tratner, *Modernism and Mass Politics: Joyce, Woolf, Eliot, Yeats* (Stanford: Stanford University Press, 1995), 117. At one time Joyce was infatuated with the Italian actress Eleonora Duse, whom he saw on stage in London in D'Annunzio's *La città morta* and *La Gioconda*.

107. Ellmann, *James Joyce*, 5.

108. Joyce, *Finnegans Wake*, 152.

109. Let us not forget that, as Harry Levin put it, "to think about Joyce is to allow our thoughts to dwell upon a buried city." Levin, *James Joyce: A Critical Introduction*, 21.

110. Edmund Wilson is right when he points out that critics have failed to recognize a plot in *Ulysses* because they failed to "recognize a progression; and the title told them nothing." Wilson, *Axel's Castle* (New York: Charles Scribner's Sons, 1931), 89.

111. Francini, "Joyce Stripped Naked in the Piazza," 28.

112. For more on this, see Edna Duffy, "Disappearing Dublin: *Ulysses*, Postcoloniality, and the Politics of Space," in Howes and Attridge, *Semicolonial Joyce*, 50.

113. Morton P. Levitt, "The Modernist Age: The Age of James Joyce," in Ehrlich, *Light Rays*, 134–36.

114. Hugh Kenner, *Modern Irish Writers*, 251.
115. Joyce, "The Home Rule Comet," in *The Critical Writings* (New York: Viking Press, 1959), 213.
116. Michael Seidel, *Epic Geography: James Joyce's Ulysses* (Princeton: Princeton University Press, 1976), 247.
117. See Pietro Pucci, *Odysseus Polutropos* (Ithaca: Cornell University Press, 1987), 124.
118. See Terence Cave, *Recognitions: A Study in Poetics* (Oxford: Clarendon Press, 1988), 407.
119. As George de F. Lord put it, "The phase of supernatural dangers and of the hostility of physical nature which comes between the departure of Odysseus from Troy and his arrival in Phaecia divides two vastly different human worlds: that of the Trojan war dominated by the heroic code of men and that of family and community life whose values are centered on several extraordinary women—Arete, Nausicaa, Penelope." Lord, "The *Odyssey* and the Western World," as reprinted in *Odysseus/Ulysses*, ed. Harold Bloom (New York: Chelsea House, 1991), 89–102.
120. Richard Ellmann, "Joyce and Homer," *Critical Inquiry* 3, no. 3 (1977): 569.
121. Maria Tymoczko, *The Irish Ulysses* (Berkeley and Los Angeles: University of California Press, 1994), 22–31.
122. Maurice Blanchot, *The Book to Come* (Stanford: Stanford University Press, 2003), 8.
123. On the symbolism of the center, see Stuart Gilbert, *James Joyce's Ulysses* (New York: Random House, 1958).
124. Jacqueline Risset, "Joyce *Traduce* Joyce," in Ruggieri, *Joyce: Poesie e Prose*, 703.
125. Irad Malkin, *The Return of Odysseus: Colonization and Ethnicity* (Berkeley and Los Angeles: University of California Press, 1998), 3.
126. See the three relevant stories in Borges, *Labyrinths: Selected Stories and Other Writings*, trans. Donald A. Yates and James E. Irby (New York: New Directions, 1964), 193–96, 242, 244–45.
127. Declan Kiberd, *Inventing Ireland* (Cambridge: Harvard University Press, 1995), 327.

CHAPTER 5

1. Calvin Bedient, *He Do the Police in Different Voices: The Waste Land and Its Protagonist* (Chicago: University of Chicago Press, 1986), 1.
2. See Elisabeth Schneider, *T. S. Eliot: The Pattern in the Carpet* (Berkeley and Los Angeles: University of California Press, 1975), 76.
3. I draw here on Denis Donoghue, *Words Alone* (New Haven: Yale University Press, 2000), 132, and William Empson, *Using Biography* (Cambridge: Harvard University Press, 1984), 193.
4. See Grover Smith, "The Making of *the Waste Land*," in *Ulysses and The Waste Land: Fifty Years After*, ed. R. G. Collins and Kenneth McRobbie (Winnipeg: University of Manitoba Press, 1972), 127–42.
5. I follow here the provocative chapter "Unifying Incompatible Worlds: The Sibyl of Cumae and Tiresias," in Jewel Spears Brooker and Joseph Bentley, *Reading The Waste Land: Modernism and the Limits of Interpretation* (Amherst: University of Massachusetts Press, 1990), 34–59.
6. T. S. Eliot, "Scylla and Charybdis," *Agenda* 23, nos. 1–2 (1985): 5.
7. Harry Levin, "The Waste Land from Ur to Echt," in Levin, *Memories of the Moderns* (New York: New Directions, 1972), 6.
8. See Grover Smith, *T. S. Eliot's Poetry and Plays: A Study in Sources and Meaning* (Chicago: University of Chicago Press, 1974), 57–59.
9. On the relationship between the two works, see Stanley Sultan, *Ulysses, The Waste Land, and Modernism: A Jubilee Study* (London: Kennikat Press, 1977).
10. For more on this, see Bedient, *He Do the Police in Different Voices*, 52–53.
11. See Kenner, "'Notes' to The Waste Land," in *A Collection of Critical Essays on "The Waste Land*," ed. Jay Martin (Englewood Cliffs, N.J.: Prentice-Hall, 1968), 36–38.
12. Jessie Weston writes that "the story postulates a close connection between the vitality of a certain King, and the prosperity of his kingdom; the forces of the ruler being weakened or

destroyed, by wound, sickness, old age, or death, the land becomes Waste, and the task of the hero is that of restoration." Weston, *From Ritual to Romance* (Cambridge: Cambridge University Press, 1920), 14.

13. Frost quoted in Elaine Barry, *Robert Frost on Writing* (New Brunswick: Rutgers University Press, 1973), 40.

14. I draw on Perry Meisel, *The Myth of the Modern: A Study in British Literature and Criticism After 1850* (New Haven: Yale University Press, 1987), 89.

15. Ezra Pound also deleted eighty-three lines from part 4 of *Death by Water*, which dealt extensively with the Homeric hero. I draw on Lois A. Cuddy, *T. S. Eliot and the Poetics of Evolution: Sub/Versions of Classicism, Culture, and Progress* (Lewisburg: Bucknell University Press, 2000), 165.

16. Ibid., 137.

17. Ibid., 127.

18. See Harry Levin, "Some Meanings of Myth," in *Daedalus: Journal of the American Academy of Arts and Sciences* (spring 1959): 228.

19. Virginia Woolf, *Between the Acts* (New York: Harcourt Brace Jovanovich, 1969), 188.

20. Bediant, *He Do the Police in Different Voices*, 8.

21. Theodore Ziolkowski, *The View from the Tower: Origins of an Anti-Modernist Image* (Princeton: Princeton University Press, 1998), 41–68.

22. Ibid., 159.

23. T. S. Eliot, *To Criticize the Critic and Other Writings* (New York: Farrar, Straus and Giroux, 1965), 126.

24. M. Keith Booker, *Literature and Domination: Sex, Knowledge, and Power in Modern Fiction* (Gainesville: University Press of Florida, 1993), 2.

25. Italo Calvino, *Invisible Cities* (Harcourt Brace, 1974), 76.

26. Italo Calvino, "Il silenzio e la città," *Franco Maria Ricci* 16 (September 1983): 70.

27. Peter Blake, *Form Follows Fiasco: Why Modern Architecture Hasn't Worked* (Boston: Little, Brown, 1977), 159.

28. Bernard Schilling, *The Hero as Failure: Balzac and the Rubempré Cycle* (Chicago: University of Chicago Press, 1968), 196–97.

29. Flaubert quoted in Eugenio Donato, *The Script of Decadence: Essays on the Fictions of Flaubert and the Poetics of Romanticism* (New York: Oxford University Press, 1993), 44.

30. Willis Barnstone calls Seferis's Odysseus "a Greek of all times" in his *Poetics of Ecstasy: Varieties of Ekstasis from Sappho to Borges* (New York: Holmes and Meier, 1983), 71.

31. George Seferis, *George Seferis: Collected Poems, 1924–1955*, trans. and ed. Edmund Keeley and Philip Sherrard (Princeton: Princeton University Press, 1967), 479.

32. Montale translated some of Eliot's early poems and wrote a short note, "Eliot and Ourselves," in *T. S. Eliot: A Symposium*, ed. Richard March (Chicago: Henry Regnery, 1949), 190–95.

33. I refer to Gian-Paolo Biasin, *Montale, Debussy, and Modernism* (Princeton: Princeton University Press, 1989), 61.

34. Glauco Cambon, "T. S. Eliot and Eugenio Montale," in March, *T. S. Eliot. A Symposium*, 248.

35. Eugenio Montale, *Cuttlefish Bones*, in *Eugenio Montale: Collected Poems, 1920–1954*, trans. Jonathan Galassi (New York: Farrar, Straus and Giroux, 1998), 41.

36. Eugenio Montale, *Seacoasts Mediterranean*, ibid., 73.

37. Helen Vendler, introduction to the Signet edition of *T. S. Eliot: The Waste Land and Other Poems* (New York: Penguin Books, 1998), xi.

38. Alfred Kazin makes this point in *An American Procession* (New York: Knopf, 1984), 316.

39. Eliot, *To Criticize the Critic*, 60.

40. I draw here on Arthur Kirsch's thoughtful study, *Auden and Christianity* (New Haven: Yale University Press, 2005), 86–87.

41. Amy Lowell, *A Critical Fable* (Boston: Houghton Mifflin, 1922), 91.

42. Eliot quoted in Lee Oser's *T. S. Eliot and American Poetry* (Columbia: University of Missouri Press, 1998), as an epigraph to the book. The preface gives a good index of the criticism on the "American" Eliot.

Notes to Pages 114–128   327

43. T. S. Eliot, "Henry James," in *The Shock of Recognition,* ed. Edmund Wilson (New York: Modern Library, 1955), 855.
44. I draw on the magisterial overview of Virgil's influence on the modern by Theodore Ziolkowski, *Virgil and the Moderns* (Princeton: Princeton University Press, 1993).
45. T. S. Eliot, "What Is a Classic?" in Eliot, *Selected Prose of T. S. Eliot* (New York: Harcourt Brace Jovanovich, 1975), 116, 130.
46. Ziolkowski, *Virgil and the Moderns,* 239.
47. T. S. Eliot, "Ulysses, Order, and Myth," in *T. S. Eliot: The Waste Land,* ed. Michael North (New York: W. W. Norton, 2001), 130.
48. I draw on Cuddy, *T. S. Eliot and the Poetics of Evolution,* 146–47.
49. T. S. Eliot, "The Music of Poetry," in Eliot, *Selected Prose of T. S. Eliot,* 112.
50. I draw on the excellent essay by Harvey Gross, "*Métoikos* in London," in Collins and McRobbie, *Ulysses and The Waste Land,* 143–44.
51. Brooker and Bentley, *A Reading of The Waste Land,* 206–7.
52. Wallace Stevens, *Wallace Stevens: Collected Poetry and Prose,* ed. Frank Kermode and Joan Richardson (New York: Library of America, 1997), 913.
53. For Alfred Kazin, London was "the purgatory—with the merest hope of salvation." Kazin, *American Procession,* 310.

CHAPTER 6

1. For Michael Issacharoff, twentieth-century experimentation was associated with "research," "audacity," "questioning." This meant that playwrights came up with the idea of "*not* putting on stage a character named in the title of a play (Beckett, Ionesco); of eliminating all characters, using instead a mouth with a spot focused on it (Beckett); of eliminating even the dialogue (Beckett), movement (Beckett), conventional signifiers (Tardieu, Stoppard), or costumes (Kenneth Tynan's *Oh Calcutta!*); of radically modifying the status of action, which is replaced by frantic movement on stage (Ionesco); and even of dispensing with decor (Beckett, Tardieu)." Issacharoff, *Discourse as Performance* (Stanford: Stanford University Press, 1989), 120.
2. Luigi Pirandello, *Six Characters in Search of an Author,* in *Naked Masks: Five Plays,* ed. Eric Bentley (New York: Dutton, 1952), 222, hereafter cited parenthetically in the text.
3. In a long study that considers Pirandello's change of titles, Giovanni Cappello mentions briefly that the drama belongs to the type of title that reveals the plot. Cappello, *Quando Pirandello cambia titolo: Occasionalità o strategia?* (Milan: Mursia, 1986), 93–94.
4. Lucio Lugnani dedicates almost two pages to an analysis of the title of *Questa sera si recita a soggetto,* in "Teatro dello straniamento ed estraniazione dal teatro in *Questa sera si recita a soggetto,*" in *La trilogia di Pirandello: Atti del convegno internazionale sul teatro nel teatro pirandelliano,* ed. Enzo Lauretta (Agrigento: Centro Nazionale di Studi Pirandelliani, 1976), 60–62. This is the kind of titological approach that I most applaud.
5. See Marjorie Perloff, *The Poetics of Indeterminacy: Rimbaud to Cage* (Princeton: Princeton University Press, 1981); and Martin Essler, *Reflections: Essays on Modern Theatre* (New York: Doubleday, 1971).
6. I draw here on the provocative book by Robert Kaplan, *The Nothing That Is: A Natural History of Zero* (Oxford: Oxford University Press, 1999), especially 20–21, 70.
7. Gérard Genette, *The Work of Art: Immanence and Transcendence* (Ithaca: Cornell University Press, 1997), 231.
8. See Kaplan, *Nothing That Is,* 70.
9. Luigi Pirandello, *To Clothe the Naked and Two Other Plays* (New York: Dutton, 1962), 84.
10. In an interview quoted in Giorgio Pullini's *Tra esistenza e coscienza* (Milan: Mursia, 1986), 176–77.
11. In Pirandello's case, the roots of disorder are somewhat genetic. Nestled between the Mediterranean Sea and the Valley of the Temples on the southern shores of Sicily, his native house

edged on a depression known as *Kaos*—Chaos. Therefore, when Pirandello writes that he was born in "Caos," he is topographically accurate and philosophically in tune with the "relativistic" culture of the times.

12. Planck quoted in Valerie D. Greenberg, *Transgressive Readings: The Texts of Franz Kafka and Max Planck* (Ann Arbor: University of Michigan Press, 1990), 203. For a contextual treatment of the subject, see "Coda: The Sign of the Four," 197–204.

13. Eugene Ionesco, *Eugene Ionesco: Four Plays*, trans. Donald M. Allen (New York: Grove Press, 1958), 59.

14. Marjorie Perloff, "The Pursuit of Numbers: Yeats, Khlebnikov, and the Mathematics of Modernism," in Perloff, *Poetic License: Essays on Modernist and Postmodernist Lyric* (Evanston: Northwestern University Press, 1990). 75.

15. My translation. In this case, the translation in the Bentley edition, 223–24, fails to convey the original, where the dialogic parallel of *narro-narrare* is linguistically and rhetorically deliberate.

16. See the fine essay by Corrado Donati, "I 'Sei personaggi' e l'orchestrazione delle incongruenze," in *Pirandello e il teatro: Atti del XXIX Convegno Internazionale*, ed. Enzo Lauretta (Milan: Mursia, 1993), 73–98.

17. In discussing *Tonight We Improvise*, Olga Ragusa has noted that "both drama and narrative are representational forms, and the techniques of the one are often found in the other. It should come as no surprise that in a writer as prolific as Pirandello in both genres there should be instances of confusion between them, an instinctive, spontaneous slipping in and out of what is in theory separate." Ragusa, *"Tonight We Improvise:* Spectacle and Tragedy," in *A Companion to Pirandello Studies*, ed. John Louis DiGaetani (New York: Greenwood Press, 1991), 247.

18. Lionel Abel, *Metatheater: A New View of Dramatic Form* (New York: Hill and Wang, 1963), 57.

19. I refer here to the fine analysis of the play by Susan Bassnett-McGuire, "Art and Life in Luigi Pirandello's *Questa sera si recita a soggetto,"* in *Drama and Mimesis*, ed. James Redmond (Cambridge: Cambridge University Press, 1980), 83, 86–87.

20. See Jana O'Keefe Bazzoni, "Seeing Double: Pirandello and His Audience," in *Review of National Literatures: Pirandello*, vol. 14, ed. Anne Paolucci (New York: Griffin House Publications, 1987), 168. On the theme of the mask as a concept, see Victor Carrabino, "Pirandello's Characters in Search of a Mask" ibid., 123–35.

21. See my *Cornucopian Mind and the Baroque Unity of the Arts* (University Park: Pennsylvania State University Press, 1990), 93, 150.

22. *The Candle Bearer*, as translated by Eric Bentley, in *The Genius of the Italian Theater*, ed. Eric Bentley, trans. Ann Paolucci (New York: New American Library, 1964), 205–6.

23. Luigi Pirandello, *Tonight We Improvise*, trans., with notes, by J. Douglas Campbell and Leonardo G. Sbrocchi (Ottawa: Canadian Society for Italian Studies, 1987), 35.

24. Ibid.

25. Luigi Pirandello, "L'azione parlata," in Pirandello, *Luigi Pirandello: Saggi, poesie, scritti varii*, 6 vols. (Milan: Mondadori, 1960), 6:981–82, 989.

26. Eric Bentley, *The Theory of the Modern Stage: An Introduction to Modern Theatre and Drama* (Baltimore: Penguin Books, 1968), 154.

27. For more on this, see Jennifer Lorch, "The 1925 Text of 'Sei personaggi in cerca d'autore' and Pitoeff's Production of 1923," *Yearbook of the British Pirandello Society* 2 (1982): 32–47.

28. On these important changes, see Alessandro Tinterri, "Two Flights of Steps and a Stage Direction: Pirandello's Staging of 'Six Characters in Search of an Author,'" *Yearbook of the British Pirandello Society* 3 (1983): 33–37.

29. A. Richard Sogliuzzo, *Luigi Pirandello, Director: The Playwright in the Theatre* (Metuchen: Scarecrow Press, 1982), 129.

30. For a translation of the play and an introduction to the *teatro del grottesco*, see Michael Vena, *Italian Grotesque Theater* (Madison: Fairleigh Dickinson University Press, 2001).

31. Luigi Pirandello, *L'umorismo*, in *Saggi, poesie, scritti varii*, 153, as translated in *On Humor*,

ed. and trans. Antonio Iliano and Daniel P. Testa (Chapel Hill: University of North Carolina Press, 1960), 139.

32. Pirandello, "Introduction to the Italian Theater," in Bentley, *Genius of the Italian Theatre*, 14. For some critics, however, there are no individual agents behind the masks. I refer to John Jones, *On Aristotle and Greek Tragedy* (Stanford: Stanford University Press, 1980), 30–38. See also Elinor Fuchs, *The Death of Character: Perspectives on Theater After Modernism* (Bloomington: Indiana University Press, 1996), 23–24.

33. Luigi Pirandello, "Note on the Scruples Involved in Controlling the Imagination," in *The Late Mattia Pascal*, trans. Nicoletta Simborowski (Garden City, N.Y.: Doubleday, 1964), 249 (my translation). This passage is so significant that I want to give the original as well: "Credo che non mi resti che di congratularmi con la mia fantasia se, con tutti i suoi scrupoli, ha fatto apparir come difetti reali, quelli ch'eran voluti da lei; difetti di quella fittizia costruzione che i personaggi stessi han messo su di se e della loro vita, o che altri ha messo su per loro: i difetti insomma della *maschera* finchè non si scopre *nuda*."

34. Eugene O'Neill, *O'Neill and His Plays: Four Decades of Criticism*, ed. O. Cargill, N. Fagin, and W. Fisher (New York: New York University Press, 1961), 116–22.

35. Pirandello, *Saggi, poesie, scritti varii*, 6:246.

36. In the case of experimental works such as *Tonight We Improvise*, Pirandello identifies the person with the role: "You must understand that, here, under this costume, Mr. . . . (he says his name) is no more; because, he promised to you to improvise tonight . . . and to make the action spontaneous, and each gesture natural; Mr. . . . (his name) must *live* the character of Rico Verri, he must *be* Rico Verri." Some characters thus take on the names of the actors who portray them. For Marvin Carlson, this device attempts "a greater conflation of actor and character than is sought in traditional theatre." Carlson, *Theatre Semiotics: Signs of Life* (Bloomington: Indiana University Press, 1990), 27. Name and personality merge in types as names—father, son, stepdaughter. The prefatory identification of each *personaggio* with a single sentiment (remorse, revenge, grief) stands out as a variation on both the expressionist drama, which takes up basic family relationships and the morality code, which removes names in order to express pure concepts.

37. As Eugene Ionesco put it: "Theatre can be nothing but theatre, although some contemporary specialists in 'theatrology' consider it not true that a thing can be identified with itself—which seems to me the most bewildering and unlikely form of paradox." Ionesco, "Experience of the Theatre," in *The Context and Craft of Drama: Critical Essays on the Nature of Drama and Theatre*, ed. Robert W. Corrigan and James L. Rosenberg (San Francisco: Chandler Publishing, 1964), 292.

38. See Claudio Vicentini, "Illustratori, attori e traduttori e il problema del teatro come arte impossibile: Proposta di una revisione critica," in *Pirandello saggista*, ed. Paola Daniela Giovannelli (Palermo: Palumbo, 1982), 284–85.

39. Rosalind E. Krauss, *The Originality of the Avant-Garde and Other Modernist Myths* (Cambridge: MIT Press, 1985), 292–93.

40. Pirandello, *Trovarsi*, ed. Marta Abba (Milan: Mursia, 1971), 49–51 (my translation).

41. Luigi Pirandello, "Eleonora Duse," in Bentley, *Theory of the Modern Stage*, 158, 169.

42. José Saramago, "How Characters Became the Masters and the Author Their Apprentice," in *Nobel Lectures: Literature 1996–2000*, ed. Horace Engdahl (London: World Scientific Publishing, 2002), 100.

43. For relationships between stories and plays, see Emanuele Licastro, *Luigi Pirandello: Dalle novelle alle commedie* (Verona: Fiorini, 1974), especially 37–48.

44. Quoted in Ann Hallamore Caesar, trans., *Characters and Authors in Luigi Pirandello* (Oxford: Clarendon Press, 1998), 45–46.

45. Bentley, *Theory of the Modern Stage*, 154–55.

46. Virginia Woolf, "Mr. Bennett and Mrs. Brown," in Michael J. Hoffman and Patrick D. Murphy, *Essentials of the Theory of Fiction*, 3d ed. (Durham: Duke University Press, 2005), 21–34.

47. Eric Bentley, *The Pirandello Commentaries* (Evanston: Northwestern University Press, 1986), 70. Renate Matthaei adds: "The entire drama of the six characters is contained in this inarticulated moment of shock. Their traumatic fate is to be chained to it and always to have to repeat it. They

try all the more urgently to put it into words and so to free themselves from the unbearable tension of its emotional pressures. But the only result is a crude violence that flashes through the play like lightning and constantly forces its back to the point of its beginning—a hysterical, speechless confusion." Matthaei, *Luigi Pirandello* (New York: Ungar, 1973), 87–88.

48. "Le messinscene dei *Sei personaggi in cerca d'autore*," in Bentley, *Pirandello Commentaries*, 65–66, 70–71.

49. Pirandello, *Saggi, poesie, scritti varii*, 6:874.

50. Emanuele Licastro reminds us that "the *personaggi* have come to recite, and they cannot recite without spectators." "Pirandello e la scienza del ventesimo secolo: suggestioni, analogie, omologie," in *Le fonti di Pirandello*, ed. Antonio Alessio and Giuliana Sanguinetti Katz (Toronto: Quaderni d'italianistica, 1990), 31.

51. On this subject, see the thoughtful essay by Emanuele Licastro, "*Six Characters in Search of an Author* and Its Critique of Traditional Theater: Mimesis and Metamimesis," in *A Companion to Pirandello Studies*, ed. John Louis DiGaetani (New York: Greenwood Press, 1991), 205–22.

52. Pirandello, "Note on the Scruples," 249.

53. See Anthony Caputi, *Pirandello and the Crisis of Modern Consciousness* (Urbana: University of Illinois Press, 1988), 116.

54. Carlson, *Theatre Semiotics*, 88.

55. Joyce Carol Oates, *The Edge of Impossibility: Tragic Forms in Literature* (New York: Vanguard Press, 1972), 5.

56. See Claudio Vicentini, *Pirandello: Il disagio del teatro* (Venice: Marsilio, 1993), 75–96.

57. Jean Baudrillard, *Art and Philosophy* (Milan: Giancarlo Politi Editore, 1991), 15.

CHAPTER 7

1. Critics have made many references to the two playwrights, but the only systematic study so far has been by Godwin Okebaram Uwah, *Pirandellism and Samuel Beckett's Plays* (Potomac, Md.: Scripta Humanistica, 1989). It contains a bibliography on the relationship between the two playwrights.

2. This term is from Benjamin Bennett, *Modern Drama and German Classicism: Renaissance from Lessing to Brecht* (Ithaca: Cornell University Press, 1979), 293.

3. Elizabeth Deeds Ermarth contextualizes the postmodern situation: "We are asked to give up logocentric, dialectical, dualistic, and other transcendental habits; we are asked to give up plot and character, history and individuality, perhaps even 'meaning' as we have long conceived it." Ermarth, *Sequel to History: Postmodernism and the Crisis of Representational Time* (Princeton: Princeton University Press, 1992), 212.

4. For Anthony Cronin, the grotesque and the absurd share characters "who were usually given little social identity and sometimes no name." Cronin, *Samuel Beckett: The Last Modernist* (New York: Da Capo Press, 1999), 424.

5. I draw here on the fine analysis in Andrew K. Kennedy, *Samuel Beckett* (New York: Cambridge University Press, 1989), 31–33.

6. Lois Oppenheim makes of this quotation the epigraph of *The Painted Word: Samuel Beckett's Dialogue with Art* (Ann Arbor: University of Michigan Press, 2000).

7. Bert O. States, *The Shape of Paradox: An Essay on Waiting for Godot* (Berkeley and Los Angeles: University of California Press, 1978), 49.

8. Eric Bentley pointedly reminds us that the English title is weaker than its French counterpart, which suggests "what happens in certain human beings *while waiting*." Ruby Cohn, *Samuel Beckett: "Waiting for Godot," a Casebook* (Basingstoke: Macmillan, 1987), 65.

9. Michel Butor, *Improvisation on Butor: Transformation of Writing* (Gainesville: University Press of Florida, 1994), 88.

10. See Dougald McMillan and Martha Fehsenfeld, *Beckett in the Theatre: The Author as Practical Playwright and Director* (London: John Calder, 1988), 1:59–60.

Notes to Pages 143–148   331

11. Samuel Becket, *Waiting for Godot* (New York: Grove Press, 1954), hereafter cited parenthetically in the text. Because this edition numbers only verso pages, quotations from recto pages will be accompanied by the letter *a* (page 42 thus becomes 41a).

12. Roland Barthes, *Writing Degree Zero* (New York: Hill and Wang, 1968), 16.

13. I draw the term from the phenomenological approach by Maurice Natanson, *The Erotic Bird: Phenomenology in Literature* (Princeton: Princeton University Press, 1998), 65.

14. Gertrude Stein, "Poetry and Grammar," in Stein, *Lectures in America* (New York: Random House, 1935), 231.

15. Samuel Beckett, *Worstward Ho*, in *Samuel Beckett: The Grove Centenary Edition*, ed. Paul Austen, (New York: Grove Press, 2006), vol. 4, *Poems, Short Fiction, Criticism*, 471.

16. Samuel Beckett, *A Beckett Canon*, ed. Ruby Cohn (Ann Arbor: University of Michigan Press, 2001), 179.

17. F. David Peat, *From Certainty to Uncertainty: The Story of Science and Ideas in the Twentieth Century* (Washington, D.C.: Joseph Henry Press, 2001), 88–89.

18. Montaigne, "Of Glory," in *The Complete Essays of Montaigne*, ed. Donald Frame (Stanford: Stanford University Press, 1971), 2:16.

19. Ludwig Wittgenstein, *Tractatus Logico-Philosophicus* (London: Routledge, 2001), 49.

20. Beckett quoted in Hannah Case Copeland, *Art and the Artist in the Works of Samuel Beckett* (The Hague: Mouton, 1975), 216. See also the fine comments by States, *Shape of Paradox*, 92–93.

21. Beckett, "Texts for Nothing," in *Beckett: Grove Centenary Edition*, 4:336. It is in this spirit that Christopher Ricks wrote *Beckett's Dying Words* (Oxford: Oxford University Press, 1993), whose "syntax of weakness" maintains that "blessed are the dead that die!" (6, 21).

22. Robert W. Corrigan, *The Making of Theatre: From Drama to Performance* (Glenville, Ill.: Scott Foresman, 1981), 264.

23. Martin Esslin, "Godot and His Children: The Theatre of Samuel Beckett and Harold Pinter," in *Modern British Dramatists: A Collection of Critical Essays*, ed. John Russell Brown (Englewood Cliffs, N.J.: Prentice-Hall, 1968), 61.

24. Beckett quoted in Alec Reid, *All I Can Manage, More than I Could: An Approach to the Plays of Samuel Beckett* (Dublin: Dolmen Press, 1968), 11. The source is an interview with Tom Driver, "Beckett by the Madeleine," *Columbia University Forum* 4, no. 3 (1961): 23.

25. Michael Issacharoff, *Discourse as Performance* (Stanford: Stanford University Press, 1989), 3–4.

26. Robert Champigny, "*Waiting for Godot:* Myth, Words, Wait," in Cohn, *Beckett: "Waiting for Godot," a Casebook*, 143.

27. To date the best effort to interpret the title of Beckett's play has been Robert Champigny's short essay cited in the previous note. Champigny writes, "the three words of the original French title of Beckett's play *En attendant Godot* can be used to introduce the three perspectives of this interpretation. The word *Godot* prompts an examination of the role of mythology in the play. While (*en* in French) waiting for Godot, the characters talk, and we shall examine their use of language. It will then remain for us to bring in the *waiting*, the existential background which the theatrical mask of myth and words does not manage to hide" (137–38). As to waiting in terms of theatrical action, Leo Bersani and Ulysse Dutoit write that "*Godot* gives us the phenomenology of those conditions; waiting for drama has become the object of dramatic representation." Bersani and Dutroit, *Arts of Impoverishment: Beckett, Rothko, Resnais* (Cambridge: Harvard University Press, 1993), 29.

28. Beckett, "Texts for Nothing," in *Beckett: Grove Centenary Edition*, 4:334.

29. Beckett, *Worstward Ho*, ibid., 4:473.

30. On modern tragicomedy, see Robert W. Corrigan, *The Making of Theatre: From Drama to Performance* (Glenville, Ill.: Scott Foresman, 1981), 127–32.

31. On pantomime, see the fine comments by Shimon Levy in *Samuel Beckett's Self-Referential Drama: The Three I's* (New York: St. Martin's Press, 1990), 28.

32. On this subject, see the concise and informative study by Martin Esslin, *An Anatomy of Drama* (New York: Hill and Wang, 1976), 10, 14.

33. Levy, *Samuel Beckett's Self-Referential Drama*, 10.
34. Katharine Worth, "The Space and the Sound in Beckett's Theatre," in *Beckett the Shape Changer*, ed. Katharine Worth (London: Routledge and Kegan Paul, 1975), 188.
35. I draw here on Ruby Cohn, "Endgame," in *Twentieth-Century Interpretations of Endgame*, ed. Bell Gale Chevigny (Englewood Cliffs, N.J.: Prentice-Hall, 1969), 42.
36. Alain Robbe-Grillet, *For a New Novel: Essays on Fiction* (New York: Grove Press, 1965), 111.
37. I refer here to Robert Scholes's insight at the end of his *Textual Power: Literary Theory and the Teaching of English* (New Haven: Yale University Press, 1985), 166.
38. Stanley Cavell, *Must We Mean What We Say? A Book of Essays* (New York: Charles Scribner's Sons, 1969), 155.
39. On the playful and clownish aspects of the tragicomedy, see Genevieve Serreau, "Beckett's Clowns," in Cohn, *Beckett, "Waiting for Godot," a Casebook*, 171–74.
40. In his review of the play, Kenneth Tynan writes that "Mr. Beckett's tramps do not often talk like that. For the most part they converse in the double-talk of vaudeville: one of them has the ragged aplomb of Mr. Buster Keaton, the other is Mr. Chaplin at his airiest and fairiest." Tynan, "New Writing," in the theater section of the *Observer* (London), August 7, 1955, 11.
41. Cohn, "Endgame, 42.
42. See Carol Rosen, *Plays of Impasse: Contemporary Drama Set in Confining Institutions* (Princeton: Princeton University Press, 1983), 267.
43. See Wolfgang Iser, "When Is the End Not the End? The Idea of Fiction in Beckett," in *On Beckett: Essays and Criticism*, ed. S. E. Gontarski (New York: Grove Press, 1986), 61.
44. Samuel Beckett, *Endgame: A Play in One Act* (New York: Grove Press, 1958), 69, hereafter cited parenthetically in the text.
45. Wolfgang Iser, *Prospecting: From Reader Response to Literary Anthropology* (Baltimore: Johns Hopkins University Press, 1993), 143.
46. See Hugh Kenner, *Samuel Beckett: A Critical Study* (New York: Grove Press, 1961), especially the chapter "The Cartesian Centaur," 117–32.
47. See Ruby Cohn, *Samuel Beckett: The Comic Gamut* (New Brunswick: Rutgers University Press, 1962), 239–40. By and large, bicycles improve the health of people and help delay deterioration.
48. Robbe-Grillet, *For a New Novel*, 111. Mercier and Camier are like two wheels sharing a common frame. But when their bicycle is stolen, they recover only a few parts chained to a railing. From that point on, even their relationship disintegrates; see Raymond Federman, *Journey to Chaos: Samuel Beckett's Early Fiction* (Berkeley and Los Angeles: University of California Press, 1965), 152–53.
49. Herbert Blau, *Directing Beckett*, ed. Lois Oppenheim (Ann Arbor: University of Michigan Press, 1997), 60.
50. See David I. Grossvogel, *Four Playwrights and a Postscript: Brecht, Ionesco, Beckett, Genet* (Ithaca: Cornell University Press, 1962), 56.
51. Beckett, *Beckett: Grove Centenary Edition*, 4:401.
52. Ibid., 4:325.
53. Samuel Beckett, *Fizzles* (New York: Grove Press, 1976), Fizzle 5, p. 37.
54. Shira Wolosky, *Language Mysticism: The Negative Way of Language in Eliot, Beckett, and Celan* (Stanford: Stanford University Press, 1995), 53.
55. A number of studies on punishment in Dante's underworld are available. I mention just two: Walter A. Strauss, "Dante's Belacqua and Beckett's Tramps," *Comparative Literature* 11 (1959): 250–61; Raymond Federman, "Beckett's Belacqua and the Inferno Society," *Arizona Quarterly* 20 (1964): 231–41.
56. I draw here on Lois A. Cuddy's thoughtful essay, "Beckett's 'Dead Voices' in *Waiting for Godot*: New Inhabitants of Dante's *Inferno*," *Modern Language Studies* (spring 1982): 48–60.
57. Samuel Beckett, *All That Fall*, quoted in Ricks, *Beckett's Dying Words*, 33.
58. Richard Gilman, *The Making of Modern Drama: A Study of Buchner, Ibsen, Strindberg, Chekhov, Pirandello, Brecht, Beckett, Handke* (New York: Farrar, Straus and Giroux, 1974), 241–42.
59. Beckett, "Texts for Nothing," in *Beckett: Grove Centenary Edition*, 4:306.

Notes to Pages 154–161   333

60. Samuel Beckett, *Malone Dies* (New York: Grove Press, 1987), 6.
61. Ibid., 51.
62. Robbe-Grillet, *For a New Novel*, 117.
63. See Catharina Wulf, *The Imperative of Narration: Beckett, Bernhard, Schopenhauer, Lacan* (Brighton: Sussex Academic Press, 1997), 9.
64. I draw here on Stephen Watt, *Postmodern/Drama: Reading the Contemporary Stage* (Ann Arbor: University of Michigan Press, 1998), 66.
65. I am reminded of Peter Brook's belief that "Beckett does not say 'no' with satisfaction." Brook, *The Empty Space* (New York: Atheneum, 1968), 58.
66. Paul Tillich, *The Shaking of the Foundations* (New York: Charles Scribner's Sons, 1950), 149, 152, 150.
67. Maurice Blanchot, *Awaiting Oblivion*, trans. John Gregg (Lincoln: University of Nebraska Press, 1997), 6, 52, 60.
68. Maurice Blanchot, *The Book to Come* (Stanford: Stanford University Press, 2003), 213.
69. Ibid., 28
70. I draw on Herbert Blau, *Sails of the Herring Fleet: Essays on Beckett* (Ann Arbor: University of Michigan Press, 2000), 47. In 1966 Miodrag Bulatovic wrote the inevitable sequel and gave it the unthinkable title *Godot Came*. The original Serbo-Croatian title, *Godot Je Dosao*, has been translated into French as *Il est arrivé* (1967). The play opens with a double curtain on which is printed GODOT HAS ARRIVED. Because it includes a train and statements about mail delivery, the idea of arrival and departure is so technological that it has replaced Beckett's tree with an electric pole. The second act opens with Godot himself, who becomes an active, middle-aged, ordinary-looking, Chaplin-like chap who interacts with Vladimir, Estragon, Pozzo, Lucky, and the Boy to the end of the performance.
71. On the matter of Beckett's familiarity with philosophers, see P. J. Murphy, "Beckett and the Philosophers," in *The Cambridge Companion to Beckett*, ed. John Pilling (Cambridge: Cambridge University Press, 1993), 222–40. Murphy does not mention Buber.
72. Martin Buber, *Between Man and Man* (London: Kegan Paul, 1947), 22.
73. Ibid., 205.
74. Martin Buber, *I and Thou* (New York: Charles Scribner's Sons, 1958), 3, 11.
75. Martin Buber, *The Knowledge of Man: A Philosophy of the Interhuman* (New York: Charles Scribner's Sons, 1965), 115–16.
76. Martin Buber, *Martin Buber and the Theater*, ed. Maurice Friedman (New York: Funk and Wagnalls, 1969), 71. This volume contains a number of translated essays and the play *Elijah*.
77. Ibid., 10.
78. Ibid., 71.
79. Roland Barthes, *A Lover's Discourse: Fragments* (New York: Hill and Wang, 1992), 37.
80. Ibid., 37.
81. Ibid., 38, 40.
82. I follow here J. Hillis Miller, *Topographies* (Stanford: Stanford University Press, 1995), 236–37.
83. Edmond Jabès, *The Little Book of Unsuspected Subversion* (Stanford: Stanford University Press, 1996), 23, 36–37.
84. Beckett, *Beckett: Grove Centenary Edition*, 4:153.

CHAPTER 8

1. Jorge Luis Borges, *Jorge Luis Borges: Selected Non-Fictions*, ed. Eliot Weinberger, trans. Esther Allen, Suzanne Jill Levine, and Eliot Weinberger (New York: Viking Press, 1999), 3.
2. Robert Woodrow Langbaum, *The Mysteries of Identity: A Theme in Modern Literature* (New York: Oxford University Press, 1977), 120–21.
3. In his thoughtful remarks on *Endgame*, Theodor Adorno writes that Beckett ignores the

fact that the philosophies of the remainder, which are meant to "subtract the temporal and contingent element of life in order to retain only what is true and eternal," have instead "turned into the remains of life, the sum total of the damages." Adorno, *Notes to Literature* (New York: Columbia University Press, 1991), 2:248.

4. See Enoch Brater, *Why Beckett?* (New York: Thames and Hudson, 1989), 54. On less is more and the theatre of the avant-garde, see Jonathan Kalb, *Beckett in Performance* (Cambridge: Cambridge University Press, 1989), 157–62.

5. I draw on Edouard Morot-Sir, "Grammatical Insincerity in *The Unnamable*," in *Samuel Beckett's Molloy, Malone Dies, The Unnamable*, ed. Harold Bloom (New York: Chelsea House, 1988), 133.

6. E. M. Cioran, *Anathemas and Admirations* (New York: Little, Brown, 1991), 131.

7. Leo Bersani and Ulysse Dutoit, *The Art of Impoverishment: Beckett, Rothko, Resnais* (Cambridge: Harvard University Press, 1993), 2.

8. T. S. Eliot, *Inventions of the March Hare* (London: Faber and Faber, 1996), 8.

9. I draw on Watson's excellent study, *Literature and Material Culture from Balzac to Proust: The Collection and Consumption of Curiosities* (Cambridge: Cambridge University Press, 1999).

10. For Jean-François Lyotard, what ensued was loss of meaning through proliferation by means of reduction; see his "Beginning to Theorize Postmodernism," *Textual Practice* 1 (spring 1987): 17; see also Lyotard, *The Postmodern Condition: A Report on Knowledge* (Minneapolis: University of Minnesota Press, 1993), xxiv.

11. Jacques Barzun, *From Dawn to Decadence: Five Hundred Years of Western Cultural Life, 1500 to the Present* (New York: HarperCollins, 2000), xvi-xvii.

12. John Barth, "The Literature of Exhaustion," in Barth, *The Friday Book: Essays and Other Nonfiction* (Baltimore: Johns Hopkins University Press, 1984), 64.

13. Ibid., 69–70.

14. On matters of plagiarism and poetics, Alvin Kernan writes: "The author has been stripped of property rights by being declared to have died, presumably intestate, and by having been denied the ownership of texts that are said to have been the products not of individual creativity but of communal attitudes. If they can be said to have been made at all, it was by the culture and its language, and therefore do not belong to any individual. 'Language writes, not the author' is a point of view that reduces the creative individual of romantic theory into little more than a factory worker assembling images, words, and ideas that are the common property of the culture and embedded in the language." Kernan, *The Death of Literature* (New Haven: Yale University Press, 1990), 113.

15. See John O. Stark, *The Literature of Exhaustion: Borges, Nabokov, and Barth*, 1.

16. John Barth, "The Literature of Replenishment," in Barth, *Friday Book*, 205, 201.

17. Emir Rodriguez Monegal, "Borges: The Reader as Writer," in *Prose for Borges*, ed. Edna Aizenberg (Columbia: University of Missouri Press, 1990), 136.

18. See Stark, *Literature of Exhaustion*, 1.

19. Barth, "Literature of Replenishment," 200.

20. Jorge Luis Borges, "The Modesty of History," in Borges, *Other Inquisitions* (Austin: University of Texas Press, 1964), 168.

21. Elizabeth Deeds Ermarth so contextualizes the postmodern situation: "We are asked to give up logocentric, dialectical, dualistic, and other transcendental habits; we are asked to give up plot and character, history and individuality, perhaps even 'meaning' as we have long conceived it." Ermarth, *Sequel to History: Postmodernism and the Crisis of Representational Time* (Princeton: Princeton University Press, 1992), 212.

22. Samuel Beckett, *Samuel Beckett: The Grove Centenary Edition*, ed. Paul Austen (New York: Grove Press, 2006), vol. 4, *Poems, Short Fiction, Criticism*, 410.

23. Beckett, "Noti," ibid., vol. 3, *Dramatic Works*, 410–11. See Carla Locatelli, *Unwording the Word: Samuel Beckett's Prose Works After the Nobel Prize* (Philadelphia: University of Pennsylvania Press, 1990), 130. See also Hersh Zeifman, "Being and Non-Being: Samuel Beckett's *Not I*," *Modern Drama* 19 (1976): 36, 82, 83.

24. Beckett, *Beckett: Grove Centenary Edition*, 3:504.
25. Michel Foucault, *The Order of Things: An Archeology of the Human Sciences* (New York: Random House, 1970), 48.
26. I draw on Raymond Federman, *Journey to Chaos: Samuel Beckett's Early Fiction* (Berkeley and Los Angeles: University of California Press, 1965), 6.
27. See Keir Elam, "*Not I:* Beckett's Mouth and the Ars(e) Rhetorica," in *Beckett at Eighty/Beckett in Context*, ed. Enoch Brater (Oxford: Oxford University Press, 1986), 127.
28. E. M. Cioran, *The Trouble with Being Born* (New York: Viking Press, 1976), 6, 193, 3.
29. See Catharina Wulf, *The Imperative of Narration: Beckett, Bernhard, Schopenhauer, Lacan* (Brighton: Sussex Academic Press, 1997), 7.
30. Martin Puchner, *Stage Fright: Modernism, Anti-Theatricality, and Drama* (Baltimore: Johns Hopkins University Press, 2002), 157.
31. Giacometti quoted in Georges Charbonnier, "Le Monologue peintre," in *Alberto Giacometti*, ed. Reinhold Hohl (New York: Abrams, 1971), 209.
32. Beckett, *Beckett: Grove Centenary Edition*, 4:412.
33. Jean-Paul Sartre, "The Search for the Absolute," in *Alberto Giacometti: Exhibition of Sculptures, Paintings, Drawings* (New York: Pierre Matisse Gallery, 1948), 6.
34. On the "hellish" dimension of Beckett's art, see Lois A. Cuddy, "Beckett's 'Dead Voices' in *Waiting for Godot:* New Inhabitants of Dante's *Inferno*," *Modern Language Studies* (spring 1982): 48–60.
35. See Jane Alison Hale, *The Broken Window: Beckett's Dramatic Perspective* (West Lafayette: Purdue University Press, 1987), 25.
36. Samuel Beckett, "Texts for Nothing," in *Beckett: Grove Centenary Edition*, 4:317–18.
37. See Matti Megged, *Dialogue in the Void: Beckett and Giacometti* (New York: Lumen Books, 1985).
38. Beckett, *How It Is* (New York: Grove Press, 1964), 7, 28.
39. For more biographical insights on this matter, see Mel Gussow, *Conversations with and About Beckett* (New York: Grove Press, 1996).
40. Samuel Beckett, *Disjecta: Miscellaneous Writings and a Dramatic Fragment*, 136.
41. Beckett quoted in an interview with John Gruen, "Samuel Beckett Talks About Beckett," *Vogue* magazine (December 1969), 210.
42. Samuel Beckett, *Bram van Velde* (New York: Grove Press, 1960), 10–13.
43. Shira Wolosky, *Language Mysticism: The Negative Way of Language in Eliot, Beckett, and Celan* (Stanford: Stanford University Press, 1995), 71.
44. Italo Calvino, *Numbers in the Dark and Other Stories* (New York: Random House, 1995), 272.
45. Beckett, "The End," in *Beckett: Grove Centenary Edition*, 4:293.
46. I draw here on Henry Glassie, *Material Culture* (Bloomington: Indiana University Press, 1999), 47.
47. I refer here to Robert Scholes's insight at the end of his *Textual Power: Literary Theory and the Teaching of English* (New Haven: Yale University Press, 1985), 166.
48. See Mary Bryden, ed., *Samuel Beckett and Music* (Oxford: Clarendon Press, 1998).
49. John Cage, "Cheap Imitation," in Cage, *M. Writings '67–'72* (Middletown: Wesleyan University Press, 1973), foreword. The matter of direct acquaintance, if not influence, between Beckett and Cage is provocative, but it falls beyond the parameters of this study.
50. John Cage, "Lecture on Nothing," in Cage, *Silence* (Middletown: Wesleyan University Press, 1960), 109, 121. The spatial arrangement of the lines has been simplified here.
51. John Cage, "Lecture on Something," ibid., 129.
52. Ibid., 195.
53. Samuel Beckett, *The Unnamable* (New York: Grove Press, 1958), 77.
54. See Brian Rotman, *Signifying Zero: The Semiotics of Zero* (Stanford: Stanford University Press, 1993), ix.
55. Robert Cowley, ed., *What If? Two Eminent Historians Imagine What Might Have Been* (New York: G. P. Putnam's Sons, 2001).

56. Victor Davis Hanson, "Socrates Dies at Delium, 424 B.C.: The Consequences of a Single Battle Casualty," ibid., 22.
57. Octavio Paz, *In Search of the Present: 1990 Nobel Lecture* (New York: Harcourt Brace Jovanovich, 1990), 30.
58. Wallace Stevens, *Wallace Stevens: Collected Poetry and Prose*, ed. Frank Kermode and Joan Richardson (New York: Library of America, 1997), 903.
59. For Jean-François Lyotard, bricolage also consists of the "multiple quotation of elements taken from earlier styles or periods, classical and modern." Lyotard, *The Postmodern Explained: Correspondence, 1982–1985* (Minneapolis: University of Minnesota Press, 1993), 8, 76.
60. Salvatore Battaglia, *Grande dizionario della lingua italiana*, 21 vols. (Turin: UTET, 1961–2002), 12:790.
61. James Joyce, *Letters of James Joyce*, ed. Stuart Gilbert, 3 vols. (New York: Viking Press, 1957), 1:297.
62. For a full discussion, see Margot Norris, *The Decentered Universe of Finnegans Wake: A Structuralist Analysis* (Baltimore: Johns Hopkins University Press, 1976), 141–48.
63. Luigi Pulci's mock epic, *Morgante maggiore*, consciously sets measure (*misura*) against mixture (*miscuglio, quazzabuglio*) in the middle of the fifteenth century. The integrity of objects is torn apart so that they can be reassembled at one's own whim:

> I left behind you a great composition
> of a thousand other sins in a concoction;
> for if I were to read you every title,
> It would strike you as too great a mixture.

Quoted in A. Bartlett Giamatti, *Exile and Change in Renaissance Literature* (New Haven: Yale University Press, 1984), 43.
64. See Albert Sbragia, *Carlo Emilio Gadda and the Modern Macaronic* (Gainesville: University Press of Florida, 1996), especially the introduction and chapter 4. Gian Paolo Biasin has written a fine essay on Gadda and the symbolism of food, *The Flavors of Modernity: Food and the Novel* (Princeton: Princeton University Press, 1993), especially 90–91.
65. Italo Calvino, *Six Memos for the Next Millennium* (New York: Random House, 1988), 124.
66. See Nabokov's *Lectures on Don Quixote* (New York: Harcourt Brace Jovanovich, 1983), 28–29.
67. Umberto Eco, *Umberto Eco on Literature* (New York: Harcourt, 2002), 122–23.
68. Arthur C. Danto, *Encounters and Reflections: Art in the Historical Present* (Berkeley and Los Angeles: University of California Press, 1986), 7.
69. John Lanchester, *The Debt of Pleasure* (New York: Henry Holt, 1996), 171.
70. To tickle the critical palate with outrageous recipes, Fredric Jameson lists "a mannerist postmodernism (Graves), a baroque postmodernism (the Japanese), a rococo postmodernism (Charles Moore), a neoclassicist post-modernism (the French, particularly Christian de Portzamparc), and probably even a 'high modernist' postmodernism in which modernism itself is the object of the postmodern pastiche." See his foreword to Lyotard, *Postmodern Condition*, xviii.
71. Jacques Derrida, "Signature Event Context," in Derrida, *Margins of Philosophy* (Chicago: University of Chicago Press, 1982), 185.
72. Jacques Derrida, *Glas* (Lincoln: University of Nebraska Press, 1986), 24. For more on the subject, see the excellent essay by Gregory L. Ulmer, "The Object of Post-Criticism," in *The Anti-Aesthetic: Essays on Postmodern Culture*, ed. Hal Foster (Port Townsend: Bay Press, 1983), 83–110.
73. E. M. Cioran has dared say that "existing is plagiarism," in *Drawn and Quartered* (New York: Arcade Publishing, 1998), 74.
74. The original French reads:

> Il y avait qu'il fallait detruire et detruire et detruire,
> Il y avait que le salut n'est qu'a ce prix.

Ruiner la face nue qui monte dans le marbre
Marteler toute forme toute beaute.

Aimer la perfection parce qu'elle est le seuil,
Mais la nier sitot connue, l'oublier morte,

L'imperfection est la cime.

Yves Bonnefoy, *New and Selected Poems* (Chicago: University of Chicago Press, 1995), 38–39.
75. Warhol quoted in David Bourdon, *Warhol* (New York: Harry N. Abrams, 1989), 10.
76. Wallace Stevens, "Notes Toward a Supreme Fiction," in Stevens, *Collected Poetry and Prose*, 334.
77. Foucault, *Order of Things*, 386; Lyotard, *Postmodern Condition*, 81.
78. Jean-François Lyotard, "Philosophy and Painting in the Age of Experimentation: Contribution to an Idea of Postmodernity," in *The Lyotard Reader*, ed. Andrew Benjamin (Oxford: Oxford University Press, 1989), 190–91.
79. Jean Baudrillard, *Art and Philosophy* (Milan: Giancarlo Politi Editore, 1991), 11–12.
80. Jean Baudrillard, *The Illusion of the End* (Stanford: Stanford University Press, 1994), 79.
81. Jorge Luis Borges, *Labyrinths: Selected Stories and Other Writings*, trans. Donald A. Yates and James E. Irby (New York: New Directions, 1964), 64.
82. A. R. Ammons, *Garbage* (New York: Norton, 1993), 8, hereafter cited parenthetically in the text.
83. William Rathje, *Rubbish: The Archeology of Garbage* (New York: Harper Collins, 1992), 2.
84. Italo Calvino, *Invisible Cities* (New York: Harcourt Brace, 1974), 115.
85. Quoted in Alexander Fiut, *The Eternal Moment: The Poetry of Czeslaw Milosz* (Berkeley and Los Angeles: University of California Press, 1990), 30–31.
86. David Harvey, *The Condition of Postmodernity* (New York: Blackwell, 1989), 16.
87. Walter Benjamin, *Illuminations* (New York: Schocken Books, 1968), 258.
88. Cioran, *Drawn and Quartered*, 12–13.
89. Giorgio Agamben, *The Man Without Content* (Stanford: Stanford University Press, 1999), 111–12.
90. See Paul Gleason, "Don DeLillo, T. S. Eliot, and the Redemption of America's Atomic Waste Land," in *UnderWords: Perspectives on Don DeLillo's Underworld*, ed. J. Dewey, S. G. Kellman, and I. Malin (Newark: University of Delaware Press, 2002), 130–43.
91. Don DeLillo, *Underworld* (New York: Scribner, 1997), 788, 791.
92. Jean Baudrillard, "Cloning Story," in Baudrillard, *Simulacra and Simulation* (Ann Arbor: University of Michigan Press, 1994), 135–37, 95.
93. On the subject of "terminal" architecture, see Martin Pawley, *Terminal Architecture* (London: Reaktion Books, 1998), especially 8, 131, 151, 162, 178.
94. Jean Baudrillard, *The Consumer Society: Myths and Structures* (London: Sage Publications, 1998), 42–43.
95. Jean Baudrillard, *Baudrillard Live: Selected Interviews*, ed. Mike Gane (London: Routledge, 1993), 95.
96. Jean Baudrillard, "The Anorexic Ruins," in *Looking Back at the End of the World*, ed. D. Kamper and C. Wulf (New York: Semiotext[e], 1989), 31.
97. Giuseppe Battista, "L'apologia della menzogna," in *Elogio della menzogna*, ed. Salvatore S. Nigro (Palermo: Sellerio, 1990), 65 (my translation).
98. Torquato Accetto's "Della dissimulazione onesta," ibid., 50–51.
99. Giorgio Manganelli, *La letteratura come menzogna* (Milan: Feltrinelli, 1967), 176.
100. Italo Calvino, *If on a Winter's Night a Traveler* (New York: Harcourt Brace Jovanovich, 1981), 159, 212, 240, 178.
101. Baudrillard, *Simulacra and Simulation*, 3.
102. Baudrillard, *The Transparency of Evil* (London: Verso, 1999), 62.
103. Baudrillard, *Simulacra and Simulation*, 4.

338   Notes to Pages 184–194

104. For E. M. Cioran, "this anomaly ceases to be one if we realize that art, on its way to exhaustion, has become both impossible and easy." Cioran, *Trouble with Being Born,* 51.
105. Or, to quote Maurice Blanchot, "there is less reality in reality." *The Book to Come* (Stanford: Stanford University Press, 2003), 95.
106. Mike Gane, *Baudrillard's Bestiary: Baudrillard and Culture* (London: Routledge, 1991), 160.
107. A. R. Ammons, *Poetics,* in *Collected Poems, 1951–1971* (New York: W. W. Norton, 1972), 199.
108. Baudrillard, *Illusion of the End,* 27, 10–11, 22, 27, 115, 78–79, 27.
109. Ibid., 4.
110. George Steiner asks, "What conceivable hypothesis can elucidate a phenomenology, a structure of felt experience, as diffuse, as manifold in its expressions, as that of 'terminality'?" Steiner, *Grammars of Creation,* 3.
111. Robert Hughes, *The Shock of the New* (New York: Knopf, 1981), 364–65. Sven Birkerts points to a sense of destabilization. Because of "so many competing isms," there "exists no definitional core to the study of literature." Birkerts, *The Gutenberg Elegies: The Fate of Reading in an Electronic Age* (New York: Ballantine Books, 1995), 186. Robert Smithson also lists, in a letter of 1967, "the Seven Deadly Isms, verbose diatribes, scandalous refutations, a vindication of Stanley Cavell, shrill but brilliant disputes on 'shapehood' vs. 'objecthood,' dark curses, infamous claims, etc." *Robert Smithson: The Collected Writings* (Berkeley and Los Angeles: University of California Press, 1996), 66.
112. E. M. Cioran confirms that we have not reached the end of one cycle, but of "all cycles" (*Drawn and Quartered,* 45). As a "supportive" criticism, I quote Gilbert Adair: "It is a moment, clearly, saturated in historical awareness; and for all its froth of brainy playfulness, of intellectual fooling and pretending, it has been accompanied by a wave of wholly serious, scholarly developments in our attitude towards the arts of the past." Adair, *The Postmodernist Always Rings Twice: Reflections on Culture in the Nineties* (London: Fourth Estate, 1992), 15.
113. Gane, *Baudrillard's Bestiary,* 160.

CHAPTER 9

1. I draw here on Georgina Dopico Black, "Canons Afire: Libraries, Books, and Bodies in Don Quixote's Spain," in *Cervantes' Don Quixote,* ed. Roberto Gonzáles Echevarría (New York: Oxford University Press, 2005), 101–2.
2. Gérard Genette, *The Architext: An Introduction* (Berkeley and Los Angeles: University of California Press, 1992), 83, 78–79.
3. Ronald J. Christ, *The Narrow Act: Borges' Art of Allusion* (New York: Lumen Books, 1995), 10–11.
4. Ludwig Wittgenstein, *Tractatus-Logico-Philosophicus* (London: Routledge, 1974), 34.
5. In the seventeenth century, Athanasius Kircher's *Turrris Babel* gave an accountant's account of the technical impossibility of ever building the tower. Too high for the workers to reach the upper floors every day, not enough wood to bake the bricks, too heavy for the earth itself to support it, etc. The technology was ill-conceived and God punished such blind daring with the plurality of languages.
6. See Stanley Corngold, "Kafka's *Die Verwandlung*: Metamorphosis of the Metaphor," *Mosaic* 3 (summer 1970): 106.
7. I refer here to the excellent study by Clayton Koelb, *Kafka's Rhetoric: The Passion of Reading* (Ithaca: Cornell University Press, 1989), 2–4.
8. Umberto Eco, *Experiences in Translation* (Toronto: University of Toronto Press, 2000), 57.
9. See Hubert Bost, *Babel: Du texte au symbole* (Geneva: Labor et Fides, 1985), 191; and Paul Zumthor, *Babel ou l'inachèvement* (Paris: Seuil, 1997).
10. Umberto Eco, *How to Travel with a Salmon and Other Essays* (London: Harcourt Brace, 1994), 83.

11. Isidore of Sevile, *The Etymologies of Isidore of Seville*, trans. and ed. Stephen A. Barney (Cambridge: Cambridge University Press, 2005), VI, 3, 3.

12. For more on this notion, see Anthony Cascardi, *The Subject of Modernity* (Cambridge: Cambridge University Press, 1992), 109.

13. Jorge Luis Borges, "The Library of Babel," in *Labyrinths: Selected Stories and Other Writings*, trans. Donald A. Yates and James E. Irby (New York: New Directions, 1964), 52, hereafter cited parenthetically in the text.

14. In *Paper Tigers: The Ideal Fictions of Jorge Luis Borges* (Oxford: Clarendon Press, 1977), John Sturrock writes, "Borges's universal library is a library of Babel because every single proposition advanced in one of its volumes is confused in another. He is not saying, surely, that Literature would be a Babel, were his fantastic project ever realized, but that it is a Babel now. He might even claim that it became a Babel the moment a second literary work was added to the first, since the second will have been composed as an answer to the first" (162).

15. We have here an unlimited view that could be visualized through one of Giambattista Piranesi *Prisons* etchings (*Carceri d'invenzione*). As George Steiner put it, "it is a beehive out of Piranesi but also, as the title indicates, an interior view of the Tower." Steiner, *After Babel: Aspects of Language and Translation* (Oxford: Oxford University Press, 1975), 69.

16. Debra A. Castillo, *The Translated World: A Postmodern Tour of Libraries in Literature* (Tallahassee: Florida State University Press, 1984), 15

17. Borges, *Labyrinths*, 190, 52–53.

18. Jorge Luis Borges, *Jorge Luis Borges: Selected Non-Fictions*, ed. Eliot Weinberger, trans. Esther Allen, Suzanne Jill Levine, and Eliot Weinberger (New York: Viking Press, 1999), 216.

19. Jorge Luis Borges, *Dreamtigers*, trans. Mildred Boyer and Harold Morland (Austin: University of Texas Press, 1964), 21.

20. Calvino extended this ideological premise to military regimes in a story by the self-explanatory title "A General in the Library."

21. Jorge Luis Borges, *Jorge Luis Borges: Selected Poems*, trans. Alexander Coleman (New York: Viking Press, 1999), 283–84.

22. W. H. Auden, *A Short Ode to a Philologist*, in *W. H. Auden: Collected Poems*, ed. Edward Mendelson (New York: Vintage Books, 1991), 753.

23. See Aleida Assmann, "The Curse and Blessing of Babel; or, Looking Back on Universalisms," in *The Translatability of Cultures: Figurations of the Space Between*, ed. Sanford Budick and Wolfgang Iser (Stanford: Stanford University Press, 1996), 99.

24. Jorge Luis Borges, *Collected Fictions of Jorge Luis Borges*, trans. Andrew Hurley (New York: Viking Press, 1998), 325.

25. Baudrillard, *Simulacra and Simulation* (Ann Arbor: University of Michigan Press, 1994), 2.

26. In Eco, *How to Travel with a Salmon*, 94.

27. Jorge Luis Borges, *Seven Nights* (New York: New Directions, 1984), 56.

28. Octavio Paz, *The Siren and the Seashell and Other Essays on Poets and Poetry* (Austin: University of Texas Press, 1976), 178.

29. Marthe Robert writes, "no sooner was it born than it created a scholarship in which the gathering, classification, and inventory of ideas took the place of real thought. The vagaries of mysticism were supposed to be dissipated by the meticulously drafted catalogue." Robert, *The Old and the New: From Don Quixote to Kafka* (Berkeley and Los Angeles: University of California Press, 1977), 66.

30. Arthur C. Danto, *Saul Steinberg: The Discovery of America* (New York: Knopf, 1992), xii.

31. Lawrence Ferlinghetti, *Americus I* (New York: New Directions, 2004), 29–30.

32. Borges quoted in Roberto Alifano, ed., *Twenty-Four Conversations with Borges, Including a Selection of Poems* (Housatonic: Lascaux Publishers, 1984), 34–35.

33. Isaac Bashevis Singer, "The Last Demon," in Singer, *The Collected Stories* (New York: Farrar, Straus and Giroux, 1982), 179–87. See Grace Farrell's discussion of the subject in *From Exile to Redemption* (Carbondale: Southern Illinois University Press, 1987).

34. Walter E. Stephens, "Un'Eco in Fabula," in Stephens, *Saggi su Il Nome della Rosa*, ed. Giovani Renato Giovannoli (Milan: Bompiani, 1999), 132–34, 139.

35. For more on Eco's adaptation of medieval sources, see Carlo Ossola, *Figurato e rimosso: Icone e interni del testo* (Bologna: Il Mulino, 1988), 283–308.

36. The translation is by Walter E. Stephens, "Ec(h)o in Fabula," *Diacritics* 13 (1983): 51.

37. Umberto Eco, *The Name of the Rose, Including Postscript to "The Name of the Rose,"* trans. William Weaver (San Diego: Harcourt Brace, 1994), 396.

38. Ibid., 500–501.

39. Umberto Eco, *The Island of the Day Before* (New York: Harcourt Brace, 1995), 1.

40. Ibid., 5.

41. Ibid., 106.

42. Umberto Eco, *Semiotics and the Philosophy of Language* (Bloomington: Indiana University Press, 1986), 81–82.

43. Michel Serres, *Genesis* (Ann Arbor: University of Michigan Press, 1995), 124.

44. Debra A. Castillo believes that we have reached a point where "the gathering and classification of ideas takes the place of real thought" in the library. Castillo, *The Translated World: A Postmodern Tour of Libraries in Literature*, (Tallahassee: Florida State University Press, 1984), 15.

45. Jacques Jouet, *Oulipo Laboratory,* trans. Harry Matthews (London: Atlas Anticlassics, 1995), 22–28.

46. Umberto Eco, introduction to *Raymond Queneau: Esercizi di stile* (Turin: Einaudi, 1983), x.

47. Raymond Queneau, *Exercices in Style* (London: Gaberbocchus Press, 1958), 79, 129, 153.

48. See Susan Stewart, *Nonsense: Aspects of Intertextuality in Folklore and Literature* (Baltimore: Johns Hopkins University Press, 1979), 62; Wendy Steiner, *The Colors of Rhetoric: Problems in the Relation Between Modern Literature and Painting* (Chicago: University of Chicago Press, 1982), 189–200.

49. What is under attack is the classical concept of language, which, in Roland Barthes's words, is "always reducible to a persuasive continuum, it postulates the possibility of dialogue, it establishes a universe in which men are not alone, where words never have the terrible weight of things, where speech is always a meeting with others." Conversely, "what modernity allows us to read in the plurality of modes of writing, is the blind alley which is its own History." Barthes, *Writing Degree Zero* (New York: Hill and Wang, 1968), 49, 61.

50. Stewart, *Nonsense,* 3.

51. Dario Fo, "*Contra Joqulatores obloquentes:* Against Jesters Who Defame and Insult," in *Nobel Lectures: Literature 1996–2000,* ed. Horace Engdahl (London: World Scientific Publishing, 2002), 55.

52. See Jean-François Lyotard, *The Postmodern Condition: A Report on Knowledge* (Minneapolis: University of Minnesota Press, 1993), 37.

53. See E. M. Cioran, *Drawn and Quartered* (New York: Arcade Publishing, 1998), 165–66.

54. Kenneth Burke, *A Rhetoric of Motives* (Berkeley and Los Angeles: University of California Press, 1969), 45; Burke, *Permanence and Change: An Anatomy of Purpose* (Berkeley and Los Angeles: University of California Press, 1954), 112–14.

55. Steve McCaffery, *North of Intention: Critical Writings, 1973–1986* (New York: Roof Books, 1990), 97.

56. Steve McCaffery, *Theory of Sediment* (Vancouver: Talon Books, 1991), 214.

57. I draw here on Koelb, *Kafka's Rhetoric,* 129–30.

58. The three stories are included in *The Tower of Babel,* ed. James G. Scott (West Burke, Vt.: Janus Press, 1975), 28–29, 31, 38.

59. Ibid., 142.

60. Ludwig Wittgenstein, *The Wittgenstein Reader,* ed. Anthony Kenny (London: Blackwell, 1994), 120.

61. Hannah Arendt, *The Human Condition: A Study of the Central Dilemmas Facing Modern Man* (New York: Doubleday, 1958), 269.

62. Even Calvino considered the novel obsolete, at least in the nineteenth-century sense of the term: "Long novels written today are perhaps a contradiction: the dimension of time has been shattered, we cannot love or think except in fragments of time each of which goes off along its own

trajectory and immediately disappears." *If on a Winter's Night a Traveler* (New York: Harcourt Brace Jovanovich, 1981), 8.

63. Salvador Elizondo, *El grafógrafo* (Mexico City: Editorial Joaquin Mortiz, 1972), 9; as quoted in Mario Vargas Llosa, *Aunt Julia and the Scriptwriter* (New York: Farrar, Straus and Giroux, 1982).

64. Georges Perec, *Species of Spaces and Other Pieces*, ed. and trans. John Sturrock (New York: Penguin Books, 1997), 9–10, 140–143.

65. As translated in Italo Calvino, *The Literature Machine: Essays* (London: Secker and Warburg, 1987), 291.

66. Shearman, *Mannerism* (Harmondsworth: Penguin Books, 1967), 19.

67. Anton Francesco Doni, *La libraria*, proem to the second trattato, in Doni, *Scritti scelti di Pietro Aretino e di Anton Francesco Doni*, ed. Giuseppe Guido Ferrero (Turin: UTET, 1950), 427 (my translation). For a complete edition, see *La libraria*, ed. Gilito (Venice, 1550 and 1551). See also Amedeo Quondam and Giulio Ferroni, *La locuzione artificiosa: Teoria ed esperienza della lirica a Napoli nell'età del manierismo* (Rome: Bulzoni, 1973), 427–30; Clayton Koelb, *The Incredulous Reader: Literature and the Function of Disbelief* (Ithaca: Cornell University Press, 1984), 55.

68. See my *Portrait of Eccentricity: Arcimboldo and the Mannerist Grotesque* (University Park: Pennsylvania State University Press, 1991), 50–52.

69. Bronzino, *Del pennello*, in *Rime in burla*, ed. Franca Petrucci Nardelli (Rome: Istituto della Enciclopedia Italiana, 1988), 233 (my translation).

70. Jean-Paul Sartre, *The Words*, trans. Bernard Frechtman (New York: George Braziller, 1964), 194.

71. I draw here on the provocative study by Marylin Randall, *Pragmatic Plagiarism: Authorship, Profit, and Power* (Toronto: University of Toronto Press, 2001), 24.

72. See Fredric Jameson, *Postmodernism, or the Cultural Logic of Late Capitalism* (Durham: Duke University Press, 1991), 44.

73. See Assmann, "Curse and Blessing of Babel," 99.

74. See Naomi Schor and Henri F. Majewski, eds., *Flaubert and Postmodernism* (Lincoln: University of Nebraska Press, 1984); Rae-beth Gordon, *Ornament, Fantasy and Desire in Nineteenth-Century French Literature* (Princeton: Princeton University Press, 1992).

75. Martha Cooley, *The Archivist* (Boston: Little, Brown, 1998), 3.

76. Jorge Luis Borges, *Ficciones* (Madrid: Alianza, 1997), 105.

77. Borges, *Selected Non-Fictions*, 216.

78. See Castillo, *Translated World*, 81.

79. See Roberto Gonzáles Echevarría, *Myth and Archive: A Theory of Latin American Narrative* (Cambridge: Cambridge University Press, 1990), 186.

80. A. R. Ammons, *Garbage* (New York: Norton, 1993), 49.

81. Robert Smithson, *Robert Smithson: The Collected Writings* (Berkeley and Los Angeles: University of California Press, 1996), 61, 78.

82. Jorge Luis Borges, *Compass*, in Borges, *Selected Poems*, 177.

83. See Assmann, "Curse and Blessing of Babel," 99.

84. Borge, *Ficciones*, 114–15.

85. Umberto Eco, *The Mysterious Flame of Queen Loana, an Illustrated Novel* (New York: Harcourt, 2004), 13, hereafter cited parenthetically in the text.

86. See Ralph Cohen, "Do Postmodern Genres Exist?" in *Postmodern Genres*, ed. Marjorie Perloff (Norman: University of Oklahoma Press, 1989), 11.

87. Maurice Blanchot, *The Infinite Conversation* (Minneapolis: University of Minnesota Press, 1993), 423.

88. Jacques Derrida, *Archive Fever* (Chicago: University of Chicago Press, 1996), 1.

89. Ibid., 3.

90. Pierre Chaunu, *Séville et l'Atlantique* (Paris: Armand Colin, 1959), 8.

91. Echevarría, *Myth and Archive*, 181.

92. See Steiner, *After Babel*, 14.

93. Derrida, *Archive Fever*, 18.

94. Geoffrey H. Hartman, *Saving the Text: Literature, Derrida, Philosophy* (Baltimore: Johns Hopkins University Press, 1981), 133.

CHAPTER 10

1. Robert Coover, *Pricksongs and Descants: Fictions* (New York: Dutton, 1969), 78.
2. I draw on Barth's "It's a Long Story: Maximalism Reconsidered," in Barth, *Further Fridays: Essays, Lectures, and Other Nonfiction, 1984–1994* (Boston: Little, Brown, 1995), 76.
3. Nowadays, this literary practice has been associated with such terms as intertextuality (Julia Kristeva), heteroglossia (Mikhail Bakhtin), or maps of misreading (Harold Bloom). See Kristeva, "Word, Dialogue, and Novel," in *The Kristeva Reader*, ed. Torik Moi (New York: Columbia University Press, 1986), 37. For a comprehensive survey of the subject, see the fine collection of essays edited by Michael Worton and Judith Still, *Intertextuality: Theories and Practices* (Manchester: Manchester University Press, 1990), especially 1–44.
4. Michel Foucault, *The Archaeology of Knowledge and the Discourse on Language* (New York: Pantheon Books, 1972), 23.
5. See Steiner's classic study, *After Babel: Aspects of Language and Translation* (Oxford: Oxford University Press, 1975), 414–15, 467.
6. Roberto Gonzáles Echevarría, *Cervantes' Don Quixote* (New York: Oxford University Press, 2005), xiv.
7. Stephen Gilman, *The Novel According to Cervantes* (Berkeley and Los Angeles: University of California Press, 1989), 13.
8. See Otis H. Green, "El ingenoso hidalgo," *Hispanic Review* 25 (1957): 175–93.
9. Gilman, *Novel According to Cervantes*, 46.
10. Insofar as Fuentes is concerned, *The Praise of Folly* is the "perfect" subtitle for *Don Quixote*. See his review of Edith Grossman's translation of the Cervantine masterpiece in the *New York Review of Books*, November 2, 2003, 15. The literary critic Walter Kaiser has drawn Erasmus and Cervantes together in the equally emblematic title *Praisers of Folly* (Cambridge: Harvard University Press, 1963). At stake here are the pathological symptoms of a culture that the art historian André Chastel has described by way of a title as symptomatic as *The Crisis of the Renaissance* (1968).
11. Miguel de Cervantes, *The Adventures of Don Quixote*, trans. J. M. Cohen (New York: Penguin Books, 1950), 6, hereafter cited parenthetically in the text.
12. Carlos Fuentes, *This I Believe: An A to Z of a Life* (New York: Random House, 2005), 207.
13. Pirandello, "Illustratori, attori e traduttori" in *Luigi Pirandello: Saggi, poesie, scritti varii* (Milan: Mondadori, 1960), 101 (my translation).
14. Harry Levin, *Grounds for Comparisons* (Cambridge: Harvard University Press, 1972), 227. Even Américo Castro and Leo Spitzer have linked the Italian playwright to Cervantes. See Castro, "Cervantes and Pirandello," in *An Idea of History: Selected Essays of Américo Castro*, ed. Stephen Gilman and Edmund L. King (Columbus: Ohio State University Press, 1977), 15–22. Spitzer refers to Pirandello in a brief but provocative footnote to his essay "Linguistic Perspectivism in *Don Quijote*," in his *Linguistics and Literary History: Essays in Stylistics* (Princeton: Princeton University Press, 1970), 84.
15. Published by *Renacimiento* in Madrid. This is the text that has been translated by Anthony Kerrigan as *Our Lord Don Quixote* (Princeton: Princeton University Press, 1976), hereafter cited parenthetically in the text.
16. Unamuno, *The Tragic Sense of Life in Men and Nations* (London: Macmillan, 1926), 298.
17. Ibid., 324.
18. Theodore Ziolkowski, *Varieties of Literary Thematics* (Princeton: Princeton University Press, 1983), 150.
19. See Daniel Balderston, *Out of Context: Historical Reference and the Representation of Reality in Borges* (Durham: Duke University Press, 1993), 138.
20. Unamuno, *Tragic Sense of Life*, 335.

21. At the level of semihagiographic textuality, Unamuno anticipated the typology of what W. H. Auden has called the Christian saint-hero; see Auden, "The Ironic Hero: Some Reflections on Don Quixote," in *Cervantes*, ed. Lowry Nelson Jr. (Englewood Cliffs, N.J.: Prentice-Hall, 1969), 73. In *The Novel According to Cervantes*, Stephen Gilman writes that Unamuno's text is more interesting "for students of Unamuno than for those who wish to bring the *Quijote* back alive" (15).
22. See Carlo Rojas, *The Garden of Janus* (Madison: University of Wisconsin University Press, 1996), 218.
23. Steiner, *After Babel*, 438.
24. Unamuno, preface to the English translation of his *Essays and Soliloquies*, trans. J. E. Crawford Flitch (New York: Knopf, 1925), vii.
25. Ibid., 459.
26. Ibid., 37.
27. Jorge Luis Borges, "Presencia de Miguel de Unamuno," in Borges, *Paginas de Jorge Luis Borges, selecionadas por el autor* (Buenos Aires, 1982), 149.
28. Jorge Luis Borges, prologue to *Discusion* (Buenos Aires: Emece Editores, 1953), 9.
29. Roberto Alifano, ed., *Twenty-Four Conversations with Borges, Including a Selection of Poems* (Housatonic: Lascaux Publishers, 1984), 89.
30. Jorge Luis Borges, *This Craft of Verse* (Cambridge: Harvard University Press, 2000), 11–12.
31. Michel Foucault puts it in ontological terms: "What is identity, partial or total, in the order of discourse? The fact that two enunciations are exactly identical, that they are made up of the same words used with the same meaning, does not, as we know, mean that they are absolutely identical." *Archaeology of Knowledge*, 143.
32. Jorge Luis Borges, "Pierre Menard, Author of the Quixote," in Borges, *Labyrinths: Selected Stories and Other Writings*, trans. Donald A. Yates and James E. Irby (New York: New Directions, 1964), 39.
33. Jorge Luis Borges, "The Lottery in Babylon," in Borges, *Collected Fictions of Jorge Luis Borges*, trans. Andrew Hurley (New York: Viking Press, 1998), 105.
34. Jorge Luis Borges, *Borges on Writing*, ed. Norman Thomas DiGiovanni, Daniel Haperin, and Frank MacShane (Hopewell, N.J.: Eco Press, 1994), 65, 54.
35. Michel Foucault, "What Is an Author?" in Foucault, *Language, Counter-Memory, Practice: Selected Essays and Interviews* (Ithaca: Cornell University Press, 1977), 124–27.
36. Borges, "Pierre Menard, Author of the Quixote," 36.
37. E. M. Cioran, *Drawn and Quartered* (New York: Arcade Publishing, 1998), 14–15.
38. Linda Hutcheon, *The Politics of Postmodernism* (London: Routledge, 1989), 80.
39. Jorge Luis Borges, *A Universal History of Infamy*, in Borges, *Collected Fictions*, 3. Hurley translates *infamy* as *iniquity*.
40. Jorge Luis Borges, *Extraordinary Tales*, trans. and ed. Anthony Kerrigan (New York: Herder and Herder, 1971), 17.
41. This suggestion was made by Anthony Kerrigan in his introduction, ibid., 12–13.
42. Jorge Luis Borges, preface to *Ficciones* (Madrid: Alianza, 1997), 2.
43. Ibid., 15–16.
44. Borges, *This Craft of Verse*, 54, 117.
45. Ibid., 43.
46. Gérard Genette asks, "Can the meaning of a text be modified without modifying the letter of it, leaving its action, for instance, untouched? Can one conceive of a purely semantic transformation unaccompanied by any pragmatic diegetic, or even formal interference?" *Palimpsests: Literature in the Second Degree* (Lincoln: University of Nebraska Press, 1997), 317.
47. Borges, *Ficciones*, 46–47, 31–32.
48. Ibid., 28.
49. Jorge Luis Borges, "Ariosto and the Arabs," in Borges, *Dreamtigers*, trans. Mildred Boyer and Harold Morland (Austin: University of Texas Press, 1964), 82–84.
50. Jorge Luis Borges, *A Soldier of Urbina*, in *Jorge Luis Borges: Selected Poems*, trans. Alexander Coleman (New York: Viking Press, 1999), 179.

51. Maurice Blanchot, "Literary Infinity: The Aleph," in Blanchot, *The Sirens' Song: Selected Essays by Maurice Blanchot*, ed. Gabriel Josipovici (Bloomington: Indiana University Press, 1982), 223.

52. Maurice Blanchot, *The Step Not Beyond* (Albany: State University of New York Press, 1992), 32.

53. The term "maximal imitation" is used by Genette in *Palimpsests*, 393.

54. Borges, "Pierre Menard, Author of the Quixote," 44.

55. Margaret Atwood illustrates this concept by analogy to music: "The printed text of a book is thus like a musical score, which is not itself music, but becomes music when played by musicians, or 'interpreted' by them, as we say. The act of reading a text is like playing music and listening to it at the same time, and the reader becomes his own interpreter." Atwood, *Negotiating with the Dead: A Writer on Writing* (Cambridge: Cambridge University Press, 2002), 50.

56. Borges, "Pierre Menard, Author of the Quixote," 44.

57. Elias Rivers suggests that Menard's "Frenchness" also echoes the central American vogue of French Parnassian fashions that surface in the *Prosas profanas* (1896) of the Nicaraguan poet Ruben Dario, who borrowed from classical mythology no less than from Paul Verlaine. Rivers, *Quixotic Scriptures: Essays in the Textuality of Spanish Literature* (Bloomington: Indiana University Press, 1983), 145.

58. Borges, *Ficciones*, ed. Anthony Kerrigan (New York: Grove Press, 1962), 15; see also Sylvia Molloy, *Signs of Borges* (Durham: Duke University Press, 1994), 28.

59. Emir Rodriguez Monegal, "Borges: the Reader as Writer," in *Borges and His Successors*, ed. Edna Aizenberg (Columbia: University of Missouri Press, 1990), especially 114–16, 143. The poem is translated by Norman Thomas DiGiovanni.

60. Jorge Luis Borges, "A Weary Man's Utopia," part of "The Book of Sand" (1975), in *Collected Fictions*, 463.

61. Norman Thomas DiGiovanni, ed., *In Memory of Borges* (London: Constable, 1988), 45.

62. Jorge Luis Borge, "Analisis del ultimo capitulo del 'Quijote,'" in Borges, *Paginas de Jorge Luis Borges*, 204.

63. Jorge Luis Borges, "A Problem," in Borges, *Labyrinths*, 244.

64. See Gary Saul Morson, *Narrative and Freedom: The Shadows of Time* (New Haven: Yale University Press, 1994), 118–19.

65. I am indebted here to the excellent introduction by Rosalind Krauss to her *Originality of the Avant-Garde and Other Modernist Myths* (Cambridge: MIT Press, 1985), 2–4.

66. Jorge Luis Borges, "A New Refutation of Time," in Borges, *Labyrinths*, 234.

67. Borges, *Borges on Writing*, 53. Leonardo Sciascia has raised the possibility that sympathetic cohorts such as Leopoldo Marechal, Adolfy Bioy Casares, and Mujica Lainez have created him. Whenever the "inexistent" Borges needs to be physically present, a second-rate actor, Aquiles Scatamacchia, is hired. Sciascia, "L'inesistente Borges," in *Leonardo Sciascia: Opere, 1984–1989* (Milan: Bompiani, 1991), 3:161–63.

68. Jacques Derrida reminds us that "every sign, linguistic or non-linguistic, spoken or written (in the current sense of this opposition), in a small or large unit, can be *cited*, put between quotation marks; in so doing it can break every given context, engendering an infinity of new contexts in a manner which is absolutely illimitable." See his "Signature Event Context," in Derrida, *Margins of Philosophy* (Chicago: University of Chicago Press, 1982), 185.

69. John Barth, *The Friday Book: Essays and Other Nonfiction* (Baltimore: Johns Hopkins University Press, 1984), 74.

70. Eric MacPhail writes, "while the historical past is irreversible, the fictional past is recurrent," in "The Use of the Past: Prophecy and Genealogy in *Don Quixote*," *Cervantes* 14 (1994): 64. The *hidalgo*, however, fails to make this distinction. For him, the literary past ought to be recurrent, if not outright continuous.

71. Borges, "The Fearful Sphere of Pascal," in Borges, *Labyrinths*, 192.

72. For background criticism, see Jean-François Lyotard, *The Postmodern Condition: A Report on Knowledge* (Minneapolis: University of Minnesota Press, 1993), xxii, 81; Frank Kermode, *History and Value* (Oxford: Clarendon Press, 1989), 133.

CHAPTER 11

1. The revival of thematics was popularized in a volume edited by Werner Sollors, *The Return of Thematic Criticism* (Cambridge: Harvard University Press, 1993).
2. Gerald Prince, *Narrative as Theme: Studies in French Fiction* (Lincoln: University of Nebraska Press, 1992), 3.
3. For a theoretical introduction to thematics and an extensive bibliography on the subject, see Theodore Ziolkowski, *Varieties of Literary Thematics* (Princeton: Princeton University Press, 1983). Ziolkowski's own scholarship is a prime example of the range and significance of literary thematics.
4. *Lazarillo de Tormes and the Swindler: Two Spanish Picaresque Novels*, trans. Michael Alpert (New York: Penguin Books, 1986), 25, hereafter cited parenthetically in the text.
5. Jacques Le Goff, *History and Memory* (New York: Columbia University Press, 1992), 13.
6. On this point, Claudio Guillén's epoch-making essays remain paradigmatic. See his *Literature as System: Essays Toward the Theory of Literary History* (Princeton: Princeton University Press, 1971).
7. For more on my approach to Lazarillo, see my *At the Margins of the Renaissance: Lazarillo de Tormes and the Picaresque Art of Survival* (University Park: Pennsylvania State University Press, 2003).
8. W. P. Ker, *Epic and Romance: Essays on Medieval Literature* (New York: Dover Publications, 1957).
9. Mikhail Bakhtin, *The Dialogic Imagination: Four Essays by M. M. Bakhtin* (Austin: University of Texas Press, 1981), 388.
10. Roberto Gonzáles Echevarría, *Myth and the Archive: A Theory of Latin American Narrative* (Durham: Duke University Press, 1998), 8–18.
11. Harry Levin, *The Gates of Horn: A Study of Five French Realists* (New York: Oxford University Press, 1963), 32–34.
12. See Peter Brooks's discussion of plot in *Reading for the Plot: Design and Intention in Narrative* (Cambridge: Harvard University Press, 1984), 113–42.
13. Honoré de Balzac, *Lost Illusions* (New York: Penguin Books, 1971), 3–4, 6.
14. I draw on Christopher Prendergast, *The Order of Mimesis: Balzac, Stendhal, Nerval, Flaubert* (Cambridge: Cambridge University Press, 1986), 87–88.
15. Jules Michelet, *History of France*, trans. G. H. Smith, 2 vols. (New York: D. Appleton, 1882), 1:3.
16. Honoré de Balzac, *The Peasants*, trans. George B. Ives (Philadelphia: George Barrie and Son, 1904), 57, hereafter cited parenthetically in the text.
17. The original title of Alessandro Manzoni's novel about an illiterate young couple on the eve of their marriage was *Fermo and Lucia*, their first names. The title was later changed to *Gli sposi promessi* and finally *I promessi sposi* (*The Betrothed*, first edition 1825–27, second edition, 1840–42). Titology thus evolved from two people to a couple embodying a family unit. By its end, the narrative presents a class of people in Spanish-dominated northern Italy during the seventeenth century.
18. José Ortega y Gasset, *Invertebrate Spain*, trans. Mildred Adams (New York: Howard Fertig, 1974), 63, 65.
19. José Ortega y Gasset, *The Revolt of the Masses* (New York: W. W. Norton, 1960), 11.
20. Ibid., 190.
21. Michel de Certeau, *The Practice of Everyday Life* (Berkeley and Los Angeles: University of California Press, 1988), v.
22. Unamuno, *The Life of Don Quixote and Sancho According to Miguel de Cervantes Saavedra, Explained and Commented on by Miguel de Unamuno*, translated by Anthony Kerrigan as *Our Lord Don Quixote* (Princeton: Princeton University Press, 1976), 331.
23. Américo Castro, *An Idea of History: Selected Essays of Américo Castro*, ed. Stephen Gilman and Edmund L. King (Columbus: Ohio State University Press, 1977), 145.

24. Miguel de Cervantes, *The Adventures of Don Quixote*, trans. J. M. Cohen (New York: Penguin Books, 1950), 567–68.
25. Victor Brombert, *In Praise of Anti-Heroes: Figures and Themes in Modern European Literature, 1830–1980* (Chicago: University of Chicago Press, 1999), 2.
26. George Lukács, *The Theory of the Novel* (Cambridge: MIT Press, 1971), 29–30.
27. Bakhtin, *Dialogic Imagination*, 366–67.
28. George Lukács, *Marxism and Human Liberation* (New York: Delta Books, 1973), 11–15.
29. Lukács, *Theory of the Novel*, 90.
30. It is here that the novel, in Milan Kundera's words, relapses and "is weighed down by 'technique,' by the conventions that do the author's work for him." Kundera, *The Art of the Novel* (New York: Harper and Row, 1988), 73.
31. The term is Theodore Ziolkowski's, in *Hesitant Heroes* (Ithaca: Cornell University Press, 2003).
32. For a thorough treatment of the Hermes motif, see Gerald Gillespie, *Proust, Mann, Joyce in the Modernist Context* (Washington, D.C.: Catholic University of America Press, 2003), 198–215.
33. See Naomi Lindstrom, *Early Spanish Narrative* (Austin: University of Texas Press, 2004), 76.
34. Alejo Carpentier, "On the Marvelous Real in America," in *Magic Realism: Theory, History, Community*, ed. Lois Parkinson Zamora and Wendy B. Faris (Durham: Duke University Press, 1995), 83.
35. Barbara Fuchs, *Mimesis and Empire: The New World, Islam, and European Identities* (Cambridge: Cambridge University Press, 2001), 1.
36. Ibid., 3.
37. Quoted ibid., 15.
38. Ibid., 13–15.
39. See the excellent discussion, with accurate references to relevant criticism, by Barbara Simerka, *Discourses of Empire: Counter-Epic Literature in Early Modern Spain* (University Park: Pennsylvania State University Press, 2003), 181–202.
40. Carlos Fuentes, *Terra Nostra*, trans. Margaret Sayers Peden (New York: Farrar, Straus and Giroux, 1975), 384.
41. Walter Reed, *The Picaresque and the Cervantine* (Chicago: University of Chicago Press, 1983), 234.
42. Carlos Fuentes, *This I Believe: An A to Z of a Life* (New York: Random House, 2005), 147.
43. Echevarría, *Myth and the Archive*, 186.
44. Guillén, *Literature as System*, 203.
45. Antonio Gramsci voices a similar complaint in his comments on popular culture and the operatic conception of life: "It is not true that a bookish and non-innate sense of life is only to be found in certain inferior strata of the intelligentsia. Among the popular classes, too, there is a 'bookish' degeneration of life which comes not only from books but also from other instruments of diffusion of culture and ideas. Verdi's music, or rather the libretti and plots of the plays set to music by Verdi, are responsible for a whole range of 'artificial' poses in the life of people." *The Antonio Gramsci Reader: Selected Writings, 1916–1935*, ed. D. Forgacs (New York: New York University Press, 2000), 373.
46. Lukács, *Theory of the Novel*, 101.
47. Fuentes, *This I Believe*, 179, 182.
48. Carlo Levi, *Christ Stopped at Eboli: The Story of a Year*, trans. Frances Frenaye (New York: Farrar, Straus and Co., 1947), 3, hereafter cited parenthetically in the text.
49. Giovanni Verga, *Rosso Malpelo*, as translated by Gregory L. Lucente in his masterly analysis of the symbolic value of onomastics in this short story, *Beautiful Fables: Self-Consciousness in Italian Narrative from Manzoni to Calvino* (Baltimore: Johns Hopkins University Press, 1986), 71.
50. James Wood describes him as "an abused abuser," in *The Irresponsible Self: On Laughter and the Novel* (New York: Picador, 2005), 114.
51. Kundera, *Art of the Novel*, 14, 58.
52. Sartre quoted in Stephen Gilman, *The Novel According to Cervantes* (Berkeley and Los Angeles: University of California Press, 1989), 195.

53. Jean-François Lyotard, *The Postmodern Condition: A Report on Knowledge* (Minneapolis: University of Minnesota Press, 1993), xxiv.

CHAPTER 12

1. "Etcetera" is the ninth story in a collection of stories entitled *A Universal History of Iniquity*, in *Jorge Luis Borges: Collected Fictions of Jorge Luis Borges*, trans. Andrew Hurley (New York: Viking Press, 1998), 53–63.
2. John Barth points to four touchstones: "Odysseus striving homeward from Troy across the wine-dark sea; Scheherazade, yarning through the night to save her neck; Don Quixote and Sancho Panza, chatting their way across the plains of La Mancha; and Huckleberry Finn, rafting down the heart-waters of America." As quoted in Heide Ziegler, *Facing Texts: Encounters Between Contemporary Writers and Critics* (Durham: Duke University Press, 1988), 285.
3. Graham Greene, *Monsignor Quixote* (New York: Simon and Schuster, 1982), 16.
4. Roland Barthes, *Roland Barthes by Roland Barthes*, trans. Richard Howard (New York: Hill and Wang, 1977), 109, 137.
5. Steve McCaffery, *North of Intention: Critical Writings, 1973–1986* (New York: Roof Books, 1990), 21.
6. As Henry Sussman puts it, "Modernism knowingly harbors the seeds of its own antiquation and its own deconstruction." *Afterimages of Modernity: Structure and Indifference in Twentieth-Century Literature* (Baltimore: Johns Hopkins University Press, 1990), 57.
7. I draw here on Ronald J. Christ, *The Narrow Act: Borges' Art of Allusion* (New York: Lumen Books, 1995), 55, 65.
8. Georges Perec, *A Void* (London: Harvill, 1994), 282.
9. Milan Kundera, *The Art of the Novel* (New York: Harper and Row, 1988), 56.
10. See the rich essay by Emir Rodriguez Monegal, "Borges: The Reader as Writer," in *Borges and His Successors*, ed. Edna Aizenberg (Columbia: University of Missouri Press, 1990), especially 114–16, 143. The poem is translated by Norman Thomas DiGiovanni.
11. e. e. cummings, *Is Five* (New York: Liveright, 1970), foreword, 2.
12. Walter Benjamin, "The Work of Art in the Age of Mechanical Reproduction," in Benjamin, *Illuminations* (New York: Schocken Books, 1968), 223, 220.
13. Michel Foucault, *The Archaeology of Knowledge and the Discourse on Language* (New York: Pantheon Books, 1972), 143.
14. Ross Chambers, *Loiterature* (Lincoln: University of Nebraska Press, 1999), 85–86, 93.
15. Umberto Eco, *The Name of the Rose, Including Postscript to "The Name of the Rose,"* trans. William Weaver (San Diego: Harcourt Brace, 1994), 511–12.
16. Umberto Eco, *Interpretation and Overinterpretation* (Cambridge: Cambridge University Press, 1992), 23, 25.
17. Umberto Eco, *Six Walks in the Fictional Woods* (Cambridge: Harvard University Press, 1994), 1–2.
18. Italo Calvino, "Il libro, I libri," in Calvino, *Italo Calvino: Saggi, 1945–1985* (Verona: Mondadori, 1995), 2:1856.
19. Italo Calvino, *If on a Winter's Night a Traveler* (New York: Harcourt Brace Jovanovich, 1981), 175–76, hereafter cited parenthetically in the text.
20. Calvino, *Saggi*, 1:215–16.
21. George Steiner, *Grammars of Creation* (New Haven: Yale University Press, 2001), 6–7.
22. Italo Calvino, *Album Calvino* (Milan: Mondadori, 1995), 155.
23. Italo Calvino, *Numbers in the Dark and Other Stories* (New York: Random House, 1995), 135–36.
24. Jean Baudrillard, *Looking Back at the End of the World*, ed. D. Kamper and C. Wulf (New York: Semiotext[e], 1989), 31.
25. Italo Calvino, *Six Memos for the Next Millennium* (New York: Random House, 1988), 124.

26. Calvino, *Saggi*, 1:1525.
27. Roland Barthes, *The Rustle of Language* (Berkeley and Los Angeles: University of California Press, 1989), 52–53.
28. Calvino, *Saggi*, 2:1852.
29. Ibid., 2:1525, 1699.
30. Calvino, *Six Memos for the Next Millennium*, 28.
31. Calvino, *Saggi*, 2:1698.
32. Roberto Alifano, ed., *Twenty-Four Conversations with Borges, Including a Selection of Poems* (Housatonic: Lascaux Publishers, 1984), 40.
33. Calvino, *Saggi*, 2:1856.
34. Italo Calvino, *The Uses of Literature: Essays* (New York: Harcourt Brace Jovanovich, 1986), 22, 258.
35. Italo Calvino, *The Castle of Crossed Destinies* (New York: Harcourt Brace Jovanovich, 1977), 3.
36. At a time when logic is rhetoric, many believe that reality and truth are defined according to the observer's personal biases. See Alvin Kernan, *The Death of Literature* (New Haven: Yale University Press, 1990), 81–82.
37. See the provocative essay by Marco Belpoliti, "Lo specchio lucido della mente," in *Italo Calvino: Enciclopedia: arte, scienza e letteratura*, ed. Marco Belpoliti (Milan: Marcos y Marcos, 1995), 233. The essay highlights mannerist features of Calvino's writings. In 1979 Giorgio Manganelli published *Centuria: Cento piccoli romanzi fiume* (Milan: Adelphi, 1998). Numbered from one to one hundred, Manganelli presents (or pretends to present) dwarfed little novels of less than two pages long. They are but outlines of potential novelistic plots. The title, or macrotitle, of the whole collection pivots in a truly mannerist fashion on the double oxymoron of little novels in the guise of fluvial length, in other words, the most restricted form in the mode of the boundless.
38. Calvino, *Six Memos for the Next Millennium*, 120.
39. Roland Barthes, *The Grain of the Voice: Interviews, 1962–1980* (Berkeley and Los Angeles: University of California Press, 1991), 26–27.
40. See the excellent discussion of Ariosto by Patricia Parker in *Inescapable Romance: Studies in the Poetics of a Mode* (Princeton: Princeton University Press, 1979), 16–53, in addition to the introduction and the epilogue.
41. Raymond Roussel, *How I Wrote Certain of My Books*, in *Oulipo Laboratory: Texts from the Bibliotheque Oulipienne* (London: Atlas Press, 1995), 6, 14.
42. See Manganelli, *Centuria*, which contains Calvino's introduction and an excellent note by Paola Italia (283–304).
43. Calvino, *Six Memos for the Next Millennium*, 51.
44. Italo Calvino, *Saul Steinberg: Still Life and Architecture, April 3–May 1, 1982*, exh. cat. (New York: Pace Gallery, 1982), text by Italo Calvino, translated by William Weaver, unnumbered page, the second of a four-page text.
45. Steinberg quoted in John Ashbery, "Callibiography," in *Narrative Art*, ed. T. B. Hess and John Ashbery (New York: Macmillan, 1970). This volume is issue no. 36 of *Art News Annual*.
46. Foucault quoted in Gilles Deleuze and Felix Guattari, *Rhizome* (Paris: Les Éditions de Minuit, 1976), 72.
47. See Debra A. Castillo, *The Translated World: A Postmodern Tour of Libraries in Literature* (Tallahassee: Florida State University Press, 1984), 15.
48. Bill Brown, *A Sense of Things: The Object Matter of American Literature* (Chicago: University of Chicago Press, 2003), 3.
49. Jorge Luis Borges, "Tlön, Ugbar, Orbis Tertius," in Borges, *Labyrinths: Selected Stories and Other Writings*, trans. Donald A. Yates and James E. Irby (New York: New Directions, 1964), 8.
50. Structurally speaking, we are reminded of Herbert Quain's *Statements* and *April-March*, in which different chapters contain different novels. Both works were known to Calvino and Borges. For more on this, see Martin McLaughlin, *Italo Calvino* (Edinburgh: Edinburgh University Press, 1998), 125.

51. Italo Calvino, "Myth in Narrative," in *Surfiction: Fiction Now and Tomorrow*, ed. Raymond Federman (Chicago: Swallow, 1975), 79.
52. Calvino quoted in Carlo Ossola, *Figurato e rimosso: Icone e interni del testo* (Bologna: Il Mulino, 1988), 81 (my translation).
53. Calvino, *Six Memos for the Next Millennium*, 124.
54. Italo Calvino, "Cibernetica e fantasmi," in Calvino, *Saggi*, 1:216.
55. In "A Note to the Text," Esther Calvino writes: "About the title. Although I carefully considered the fact that the title chosen by Italo Calvino, 'Six Memos for the Next Millennium,' does not correspond to the manuscript as I found it, I have felt it necessary to keep it. Calvino was delighted by the word 'memos,' after having thought of and dismissed titles such as 'Some Literary Values,' ' Choice of Literary Values,' 'Six Literary Legacies'—all of them ending with 'for the Next Millennium.'" Ibid. In Italian they are called *lezioni americane*.
56. Calvino, *Six Memos for the Next Millennium*, 119, 51. Calvino admires Borges's stories "because they are texts contained in only a few pages, with an exemplary economy of expression."
57. Calvino, *Castle of Crossed Destinies*, 124.
58. See Calvino's short piece "Un progetto di pubblico," in Calvino, *Una pietra sopra: Discorsi di letteratura e società* (Turin: Einaudi, 1980), 279.
59. Calvino, *Castle of Crossed Destinies*, 124.
60. Ibid., 39.
61. Italo Calvino, *Why Read the Classics?* (New York: Pantheon Books, 1999), 62.
62. Italo Calvino, *Mr. Palomar* (New York: Harvest Books, 1986), 162. See the introduction—*presentazione*—to his commentary to *Orlando furioso di Ludovico Ariosto raccontato da Italo Calvino* (Milan: Mondadori, 1995), 23–24, where he writes that the defect of any introduction to the book is that one has to begin by saying that it is a continuation of a cycle of innumerable poems.
63. Jorge Luis Borges, *Jorge Luis Borges: Selected Poems*, trans. Alexander Coleman (New York: Viking Press, 1999), 123.
64. Calvino, *Orlando furioso*, 70.
65. Calvino, *Saggi*, 1:87.
66. The very structure of *Six Memos for the Next Millennium* echoes Hermogenes's seven ideals of style, so much so that John T. Kirby titles them "Seven Memos for the Postclassical Orator." See Kirby, *Secret of the Muses Retold: Classical Influences on Italian Authors of the Twentieth Century* (Chicago: University of Chicago Press, 2000), 86.
67. Maurice Blanchot, "The Book to Come," in his collection of essays *The Sirens' Song: Selected Essays by Maurice Blanchot*, trans. Sacha Rabinovitch (Bloomington: Indiana University Press, 1982), 232.
68. Calvino, *Six Memos for the Next Millennium*, 4, 7.
69. Calvino, preface to *Numbers in the Dark*, 2.
70. Calvino, *Saggi*, 1:8 (my translation).
71. Calvino, *Uses of Literature*, 85.
72. Italo Calvino, "Level of Reality in Literature," in Calvino, *The Literature Machine: Essays* (London: Secker and Warburg, 1987), 104.
73. Macedonio Fernández, *Macedonio Fernández: Selected Writings in Translation*, ed. and trans. Jo Anne Engelbert (Forth Worth: Latitude Press, 1984), 91.
74. Calvino, "Cibernetica e fantasmi," in Calvino, *Saggi*, 1:216.
75. Calvino, *Literature Machine*, 13.
76. Italo Calvino, *Letters: A Novel* (New York: G. P. Putnam's Sons, 1979), 654.
77. This is undoubtedly one of the reasons why Karsten Harries writes that postmodernism "is today's Mannerism." Harries, "Nietzsche's Labyrinths: Variations on an Ancient Theme," in *Nietzsche and the "Architecture of Our Minds,"* ed. Alexandre Kostka and Irving Wohlfarth (Los Angeles: Getty Research Institute Publications and Exhibitions, 1999), 42, 45.
78. Umberto Eco, *The Island of the Day Before* (New York: Penguin Books, 1995), 482; Eco, *Six Walks in the Fictional Woods*, 3.
79. John Barth, *Chimera* (New York: Random House, 1972).

80. John Barth, *Countdown: Once upon a Time*, in Barth, *On with the Story: Stories* (Boston: Little, Brown, 1997), 225.
81. John Barth, "The Literature of Replenishment," in Barth, *The Friday Book: Essays and Other Nonfiction* (Baltimore: Johns Hopkins University Press, 1984), 38.
82. John Barth, "Life Story," in *Lost in the Funhouse* (New York: Doubleday, 1969), 118.
83. Barth, *Countdown*, 255–56.
84. John Hollander, *The Figure of Echo: A Mode of Allusion in Milton and After* (Berkeley and Los Angeles: University of California Press, 1981), ix.
85. Barth, "Echo," in *Lost in the Funhouse*, 97.
86. Roland Barthes, *North of Intention: Critical Essays, 1978–85* (New York: Roof Books, 1986), 135.
87. John Updike, *Still Looking: Essays on American Art* (New York: Knopf, 2005), 213.
88. In *All Except You* (France: Galerie Maeght, 1983), 38.
89. D. F. McKenzie, *Bibliography and the Sociology of Texts* (London: British Library, 1986), 10.
90. Borges, *Labyrinths*, 249.
91. Barthes, *Rustle of Language*, 52–53.

CHAPTER 13

1. Warren Motte, preface to Marcel Benabou's *Why I Have Not Written Any of My Books* (Lincoln: University of Nebraska Press, 1996), xv.
2. Arthur C. Danto, *After the End of Art: Contemporary Art and the Pale of History* (Princeton: Princeton University Press, 1997), xiii–xiv.
3. I draw here on Genette, *Paratexts: Thresholds of Interpretation* (Cambridge: Cambridge University Press, 1997), 368.
4. Wallace Stevens, *Wallace Stevens: Collected Poetry and Prose*, ed. Frank Kermode and Joan Richardson (New York: Library of America, 1997), 913.
5. Michel Foucault, *Language, Counter-Language, Practice: Selected Essays and Interviews* (Ithaca: Cornell University Press, 1977), 109.
6. Michel Butor, *Portrait of the Artist as a Young Ape*, trans. Dominic DiBernardi (Normal Ill.: Dalkey Archive Press, 1995), 29.
7. On this subject, see the fine essay by Walter E. Stephens, "Un'Eco in Fabula," in Stephens, *Saggi su Il Nome della Rosa*, ed. Giovani Renato Giovannoli (Milan: Bompiani, 1999), 132–34, 139.
8. See Terence Cave, *The Cornucopian Text: Problems of Writing in the French Renaissance* (Oxford: Clarendon Press, 1979), 23.
9. William H. Gass, *A Temple of Texts: Essays* (New York: Knopf, 2006), 44.
10. Italo Calvino, *If on a Winter's Night a Traveler* (New York: Harcourt Brace Jovanovich, 1981), 178, 212, 240.
11. Theodore Ziolkowski, *The Sin of Knowledge: Ancient Themes and Modern Variations* (Princeton: Princeton University Press, 2000), xii.
12. Jean Baudrillard, *Paroxysm: Interviews with Philippe Petit* (London: Verso, 1998), 12.
13. Umberto Eco, *Setti anni di desiderio* (Milan: Bompiani, 2004), 246.
14. Hillel Schwartz, *The Culture of the Copy: Striking Likenesses, Unreasonable Facsimiles* (New York: Zone Books, 1996).
15. K. K. Ruthven, *Faking Literature* (Cambridge: Cambridge University Press, 2001), 200.
16. Bénabou, *Why I Have Not Written*, 55, 43.
17. Finally, Gilbert Adair gave novelistic form to the critical debate in his own *Death of the Author* (1992): "*Who cares what Yeats meant? His poems mean*—my insistence, just as my fellow critics were straining to isolate *the* interpretation, that literary meanings were generated not by their nominal author but from an accumulation of linguistic conventions and codes." Adair, *The Death of the Author* (London: Heinemann, 1992), 23, 28.
18. Bénabou, *Why I Have Not Written*, 55.

Notes to Pages 288–292   351

19. Marcel Bénabou, *Dump This Book While You Still Can!* (Lincoln: University of Nebraska Press, 2001). I quote Motte's introduction to Bénabou's *Why I Have Not Written*, xiv.
20. Bénabou, *Why I Have Not Written*, 23, 28, 105–6.
21. Gérard Genette, *Palimpsests: Literature in the Second Degree* (Lincoln: University of Nebraska Press, 1997), 33.
22. Mike Gane, *Baudrillard's Bestiary: Baudrillard and Culture* (London: Routledge, 1991), 160.
23. E. M. Cioran, *Drawn and Quartered* (New York: Arcade Publishing, 1998), 45.
24. To Baudrillard's dead end and my own marginality, Achille Bonito Oliva adds *lateralità*, laterality versus *frontalità*, frontality, in *L'ideologia del traditore: Arte, Maniera, Manierismo* (Milan: Feltrinelli, 1976), 15.
25. Quoted in Michael North, *Reading 1922: A Return to the Scene of the Modern* (Oxford: Oxford University Press, 1999), 60. See also Hugh Kenner, *The Pound Era* (Berkeley and Los Angeles: University of California Press, 1971), 95–97.
26. José Ortega y Gasset, *Velázquez, Goya, and the Dehumanization of Art*, trans. Alexis Brown (New York: W. W. Norton, 1972), 70.
27. Michel Foucault, *The Archaeology of Knowledge and the Discourse on Language* (New York: Pantheon Books, 1972), 14. The eminent anthropologist Henry Glassie writes: "While we seek new people and new sources, we accept them only insofar as they can be accommodated by the rules of narration implicit in the old story we tell. To get the story told, we continue to search for signs of change, for devices we can use to compose our myth, segmenting linear time, then linking the segments along the arc of progress that leads, inevitably, to us." Glassie, *Material Culture* (Bloomington: Indiana University Press, 1999), 7.
28. José Ortega y Gasset anticipated all this when he wrote, "In short, I believe that the genre of the novel, if not irretrievably exhausted, has certainly entered its last phase, the scarcity of possible subjects being such that writers must make up for it by the exquisite quality of the other elements that compose the body of the novel." *The Dehumanization of Art and Other Essays of Art, Sculpture, and Literature*, trans. Willard Trask (Princeton: Princeton University Press, 1968), 56.
29. See Ronald Sukenick, *The Death of the Novel and Other Stories* (New York: Dial Press, 1969); and Jerome Klinkowitz's first chapter in *Literary Disruptions: The Making of a Post-Contemporary American Fiction* (Urbana: University of Illinois Press, 1975).
30. Alvin Kernan, *The Death of Literature* (New Haven: Yale University Press, 1990), 2. The passage continues: "Internally, the traditional romantic and modernist literary values have been completely reversed. The author, whose creative imagination had been said to be the source of literature, was declared dead or the mere assembler of various bits of language and culture into writings that were no longer works of art but simply cultural collages or 'texts.' The great historical tradition extending from Homer to the present has been broken up in various ways. The influence of earlier poets on their successors has been declared no longer beneficial but the source of anxiety and weakness. The literary canon has been analyzed and disintegrated, while literary history itself has been discarded as a diachronic illusion, to be replaced by a synchronic paradigm."
31. Mary Roach, *Stiff: The Curious Lives of Human Cadavers* (New York: W. W. Norton, 2003), 292.
32. Roland Barthes, "The Death of the Author," in Barthes, *Image, Music, Text* (New York: Hill and Wang, 1977), 145, 148.
33. Roland Barthes, *Roland Barthes by Roland Barthes*, trans. Richard Howard (New York: Hill and Wang, 1977), 92–93, 187.
34. Roland Barthes, *The Rustle of Language* (Berkeley and Los Angeles: University of California Press, 1989), 18.
35. Italo Calvino, *The Literature Machine: Essays* (London: Secker and Warburg, 1987), 120.
36. Roland Barthes, *The Responsibility of Form* (New York: Hill and Wang, 1985), 119.
37. Ibid., 154–56.
38. Michel Foucault, *The Order of Things: An Archeology of the Human Sciences* (New York: Random House, 1970), 386; Jean-François Lyotard, *The Postmodern Condition: A Report on Knowledge* (Minneapolis: University of Minnesota Press, 1993), 81.

39. See Christine Buci-Glucksmann, *Baroque Reason: The Aesthetics of Modernity* (London: Sage Publications, 1994), 70–71.
40. Octavio Paz, *Alternating Current* (New York: Viking Press, 1973), 69.
41. I refer here to the excellent essay by Thomas J. Otten, "Jorie Graham's ——S," *PMLA* 118, no. 2 (2003): 239–53.
42. Barthes, *Responsibility of Form*, 158–59.
43. Arthur C. Danto, *The Madonna of the Future: Essays in a Pluralistic Art World* (Berkeley and Los Angeles: University of California Press, 2000), 91.
44. See Robert Rosenblum, *On Modern American Art* (New York: Harry N. Abrams, 1999), 141–46.
45. Jed Perl, *Eyewitness: Reports from an Art World in Crisis* (New York: Basic Books, 200), 38.
46. Maurice Blanchot, *Le livre a venir* (Paris: Gallimard, 1959), 267.
47. Georges Perec, *Species of Spaces and Other Pieces*, ed. and trans. John Sturrock (New York: Penguin Books, 1997), 91 (written in 1973–74).
48. Foucault, *Order of Things*, 386; Lyotard, *Postmodern Condition*, 81.
49. Borges quoted in Jorge J. E. Gracia, Carolyn Korsemeyer, and Rodolphe Gasché, eds., *Literary Philosophers: Borges, Calvino, Eco* (New York: Routledge, 2002), 109.
50. Charles Jencks, "Death for Rebirth," in *Post-Modernism on Trial*, ed. Andreas C. Papadakis (New York: St. Martin's Press, 1990), 6–9.
51. Foucault, *Archaeology of Knowledge*, 7
52. "Our modernity," Leo Bersani writes thoughtfully, "makes absolute the notion of discontinuity implicit in all discourses on modernity, reformulates discontinuity as a loss of the aptitude for continuities." *The Culture of Redemption* (Cambridge: Harvard University Press, 1990), 48.
53. See Paul Shehaan's excellent study, *Modernism, Narrative, and Humanism* (Cambridge: Cambridge University Press, 2002), 19.
54. Bill Bryson, *A Short History of Nearly Everything* (New York: Broadway Books, 2003), 478.

CHAPTER 14

1. Petrarch, *Letters from Petrarch*, trans. Morris Bishop (Bloomington: Indiana University Press, 1966), 296.
2. Jean Paul, *Jean Paul: A Reader*, ed. Timothy J. Casey (Baltimore: Johns Hopkins University Press, 1991), 86.
3. Quoted in a 1956 interview with Israel Shenker, in John Fletcher, *Beckett: A Study of His Plays* (New York: Hill and Wang, 1972), 25.
4. Robert Champigny, "Adventures of the First Person," in *Samuel Beckett Now*, ed. Melvin Friedman (Chicago: University of Chicago Press, 1970), 122.
5. Gertrude Stein, "Poetry and Grammar," in Stein, *Lectures in America* (New York: Random House, 1935), 235.
6. Samuel Beckett, *Three Novels by Samuel Beckett: Molloy, Malone Dies, The Unnamable* (New York: Grove Press, 1955), 308, 414.
7. Maurice Blanchot, "Where Now? Who Now?" *Evergreen Review* (winter 1959): 222–29, reprinted in *Critical Essays on Samuel Beckett*, ed. Lance St. John Butler (Aldershot: Scolar Press, 1993), 86.
8. Italo Calvino, *If on a Winter's Night a Traveler* (New York: Harcourt Brace Jovanovich, 1981), 258–59.
9. *Jane Hammond: The John Ashbery Collaboration, 1993–2001*, exh. cat., curated by Jill Snyder, ed. Frank Kermode and Joan Richardson (Cleveland: Cleveland Center for Contemporary Art, 2001), 7.
10. Wallace Stevens, *Wallace Stevens: Collected Poetry and Prose*, ed. Frank Kermode and Joan Richardson (New York: Library of America, 1997), 899.
11. John Ashbery, *As We Know* (New York: Penguin Books, 1979), 93–94.

12. Quoted in David Lehman, "The Shield of Greeting: The Function of Irony in John Ashbery's Poetry," in *Beyond Amazement: New Essays of John Ashbery,* ed. David Lehman (Ithaca: Cornell University Press, 1980), 111.

13. Geoffrey H. Hartman, *Saving the Text: Literature, Derrida, Philosophy* (Baltimore: Johns Hopkins University Press, 1981), xxiv.

14. John Barth, *The Friday Book: Essays and Other Nonfiction* (Baltimore: Johns Hopkins University Press, 1984), x.

15. Ibid., 116.

16. Ferial J. Ghazoul, *Nocturnal Poetics: The Arabian Nights in Comparative Context* (Cairo: American University in Cairo Press, 1996), especially 121–23, 150–52.

17. Michel Foucault, *Language, Counter-Memory, Practice: Selected Essays and Interviews* (Ithaca: Cornell University Press, 1977), 53.

18. Jorge Luis Borges, *Seven Nights* (New York: New Directions, 1984), 57, 45.

19. Barth, *Friday Book,* 264. For William H. Gass, the title's *1001* means "for a very long time, and then some." Gass, *A Temple of Texts: Essays* (New York: Knopf, 2006), 94.

20. W. H. Auden, *W. H. Auden: Collected Poems,* ed. Edward Mendelson (New York: Vintage Books, 1991), 601–3.

21. Harold Rosenberg, *The Definition of Art: Action Art to Pop to Earthworks* (New York: Horizon Press, 1972), 203–4.

22. See Brian Rotman, *Signifying Zero: The Semiotics of Zero* (Stanford: Stanford University Press, 1993), ix.

23. John Barth, *Lost in the Funhouse* (New York: Doubleday, 1969), 102.

24. Alfred Apple, "Lost in the Funhouse," in *Critical Essays on John Barth,* ed. Joseph J. Waldmeir (Boston: G. K. Hall, 1980), 180.

25. Stan Fogel and Gordon Slethaug, *Understanding John Barth* (Columbia: University of South Carolina Press, 1990), 121.

26. Barth, *Lost in the Funhouse,* 105, 110.

27. Maurice Blanchot, *The Space of Literature* (Lincoln: University of Nebraska Press, 1982), 89.

28. Robert Kaplan, *The Nothing That Is: A Natural History of Zero* (Oxford: Oxford University Press, 1999), 1.

29. For an analysis of the story, see Matei Calinescu, *Rereading* (New Haven: Yale University Press, 1993), 3–8.

30. Jorge Luis Borges, *A Personal Anthology* (New York: Grove Press, 1967), 146–47, 150.

31. Marjorie Perloff, *Twenty-firstt-Century Modernism: The New Poetics* (Oxford: Blackwell, 2002), 2.

INDEX

Abel, Lionel, 130
Abrams, Harry H., 177
Accetto, Torquato, 183
Achilles, 82
Adorno, Theodor, 61, 62, 141
Aeneas, 82, 83, 89, 91, 101, 112, 120
Aeschylus, 164
Agamben, Giorgio, 179
Ahab, 91
Ajax, 82
Alexander the Great, 190
Alter, Robert, 124
Alberti, Leon Battista, 13, 31, 39, 54
Alcott, Louisa May, 200
Alemán, Mateo, 1, 33, 244, 253
Amadis de Gaula, 32, 33, 38, 42, 253
Ammons, A. R., 175, 184, 214, 292
Anchises, 120
Andreuccio, 42
Angelica, 243
Anouilh, Jean, 141
Antigones, 76, 136
Apollinaire, Guillaume, 110
Apollo, 20, 98
Aquinas, Thomas, 73, 200
Arcimboldo, Giuseppe, 208, 209, 213
Arendt, Hanna, 206
Ariosto, Ludovico, 15, 222, 235, 267, 275, 276
Aristocrat, 80
Aristotle, 24, 75, 80, 222
Arnheim, Rudolph, 263
Ashbery, John, 302, 303
Astolfo, 275
Athena, 24, 25, 87, 88
Auden, W. H., 67, 113, 115, 116, 197, 305
Auerbach, Erich, 5
Augustine, 54, 93, 144, 191
Augustus, 67
Autolycus, 70

Avellaneda, Alonso Fernandez de, 225, 230, 250

Babbitt, Irving, 112
Bach, Johann Sebastian, 200
Bacon, Francis, 54, 61
Bakhtin, Mikhail, 41, 58, 77, 242, 252, 255
Balzac, Honoré, 1, 33, 37, 109, 162, 245, 246, 247
Barth, John, 163, 164, 257, 278, 279, 280, 284, 303, 304, 305, 306
Barthes, Roland, 3, 35, 46, 61, 66, 143, 154, 158, 263, 281, 283, 290, 292, 294, 301, 306
Barzun, Jacques, 4, 163
Battista, Giuseppe, 183
Baudelaire, Charles, 106, 113
Baudrillard, Jean, 5, 140, 160, 180, 182, 184, 185, 198, 217, 284
Beach, Sylvia, 77
Beckett, Samuel, 107, 110, 140, 141, 142, 143, 144, 145, 146, 147, 148, 150, 151, 152, 153, 154, 155, 156, 158, 159, 160, 161, 164, 165, 166, 167, 168, 169, 170, 171, 300
Bedient, Calvin, 95, 118
Bellini, Giovanni, 19
Bellow, Saul, 257
Bembo, Pietro, 28, 29
Bénabou, Marcel, 287, 288
Benjamin, Walter, 72, 179, 265, 286
Bernal Díaz del Castillo, 253
Bernard of Cluny, 200
Bernini, Gianlorenzo, 131
Bettino da Trizzo, 208
Bion, 11
Blake, William, 93, 118
Blanchot, Maurice, 91, 156, 160, 217, 236, 277, 295, 300, 306
Blasing, Mutlu Konuk, 95
Blau, Herbert, 144, 152
Blin, Roger, 141

Bloom, Leopold, 66, 71, 72, 73, 74, 76, 77, 81, 89, 90, 91, 101, 112, 301
Bloohoom, 77
Boccaccio, Giovanni, 11, 41, 49, 68
Boiardo, Matteo Maria, 10
Bonaparte, Charles-Louis-Napoleon, 1
Bonaparte, Napoleon, 1, 65, 215
Bonaventura, 39
Boni, Giacomo, 84
Bonnefoy, Yves, 174
Bonvicinus, 39
Borges, Jorge Luis, 61, 79, 93, 160, 163, 164, 172, 175, 186, 189, 191, 194, 195, 196, 197, 198, 200, 202, 204, 205, 206, 212, 214, 215, 216, 217, 218, 220, 221, 229, 231, 232, 233, 234, 235, 236, 237, 238, 262, 272, 274, 275, 276, 278, 282, 283, 286, 295, 304, 307
Bosch, Hieronymus, 255
Bounderby, Josiah, 244
Bouvard, 286
Bovary, Emma, 81, 229, 270
Bovary, Charles, 45
Bracciolini, Poggio, 53
Branca, Vittore, 68
Brancusi, Constantin, 264
Brant, Sebastian, 60, 222, 255
Braudel, Fernand, 240
Brilliant, Richard, 18
Broch, Hermann, 102
Brombert, Victor, 33, 251
Bronzino, Angelo, 210
Brooks, Peter, 156
Brown, Daniel, 204
Browning, Robert, 28
Brueghel, the Elder, 191
Bruni, Leonardo, 11, 30, 93
Bruno, Giordano, 53, 56, 57, 59, 132, 222
Brryson, Bill, 298
Buber, Martin, 107, 156, 158
Burckhardt, Jacob, 46, 93
Burgos, Jorge de, 200, 212
Burke, Kenneth, 50, 204
Burton, Richard, 136
Burton, Robert, 261
Buscón, Pablos, 40
Butor, Michel, 1, 61, 143, 285, 286

Cage, John, 171, 292
Callimachus, 189
Calypso, 89
Calvino, Italo, 5, 108, 170, 173, 178, 183, 189, 190, 208, 257, 260, 267, 268, 269, 270, 271, 272, 273, 274, 276, 277, 279, 280, 282, 290, 301, 305

Campbell, Joseph, 77
Campanella, Tommaso, 30, 255
Camus, Albert, 261
Camus, Renaud, 285
Canini, 51
Canova, Antonio, 85
Caracciolo, Gian Francesco, 14
Cariteo di Barcellona, 14
Carpentier, Alejo, 253
Carroll, Lewis, 203
Cassandra, 113
Cassirer, Ernst, 61
Castelli, Leo, 174
Castiglione, Baldassar, 28, 29, 61, 223
Castillo, Debra A., 196
Castro, Américo, 250
Cather, Willa, 66
Cavafy, Constantine, 88, 107
Cavalcanti, Guido, 208
Cavell, Stanley, 150
Ceriol, Furió, 254
Cervantes, Miguel de, 2, 32, 34, 58, 201, 209, 210, 216, 220, 221, 222, 223, 224, 228, 229, 230, 231, 233, 234, 235, 236, 237, 240, 244, 249, 250, 251, 256, 260, 261, 267. 286
Chambers, Ross, 267
Champigny, Robert, 147, 300
Charles V, 69, 189, 243, 250, 253
Chaunu, Pierre, 218
Checkhov, Anton, 137
Chiarelli, Luigi, 134
Ciappelletto, 68
Cicero, 43, 48, 244, 299
Cid, El, 32, 33
Cide Hamete Benengeli, 221, 223, 228, 235
Cioran, E. M., 62, 161, 166, 179, 233, 284, 288
Clark, Kenneth, 18
Claudel, Paul, 21
Clov, 149, 151
Coleridge, Samuel Taylor, 60
Colón, Fernando, 189
Columbus, Christopher, 69, 91, 189, 198
Concolorcorvo (Alonso Carrio de la Vandera), 253
Conrad, Joseph, 96
Cooley, Martha, 212
Coover, Robert, 220, 278
Copernicus, 4
Coriolanus, 74
Corrigan, Robert W., 145
Cornaro, Caterina, 28
Cortés, Hernan, 241
Cotroneo, Roberto, 279

Index   357

Cowley, Robert, 172
Croce, Benedetto, 259
Cuddy, Lois A., 102
cummings, e. e., 264
Cyrano, 136

Daedalus, 73, 77, 78
Daidalus, 77
D'Annunzio, Gabriele, 85, 124, 137
Dante, 11, 12, 68, 69, 71, 89, 102, 107, 153, 154, 256
Danto, Arthur C., 173, 198, 284
Darius, 190
Darwin, Charles, 102, 248
Dauriat, 245
De Certeau, Michel, 248
De Chirico, Giorgio, 116
Dedalus, Stephen, 74, 75, 77, 78, 85, 87, 90, 91, 92, 112, 301
De Kooning, William, 295
DeLillo, Don, 179
Della Casa, Giovanni, 51
Della Griva, Roberto, 201
Derrida, Jacques, 3, 30, 174, 217, 218
Descartes, René, 59
Detwiler, Jesse, 179
Dickens, Charles, 1, 2, 46, 95, 244, 245
Didi, 142, 143, 145, 146, 149, 150, 151, 153, 156, 158, 159, 166
Divitia, 39
Donata, 137
Don Cirincio, 135
Doni, Anton Francesco, 209
Donne, John, 54, 60, 76
Doyle, Arthur Conan, 200
Duchamp, Marcel, 65, 100, 125
Dulcinea del Toboso, 229, 243
Duse, Eleonora, 137, 157

Eagleton, Terry, 252
Eco, Umberto, 73, 80, 173, 194, 198, 200, 201, 215, 216, 260, 267, 278, 279, 287
Edmund, 75
Egan, Patricia, 29
Eliot, T. S., 3, 66, 73, 76, 90, 93, 95, 96, 97, 99, 100, 101, 102, 103, 104, 106, 107, 108, 109, 111, 112, 113, 114, 115, 116, 117, 118, 119, 120, 121, 122, 145, 146, 160, 161, 162, 163, 175, 182, 190, 191, 195, 212, 278, 289
Elizondo, Salvador, 207
Ellmann, Richard, 84, 90
Emerson, Ralph Waldo, 61, 122
Eneas, 82

Erasmus, Desiderius, 44, 45, 53, 189, 222, 255, 286
Ergasto, 15
Espinel, Vicente, 244
Estragon, 146, 148
Eurycleia, 70
Euterpe, 24

Faulkner, William, 2, 257
Faust, 164, 191, 237
Fauré, G., 110
Federigo da Montefeltro, 48
Ferlinghetti, Lawrence, 198
Fernández, Macedonio, 278
Ficino, Marsilio, 54
Fiedler, Leslie, 289
Fileno, 137
Fitzgerald, F. Scott, 66
Fish, Stanley, 55
Flannery, Silas, 274
Flaubert, Gustave, 2, 45, 74, 110, 147, 191, 211, 286, 292
Fo, Dario, 204
Folengo, 173
Fontana, Lucio, 292
Foscolo, Ugo, 67
Foucault, Michel, 154, 165, 232, 262, 267, 273, 289, 292, 297, 304
Frame, Donald, 49
France, Anatole, 110
Francesca, 270
Francesca, Piero della, 19, 256
Francken, Frans, 191
Franckenstein, 191
Freccero, John, 69
Freedberg, Sidney, 22
Friedman, Thomas L., 198
Fronimo, 15
Frost, Robert, 100, 278
Frye, Northrop, 60
Fuchs, Barbara, 253
Fuentes, Carlos, 1, 220, 223, 237, 254, 255, 257, 261
Fuentes, Larry, 177
Funes the Memorious, 215, 216

Gadda, Carlo, 173
Galilei, Galileo, 54, 59, 200
Gallarati-Scotti, Tommaso, 137
Gallus, 10
Gass, William, H., 286
Gehry, Frank, 218
Genette, Gérard, 67, 189, 220

Gerontion, 102, 146
Giacometti, Alberto, 167, 168, 169
Gibbon, Edward, 67, 117
Gibson, Mel, 136
Gide, André, 60, 110
Gilman, Stephen, 222, 261
Ginés de Pasamonte, 34
Ginesillo de Parapilla, 34
Giorgione, 10, 18, 22, 99
Giraudoux, Jean, 110
Godel, Kurt, 128
Godet, 146
Godin, 146
Godot, 142, 143, 144, 145, 146, 147, 148, 150, 153, 157, 158, 159, 217, 258, 298
Gogo, 142, 143, 145, 146, 149, 150, 151, 153, 156, 158, 159, 166
Gonzáles Echevarría, Roberto, 189, 218, 221, 243
Goya, Francisco, 296
Graham, Jorie, 292
Gramsci, Antonio, 36
Greenblatt, Stephen, 4, 47
Greene, Graham, 262
Guercino, 22
Guicciardini, Francesco, 51, 53, 115
Guillén, Claudio, 47, 221, 255
Guzmán de Alfarache, 31, 32, 33, 37, 244, 255
Guzmánillo, 34

Hadrian, 112
Hamm, 146, 148, 151, 152, 167, 168
Hamlet, 60, 101, 136, 164
Hammond, Jane, 302
Hannibal, 48
Hartman, Geoffrey, 15, 218, 303
Haskell, Francis, 18
Hassan, Ihab, 289
Heidegger, Martin, 212, 249
Helen, 89
Heliodorus, 15
Hemingway, Ernest, 113
Heney, Seamus,
Hercules, 68, 69
Herms, George, 213
Hero, 293
Herodotus, 93
Hesiod, 25
Higden, Betty, 95
Hinkfuss, 131, 132
Hollander, John, 20, 281
Homer, 73, 80, 81, 82, 87, 89, 91, 102, 154
Horace, 154
Hughes, Robert, 185, 186

Huizinga, Johan, 13
Hunter, 83
Husserl, Edmund, 249
Hutcheon, Linda, 233
Huysmans, Joris-Karl, 162

Ibsen, Henrik, 79
Ionesco, Eugene, 128, 152
Iser, Wolfgang, 151, 274
Isidore of Seville, 194
Isozaki, Arata, 264

Jabès, Edmond, 158, 299
Jakobson, Roman, 230
James, Henry, 2, 114
Jameson, Fredric, 91, 252
Janus, 103
Jarry, Alfred, 203
Jefferson, Thomas, 124
Jencks, Charles, 296
Jennaro, Jacopo de, 10
Jerome, 1
Jesus, 62, 262
Johns, Jasper, 210, 294
Jones, Tom, 81
Jouet, Jacques, 203
Joyce, James, 2, 66, 67, 68, 70, 71, 72, 73, 74, 75, 76, 77, 78, 79, 80, 81, 82, 83, 84, 85, 86, 87, 89, 90, 91, 92, 93, 94, 97, 98, 101, 107, 110, 112, 117, 152, 154, 179, 190, 200, 216, 240, 257, 278
Joyce, Lucia, 78
Julius II, 174

Kafka, Franz, 205, 206, 220, 270
Kandinsky, Wassily, 169, 170, 292
Kaplan, Robert, 306
Keats, John, 17, 22, 67
Kenner, Hugh, 78, 80
Ker, W. P., 242
Kernan, Alvin, 289
Kiberd, Declan, 94
Klee, Paul, 179
Krapp, 168
Krauss, Rosalind E., 136
Krull, Felix, 253
Kundera, Milan, 240, 261, 263

Laforgue, Jules, 113
Lamb, Charles, 83
Langbaum, Robert, 160
Las Casas, Bartolomé de, 254
Lazarillo de Tormes (Lázaro), 32, 33, 34, 35, 36, 37, 38, 39, 40, 42, 43, 44, 45, 47, 48, 81, 112,

225, 241, 242, 243, 244, 245, 246, 252, 253, 255,
256, 257, 261
Lazarus, 40, 41, 258
Leander, 293
Lear, Edward, 203
Lebrun, Charles, 18
Le Goff, Jacques, 242
Lehman, David, 303
Lemuel, 168
Léon, Luis de, 33.
Leopold, 77
Levi, Carlo, 258, 259, 260
Levin, Harry, 3, 97, 225, 245
Lewis, R. W.B., 257
Linati, Carlo, 83
Lipsius, Justus, 54
Livy, 244
Loman, Willie, 156
Longley, Michael, 68
Lopez de Hoyos, 223
Lowell, Amy, 113
Loyola, Ignatius de, 222, 230
Lucan, 154
Lucien, de Rubempré, 1, 246
Lucky, 152
Ludmilla, 276, 277
Lugones, Leopoldo, 196
Lukács, Georg, 61, 251,252
Lycoris, 10
Lyotard, Jean-François, 261, 284

Machiavelli, Niccolò, 45, 51, 52, 95, 115, 222
Macbeth, 164
MacHugh, 78, 79, 85, 86
Madama Pace, 127, 130
Magellan, 189
Magritte, René, 5
Malevich, Kazimir, 213
Mali, Joseph, 93
Malone, 152, 154
Mallarmé, Stephane, 113, 147, 200
Malpelo, 259
Malraux, André, 49
Manet, Edouard, 10, 99
Manganelli, Giorgio, 183, 271
Mann, Thomas, 93, 113, 252, 253, 257
Mantegna, Andrea, 16
Manzoni, Alessandro, 200, 247
Marconi, Guglielmo, 124
Marcuse, Herbert, 249
Marino, Giambattista, 58
Marot, Clement, 209
Marx, Karl, 247

Masson, André, 292
McCaffery, Steve, 205, 263
McChoakumchild, 46
McKenzie, D. E., 282
Medea, 76, 147
Melville, Herman, 91
Menard, Pierre, 232, 233, 234, 236, 238, 261, 280, 282, 301
Menelaus, 89
Meredith, George, 75
Michelangelo, Buonarroti, 119, 175
Michelet, Jules, 93, 246
Miller ,J. Hillis, 68
Milosz, Czeslaw, 178
Minotaur, 217
Miranda, Don Diego de, 251
Mnemosyne, 23
Molly Bloom, 80, 90, 112, 152
Mondrian, Piet, 170, 292
Moneta, 39
Montaigne, Michel de, 45, 47, 48, 49, 50, 51, 52, 53, 54, 55, 56, 57, 58, 59, 60, 61, 62, 71, 76, 144
Montale, Eugenio, 111
Montemayor, Jorge de, 10
More, Thomas, 3, 10, 255
Moore, Henry, 121
Moore, Thomas, 86, 243
Morelli, Giovanni di Pagolo, 53
Morny, 1
Morson, Gary Saul, 59
Moscus, 11
Moses, 38, 79
Motte, Warren, 284
Mujica Lainez, Manuel, 233, 237
Mulligan, Buck, 71, 72
Muret, Marc-Antoine, 54
Murillo, 32
Murphy, 152
Murray, William Mrs., 83
Musil, Robert, 251
Mussolini, Benito, 124

Nabokov, Vladimir, 173
Nagg, 149, 151
Namar, 80
Naselli, 51
Nebrija, Antonio, 35
Nebuchadnezzar II, 105
Nell, 149
Nietzsche, Friedrich, 212
Nimrod, 191, 194
Nomad, 80

Nomon, 80
Numah, 80

Oedipus, 136, 147
Odysseus, 66, 68, 70, 71, 72, 73, 75, 76, 77, 81, 82, 85, 87, 88, 89, 90, 91, 101, 107
Oedipus, 76
Olivier, Laurence, 136
Olusseus, 82
Olympia, 99
O'Neill, Eugene, 135
Ops, 286
Orlando, 34
Ortega y Gasset, José, 190, 247, 248, 249, 289
Ovid, 154

Pablillos, 34
Pan, 10, 11, 15
Panofsky, Erwin, 12
Panza, Sancho, 2, 224, 225, 226, 227, 231, 248, 249, 250
Paolo, 270
Paris, 89
Parnell, Charles, Stewart, 79
Pascal, Blaise, 54, 60, 61
Pater, Walter, 22, 27, 46, 74
Paul, Jean, 299
Paz, Octavio, 1, 172, 198, 292
Pécuchet, 286
Peer Gynt, 164
Perec, Georges, 207, 263, 295
Pelasgus, 11
Penelope, 87, 88
Perl, Jed, 294
Perloff, Marjorie, 128, 307
Persigny, 1
Pessoa, Fernando, 160
Petrarch, 30, 48, 54, 189, 191, 243, 299
Petronius, 98
Perugino, 19
Philip II, 255
Picasso, Plabo, 125
Pip, 1, 245
Pirandello, Luigi, 124, 125, 126, 127, 128, 130, 132, 133, 134, 135, 136, 137, 138, 139, 140, 141, 142, 164, 224, 238
Piranesi, Giambattista, 117, 205, 296
Pistoletto, Michelangelo, 182
Pitoeff, Georges, 133, 142
Pius II, 286
Pizarro, Francisco, 241
Pynchon, Thomas, 301
Planck, Max, 128

Plato, 102
Plautus, 80
Pliny, 43, 44, 45, 48
Poe, Edgar Allan, 113
Poggioli, Renato, 9, 27
Pollio, 10
Pollock, Jackson, 5
Polybius, 10, 13
Polyphemus, 71
Pontano, Giovanni, 13
Poseidon, 88
Poulet, Georges, 263
Pound, Ezra, 66, 74, 93, 97, 98, 100, 110, 113, 116, 122, 124, 278
Poussin, Nicolas, 22
Pozzo, 146, 148, 152
Praga, Marco, 137
Praz, Mario, 111
Prince, Gerald, 240
Prometheus, 77
Proteus, 72
Proust, Marcel, 103, 162, 257
Prufrock, J. Alfred, 99, 101, 102, 107, 110, 113, 118
Puchner, Martin, 167
Pulci, Luigi, 173

Queneau, Raymond, 203, 271
Quesada, 34
Quevedo, Francisco de, 32, 33, 40, 249
Quexada, 34, 222
Quijano, Don, 34, 222, 223, 224, 225, 230, 250
Quijote, Don 34
Quintilian, 80
Quixano, 225, 230
Quixote, Don, 32, 34, 58, 189, 201, 221, 222, 223, 224, 225, 226, 227, 228, 229, 231, 232, 234, 235, 237, 239, 242, 248, 249, 250, 256, 257, 261, 270

Rabelais, 60, 144, 173, 200, 216, 267
Racine, Jean, 125
Raphael, 20, 26, 175, 307
Rauschenberg, Robert, 100, 162, 175, 182, 217, 294, 295
Ray, Man, 100
Remus, 38
Ribadeneira, Pedro de, 230
Ribera, 32
Rilke, Reiner Maria, 105
Risset, Jacqueline, 92
Roach, Mary, 289
Robbe-Grillet, Alain, 154
Rojas, Fernando de, 32
Roland, 34

Index 361

Romulus, 38
Ronsard, Pierre de, 243
Rooney, 154, 168
Rosenberg, Harold, 305
Rossetti, Dante Gabriel, 29
Rotolando, 34
Roussel, Raymond, 271
Rudy Bloom, 112
Russell, Betrand, 99
Ruthven, K. K., 287
Ruzante (Angelo Beolco), 26

Saint Stephen, 78
Salinas, Pedro, 45
Sandburg, Carl, 109
Sannazaro, Jacopo, 10, 11, 12, 13, 15, 16, 18, 22, 25, 26, 27, 29, 223, 243
Santayana, George de, 102, 112
Saramago, José, 137
Sarpi, Paolo, 54
Sartre, Jean-Paul, 168, 210, 261
Satan, 153
Schoenberg, Arnold, 170
Scott, Walter, 245, 246
Segismundo, 164
Seneca, 54
Senn, Fritz, 82
Sepheris, George, 71
Serres, Michel, 48
Shahryar, 304
Scheherazade, 261, 304
Schiller, Friedrich, 29
Schilling, Bernard, 109
Scipio, 48
Schwartz, Hillel, 287
Seferis, George, 110
Seidel, Michael, 2, 87
Serres, Michel, 201
Shakespeare, William, 72, 73, 89, 136, 235, 283
Shaw, Bernard, 86
Shearman, John, 208
Shih Huang Ti, 197
Sidney, Philip, 10, 11, 75
Silone, Ignazio, 257
Sincero, 14
Singer, Isaac Bashevis, 200
Siopold, 77
Sisyphus, 40
Smithson, Robert, 214
Snell, Bruno, 10
Soane, John, 116
Socrates, 62, 172, 191
Sollers, Philippe, 301

Sontag, Susan, 61
Sophocles, 71, 118
Sosostris, Madame, 98
Spagnoli, Battista, 25
Spencer, Herbert, 102
Spengler, Oswald, 66, 103
Spitzer, Leo, 3
Stanford, W.B., 82
Stanislaus, 70
Stanislawsky, Konstantin, 137
States, Bert O., 142
Stein, Gertrude, 113, 144, 162, 300
Steinberg, Saul, 198, 273, 281, 282, 306
Steiner, George, 9, 62, 230, 268, 289
Stevens, Wallace, 3, 92, 122, 172, 175, 257, 285, 302
Stewart, Susan, 204
Stoom, 77
Suarez Miranda, J. A., 198
Summonte, Pietro, 14
Svevo, Italo, 99
Swedenborg, Imanuel, 262
Swift, Jonathan, 194

Tasso, Torquato, 189
Tassoni, Alessandro, 58, 222
Telemachus, 112
Tesauro, Emanuele, 58
Theocritus, 10, 11, 13
Theresa, Saint, 222
Tillich, Paul, 155
Tinguely, Jean, 100, 217
Tiresias, 97, 100, 102, 112, 119, 146
Titian, 10, 17, 18, 21, 22, 25, 29
Tomé, 241
Twist, Oliver, 81
Twombly, Cy, 292, 293, 294
Tzara, Tristan, 65

Ulisse, 66, 69, 77, 83, 85
Ulixes, 66, 67, 68, 77, 82, 83, 85
Ulysses, 66, 68, 69, 70, 71, 72, 73, 74, 75, 78, 80, 81, 83, 85, 87, 90, 91, 92, 101, 102, 107
Unamuno, Miguel de, 220, 221, 226, 227, 228, 229, 230, 231, 232, 233, 248, 249, 262
Updike, John, 301
Uruk, 194

Valadier, Giuseppe, 85
Valdés, Juan de, 222
Valéry, Paul, 65, 93, 110, 113, 191, 237, 293
Vattimo, Gianni, 5
Velázquez, 32

Velde, Bram van, 169
Vendler, Helen, 3, 112, 118
Venus, 99, 182
Verdanel, Jean, 101
Verga, Giovanni, 124, 246, 259
Vico, Giambattista, 13, 70, 89, 93, 117
Victor Emmanuel II, 307
Vinci, Leonardo da, 21
Virgil, 10, 13, 15, 18, 25, 61, 67, 71, 82, 115, 116, 154, 194, 293
Vittorini, Elio, 173
Vives, Juan Luis, 254
Vladimir, 146, 148

Warhol, Andy, 162, 175, 212, 213, 265, 281, 282, 285, 286
Watson, Janell, 162
Watteau, 10
Webber, Joan, 54

Weinstein, Arnold, 39
Weston, Jessie, 99
Whitman, Walt, 122
Wilde, Oscar, 79, 183
Wilkins, David J., 18
Wilson, Edmund, 65
Winckelmann, Johan, 20, 67
Winnie, 153
Wittgenstein, Ludwig, 144, 190, 206, 289
Wolosky, Shira, 153
Woolf, Virginia, 65, 103, 105, 138

Yamasaki, Minoru, 180
Yambo, 215, 216
Yeats, W. B., 79, 87, 93, 105, 118, 263
Yourcenar, Marguerite, 233

Ziolkowski, Theodore, 105, 116, 229, 286
Zola, Emile, 85

www.ingramcontent.com/pod-product-compliance
Lightning Source LLC
Chambersburg PA
CBHW021352290426
44108CB00010B/204